MIDNIGHT MARQUEE ACTORS SERIES

BORIS KARLOFF

W9-BEL-973

Edited by Gary J. and Susan Svehla

MIDNIGHT MARQUEE PRESS, INC.

BALTIMORE, MARYLAND

ISBN 1-887664-07-6
Library of Congress Catalog Card Number 96-75975
Manufactured in the United States of America
Printed by Kirby Lithographic Company, Arlington, VA
First Printing by Midnight Marquee Press, Inc., October, 1996

Acknowledgments: John Antosiewicz Photo Archives, Ronald V. Borst/ Hollywood Movie Posters, Michael Brunas, Jim Clatterbaugh, Richard Gordon, Leonard Kohl, Frank Lidinsky, Greg Mank, Mark Miller, John Parnun, John Soister, Tom Weaver

Front Cover: David L. Daniels' rendering of Boris Karloff from *Die, Monster, Die!* Cover copyright © by David L. Daniels.

for Boris Karloff

TABLE OF CONTENTS

INTRODUCTION

After profiling arch bogeyman Bela Lugosi in our initial installment of the *Midnight Marquee Actors Series* one year ago, we have decided to make his counterpart, Boris Karloff, the focus of this second installment. While Lugosi is considered to be the more colorful personality of the two, Boris Karloff has always been considered the more versatile *actor*. Our purpose is not to start a Karloff/Lugosi debate within our pages, for our writers love *both* horror film icons (if not equally, well, that's not the point, is it!).

As profiled in Bob Madison's *Mad Monster Party?* chapter, Karloff was the dominant horror movie personality during the decade of the 1960s (as he had been since the 1930s) when I first premiered my magazine *Gore Creatures*, later *Midnight Marquee*, in the summer of 1963 (I had just turned 13-years-old). Seeing those beloved Universal horror classics on television late at night (with fuzzy reception making the viewing experience an almost mystical one) and catching the latest Karloff feature at theaters during Saturday afternoon matinees: *The Raven* (I saw it in 1963 at the Boulevard Theater with a live Spook Stage Show), *Black Sabbath*, *The Terror*, *The Comedy of Terrors*, etc., Karloff was seen everywhere, even on variety programs on television. Boris Karloff, more so than any other horror film personality, became the definitive horror movie icon to me. Whether that was because of his variety of roles, his depth of acting talent, his cinematic personality (bowed legs, lisp, sinister smile, intense eyes, expressive mouth), or the stellar films in which he appeared, I do not know. But for me, Karloff represented all that was grand about horror movies. While Boris does not instill the passion that Lugosi does, Boris represents the regality and refinement of a choice wine to Bela's whiskey personality. Boris Karloff represents that refinement that he, more so than anyone else, used to elevate horror cinema to popular art.

Again, a note of explanation as to what the *Midnight Marquee Actors Series* is and is not. Our intention was not to be definitive and include every one of Karloff's features. The approach to the *Actors Series* is simple. We solicited written chapters from our stable of expert film writers on the Karloff film or films which they most desired to shed ink. Granted, these selections might not be Karloff's best films nor his more memorable. Many writers chose to select Karloff films on which precious little has been written. Others decided to select a favorite Karloff film, but one that is not necessarily his best. Others opted to address the classics—*Frankenstein, Bride of Frankenstein, The Black Cat, The Body Snatcher*—to try to create a new slant, a new angle on films so often critiqued. Interestingly enough, writers frequently comment on Karloff films other than their one focus title, and after editing chapters and placing them in chronological order, all these individual chapters magically meld into a definitive history of Karloff's film work and life.

Each writer brings his/her biases, opinions, and expertise to the table. By combining such opinionated visions and varied interpretations, this volume becomes a better balanced vehicle by which to judge Karloff the man, his work, and his overall contribution to film.

Gary J. Svehla, October 1996

FRANKENSTEIN (1931)

by Don G. Smith

At last check there were over 24 editions of Mary Shelley's *Frankenstein* in print. In addition, the homunculus theme has been a staple of the cinema since Edison's silent *Frankenstein* (1910). But when the world thinks of the Frankenstein monster, it immediately conjures the image of Boris Karloff: KARLOFF—the loping creature with the sunken eyes, the square head, and the bolt through his neck. Impressions left by Karloff's creature in 1931 have been indeed long-lasting. In fact, I would argue that it is Karloff's interpretation of the creature that largely accounts for the film having passed from 1931 potential ephemera to world popular culture. But what kind of creature does Karloff play, and why is his interpretation so successful? The answer lies in the fact that Karloff plays the creature as a child.

Shortly before writing *Frankenstein*, Mary Shelley read the novel *Emile* by Jean Jacques Rousseau. According to Rousseau, children have their own inner potential for learning. Children will develop according to their own natures. Rousseau, however, rejects the common Judeo-Christian assumption that children are tainted with original sin. Rousseau writes instead that "God makes all things good; man meddles with them and they become evil." Rousseau writes further that the child develops from his pristine state following an inner pattern, subject to education:

> "Plants are fashioned by cultivation, man by education... All that we lack at birth, all that we need when we come to man's estate, is the gift of education. This education comes to us from nature, from man, or from things. The inner growth of our organs and faculties is the education of nature, the use we learn to make of this growth is the education of men, what we gain by our experience of our surroundings is the education of things."

This, I believe, is the secret of the success of Mary Shelley's novel, and it is also the secret of Karloff's success as the creature. In essence, Karloff's creature is a child. As such, he does receive education from nature, from man, and from things. Reflect for a moment on Karloff's first appearance in the film.

When Frankenstein (Colin Clive) turns out the lights, the creature backs into the room through a doorway. He turns, and the camera relays successive portraits of the creature's face, each in greater close-up than before. The impression is one of a maltreated child, its cheeks hollowed and its eyes sunken like those that stare back at us from charity relief posters.

As the creature enters the room, it does so with baby steps. Karloff is "a toddler"—a creature with a brain answering to Locke's *tabula rasa* or blank slate; a creature essentially reaching out to the world around it, reaching out for the education of man and the education of things. Karloff is a "toddler" with the body of a giant. It is essentially this that elicits audience sympathy because Karloff's toddler is being mistreated. Deprived of light and human warmth, the creature/toddler is obviously depressed. Such are the results when a child is deprived of education from both things and from man. Were it not for the powerful body given it by Frankenstein, the creature would suffer the deprivation woes experienced by unattended infants in some orphanages. Like a neglected toddler, the creature has not learned a language that allows it verbally to communicate its emotional response to the world.

Frankenstein then allows the creature for the first time to experience sunlight through an opening in the roof. The creature, obviously yearning for the light, basks momentarily in the warmth. Then Frankenstein closes the opening, and the sunlight is gone, leaving the creature to gesture and plead silently with its hands as a child would. As Emerson writes: "The sun illuminates only the eye of the man, but shines into the eye and heart of the child." Karloff illustrates Emerson's point beautifully with heartbreaking pathos.

Arthur Edeson's camera often draws attention to Karloff's hands as they grope, search, plead, and at times brutally murder. The hands are the feeders of the creature's intellect and emotions. They attempt communication, but the response they receive is usually rejection and pain. Frankenstein's assistant, Fritz (Dwight Frye), often frightens and torments the creature with fire for no apparent reason. When the world does not return the love of a child, the child responds in anger. Consequently, the creature kills Fritz and Dr. Waldman (Edward Van Sloan). Karloff perfectly summons the facial expressions and body movements necessary to communicate the creature's distrust of the world around it. Note the violent swing of the arms meant to banish fearful objects and threatening people. Note the animal-like growl of the pre-verbal child.

Let us return now to Rousseau, whose *Emile* helped inspire Shelley's masterpiece. The novel *Frankenstein* has survived for well over a century largely because of its success in exploring ambiguities suggested by several contradictory ideas and possibilities. Is Frankenstein's creature a "failure" because a prideful Prometheus insists on usurping the power of God? Or is the creature really Rousseau's noble savage, its true nature twisted and perverted by the cruelties of human society? The novel plays fair with these crucial ideas, but

Arthur Edeson's camera often draws attention to Karloff's hands as they grope, search, plead, and at times brutally murder.

the film is not so honest. The film was adapted by John L. Balderston from the play by Peggy Webling. The screenplay itself was penned by Garrett Fort, Francis Edwards Faragoh, John Russell (uncredited), and Robert Florey (uncredited). When Universal replaced director Robert Florey with James Whale, the former's contributions to the film were excised from the credits. One of Florey's reputed uncredited contributions to the film is the idea of Fritz's mistaken delivery of a criminal brain to Frankenstein. It is, of course, this malfunctioning brain that finds its way into the skull of the creature.

11

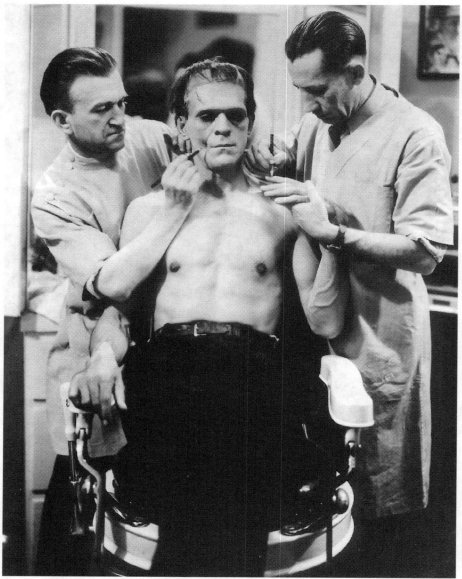

Boris Karloff's performance, along with Jack Pierce's makeup, is one of the main reasons for the success of *Frankenstein*.

But this is a cheat. Florey's "contribution" allows us to skirt all the philosophical ambiguities suggested by the novel. We can simply drop all deeper consideration of why the creature becomes a monster by blaming the problem on the criminal brain. Then the problem simply becomes one of human error, allowing audiences to safely ignore questions of human development, of God, and of society. But Karloff's interpretation, as suggested by the final screenplay, does not allow Florey to cheat us. The creature's brain is Locke's *tabula rasa*, not a brain apparently inclined to murder. Karloff, in playing the creature as a child, shows no signs of undue aggression or organic mental malfunction. He is not the criminal whose "spirit" once inhabited a malfunctioning brain. The criminal spirit is gone; only the brain itself remains. Karloff simply acts and reacts as a pre-verbal child would. In other words, any organically sound child treated as Karloff is treated in the film would likewise become a monster—especially if that child had Karloff's size and strength, and if its role models were a negligent Frankenstein, a sadistic Fritz, and a right-meaning but deadly Dr. Waldman.

Still, even the most perceptive critics sometimes manage to miss the obvious. According to *Film Weekly* (January 23, 1931), "Boris Karloff's portrayal of a synthetic monster... is an astonishing piece of work. His make-up alone is masterly, and he depicts the awkwardness, the bewilderment, and the fiendish instincts of the creature with restrained power." All of that is true except for one thing: Karloff never depicts fiendish instincts! In truth, he never exhibits aggression against another human being before someone else first aggresses against him. Perhaps *Film Weekly* refers to the creature's drowning of a little girl, the act itself being cut from the original print. Only from those scenes, with its most important elements cut, could one conclude that the creature exhibits fiendish instincts. But let us examine the scene carefully.

The creature is confusedly lurching through the forest when he encounters a little girl beside a pond. As any parent knows, children are almost instinctively drawn to other children. Such is the case with the creature, who shyly shambles forward hoping to make his first real friend. Until the creature runs out of flowers, both "children" are quite happy tossing flowers into the lake and watching them float. The creature, who previously smiled innocently, looks down at his empty hands and becomes unhappy. He then reaches out for his friend. Universal cut from the original print the scenes immediately following. Operating on the lowest levels of Piaget's cognitive development, the creature tosses his little friend into the lake and stands helplessly by as she fails to float. The creature has learned a valuable lesson from "things," one that unfortunately brings much pain and sorrow. Since the drowning itself was cut from the original print, the mistaken impression may have been left with the *Film Weekly* that Karloff, in those scenes, depicts fiendish instincts.

When the creature came into the world, he was a child as described by Nietzsche—an "innocence and forgetting, a new beginning, a play, a self-propelled wheel, a first movement, a holy yes-saying." But the creature's human environment answered NO! In James Whale's *Frankenstein*, society does indeed take an innocent creature and turn it into a monster. So forget the clumsy, cheating device of Florey's criminal brain. Though not to the same extent as Mary Shelley, Whale, and Karloff make us confront real ideas.

Karloff as Frankenstein's Monster brought to celluloid life one of the world's most endearing monster portrayals.

We might argue that Karloff's creature quickly becomes an adolescent, at which point the film raises other issues. In scenes that seem to lack motivation, the creature enters the bedroom of Elizabeth (Mae Clarke), Frankenstein's fi-

The image of Karloff's creature is an indelible part of world popular culture.

ancee, and stalks her with apparently maleficent intentions. Frankenstein hears her screams and rushes to the rescue. When he opens the door he finds the creature gone and his fiancee sprawled upon the bed. The last we saw of her, she was backed up in fear against the bedroom door. How did she get to the bed? Obviously the creature carried her there. But why? As in the original novel, the creature's assault on Elizabeth can be explained as revenge against Frankenstein. But in the novel the motivations are much stronger. There, the creature enters Elizabeth's bedroom and actually kills her because Frankenstein

15

In James Whale's *Frankenstein*, society takes an innocent creature and turns it into a monster.

broke his promise to create a mate for the creature. If the creature cannot have a mate, neither can Frankenstein. But the creature's motivation is very flimsy in the film. Elizabeth has never harmed the creature, so what does he want with her. Well, he doesn't try to kill her. Instead he carries her to a bed, so you figure it out.

In the bedroom scenes we have a creature, or adolescent, who has been learning from "nature." The creature desires a mate. Karloff approaches Mae Clarke clumsily, indicating the approach of an inexperienced adolescent intent on rape. As such, Karloff perfectly captures the purpose and confusion of the delinquent adolescent whose natural urges lead him toward a violent act.

As the film winds to its conclusion, Karloff's creature is a maladapted adolescent unable to speak. As a result of vicious childhood neglect, the creature is now a monster indeed. The fire in the windmill, however, cuts short all speculation as to what hope might exist. In these scenes, Karloff portrays the creature as a sub-human animal—for that is what he has become. As Aristotle noted, any human being who lives outside of society must be either a god or a beast. Karloff has become a beast. As the fire moves closer and people cry out for his death, he lurches about the enclosed windmill like a trapped animal. The only other actor in the entire Frankenstein film genre remotely to approach in quality Karloff's portrayal of synthetic creature as animal is Christopher Lee in *The Curse of Frankenstein* (1957).

Though the film has proven wildly effective by cinematic standards, by cutting off the creature as an adolescent unable to speak (or as essentially a hunted animal), the 1931 horror film does not allow Shelley's themes to be explored in a very honest way. In Shelley's novel, the creature learns to speak and to read. In fact, having seriously digested such classics as Milton's *Paradise Lost* and Goethe's *The Sorrows of Young Werther*, he probably emerges better-read and more intellectually cultivated than most of today's American high school students. So much for Universal's clumsy, speechless adolescent. James Whale does attempt some exploration of these themes in his sequel, *Bride of Frankenstein* (1935), in which the creature at least learns to speak, if not to read. Though taken as a unit, *Frankenstein* and *Bride of Frankenstein* raise some of the key issues inherent in the novel, the combination still falls far short of the novel in philosophical complexity. In the novel, as in the films, the creature is cruelly abandoned and elicits our sympathy. On the other hand, as he matures, he commits unforgivable crimes in a cunning manner. Can we still identify with his pain? Can we at all morally justify his actions? In Shelley's novel, is Frankenstein the flawed romantic hero? As a "modern Prometheus" who is not a demi-god, he dies for his flaws. In Whale's *Frankenstein*, audiences are spared Frankenstein's death. Is he the hero of the film? Apparently so. At least he appears to be given the last minute, tacked-on happy ending. Elizabeth even delivers to Frankenstein a new child to take the place of the one he created and lost. But what does this say of the creature's status? Again, the film cheats where the novel does not.

Interestingly, as the *Frankenstein* series progressed, it increasingly cheated regarding the issues raised in the novel by relying on Florey's criminal brain as a source of the creature's motivation. In *Son of Frankenstein*, the creature (Boris Karloff) is regarded as "sick," and Ygor (Bela Lugosi) becomes the creature's evil master, the creature becoming little more than Ygor's avenging angel. Interestingly, in that film, the creature regains just a bit of the malevolent motivation present in Shelley's novel when he decides to kill the child of Dr. Frankenstein (Basil Rathbone) because the doctor has killed the creature's companion, Ygor. In *The Ghost of Frankenstein*, Ygor takes the creature (Lon Chaney, Jr.) to another of Frankenstein's relatives, who specializes in diseases of the mind. In that film, the creature is again drawn to the friendship of a little girl, though the motivation for such a relationship does not follow from the previous two films. In *Frankenstein Meets the Wolf Man,* the creature (Bela Lugosi) is at

first befriended by the Wolf Man, and the series departs almost entirely from the Mary Shelley orbit. *House of Frankenstein* and *House of Dracula* find the creature as a mere parody of its former self, a stiff-legged, generally ineffectual

18

monster that lies about in a state of illness waiting for some scientist to give it strength. The finale of the series, *Abbott and Costello Meet Frankenstein*, reduces the creature to Dracula's slave, an automation awaiting the brain of comedian Lou Costello. How far from Karloff's powerful child we came! How far from Mary Shelley's world of ideas we devolved!

I think that we must conclude that in the hands of Florey and Lugosi (Universal's first choice to play the creature), the *Frankenstein* film mythology may never have received the relatively strong foundation given it by James Whale and Boris Karloff. Though unlikely, it conceivably could have been a one-shot wonder. As it stands, Universal's *Frankenstein* served as a strong foundation for at least two or three good sequels, and the image of Karloff's creature is an indelible part of world popular culture. Still, in our evolving post-literate culture, I must, despite Boris Karloff's great performance (which he equals only in *The Black Room* and *The Body Snatcher*), steer readers of this chapter to Mary Shelley's novel. While any true horror aficionado has read *Frankenstein*, the vast majority of people believe they "know" *Frankenstein* because they have seen the films. Nothing could be further from the truth. Then again, if Karloff's portrayal serves to lead audiences to the novel, as it did me, literature and culture will owe him a great debt. But even if that never happens, we already owe Karloff a great debt—for bringing to celluloid life one of the world's most enduring screen portrayals, a thespian masterpiece based on some of the world's most important ideas.

CREDITS: Producer: Carl Laemmle, Jr.; Director: James Whale; Writers: Garrett Fort, Francis Edwards Faragoh, John Balderston, Robert Florey; based on the novel by Mary Shelley and the play by Peggy Webling; Cinematographer: Arthur Edeson; Editor: Maurice Pivar, Clarence Kolster; Music Composer: David Broekman; Art Design: Charles D. Hall; Special Effects: John P. Fulton; Set Design: Herman Rosse; Makeup: Jack Pierce; Universal, 1931; 71 minutes

CAST: Boris Karloff...the Monster, Colin Clive...Henry Frankenstein, Mae Clarke...Elizabeth, John Boles...Victor Moritz, Edward Van Sloan...Dr. Waldman, Dwight Frye...Fritz, Frederick Kerr...Baron Frankenstein, Lionel Belmore...Herr Vogel, Michael Mark...Ludwig, Marilyn Harris...Maria

Don G. Smith is an associate professor in history and philosophy of education at Eastern Illinois University. He has published in *Midnight Marquee, Scarlet Street, Filmfax, Movie Collector's World,* etc. He is the author of *Lon Chaney, Jr.* (McFarland and Company, 1995), and is currently writing *The Cinema of Edgar Allan Poe,* also for McFarland.

[Courtesy Ronald V. Borst/Hollywood Movie Posters]

BEHIND THE MASK (1932)
SCARFACE (1932)

by Dennis Fischer

With the advent of sound, every rat-a-tat of the machine gun and every tinkling bit of breaking glass of the gangster film could finally be captured, and a new film genre was launched. Naturally, Boris Karloff contributed to this genre in his own inimitable fashion.

Early in his career, fresh from the Canadian stage, Karloff was typecast in several films as a Canadian-French fur trapper. Later in the '20s, he essayed parts as criminals and hoods, consequently it wasn't long before he graduated to portraying gangsters beginning with *Smart Money*.

According to Michael Brunas, John Brunas, and Tom Weaver in *Universal Horrors*, "In the early '30s Karloff played gangland characters in a number of Hollywood films, with mixed results. With his British accent and lisp, Karloff was not suited to play American gangsters.... It's quaint and enjoyable to see Karloff as a mug or a racketeer in pictures like *Smart Money* (1931), *Scarface* (1932) and others, but his presence effectively robs them of what verisimilitude they had."

While these authors try to ameliorate this slight by pointing out that Edward G. Robinson would have made a lousy mummy, the main problem with this assertion is that it isn't quite true. While prominent gangsters came largely from Italian and Jewish immigrant backgrounds, thirties' America was still quite a melting pot, particularly in the major urban centers, and uncultured British accents would not have been wholly out of place. Karloff tackled his gangster roles with aplomb and verve, employing a naturalistic style that won good notices from contemporary critics.

Karloff would play Tony Ricca in Columbia's *The Guilty Generation*, going on to appear in gang-related roles in Howard Hawks' classic *Scarface*, as well as *Graft, Behind the Mask, The Miracle Man, Night World, Dick Tracy Meets Gruesome,* and *The Secret Life of Walter Mitty.* Although *The Criminal Code* is a prison film, it is very important in Karloff's filmography because it is quite likely that Karloff's portrayal of Ned Galloway is what convinced James Whale to cast him as the Frankenstein monster. The body movements of Galloway when he is about to kill an informant are identical to those he used in *Frankenstein*, something Peter Bogdanovich emphasized in his Karloff tribute film *Targets*, where he shares a scene with Karloff as they watch this early Howard Hawks effort.

Let's take a closer look at Karloff's two best gangster films, both released in 1932.

Behind the Mask was sold as a horror film with at least some justification, although the source of horror in the film isn't Karloff who has a supporting role as a stooge, but that old nemesis of evil, Edward Van Sloan, best known for playing Van Helsing in *Dracula* and *Dracula's Daughter*, Dr. Waldman in *Frankenstein*, and Professor Muller in *The Mummy*. As Dr. August Steiner, Van Sloan gives one of his best and most sinister performances.

While filmed in 1931, *Behind the Mask* wasn't released until February 1932. It opens at Sing Sing where Henderson (Karloff) tells his cellmate Quinn (who is actually Jack Hart, a member of the secret service sent to prison to infiltrate a drug ring) to see a man named Arnold who will set him up after Quinn breaks out. Henderson reveals that he is hooked up with a big man who will get him released from prison shortly; however, he refuses to reveal the identity of his mysterious patron.

That night, during cell check, Quinn (Jack Holt) is missing. Henderson laughs and says, "Quinn, now where have I heard that name before?" much to the merriment of the inmates. While sirens blare, Henderson gives the coppers the horselaugh.

A horrific atmosphere is set up subsequently with shots of a dark and stormy night, a mysterious and somewhat Gothic house, and the skittish Arnold (Claude King) discovering that the housekeeper, Edwards (Bertha Mann), has been listening in on his conversation with a man named Burke. Edwards phones an old-fashioned cylinder recorder and reports to a mysterious superior that Burke phoned Arnold.

Hart after his "jailbreak" meets up with an agent in the rain and asks for a cigarette. To make it look good, he asks that the man shoot him in the arm and then fire his gun several times, a request with which the man complies. The now wounded Hart breaks into the house where he meets Arnold's daughter Julie (Constance Cummings) who bandages his wound. "I'd do the same for any animal that was injured," she tells him. Hart tells Arnold that Henderson sent him.

Burke is an underling of Captain Hawkes (Willard Robertson) who has been working to break a drug ring. Hawkes asks him to tail Henderson once he's released. Henderson immediately heads for the office of Dr. August Steiner, whose office is filled with menacing medical apparatus more appropriate to a mad scientist's laboratory.

The bearded, malevolent Steiner tells Henderson that the man they have been working for is displeased with him because of his curiosity, and that's why he was framed and sent to prison. Henderson is to take over from Arnold.

The bearded, malevolent Steiner (Edward Van Sloan) tells Henderson (Karloff) he is to take over for Arnold.

Just as Henderson is leaving, he spots Burke tailing him, rushes back, and informs Steiner. Karloff carefully conveys Henderson's fear of making a fatal mistake, a clear contrast to the cool, collected Steiner.

Burke pretends to be a potential patient and Steiner agrees to see him, placing him behind a fluoroscope which allows Steiner to use X-rays to see the badge that Burke has concealed in his pocket. Steiner makes an appointment to see Burke the next day. Recalling Henderson to his office, Steiner tells him, "I made an appointment for 11 tomorrow morning—make certain he doesn't keep it."

Burke calls Hawkes saying he has discovered the identity of Mr. X and will reveal it at four. However, Burke fails to appear. Several minutes later a messenger arrives with a taunting message from Mr. X and Burke's badge, indicating that Burke has been killed.

Hart, working for Arnold as a chauffeur, takes Arnold to his office only to discover Henderson there. Henderson is surprised and pleased to see his old pal, "Quinn," and tells Arnold that he will take over and there are big plans for

Karloff tackled his gangster roles with aplomb and verve, employing a naturalistic style that won good notices from contemporary critics.

Arnold in the organization. As Arnold leaves, Henderson menacingly bids him, "So long… pal."

Hart is assigned to pick up a shipment for Henderson and leaves. (Karloff shows he was always adept at sinister entendres.)

Steiner arrives and initially becomes furious, revealing to Henderson that "Quinn" is actually a secret service agent. "How do you know he's a federal?" asks the taken aback Henderson who suddenly realizes the extent of his blunder. Henderson offers to kill Hart, but Steiner begins to enjoy the irony of having Hart transport drugs for them.

Hart bids Julie adieu and explains her father is in the dope business and to get him out of it as quickly as possible. He leaves and Arnold arrives informing Julie that Hart is a secret service man who has been marked for death. Desperately Julie rushes to the site of the seaplane to warn Hart before he takes off, but she just misses him.

Two hundred miles out, Hart rendezvous with a ship and picks up the shipment which he takes to Henderson's boat. Henderson warns him that the feds are about and that he'd better ditch the plane and parachute out of it. After

24

promising to pick Hart up, Henderson sees a parachute in the distance as the plane dives down and he abandons the apparently hapless agent.

Julie goes to Hawkes' office to tell him what happened, but Hart shows up and reveals that he suspected something, and quickly rigged a dummy with a parachute, getting away safely. Hawkes orders Hart to bring Arnold in, but when they get to his place, they find he's been sent to Eastland Hospital where Steiner is performing an appendicitis operation. Unsurprisingly, Arnold does not pull through.

Henderson asks him, "All right, doctor?" to which Steiner responds significantly, "Yes, he's all right." Hart tells Julie to be brave when they go into Arnold's room and he asks to speak with Arnold. Edwards covers Arnold's face instead—dead men tell no tales—and Edwards later informs the recording device that "Quinn" has somehow survived.

Hart breaks into Steiner's office and discovers the recording device and some recently recorded cylinders, which he takes to Hawkes. There's enough information to indict Steiner for Arnold's murder if they exhume Arnold's body and prove he didn't die from peritonitis.

However, when opening the coffin, they discover the drug shipment rather than Arnold's body.

Hart rushes back to where he left Julie only to be informed that she has been taken to Eastland Hospital. After Hart leaves, Edwards makes a call announcing his imminent arrival. Just as Hart reaches Julie, he is overpowered from behind. Steiner informs him that he will conduct an operation which, alas, Hart will not survive. Hart tells him that the police have Henderson.

Van Sloan gets the finest and most shudder-producing moment in the film when he delivers the following monologue: "Has it ever occurred to you, Mr. Hart, that you can commit almost any crime if you select the proper environment? For example, if I were to stick a knife into you in the street, it would attract attention, I might have to answer embarrassing questions. But when I stick a knife into you here, on the operating table, nothing will happen… to me…. The pain when I am going through the layers of skin will not be unendurable. It is only when I begin to cut on the *inside* that you will realize that you are having an experience. Wasn't it Nietzsche who said that unendurable pain merges into ecstasy? We shall find out whether that was an epigram or a fact. For my part, I know it will be ecstasy."

Steiner is just about to begin his first, anesthetic-less incision when a nurse comes in whom Steiner assumes to be Edwards. Instead, it is Julie who fires and kills the masked surgeon. Steiner, it is revealed, is Dr. Monsell, an anti-crime fighting doctor who adopts a beard to take on the alter ego of Steiner, the man behind the mask. Julie and Hart plan on marriage at the happy fade-out.

Karloff makes a game try at an American accent in the film, but his soft-spoken familiar British accent keeps coming through. Henderson's capture takes place off-camera, giving Karloff no exciting action scenes in which to shine. Nevertheless, he does a good job of conveying a ruthless underling who lives in fear of his unknown master.

That the sinister Steiner is really Mr. X is no big surprise—his references to working for a superior are an obvious red herring; however, his dual role as Dr. Monsell is harder to spot since Van Sloan's usual thick accent and looks have been altered effectively. Van Sloan makes the most of his menacing dialogue and proves he could be the equal of Lionel Atwill when playing sinister surgeons.

Van Sloan continued playing doctors and professors throughout most of his career. He reteamed with Karloff in 1935 for *The Black Room* and in 1940 for *Before I Hang,* and made memorable appearances in *Deluge, Death Takes a Holiday, The Scarlet Empress, The Last Days of Pompeii, The Story of Louis Pasteur,* the serial *The Phantom Creeps,* and made his best appearance in the '40s *The Mask of Diijon.* He has rightfully been called the "Elder Statesman of Horror."

The screenwriter, Jo (Joseph) Swerling, may be best known for co-crafting the play *Guys and Dolls.* He worked with some of Hollywood's top directors and provided quite versatile, writing the scripts for *It's a Wonderful Life, Lifeboat, The Westerner, Blood and Sand, Leave Her to Heaven* and *The Pride of the Yankees.*

Director John Francis Dillon would work again almost immediately with Karloff on *The Cohens and Kellys in Hollywood,* the sixth in the insipid series about the competition between a Jewish and an Irish family. Karloff has a mere cameo in the film, appearing as a star at the famous Coconut Grove in the company of Universal stars Tom Mix and Lew Ayres, in this, Karloff's first Universal film after *Frankenstein.* Dillon had an extensive career, both as an actor (as Jack Dillon) and as a director of silent films, during which time he specialized in comedies and romantic dramas. He only made a few more films before his death in 1934.

Millionaire turned film producer Howard Hughes wanted to make a gangster epic that would surpass all others. To that end, he purchased the rights to Maurice Coons' novel *Scarface,* which was written under the pseudonym Armitage Trail. He also hired Fred Pasley, a *New York Daily News* reporter who was an expert on Al Capone, as technical adviser. Pasley ended up sharing screen credit with the top screenwriters in Hollywood.

Hughes hired Howard Hawks, whose film *Dawn Patrol* aviation buff Hughes greatly admired. Hawks in turn hired Ben Hecht, who had been much acclaimed for his work on Von Sternberg's *Underworld.* Hawks proposed that the Capone family be portrayed as if they were the Borgias set down in Chicago. Hecht worked on the story for 11 days at $1,000 a day before leaving the final polishing to other hands.

James Cagney couldn't do it any better than Karloff does in these classy crime productions, such as *Scarface*.

While Karloff only has a small part as Gaffney, he nonetheless makes a significant contribution to this great all-time gangster classic. Of the many gangster films of the '30s, *Scarface* is by far the sexiest and most violent, which led to trouble with the Hays Office.

The film made a star out of its lead, former stage actor Paul Muni, who came to be considered one of the greatest actors of the thirties (though much of his work seems phony and affected today), and, apart from *Scarface*, he is best remembered for his film biographies in *I Am a Fugitive From a Chain Gang, The Story of Louis Pasteur*, and *The Life of Emile Zola*, earning an Oscar nomination for each and winning for *Pasteur*.

Muni's Tony Camonte was based on Al Capone, the famous thirties' gangster, who became such a fan of the film that he obtained his own private print. Muni's Camonte is a semi-simian pixilated creation, mixing humor with hard-as-nails toughness. He portrays his character as an uncouth, swaggering hick who has made the big time and revels in it. As he makes his way to the top, he loses some of his vaudevillian Italian accent and garbs himself in gaudy fashions being incapable of recognizing his own bad taste.

In addition to Muni and Karloff, *Scarface* has a great supporting cast. Two particular stand-outs are Osgood Perkins, Tony Perkins' father, as Johnny Lovo, Camonte's new boss who uses the hood to do his dirty work and then finds he can't keep the ever-ambitious Camonte in line, and Vince Barnett, who is hilarious as Camonte's illiterate social secretary who tries to take a message over machine gun fire, can't master how to work a phone, and is kept behind at a stage production of *Rain* because his boss wants to find out who Sadie Thompson will choose at the end. (Later when Barnett tells him, "She climbed back in the hay with the Army," Muni replies, "That's-a fine. She's-a smart girl, that one.")

Where Cagney's Tom Powers (*Public Enemy*) was overprotective of his sister, Muni's Camonte has an unresolved incestuous fixation with his sister Cesca (Ann Dvorak). He is jealous of any other man paying attention to her, which prods her to try and get out from under her brother's thumb by being even more flirtatious. (This trend of gangsters having unnatural sexual fixations reached its apex with Cagney's obsessive mother love in *White Heat*.)

In fact, Camonte even kills his best friend Guido Rinaldo (George Raft) when he finds the pair in a hotel room together, not waiting to learn that they have been legally married. Throughout the film Rinaldo flips a coin to pass the time. This bit of business became a Raft trademark and was spoofed years later in Billy Wilder's superb comedy, *Some Like It Hot*, where Raft plays a gangster named "Spats" Baxter who approaches a coin-flipping hood and asks him where he learned that cheap trick.

Hawks noted the motif of "X" marks the spot of the murder imposed on newspaper photographs and decided to play a game with the audience in the film. Every killing in *Scarface* is preceded by the appearance of an "X" somewhere in the frame, beginning with the killing that opens the film in which the camera starts on a window with four panes, the supports to which form an X. (Another example would be Raft's hotel room which bears the Roman numeral X on its door.)

Karloff doesn't appear until 40 minutes into the film just after Camonte has killed O'Hara, the leader of the North Side. He is shown opening pineapple crates which have been used to smuggle Tommyguns. The Gaffney character he portrays is based on real-life gangster Bugs Moran.

"Camonte thinks he's going to run this side of town now that he's got O'Hara," Gaffney sneers.

"He's getting too big," agrees Gaffney's subordinate.

"Yeah? He won't get any bigger. We'll take him before he finds out about these guns," says Gaffney, caressing the deadly steel of the machine gun. "Three hundred slugs a minute. Get the rest of them unpacked," he snaps.

"How many we got?"

"Plenty. And there's a lot more coming. O'Hara had them run across the line last night."

"We'll have the cops around our necks."

"Forget it," assures Gaffney with disdain. "They can't do anything about it. There's no law against bringing guns into the state and we can buy all we want."

"What a cinch."

"You said it," agrees Gaffney, who is then informed that Camonte has left headquarters and mobilizes his gang to attempt to rub him out.

Next time Gaffney appears is just after the St. Valentine's Day Massacre, and his cockiness is now replaced with nervousness as the police bring him to the scene of the crime for questioning.

"Well, I was on my way here to the garage to keep an appointment, and I was late," the daunted bootlegger tells them.

"Yeah?" prompts the tough-talking cop.

"And a car drives up and some guys pile out. Two of 'em was cops, at least they was dressed like cops."

"Cops? That's a new gag. Then what?"

"Well, it looked like a pinch," Gaffney continues, "so I beat around the block until it was over. Then he picked me up." Gaffney is clearly unsettled after being shown his comrades in arms, now a pile of corpses.

Karloff goes from daunted to disheveled, from nervous to outright fearful in the subsequent scene set at Gaffney's hideout. Two lines of white light cross to form an X above Gaffney's bed, indicating that he's doomed. He lights a cigarette, and says, "Seven of 'em, lined up against a wall. Mowed down just like that." He gets to his feet and starts to pace. "Didn't have a chance," he mourns.

"Sit down," advises one of his hoods. "You're wearing out the carpet."

"Oh yeah?" he responds. "Well, I'm the only one left. Thinks he'll get me, huh? Fat chance." Just then McArthur from the *Journal* arrives, having figured out where Gaffney is holed up. Gaffney decides he wants McArthur to stay, presumably to fill him in on what Camonte has been doing, which indicates where reporters get some of their inside information.

Gaffney is killed by Camonte and his gang a short time later while bowling in a bowling alley, just after he marks a "strike" (the familiar fatal X) on his scorecard. He is shot just as he releases the ball, which scores a strike. A single remaining pin wobbles, more machine-gun fire is heard, and it falls, representing Gaffney's final fall. (In reality, Moran turned to bankrobbing and spent most of his remaining years in prison.)

Hawks' direction is actually more expressionistic than most horror films of the period with impressive chiaroscuro lighting, darkened rooms, bodies silhouetted by blinds, and pools of light that hold no promise of safety. The excit-

While Karloff only has a small part as Gaffney, he nonetheless makes a significant contribution to the great gangster classic *Scarface*.

ing car chase gun battles in the film provided stock footage fodder for many later gangster melodramas, notably Monogram's *Dillinger* starring Lawrence Tierney. These scenes are some of the most exciting and kinetic in '30s' cinema.

The Hays Office offered up numerous objections to the film, including deleting a scene which made the incest theme more explicit, another showing Camonte on a yacht (crime could not be shown to pay), and another showing him buying his mother a thousand dollar lamp.

To ameliorate the Hays office, four changes were inaugurated: an opening crawl was written that indicated that the film was meant to expose a growing social problem, the subtitle *Shame of a Nation* was added, Hawks' assistant Richard Rosson was assigned to film an extraneous scene where reform-minded city officials band together to decry gangsterism, and Hawks himself inventively shot a second ending depicting Camonte being hanged (without the use of Paul Muni's services, as Muni was appearing in *Counselor-at-Law* on Broadway at the time). The ending shown depended on what each state's censorship board decided, though the MCA laserdisc provides both endings.

Gaffney will meet his doom at the local bowling alley after he rolls this strike in *Scarface*.

The film was unavailable for years as Howard Hughes owned all rights and acquired all prints. Universal bought the rights to the film for Brian De Palma and Oliver Stone's overblown, updated remake, and fortunately the original was finally released to video where it could enchant a new generation with its thrilling and amusing fare.

There is a wealth of talent behind *Scarface*'s screenwriting credits including Seton I. Miller, who worked with Hawks on the original *Dawn Patrol* and *The Criminal Code*. He won an Academy Award for co-writing the classic fantasy *Here Comes Mr. Jordan* and his other scripts include *The Adventures of Robin Hood*, the remake of *Dawn Patrol, The Sea Hawk, The Black Swan*, and Vincent Price's *Confessions of an Opium Eater*. He became a producer with Fritz Lang's *Ministry of Fear*, which he also scripted.

W. R. Burnett is a highly respected crime writer who wrote the novels that were the bases for *Beast of the City, Little Caesar,* and *The Asphalt Jungle*, and would co-script *High Sierra, This Gun For Hire, Captain Lightfoot* (which Michael Cimino ripped off as *Thunderbolt and Lightfoot* with Clint Eastwood and Jeff Bridges), and *The Great Escape*.

John Lee Mahin was brought out to Hollywood by Ben Hecht and become one of the great Hollywood script doctors, working uncredited on *A Star Is*

31

Born (1937), *The Wizard of Oz, Gone With the Wind, Foreign Correspondent, Woman of the Year*, and *The Yearling*. He was nominated for an Academy Award for *Captains Courageous* and *Heaven Knows, Mr. Allison*. He helped found the Screenwriters Guild in 1933 and his own script work includes *Bombshell, Treasure Island* (1934), *Boom Town, Dr. Jekyll and Mr. Hyde* (1941), and *The Bad Seed*.

Ben Hecht himself is one of the greatest screenwriters and script doctors Hollywood has ever known with credits too numerous to mention. That he received script credit for *Queen of Outer Space*, which he did not work on, but no screen credit for *The Thing*, which he did, is only one of many ironies in his career. He wrote, produced, and directed three fascinating but seldom seen films which should all be revived: *Crime Without Passion, The Scoundrel*, and *Spectre of the Rose*.

Howard Hawks enjoys a well-deserved reputation as one of the greatest directors of all time and is responsible for such classics as *Bringing Up Baby, Ball of Fire, His Girl Friday, The Big Sleep, Red River*, and *Rio Bravo,* among many others, though he is perhaps better known to many horror fans as the producer/uncredited director of *The Thing*. *Scarface* ranks with his very best, most exciting, and funniest films.

Karloff, of course, made a greater impact on the world of horror films than he did in gangster dramas, but a portrait of his career would be incomplete without acknowledging this separate side of his film characterizations.

Still, one piece of evidence as to the impact he made in his time is in *Night World*, which afforded Karloff one of his most suave roles as "Happy" MacDonald, a handsome nightclub owner who runs afoul of some bootleggers who insist that he buy his hooch from them. Former silent star Bert Roach cuts up as "Tommy" and flirts with a pair of flappers who decorate him gaudily with makeup. He turns to the camera and complains that he has been changed into a "Frankenstein," indicating that Karloff's creation had been integrated into the American consciousness mere months after the film's release.

Karloff, like any great actor, played many different parts in his career. In these films, he played tough guys who suddenly find themselves surrounded by the stress of dealing daily with death, of risking the displeasure of those who wouldn't hesitate to terminate with extreme prejudice. He clearly limns the characters' posturings, the veneer of violence which is meant to keep the world at bay, but he also shows these men's vulnerability and fear, their craven souls as they come face to face with those who prove even more maliciously malfeasant than they are.

It remains a timely lesson on why the life of a criminal is undesirable, that crime truly doesn't pay but takes its toll on a person's heart and soul, and that violence only begets more violence. Gangster great James Cagney couldn't do it any better in *Angels With Dirty Faces* than Karloff does in these classy crime productions.

Behind the Mask

CREDITS: Directed by John Francis Dillon; Producer: Harry Cohn; Screenplay: Jo Swerling from his story "In the Secret Service"; Continuity: Dorothy Howell; Photography: Teddy Tetzlaff; Editor: Otis Garrett; Sound: Glenn Rominger; Filmed in November 1931; Released by Columbia Pictures on February 25, 1932; 69 minutes

CAST: Jack Holt...Jack Hart, Constance Cummings...Julie Arnold, Boris Karloff...Jim Henderson, Claude King...Arnold, Bertha Mann...Edwards, Edward Van Sloan...Dr. August Steiner, Willard Robertson...Captain E. J. Hawkes

Scarface

CREDITS: Directed by Howard Hawks; Producer: Howard Hughes; Screenplay: Seton I. Miller, John Lee Mahin, W. R. Burnett, Fred Palsey, based on novel by Armitage Trail; Adapted for the screen by Ben Hecht; Photography: Lee Garmes and L. W. O'Connell; Editor: Edward Curtiss and Douglas Biggs; Assistant Director: Richard Rosson; Sound: William Snyder; music: Adolph Tandler and Gus Arnheim; Art Direction: Harry Oliver; Filmed May to November 1931; 99 minutes; Released by United Artists on March 26, 1932

CAST: Paul Muni...Tony Camonte, Ann Dvorak...Cesca Camonte, Karen Morley...Poppy, Osgood Perkins...Johnny Lovo, Boris Karloff...Gaffney, C. Henry Gordon...Guardino, George Raft...Rinaldo, Purnell Pratt...Publisher, Vince Barnett...Angelo, Inez Palange...Mrs. Camonte, Edwin Maxwell...Commissioner, Tully Marshall...Managing Editor, Henry Armetta...Pietro, Bert Starkey...Epstein, Harry J. Vejar...Big Louis Costello, Maurice Black...Sullivan, Charles Sullivan, Harry Tenbrook...Bootleggers, Hank Mann...Worker, Paul Fix...Gaffney Hood, Howard Hawks...Man on Bed, Dennis O'Keefe...Dance Extra

Dennis Fischer is the author of the book *Horror Film Directors* (McFarland, 1991) and is currently working on a follow-up on science fiction directors. He has contributed to many film magazines including *Filmfax, Cinefantastique*, and *Midnight Marquee*.

34

THE MASK OF FU MANCHU (1932)

by David J. Hogan

In 1932 Boris Karloff stood poised on the brink of major stardom. He had shocked and astonished audiences the year before as the Monster in *Frankenstein*, and the releasing studio, Universal, realized it might have stumbled onto the new Lon Chaney. But Karloff was not yet locked in at Universal, so the nine films he did in 1932 were produced by a variety of studios: Columbia (*Behind the Mask*); Fox (*Business and Pleasure*); United Artists (*Scarface*); Paramount (*The Miracle Man*); MGM (*The Mask of Fu Manchu*); and Universal (*The Cohens and Kellys in Hollywood, Night World, The Old Dark House*, and *The Mummy*).

For Karloff, the loan-out to MGM was a step up; *The Mask of Fu Manchu* offered him his first top-billed speaking part (he had had top billing in his previous picture, James Whale's *The Old Dark House*, but the character he played was mute). Nearly as important to Karloff's career was that MGM was one of the most respected and successful studios in Hollywood. Smart management by Nick Schenck at the parent company, Loew's Consolidated Enterprises, had guided MGM through the industry changes that marked the close of the silent era and the early years of the Depression. Because Loew's owned fewer theaters than Fox, Warner, and Paramount, it handled the mass conversion to sound with relative ease, and did not have to dip deeply into assets earmarked for production. Because of this, MGM had the wherewithal to roll confidently into the thirties, pursuing a strategy of A-pictures that would cement its position (with Paramount) as one of the two top studios in town.

After 1930 MGM became well known to the public for its expanding roster of big-name star players that brought prestige and impressive box-office. "More stars than there are in heaven" was MGM's boast, and it was not a hollow one; Clark Gable, Joan Crawford, Robert Taylor, Greta Garbo, Mickey Rooney, Jean Harlow, Lionel Barrymore, Spencer Tracy, and William Powell were just a few of the MGM family.

The studio's leading directors offered high levels of polish and efficiency, and included George Cukor, Victor Fleming, Edmund Goulding, W. S. Van Dyke, Sidney Franklin, Clarence Brown, and Jack Conway.

Nearly as significant was the studio's revolving staff of well-known writers, which included numerous transplanted novelists and journalists. At various times in the thirties, the studio employed Ben Hecht, Robert Benchley (who also starred in a successful series of MGM shorts), F. Scott Fitzgerald, S. J. Perelman, Dorothy Parker, and Maxwell Anderson.

Added to this plentitude of talent was an outstanding support staff of cinematographers (Karl Freund, George Folsey, Harold Rosson), costume designer Gilbert Adrian, art director Cedric Gibbons, makeup artists Cecil Holland and Jack Dawn, and soundman Douglas Shearer.

Although MGM management (that is, Louis B. Mayer and Irving Thalberg) did not consider *The Mask of Fu Manchu* a prestige release, the project had novelty, the potential box-office appeal of Karloff, and an enormous, built-in audience that had been cultivated by Fu Manchu's creator, Sax Rohmer, a novelist whose real name was Arthur Henry Ward.

Ward was a Briton with dark, heavy eyebrows and dark hair that receded slightly from his forehead. He was handsome in a diffident sort of way, and like many Englishmen he affected a pipe. He was born in Birmingham in 1883. His father was an Irish clerk, his mother an alcoholic who was convinced she was related to the 17th-century Irish general Patrick Sarsfield. Ward liked the name, and joined it to his own, calling himself Arthur Henry Sarsfield Ward.

Bright but frequently undisciplined, Ward had trouble keeping to schedules imposed by others, and decided to be a writer after a brief period in London's financial district and a longer stint as a journalist.

Literary acceptance did not come easily. The young Ward was eventually able to paper an entire room with rejection slips, and later remembered, "In order to complete the color scheme, I sent the same manuscript to the same magazine three times. But the third time they lost it."

Ward had long been curious about Egypt and the Middle East, and had a keen interest in the occult, which led him to join Aleister Crowley, Arthur Machen, and W. B. Yeats as a member of the Hermetic Order of the Golden Dawn.

Newspaper accounts of China's Boxer Rebellion, the overthrow of the Manchu dynasty, and the Asian drug trade helped stimulate Ward's interest in the Far East. He became fascinated by the region after a newspaper assignment took him to London's Chinatown, located in the shadowy Limehouse district. There, he became aware of the mysterious "Mr. King," who reputedly controlled all of Chinatown's illegal activity.

Ward took much of what he had learned about Mr. King and melded it with current events and his own vivid imagination to create the sinister genius Dr. Fu-Manchu (the name was hyphenated early on), who was introduced in a 1913 novel called *The Mystery of Dr. Fu-Manchu* (American title, *The Insidious Dr. Fu-Manchu*). Partly because of the urging of his wife, a gorgeous entertainer named Rose Elizabeth Knox, Ward adopted the pseudonym "Sax Rohmer"; in time, he would use the name in his everyday dealings as well as on his books.

The Mask of Fu Manchu **provided Karloff his first top-billed** *speaking* **part.**

The Mystery of Dr. Fu-Manchu was not Rohmer's first book; he had anonymously co-written with George Robey a novel called *Pause!* in 1910. But *Fu-Manchu* was his first hit, and Rohmer would produce a total of 14 Fu novels until his death in 1959. Two additional Fu adventures were published posthumously, in 1970 and 1973.

In that first novel, Rohmer wrote, "Imagine a person, tall, lean and feline, high-shouldered, with a brow like Shakespeare and a face like Satan, a close-shaven skull, and long, magnetic eyes of true cat-green. Invest him with all the cruel cunning of an entire Eastern race, accumulated in one giant intellect... Imagine that awful being, and you have a mental picture of Dr. Fu-Manchu, the yellow peril incarnate in one man."

The novels are marked not just by Fu's fiendish characterization and a high adventure quotient, but by Rohmer's almost fanatical attention to detail. Weaponry, animal life, geography—all of these and more were scrupulously researched. Rohmer also revised and rewrote extensively, honing a book until it was precisely what he wanted.

By the thirties, Fu Manchu had become a phenomenon that encompassed magazines (*Collier's* serialized Fu novels for years), radio series in Britain and America, and motion pictures. The screen's first Fu Manchu was Harry Agar Lyons in 1923; other actors in the role include Warner Oland (in numerous films), Boris Karloff, Henry Brandon (in a Republic serial), Manuel Requena (in a 1945 Mexican feature), Christopher Lee (in a series that started out promisingly but grew progressively worse), and Peter Sellers (in a misfired parody).

Television was one medium that Fu could not bend to his will. A 1952 pilot produced by Fox Movietone, directed by William Cameron Menzies, and starring John Carradine as Fu Manchu and Sir Cedric Hardwicke as Fu's antagonist, Sir Denis Nayland Smith, did not sell. In 1956 Republic's *The Adventures of Dr. Fu Manchu*, starring an inappropriately low-key actor named Glen Gordon, lasted just 13 episodes in syndication. (The show's primary appeal is beautiful Laurette Luez, well cast as Fu's sultry aide, Karamenah.)

Despite the trouble with TV, Fu was a compelling and popular creation that, by rights, should have made Rohmer a wealthy man. Two things conspired against the author: an agent who cheated him of royalties for 15 years, and the spendthrift ways of Rohmer and his wife. As quickly as the advances and (skimmed) royalties arrived in the post, Rohmer and Rose squandered them.

Late in Rohmer's career, he and his wife lived in an unheated New York apartment, and when things became unbearably tight, Rose would purposely anger her husband, then lock him in his study until he vented his fury by banging out a salable story.

The delicious melodrama that propels Rohmer's work is not without controversy. Asians have disliked the Fu stories for generations, and with good reason, for Rohmer's view of the Orient is distorted and purposely distasteful. In Fu's world, Asians are clever but unprincipled; industrious but easily led; ambitious but eager mainly to conquer and terrorize the white race. They are ingenious in the ways of subterfuge and torture, and although they loathe the white man, they lust for white women.

It's easy but pointless to excoriate Rohmer for the vulgar racism of the Fu stories. Born late in the Victorian era, Rohmer was very much a product of his time. The sun never sets on the British Empire, the saying went, and Rohmer's interpretation of the "yellow peril" (a presumed menace completely at odds

The significance of Karloff's participation in *The Mask of Fu Manchu* is very nearly obscured by the film's celebration of the sadistic, the immoral, and the revolting.

with British self-image and colonial ambition) was neither surprising nor without antecedent. M. P. Shiel's 1898 novel, *The Yellow Danger*, for instance, revolves around the Chinese warlord Yen How, and his plans for world conquest. Sorcery and the supernatural inform Allen Upward's *The Yellow Hand* (1904).

Prominent Asian menaces of the period's pulp fiction include Roland Daniel's Wu Fang, Eugene Thomas's Chu-Sheng, Jack Wylde's Fan Chu Fang, Walter B. Gibson's Shiwan Khan (a nemesis of the Shadow), Anthony Rud's Wun Wey (!), and Nigel Vane's Li Sin. Rohmer himself added to the list with Sumuru, a female version of Fu Manchu.

Characterizations of this sort flourished primarily because of the understandable ignorance of European and American readers. In that pre-TV era, westerners had no sense of connection to Asia and little knowledge of the people who lived there. But this observation allows the period's readers to wriggle off the hook too easily. The fact is that Fu Manchu and similar Oriental fiends were popular because the characters gave American and European readers what they wanted—and what they wanted to believe. Americans, in particular, living in an isolationist, superficially homogeneous society that was strictly segregated, were self-absorbed and often narrow-minded. If Sax Rohmer and other writers said that Chinamen were inscrutable and dangerous, Americans were willing to believe it.

The brutal Japanese adventurism that exploded across Asia in the early thirties (and that, paradoxically, allowed Americans to view the Chinese with sympathy) only cemented old prejudices, and seemed to confirm them as being correct. The Asian image couldn't catch a break.

By the early fifties, the Japanese had been subdued but the Chinese (now termed the *Red* Chinese) were once again cast as bogeymen in the western consciousness, so Fu's perverse appeal—and apparent relevance—did not diminish in the postwar era. (In an odd twist, though, some of the later Fu novels cast him as a zealous anti-Communist.)

In 1955 newspapers reported that Rohmer had sold the film, TV, and radio rights to Fu Manchu for $4 million. It was a good story, but completely fabricated, for Rohmer came away with an incredibly paltry $8,000. Over the years, he had supplemented his income by working as a "hired gun" for music-hall sketch comics, and by writing books of non-fiction, notably *The Romance of Sorcery*, a study of the occult published in 1914. Despite these sideline activities, Rohmer's ultimate financial disarray was irrevocable.

Movie sales brought temporary relief to Rohmer's perilous situation. MGM, anxious in 1932 to locate an exploitable vehicle for Boris Karloff, chose Rohmer's 1932 novel, *The Mask of Fu Manchu*. From the outset, producer Hunt Stromberg knew he wanted the film to emphasize sex—not the cheeky, carefree sort offered by MGM's inimitable Jean Harlow, but a dark, perverse sexuality grounded in sadism. Screenwriters Irene Kuhn, Edgar Allan Woolf (later a contributor to MGM's *The Wizard of Oz*), and John Willard (writer of 1927's *The Cat and the Canary*) had clear instructions, and ran with them.

Inside London's British Museum, Sir Denis Nayland Smith (Lewis Stone) meets with Sir Lionel Barton (Lawrence Grant) to discuss an expedition that

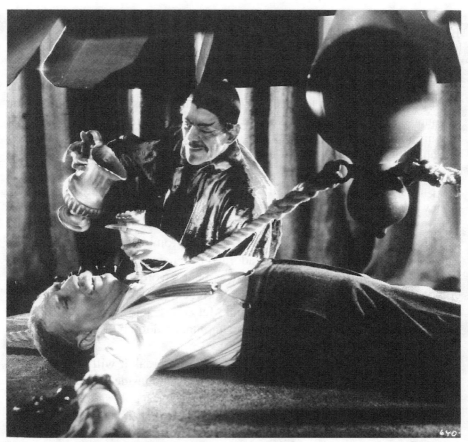

Fu torments Barton (Lawrence Grant) with water that turns out to be saltwater. Barton still won't crack.

will take them to the edge of the Gobi Desert and to the tomb of Mongol conqueror Genghis Khan. Among the artifacts inside are a golden mask and scimitar—valuable treasures in the west and absolutely vital to the plans of Fu Manchu to consolidate his power in the Orient and conquer the rest of the globe. "He'll lead hundreds of millions of men to sweep the world!" Smith cautions.

Barton can't believe it. "A Chinaman beat me? He couldn't do it!"

But the "Chinamen" are more clever than Barton believes, for in Smith's very office human eyes move behind the mask of a sarcophagus, observing the discussion. And later, while leaving the museum, Barton is abducted.

His daughter, Sheila (Karen Morley), is understandably upset by her father's disappearance, and insists that she be included in a rescue expedition after Smith receives a telegram: "Barton believed captive of Fu Manchu near Liangchow."

Help can't arrive too soon, for Fu insists that Barton reveal the location of Genghis Khan's tomb. Barton, for the moment, is keeping mum. Fu offers riches to his captive, and even his beautiful daughter, Fah Lo See (Myrna Loy), if Barton will talk. Still Barton refuses.

Fu's patience, slender to begin with, frays and snaps. He orders Barton roped to a stone platform, over which hovers an enormous bell with a gigantic clapper operated by a pair of coolies. Well, it's better than hot pokers—or is it? "Just a bell ringing," Fu leers to Barton, "but the percussion and repercussion of sound against your eardrums will soften and destroy them, until the sound is magnified a thousand times. You can't move, you can't sleep, you will be frantic with thirst. You will be unspeakably foul. But here you will lie, day after day, until you tell."

Barton is made of stern stuff, and remains silent during days of torture, even when Fu torments him with fresh fruit and allows him to drink from a cup of saltwater.

Meanwhile, Smith's expedition arrives at the tomb, uncovers it, and enters. The doors of the inner sanctum are adorned by a pair of gilded, bas-relief warriors, splendid in battle dress, their knees bent, swords at the ready. Smith's companions—Sheila, handsome young Terrence Granville (Charles Starrett), Professor von Berg (Jean Hersholt), and McLeod (David Torrence)—are suitably impressed. "You're standing in the unplundered tomb of a king who died 700 years ago!" the professor exclaims.

Although the tomb's seal warns that any who break it will be cursed, the group is not deterred. The doors are cracked wide and inside, astride a splendid throne, is the skeleton of Genghis Khan, the mammoth gold scimitar across its lap and the graceful gold half-mask covering the skull. When Granville lifts the artifacts from the bones, the expedition's coolies retreat in fear, and only Smith's quick pistol shots into the air restrain them from bolting.

Meanwhile, Fu reasons that it's only a matter of time until Barton cracks. Then, the expedition will be routed, the sword and mask stolen, and Fu's march to conquest begun. In a great meeting hall, Fu addresses the assembled chieftains who will help him carry out his plan. "I have heard the shouts of the dead and dying drowned by the cries of our victorious people!"

Artifacts in hand, the Smith expedition has left the tomb and now rests overnight in an abandoned temple. Smith wonders aloud why the Chinese can be impressed by a mere "bauble" such as the sword. "Will we ever understand these eastern races?"

McLeod agrees to take the first watch, unaware that Chinese loyal to Fu are silently scampering about the temple. In a particularly gruesome moment, Mac takes a dagger in the back. Although mortally wounded, he manages to get off a shot, killing his assassin and rousing Smith and the others.

Smith orders the expedition to pack up and leave immediately. "You suppose for a moment Fu Manchu doesn't know we have a beautiful white girl with us? Fu knows everything that's happening. His spies are everywhere."

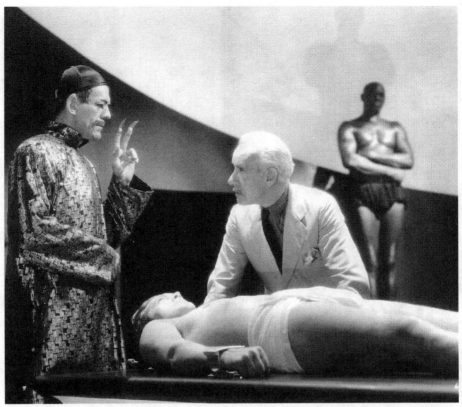

Fu has mesmerized Granville (Charles Starrett). He promises Smith (Lewis Stone) he won't be as lucky.

In the temple garden, Granville is almost hit on the head by a human hand that wears a signet ring. Sheila identifies the ring as her father's, leaving little doubt as to the identity of the unlucky owner of the hand. Moments later Granville and Sheila are visited by one of Fu's messengers, who boldly shows up at the garden gate. He calmly explains that unless the gold artifacts are handed over, Barton will be killed.

Acting without Smith's permission, young Granville agrees. He takes the artifacts and travels with the messenger to Fu, who gleefully accepts the prizes. But the sword, Fu discovers, is a fake. Furious, he hands Granville over to Fah Lo See, who orders the young man stripped and flayed. After Granville is whipped into semi-consciousness, the girl orders him cut down. He slumps in her arms and she gazes at him with undisguised lust before kissing him.

"He is not entirely unhandsome, is he, father?"

Fu is only mildly impressed: "For a white man, no."

At the temple, the group is shocked when Barton's body is unceremoniously dumped in the garden. Smith understands at once what has happened,

"It will be your pleasure to be the first white martyrs to perish at the hands of the new Genghis Khan!"

and reveals that he had had a fake sword made, with the intention of using it later as a bargaining chip. But Granville's impetuous act has ruined that plan, and precipitated the death of Sheila's father.

Using bluff and subterfuge, Smith discover an entrance to Fu's headquarters. In a narrow passageway, Smith is halted by an imperious voice: "The slightest move will send a bullet crashing through your stiff British spine."

It is Fu, of course, who reveals himself a moment later. He and Smith confront each other—two great adversaries, with Smith at an admitted disadvantage. Fu has mesmerized Granville, who has become the chosen one of Fah Lo See. The young man's hypnotized condition will become permanent after Fu injects him with a nasty serum distilled from the blood of snakes, spiders, and Fu himself.

Fu promises Smith that neither he nor the others will be as fortunate as Granville. But first, Fu must get his hands on the real sword. Von Berg is tricked, and removes it from its ghoulish hiding place: Mac's grave.

Fu eagerly takes the gilded weapon and determines it is real. Exultant, he addresses the captives: "It will be your pleasure to be the first white martyrs to perish at the hands of the new Genghis Khan! I congratulate you!"

Sheila has three words: "You yellow monster!"

The interlopers are taken away for final disposition. Von Berg is strapped to a seat where he will be skewered by moving walls of heavy chromium spikes; Sheila is dressed in a white gown and prepared for ritual sacrifice; and Smith is tied to a teeter-board that slowly lowers him into a pit of crocodiles.

Fortunately (and was there ever any doubt?), Smith and Granville manage to escape their respective pickles. The pair struggle with Fu's ebony body-guards, then rescue von Berg seconds before his all-over body piercing. In a room above the great hall, Smith activates an enormous death ray and plays it across the crowd of chieftains below. Men scream, burst into flame, and fall dead.

Smith spies Fu and exclaims, "Wherever you are, Genghis Khan, I give you back your sword!" The deadly ray coruscates along the gold blade and into Fu's body. The evil genius is electrocuted, the threat to the British Empire and the white race eliminated.

The shoot of *The Mask of Fu Manchu* began on August 6, 1932, with the script not yet complete. And when enough pages did come down so that the cast could get an idea of what was going on, the stars reacted with surprise. In a 1969 interview with the *New York Times*, Myrna Loy recalled, "I carried around a pet python and whipped a young man tied to a rack and all sorts of dreadful things. Now I had been reading a little Freud around that time, so I called the director [Charles Vidor] over one day and said, 'Say, this is obscene. This woman is a sadistic nymphomaniac!' And he said, 'What does *that* mean?' We did it all before these kids today ever thought of it, and we didn't even know what we were doing!"

Karloff's first look at a lengthy speech by Fu that opens the film came as the actor was sitting in Cecil Holland's makeup chair, undergoing the two-and-a-half-hour process that would transform him into Fu. Karloff was astonished that he was expected to memorize the speech on short notice, and even more astonished after leaving the chair, when the pages were taken from him and replaced with rewritten ones.

The cast soldiered on for about two weeks. Then, after eyeing the rushes with alarm, the MGM front office shut down production and fired Hungarian director and UFA veteran Charles Vidor (1900-59). Although he did not direct again until landing a job at Monogram two years later, his career eventually flourished and he remained an active, A-picture director until his death. He also wed *Fu Manchu* leading lady Karen Morley late in 1932, and chose not to let MGM know for a month—a bit of revenge, perhaps, for what he perceived as bad treatment.

Mayer and Thalberg apparently were worried that Vidor's take on the story was *so* grotesque that it would culminate in a box-office disaster on the order of

Tod Browning's *Freaks*—a brilliant but undeniably peculiar thriller, released in February 1932, that aroused the vitriol of critics, confused and alarmed the public, and was a big money-loser. That concern was legitimate, but it's likely that Vidor became the *Fu Manchu* fall guy through little fault of his own; if Mayer and Thalberg ever realized that Vidor had merely delivered the sort of queasy ambience that had been insisted upon by Hunt Stromberg, they chose to discount the fact, and to replace the director rather than the producer.

Elsewhere at the studio, director Charles Brabin was struggling with *Rasputin and the Empress*. Brabin (1883-1957) was a talented but problematic director whose working habits undercut and ultimately shortened his film career. He was born in Britain and was a stage actor in the States before 1908. His first work as a director was for the Edison Company in 1911. Later, he directed two vehicles of screen vamp Theda Bara, whom he married in 1921.

Brabin's greatest critical success was a rural melodrama called *Driven* (1923). So highly regarded was the picture that Brabin was selected to direct *Ben-Hur* (1925), but after thousands of feet of film had been exposed with unsatisfactory results, he was pulled from the film and replaced by Fred Niblo. The multi-million-dollar suit that Brabin subsequently brought against MGM was evidently resolved to everyone's satisfaction, for the director was again hired by the studio in 1930. While there, Brabin directed *The Beast of the City* (1932), a startlingly effective urban crime melodrama starring Walter Huston and Jean Harlow.

Trouble asserted itself again later in 1932, however, when Brabin ran afoul of John, Lionel, and Ethel Barrymore on the set of *Rasputin and the Empress* and was replaced by Richard Boleslawski. Brabin, in turn, was tapped to fill Charles Vidor's spot on *Fu Manchu*. Little, if any, of Vidor's footage was retained, and cast and crew began again.

None of this made the *Fu Manchu* set any calmer, and certainly did not make MGM a congenial place, particularly since the studio was still reeling from the July death of Jean Harlow's husband, MGM producer Paul Bern. His apparent suicide generated unsavory (and probably untrue) sexual rumors, and threatened Harlow's incipient stardom. The whole situation was an ongoing distraction for *Fu Manchu* producer Hunt Stromberg, who was also producing *Red Dust* and trying to keep Harlow, that film's star, up and working.

On the *Fu Manchu* set, key scenes were routinely altered in the middle of production. For example, an early draft of the script called for Smith, not von Berg, to be strapped to the spike device (stills exist of Lewis Stone in the seat), but according to an oft-told story, studio executives reasoned that to have a fat man (Hersholt) in the predicament would be more unnerving for audiences than to imperil a slim one (Stone)—hence Hersholt's meeting with the walls of spikes. The decision has a certain twisted logic until one realizes that von Berg was probably the character menaced by the crocodiles in the unamended script,

Karloff and Stone in the filmed torture scene that was changed to put Jean Hersholt in the hot seat.

and that the animals' consumption of a fleshy fat man is infinitely more gross than a quick nibble on a lean one!

Following the false start, plus an inordinate amount of reshoots and added scenes, filming of *The Mask of Fu Manchu* finally wrapped on October 21, at a total cost of about \$325,000. Charles Brabin directed only two more films—*Day of Reckoning* (1933) and *A Wicked Woman* (1934)—before his retirement in 1934. He spent most of the rest of his life in Manhattan.

The significance of Karloff's participation in *The Mask of Fu Manchu* is very nearly obscured by the film's celebration of the sadistic, the immoral, and the revolting—and that's not bad, because it's all in (nasty) fun, and precisely what producer Stromberg wanted.

The picture is a virtual primer of sexual sadism, and the way in which the predilection can be buffed to a gloss as high as that of the chromium spikes that threaten to impale von Berg. A real-life Fu Manchu and Fah Lo See would provide an army of clinical researchers with a lifetime of study.

Our first look at Fu is a closeup on his face, and its simultaneous reflection in a peculiar concave mirror that distorts his features in the flashing lights of his laboratory. The moment has a grotesque funhouse aspect, and it's clear from the start that the adventure will be concerned as much with twisted psychology as with high adventure.

Fu's tortures—a catalog of spearings, piercings, and other bodily violations—have undeniable sexual overtones. Even the crocodile pit, which offers to male victims the prospect of being eaten alive (a sort of vaginaphobia well known to psychoanalysts) is darkly sexual.

Fah Lo See is no less unbalanced, as she orders Granville whipped into insensibility and then caresses his naked torso after he slumps to the floor. Later, she is willing to allow the sacrifice of Granville's mind if it will guarantee her possession of his splendid body.

Miscegenation—a completely artificial racialist notion that has no basis in human biology—frightened many in 1932, and has the power to rankle regressive minds even today. One can only imagine the revulsion felt by audiences of 1932 as Fah Lo See ogles Granville, and as Fu exploits his followers' desire for white women. The gathered chieftains are randy enough when in the presence of a beautiful Asian doll (their predatory expressions as Fu introduces Fah Lo See can make viewers shiver), and the group works itself into a fine froth over the prospect of defiling the world's white maidens. Fu expertly manipulates the group, urging them to "Rain down on the white race and burn them!" He pauses to acknowledge Sheila, his demure blonde captive. "Would you all have maidens such as this for your wives?" The crowd roars its assent. "Then conquer and breed! Kill the white man and take his women!"

The aspect of Fu's character that many viewers find particularly disturbing is his disdain for all things Christian. He mockingly promises to turn Smith and the others into "white martyrs" and to send them to their "saintly Christian paradise." He is not a very respectful fellow at all, and so to see him receive his comeuppance is extremely satisfying. Wherever his black soul is destined, the place is unlikely to be a "paradise."

All of this is presented in a stew concocted from our subconscious revulsion for needles, spiders, snakes—and people who are not like us. Fu's world is an alien, intimidating one, emphatically so thanks to Gilbert Adrian's exotic costumes, Cedric Gibbons's deco set and furniture designs, and Tony Gaudio's evocative, high-contrast monochrome cinematography. Two camera setups are particularly striking: a silhouetted long shot of Smith as he ascends a steep staircase in Fu's lair, and a marvelous tableau of the mesmerized Granville stretched atop a stone bier, illuminated by a broadening triangle of light that falls from an unseen source far above him. If *The Mask of Fu Manchu* is about xenophobia and sexual pathology, it's also about sleek decadence, thirties-style.

Interestingly, Brabin (or is it Vidor?) tossed in some effective sequences that are straight out of traditional gothic horror. The genuine sword is removed from Mac's grave at night in a howling thunderstorm, *a la* the nocturnal activities of Dr. Frankenstein and Fritz, or Burke and Hare. And the sword is not transported in some sleek roadster along a superhighway, but in a horse-drawn covered wagon that churns and struggles along a muddy, rutted path.

Electrical effects by *Frankenstein* contributor Kenneth Strickfaden are completely gratuitous—and perfectly marvelous. There's no logical reason for Fu to test the authenticity of the swords by standing with them in coruscating feelers of electricity, but you're nevertheless swept away by the noisy, crackling drama of the displays. Similarly, the enormous death ray that figures in the climax is far from discreet, but when its nozzle emits a ropy burst of electricity that destroys Fu and his followers, your heart races with pleasure and horror. (Strickfaden doubled for Karloff in some of these high-voltage sequences.)

Karloff seems to have had fun playing Fu, and while audiences of 1932 may have "bought" the illusion of the lisping English actor as a Chinese, the passing of the years has turned the illusion completely around, so that now Karloff's performance is a campy masquerade. Hindsight allows us to exclaim, "Whee! It's Boris Karloff!" and to giggle a bit at the showy but very theatrical makeup Cecil Holland devised for Karloff.

The performance is among Karloff's most enjoyable; seldom did he let himself go with such abandon. You'll never see a leer more fiendish than those summoned by Fu Manchu, or a greater sense of wicked triumph as he hefts the true sword of Genghis Khan. Watching as Karloff happily imposes himself on the film, you can't help reacting with a shudder and a smile.

Typical of MGM product of the period, *The Mask of Fu Manchu* has a solid supporting cast. Lewis Stone (1879-1953) is well known to generations of film fans as kindly Judge Hardy in MGM's enormously popular Andy Hardy films of 1937-46. The sum of his film career, though, is considerably more varied, encompassing romance, drama, and costume adventure from 1915 until his death. Stone remained popular throughout his life, and MGM hung on to him jealously; most of the actor's sound films were produced by that studio.

Stone is ideally cast as Sir Nayland Smith. Although not a young man, he gives the impression of being a vigorous one. This, coupled with the actor's inherent dignity, make this Smith an adversary worthy of Karloff's demented Fu.

Famed Hollywood glamour photographer George Hurrell once described Karen Morley's appeal as "cerebral" rather than "emotional." That's an apt summation of this talented actress, who won third billing in *Fu Manchu*. Blonde, big-eyed, and with a delicate, almost neurotic air, Morley (born 1905) was not a typical Hollywood leading lady. The first part of her film career spanned 1931 to 1940, after which she worked mainly on the stage, with occasional film roles. Throughout her career, she was known as one of Hollywood's premier political activists. She had a highly developed social conscience, and was keenly interested in workers' rights—to her own detriment, for when she was summoned by the House Un-American Activities Committee (HUAC) in 1953 to testify about alleged Communist infiltration of the film industry, she invoked her Fifth Amendment right against self-incrimination. That was sufficient for the Hollywood establishment, which had been soundly spooked by the committee and had caved in to its absurd, Red-baiting excesses: After 1953, Karen Morley did not work in film again.

Morley made solid impressions in numerous high-profile films of the thirties and forties, notably *Our Daily Bread* (1934), in which she's wonderful as the farm woman who dedicates herself to the creation of a commune. In *Fu Manchu*, she's effective as Sheila Barton, less for what the character does (Sheila mainly frets and wrings her hands) than for the sensitivity and intelligence that Morley managed to bring to the thinly scripted character. If there is a quiet surprise in *Fu Manchu*, it is Karen Morley.

B-movie cowboy stardom was in the cards for Charles Starrett (1903-86), a strapping, ex-Dartmouth football star who began as a movie extra in 1926, left films for the stage, and returned to movies in 1930. His cowboy career began at Columbia in 1936 and lasted until 1952. As the sex object Granville in *Fu Manchu*, Starrett is appropriately handsome (and a wee bit dim), a nice fellow in a milieu in which niceness doesn't carry much weight.

Like Lewis Stone, Myrna Loy (1905-93) had a varied career but remains best known for a single role: the sophisticated Nora Charles opposite William Powell's Nick Charles in MGM's Thin Man series (1934-47). So powerful (and influential) was Loy's impact as the bright, glib Nora that casual movie fans are probably unaware that the actress spent the first decade of her film career typecast as a dark seductress, often of Asian background. Following experience as a dancer, Loy broke into pictures in 1925 with a small part in *Ben-Hur*. By 1932, she was under contract to MGM and working steadily, but seemed unlikely to break into the pantheon. Indeed, the same year that Loy took the part of Fah Lo See, she starred in *Thirteen Women* as a vengeful Eurasian beauty

Karloff seems to have had fun playing Fu.

who uses her powers of hypnosis to pay back the ex-sorority sisters who had once tormented her.

Fah Lo See is the sort of showy, campy role a good actress can dive into, and Loy did so with relish, exuding sadistic excess and blasts of pheromones in about equal measure.

Actors cast as other members of Smith's expedition are competent character players: Jean Hersholt (1886-1956), a popular industry activist who founded the Motion Picture Relief Fund; Lawrence Grant (1870-1952), whose stolid demeanor served him well in *The Cat Creeps* (1930), *Werewolf of London* (1935), *Son of Frankenstein* (1939), and *The Ghost of Frankenstein* (1942); and David Torrence (1880-1942), a Broadway actor who has supporting roles in *Five Star Final* (1931), *Captain Blood* (1935), and *Lost Horizon* (1937).

Finally, in a film in which every Asian speaking role but one is taken by a Caucasian actor, there is round-faced Willie Fung (1896-1945), active in motion pictures from 1926 to 1942, who shows up in the final scene of *The Mask of Fu Manchu* to provide low-comedy relief as a foolishly grinning ship's porter who summons Smith and the others to supper. Fung took a similar—and even more moronic—role in Victor Fleming's *Red Dust*, released the same year as *Fu Manchu*.

Box-office reaction to *The Mask of Fu Manchu* was acceptable but not outstanding. Combined domestic and worldwide gross was $625,000—good enough, according to historian Gregory William Mank, for a net profit of $62,000.

Not surprisingly, critical response varied. "And still the cinema goes busily about its task of terrorizing the children," sniffed the *New York Times*. "The latest of the bugaboo symposiums arrived at the Capitol yesterday under the fairly reticent title of *The Mask of Fu Manchu*. Its properties include Boris Karloff, one well-equipped dungeon, several hundred Chinamen, and the proper machinery for persuading a large cast...."

England's *Film Weekly* described the picture as "A blood-and-thunder thriller of nightmare dimensions.... [Karloff] is allowed to indulge in an orgy of organized torture that would have been the envy of any medieval monarch."

On the down side, *Variety* reported that audiences laughed at inappropriate moments, said Karen Morley was miscast, and inexplicably claimed that Myrna Loy "is playing stock." And Karloff, *Variety* concluded, "is still doing the Frankenstein Monster."

Mass-market film guides of the present day are positive in their assessments. "Highly satisfactory," says *Halliwell's Film Guide*, "very good to look at." Leonard Maltin's *Movie and Video Guide* calls the film "Elaborate," adding that it is "ornate and hokey, but fun; Loy is terrific as Fu's deliciously evil daughter."

Politically correct special-interest groups (that is, resentful, grudge-filled people with no sense of historical perspective) skewered *The Mask of Fu Manchu* during its 1972 re-release. The film was many years coming to home video, and when it did in 1992, it was in a truncated version that eliminated most of the references to race, sex, and Christianity. A historian's best hope to own a complete version is to tape a local-station broadcast of an older print.

In the meantime, we can only hope that those who would deny and obscure cultural history, and the corporate rabbits who are intimidated by the revisionists' cries, will one day come to their senses and return MGM's Fu Manchu to his grandly melodramatic glory.

CREDITS: Producer: Hunt Stromberg; Director: Charles Brabin (uncredited: Charles Vidor); Screenplay: Irene Kuhn, Edgar Allan Woolf, and John Willard, from the novel *The Mask of Fu Manchu* by Sax Rohmer; Cinematographer: Tony Gaudio; Art Director: Cedric Gibbons; Editor: Ben Lewis; Makeup: Cecil Holland; Sound Recorder: Douglas Shearer; Special Electrical Properties: Kenneth Strickfaden; Running Time: 68 minutes; Metro-Goldwyn-Mayer/Cosmopolitan Productions; Released December 2, 1932

CAST: Boris Karloff...Dr. Fu Manchu, Lewis Stone...Sir Denis Nayland Smith, Karen Morley...Sheila Barton, Myrna Loy...Fah Lo See, Charles Starrett...Terry Granville, Jean Hersholt...Prof. von Berg, Lawrence Grant...Sir Lionel Barton, David Torrence...McLeod, E. Alyn Warren...Goy Lo Sung, Ferdinand Gottschalk...British Museum official, C. Montague Shaw...British Museum official, Willie Fung...Ship's steward

Sources: *Encyclopedia of Mystery and Detection* by Chris Steinbrunner and Otto Penzler, McGraw-Hill, 1976; *The Film Encyclopedia* by Ephraim Katz, Perigee Books, 1979; *Hollywood Cauldron* by Gregory William Mank, McFarland, 1994; *Karloff* by Denis Gifford, Curtis Books, 1973; various novels by Sax Rohmer.

David J. Hogan has contributed to a variety of magazines including *Cinefantastique, Moviegoer, Photon, Filmfax*, and *Outré*. His essays have appeared in editions of *Magill's Cinema Annual* and he has authored three books: *Who's Who of the Horrors and Other Fantasy Films, Dark Romance: Sexuality in the Horror Film*, and *Your Movie Guide to Drama Video Tapes and Discs*. He is Publisher, Special Projects, with Chicago-based Publications International, Ltd. Hogan lives with his wife Kim and three children in a rambling house filled with books, music, and movies.

[Courtesy Ronald V. Borst/Hollywood Movie Posters]

THE MUMMY (1932)

by Paul M. Jensen

Although Boris Karloff is probably best known for his performance as the Frankenstein Monster, that dangerous but innocent brute does not represent the actor at his most typical, nor does the role display all of his strengths. The first true showcase for Karloff was MGM's *The Mask of Fu Manchu* (1932), in which he played an articulate, sardonic sadist. However, that film's production was too chaotic to result in a truly satisfying work. Only with *The Mummy* did the actor receive a context which set off his physical and vocal talents to perfection. Here, Karloff's presence dominates, but it doesn't stand apart, for all of the other creative elements mesh to produce a truly balanced film experience.

In general, Karloff's gaunt features, his angular form, and his lisping articulation make such an immediately powerful impression that no matter what he does or says, he automatically runs the risk of overemphasis. Because of this unusual, larger-than-life aura, Karloff tends to be most convincing when he plays an understated and restrained character. On such occasions, his extraordinary appearance and voice suggest that behind the restraint lie a bitter intelligence and an unrelenting will, which could at any moment break free with overwhelming power. The key to Karloff's personal success in *The Mummy* is the fact that the title character—the reanimated and unwrapped corpse of Imhotep, an ancient Egyptian priest—has a physical fragility that makes him resist physical activity or even contact. Holding his body still and erect, with his arms at his sides, Karloff becomes the quietly forceful center of attention in every scene. By doing nothing, he manages to seem constantly in control, both of himself and of the situation. Similarly, Karloff's voice gives his understated dialogue a haunted and haunting resonance, while his tone of ironic politeness lends a sophisticated dignity to his inner frustration and menace.

At the same time as Imhotep conveys, and takes for granted, the power surging below the reserved surface, Karloff's restraint also suggests the physical and emotional suffering of the character, as well as his unwavering love for Anckesenamon, an emotion which so transcends mere feeling that it has become his entire nature. The tragedy of Imhotep is not his suffering at having been buried alive, but his isolation and solitude, an isolation made especially poignant by the fact that the woman for whom he had sacrificed all has been reincarnated as Helen Grosvenor (Zita Johann), to whom he is a stranger.

Thanks to the skill and sensitivity of its makers, *The Mummy* consistently exemplifies what is best in the horror films of the early 1930s, but two moments stand out. These moments, significantly, make use of Karloff, but do not entirely depend on his presence. The return to life of the mummy, in the film's first scene, is perhaps Hollywood's best illustration of how to use the film medium—images and sound—to evoke a horrific situation through implication. Although Karloff spent long hours being made-up and wrapped-up for this scene, the filmmakers reveal an amazing degree of restraint, for they show only Karloff's face as his eyes open slightly, his chest as his arms unfold, his hand as he touches a parchment, and a few strands of wrappings as they trail through a doorway. The horror is felt through the oppressive lack of background music; through the stately rhythm of the editing between the archeologist (Bramwell Fletcher), intent on reading the Scroll of Thoth, and the mummy in his upright sarcophagus, responding to the incantation; through the sense of dreadful anticipation created by the camera's movement across the room; and through the unpredictable appropriateness of the archeologist's insane laughter when he sees what we do not—the living mummy standing before him.

In this scene, the heavily made-up Karloff is just a face and arms and a hand, but later he is fully visible and audible as he sits by his pool of memory and tells Helen of his austere passion, his ancient torment. "Anckesenamon," he says, "my love has lasted longer than the temples of our gods. No man ever suffered as I did for you. But the rest you may not know, not until you are about to pass through the great night of terror and triumph, until you are ready to face moments of horror for an eternity of love." Karloff speaks these lines in an almost flat tone that nonetheless captures the rhythmic musicality of the syllables ("my love has last-ed long-er than the tem-ples of our gods"), the alliteration ("ter-ror and tri-umph"), and the contrast between the brevity of "moments" and the extensiveness of "e-*ter*-ni-ty." What a pleasure it must be for an actor to speak such well-phrased dialogue, especially when that dialogue is so attuned to the echoes of dry intensity in that actor's own voice.

Imhotep is a menace, a single-minded obsessive who possesses the power to implement his obsession, but he is also a sympathetic figure, a man who once dared the gods' wrath in an attempt to return his lover to life, and who now, 3,700 years later, finds himself given a second chance. His suffering is strongly felt, as is his love, of which he has become the victim, for it has taken possession of him and now it, and only it, defines him.

Boris Karloff is the centerpiece of *The Mummy*. One cannot imagine the film existing without him. Other actors might have had the necessary stature—Bela Lugosi, perhaps, or John Barrymore—but their charisma would have been overwhelming. Still others—such as Fredric March or Paul Muni—might have played the character well, but they would have acted the part, not embodied it. Karloff, however, did not create this film alone. Rather, he was handed the part,

Boris Karloff is the centerpiece of *The Mummy.*

and the cinematic context which makes it shine, by two other creative sensibilities. The collaboration of John L. Balderston and Karl Freund made *The Mummy* possible, and the evolution of this film dramatizes how difficult it is for such a thoroughly accomplished motion picture ever to materialize.

The process began when Universal Studios hired the writer Nina Wilcox Putnam, long a popular and prolific author of stories for magazines such as *The Saturday Evening Post*. Independent in her life and assertive in her opinions, Putnam was an early advocate of women's rights. Among her many books are *It Pays to Smile* (1920), *Tomorrow We Diet* (1922), *The Bear Who Went to War* (1928), and an autobiography, *Laughing Through* (1930). As a writer, she was known for dealing with women's domestic and professional lives in a humorous style, so it is surprising that for Universal she supplied the original stories

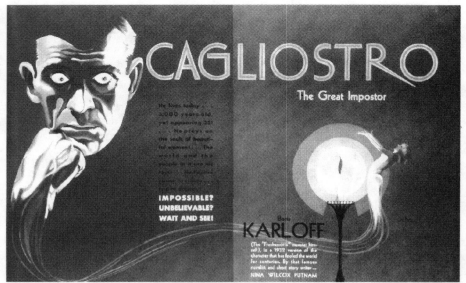

Cagliostro, a nine page story, was developed into a more extended treatment before John L. Balderston turned it into *The Mummy*. [Courtesy Ronald V. Borst/ Hollywood Movie Posters]

for a Tom Mix western (*The Fourth Horseman*, 1932) and a Boris Karloff horror film. By the first week of February, 1932, Putnam had completed *Cagliostro*, a nine-page story which the head of Universal's scenario department, Richard Schayer, quickly developed into a more extended treatment, dated February 19. The summary of *Cagliostro* retained in the studio's files, although credited to Putnam alone, is probably derived from that treatment.

The real Cagliostro was a poor Italian who gave himself the title of count and, just prior to the French Revolution, passed himself off as a magician and alchemist. For several years, his seances were popular in Parisian high society. Finally, in 1789, he was convicted of heresy by the Inquisition and he died in prison six years later. (Orson Welles portrayed Cagliostro in the 1949 film, *Black Magic*.) Universal's plot summary, however, calls Putnam's title character a "great Egyptian magician," which is the story's only link with Egypt, while an item in *Variety* (2/9/32, p. 6) identifies him as "jester to Louis XIV," which would place him in early 18th century France. Evidently, Putnam used only the name and the idea of his being a magician, and no one yet had a clear idea of the character's origin.

Set in modern San Francisco, the story devised by Putnam establishes that Cagliostro solved the secret of longevity by injecting himself with nitrates. Having been betrayed by his lover, he spends the next thirty centuries seeking out women who resemble her and destroying them in revenge. "His great intelligence keeps him ever ahead of scientific discovery so he has improved radio and television for purposes of robbery, to keep him wealthy," and as a way of eliminating "enemies, guards and detectives." Arriving in San Francisco with "a giant dumb Nubian as attendant," he poses as the blind, long-lost uncle of heroine Helen Dorrington, who happens to resemble his ancient mistress.

"Because of the depression, Helen is now a ticket-seller at a small movie house, knowing joy only through her love for young Dr. Jack Foster, almost as poor as she. By a strange chance Jack will come into a fortune in six months' time: he was physician to millionaire H. G. Whemple, who died under mysterious circumstances (really Cagliostro's death ray). Whemple, deeply religious, resented as sacrilege the brilliant archaeological accomplishments of his only relative, a brother, Professor Whemple, and therefore left his money in trust to Jack. Cagliostro rents H. G.'s mansion and through lawyers gets Helen to live with him and care for him. Helen consents because she is given enough money to support her mother royally. She likes her uncle, but senses something uncanny in the house, and notices that wherever her uncle's hand rests, a dusty imprint is left.

"Meanwhile a series of sensational and inexplicable robberies take place, and both Jack and the Professor are on the case. The Professor suspects the truth, and communicates his fears for Helen to Jack. Helen takes fright and tries to leave, but is imprisoned in the cellar by the Nubian. One of the robber gang operated by Cagliostro through radio breaks down and confesses that the next theft is to be the supply of nitrates in a safe deposit vault... The Professor secretly invades his brother's home and steals the hypodermic and nitrate supply in Cagliostro's room. Then he seeks out the magician finding him operating the radio robbery. The theft is not completed, but the Professor is thrown in the cellar with Helen, whence they are rescued by Jack when Cagliostro crumbles to dust without his nitrates."

One can find very little resemblance to *The Mummy* in this highly unpromising tangle of arbitrary events and contrived character relationships, which are presented in an unstructured, haphazard fashion. Clearly, something radical had to be done to impose dramatic coherence on *Cagliostro*. Wisely, Universal sought out John L. Balderston. This former journalist had written the popular play, *Berkeley Square*, a romantic fantasy which premiered in London in 1926. He had also adapted Hamilton Deane's play, *Dracula*, for American audiences and did the same for Peggy Webling's theatrical version of *Frankenstein*; both of these works provided Universal with the basis for successful films in 1931.

Balderston arrived in Hollywood near the end of March, 1932, and set to work transforming the muddle that was *Cagliostro* into a viable story. He retained only a few minor elements of Putnam's plot, which he mixed with inspirations drawn from other sources and his own imagination, and it took him about three months to develop a screenplay. Balderston's first, incomplete script—dated June 30—was soon followed by a complete version (July 13), then five more (August 3, August 19, undated, September 6, and September 12). Although only the last is available for examination, published by MagicImage Filmbooks in 1989, the fact that all are of nearly the same length suggests that he had solved his major plot problems by the end of June.

In one major adjustment, he used the references to Cagliostro being an ancient Egyptian and to Professor Whemple being an archeologist as a starting point and elaborated on that aspect, drawing on news reports about the intact tomb of Pharaoh Tutankhamon for inspiration. Balderston was a reporter covering the discovery of Tut's tomb, thus his final screenplay refers to the Semiramis Hotel, *The Egyptian Gazette*, and the Shari'a el Hami, a Cairo street. Dialogue in the script also mentions native diggers from Kerna (also spelled Kurna, Qurna, Gurna, and Gourna), a village which traditionally supplied labor for excavations in the Valley of the Kings—and whose inhabitants also made a living by plundering tombs.

Tutankhamon's tomb had been discovered on November 26, 1922, but Howard Carter's excavation was methodical. The inner chamber was not even opened until February 17, 1923, and the pharaoh's mummy was not unwrapped until November 11, 1925. Items from the tomb were first displayed in the Egyptian Museum, Cairo, in 1929, and Carter didn't finish clearing the tomb until February 1932—just a month before Balderston began working on his script. Thus, although the tomb's discovery occurred a full decade earlier, it remained a developing event and *The Mummy* reveals Balderston's awareness of it by the fact that the film's prologue is set in 1921; then, ten years later, when the revived mummy of Imhotep shows an archeologist where to dig for the tomb of Princess Anckesenamon, he says, "Permit me to present you with the most sensational find since that of Tutankhamon."

But the events surrounding Tutankhamon's tomb did more than supply Balderston with an exotic setting; they also contributed to his new plot, as he turned Cagliostro, who had lived for three thousand years, into Imhotep, who was buried alive and is centuries later returned to life by the reading aloud of the Scroll of Thoth, which contains the spell by which the goddess Isis had raised Osiris from the dead.

Also, ever since the discovery of Tutankhamon's tomb, news reports had fueled popular interest with speculation about a curse being attached to the tomb, and whenever someone even remotely connected with it died, the story was revived. In 1924, for example, the *New York Times* reported that Dr. J. S. Mardrus, a French Egyptologist, warned of the need "to take certain precautions, both against the visible and invisible." For one thing, he "would have spoken words of incantation necessary to guard against the dangerous surrounding of the tomb, notably against the Pharaoh's Ka, which appears to play the chief part in protecting the Pharaoh's mummy." (2/6/24, p. 4)

Two years later, Dr. Mardrus's warning was repeated by the *Times* in a front page article with the headline: "Sixth Tomb Hunter Succumbs in Egypt; Dr. Mardrus Advances Theory of Strange Force." Mardrus spoke of these men having "succumbed to an inexplicable malady. This is no childish superstition which can be dismissed with a shrug of the shoulder. We must remember that the Egyptians during a period of 7,000 years... practiced magical rites the power of which held no doubts for them. I am absolutely convinced that they knew how to concentrate upon and around a mummy certain dynamic powers of which we possess very incomplete notions... It is a deep mystery, which it is all too easy to dismiss by skepticism." (3/28/26, p. 1) As late as March 9, 1930, the *Times* carried an article summarizing the deaths supposedly related to Tutankhamon's tomb.

A 1924 report about a separate incident, the suicide in London of Egyptologist H. G. Evelyn White, may also have inspired Balderston. According to the *Times*, White "was some years ago introduced by a monk into a secret room in an Egyptian monastery where he found and removed fragments of apocryphal books, some previously unheard of and of inestimable value." At the inquest into White's death, a letter in his handwriting was read, which said, "I knew there was a curse on me, though I had leave to take those manuscripts to Cairo. The monks told me the curse would work all the same. Now it has done so." (9/12/24, p. 21)

Balderston provided *The Mummy* with a curse—"Death, eternal punishment, for anyone who opens this casket, in the name of Amon-Ra, the King of the Gods"—which is engraved on the box containing an ancient manuscript, the Scroll of Thoth. In addition, the character of Dr. Muller (Edward Van Sloan) is, like Mardrus, an expert on the Egyptian occult and he voices similar ideas when he warns, "The Gods of Egypt still live in these hills, in their ruined temples. The ancient spells are weaker, but some of them are still potent." Later, Muller asserts, "When we fight this creature, we must ask protection from the forces of old it defied." Ultimately, he is proven correct, for he is helpless against Imhotep and it is the goddess Isis herself who destroys the reanimated mummy.

In *The Mummy*, however, the presence of a curse is more misleading than meaningful, for by opening the box and reading the scroll the archeologists do Imhotep a service by bringing him back to life. Once revived, Imhotep's goal is not to gain revenge for sacrilege; to him, the archeologists are useful as a way of unearthing the mummy of his lost lover, Princess Anckesenamon. As he explains, "We Egyptians are not premitted to dig up our ancient dead—only foreign museums." Later, when he attacks someone, it is only because that person stands in the way of his goal, either by attempting to burn the scroll or by keeping Helen from him.

This goal—the essence of the film's plot and its sensitive characterizations—is a complete reversal of the comparable character's motivation in Nina

The Mummy **juxtaposes an ancient romance with a modern one in which one person survives from the past and the other has been reincarnated in a new body.**

Wilcox Putnam's original story. Balderston took Cagliostro's negative urge, the avenging of his lover's betrayal in the ancient past by destroying Helen in the present, and turned it into a positive one, Imhotep's determination to be reunited with the woman from the past with whom he had shared a powerful, enduring love. This change evokes the central situation of Balderston's play, *Berkeley Square*, in which a contemporary Englishman periodically finds himself in 18th century London, where he falls in love with a woman from the past. To this element of love across time, Balderston added the fact that Anckesenamon's soul has been reincarnated in Helen, which complicates matters by creating within her a struggle between her ancient self and her modern one.

This reincarnation aspect derives from a fateful coincidence. At some point after he started to work on *Cagliostro*, Balderston received a second assignment from Universal—to adapt *She*, H. Rider Haggard's 1887 novel of adventure, love, and fantasy. Balderston worked on both projects simultaneously and submitted his first, 33-page treatment of *She* on July 17, just four days after completing the second version of his *Mummy* script. This was followed by a second treatment of *She* (dated August 2). He then concentrated on *The Mummy*, and did not complete a screenplay of *She* until October 17, while *The Mummy* was in production.

Universal no doubt shelved its plan to produce *She* because the budget would have been too high, but it may also have realized that Balderston had included in *The Mummy* so many elements from *She* that a resemblance between the two films would have been evident. Finally, on May 31, 1934, Universal sold its rights to *She* to RKO (for $20,000) and transfered to that studio Balderston's treatments and screenplay. Although Merian C. Cooper's 1935 film of Haggard's novel does not credit Balderston, some of its dialogue echoes that in *The Mummy* and may derive from his work.

It is from *She* that Balderston clearly drew the basic situations and motivations which he added to *Cagliostro*. Haggard's novel, like *The Mummy*, juxtaposes an ancient romance with a modern one in which one person survives from the past and the other has been reincarnated in a new body. In ancient Egypt, Kallikrates was a priest of Isis who committed sacrilege, breaking his vow of celibacy by loving the Princess Amenartas. After the two fled from Egypt, they crossed paths with Ayesha (known to the natives she rules as She-who-must-be-obeyed). Ayesha fell in love with Kallikrates but, because he loved another, she killed him in a fit of jealous anger. Amenartas then escaped with Kallikrates's child. Because Ayesha gained immortality by bathing in a mysterious flame, she lived on, awaiting the return of her beloved. And return he does, 2000 years later, in the form of Leo Vincey, the descendant and, in a sense, the reincarnation of Kallikrates.

By blending Amenartas and Ayesha into a single character and then reversing the lovers' sexes, Balderston turned this situation into the forbidden love of Princess Anckesenamon, a priestess of Isis who broke her vows as a vestal virgin, and Imhotep, High Priest of the Temple of the Sun at Karnak. No jealousy is involved in this situation, however, and Anckesenamon, unlike Kallikrates, died of natural causes. At her death, Imhotep compounded his sacrilege by stealing the Scroll of Thoth from the temple and trying to use it to return her to life. Interrupted, he is punished by being buried alive, but 3,700 years later he is accidentally revived and sets out to regain his lost love. Thus, whereas Ayesha remained alive over the centuries, suffering solitude as her love endured, Imhotep's suffering was more immediate and physical, but also more temporary. Their basic needs and goals, however, are the same.

Before Ayesha can be reunited with Kallikrates-in-Leo, he must undergo a process of death and rebirth by bathing in the eternal flame, thus becoming immortal, like her. As a first step, she destroys Kallikrates's preserved body, which she has kept through the centuries. Similarly, Imhotep tells

Anckesenamon-in-Helen that they may not love "until the great change," which involves killing Helen, mummifying her body, and then using the scroll to revive it to eternal life. First, though, he burns Anckesenamon's mummy. "I destroy this lifeless thing," he tells Helen. "Thou shalt take its place but for a few moments, and then rise again even as I have risen... For thy sake I was buried alive. I ask of thee only a moment of agony. Only so can we be united." In another link between *The Mummy* and *She*, both Imhotep and Ayesha reveal to others images of the past in the surface of a pool of water.

Although Ayesha is beautiful and Imhotep is certainly not handsome, the two characters share a similar mixture of attraction and repulsion, of malevolence and suffering. Each, too, is (in Haggard's words) "a being who, unconstrained by human law, is also absolutely unshackled by a moral sense of right and wrong." They are passionately devoted to their goals, to satisfying the long-denied need to be with their beloveds.

In *She*, a conflict arises because a native girl, Ustane, has fallen in love with Leo. Ayesha, who can "slay with mine eyes and by the power of my will," kills her new rival: "Ayesha said nothing, she made no sound, she only drew herself up, stretched out her arm, and... appeared to look fixedly at her victim. Even as she did so Ustane put her hands to her head, uttered one piercing scream, turned round twice, and then fell backward with a thud—prone upon the floor." Both Ayesha's method and her casual ruthlessness ("she stood between me and thee, and therefore have I removed her") are transferred to Imhotep, who does not even need to be in his victim's presence to cause his death and who attempts to destroy Frank Whemple (David Manners), "that boy for whom love is creeping into your heart. Love that would keep you from myself."

In the 1935 film, *She*, Ustane becomes the more articulate Tanya, who tells Ayesha that she has a stronger hold on Leo "because I'm human and you're not, because I'm young and you know love belongs to the young. Your magic makes you seem young, but in your heart you're old, old. You were young once, like me, but now you're old and it's too late for love forever." This change in the character may have originated in Balderston's script of *She*, because Tanya here sounds very much like Anckesenamon-as-Helen who, in *The Mummy*'s climax, tells Imhotep, "I'm alive! I'm young! I won't die! I loved you once, but now you belong with the dead. I am Anckesenamon—but I—I'm somebody else, too. I want to live, even in this strange new world."

All of this material from *She* takes on a new identity when placed in the context of Egypt, and it certainly gives *The Mummy* the emotional substance and dramatic power that cannot even be glimpsed in the *Cagliostro* plot summary. But in adapting these elements to their new form, Balderston drew on still another influence to flesh out the relationships and develop the plot. That influence was his own theatrical adaptation of *Dracula*. Thus, both films present an un-dead creature who seductively threatens the heroine with death, while offering a kind of eternal life, thereby endangering both her life and her soul. In each case, the creature's manner is reserved, mixing politeness with irony, and he can influence others with a hypnotic force. Combatting him are the young man who loves the heroine and an older expert in the occult (played in both films by David Manners and Edward Van Sloan, respectively). Each film even includes a pivotal scene in which the expert tests his suspicions, using a mirror in *Dracula* and a photograph in *The Mummy*, which prompts the creature to drop his pose of civility. In both cases, too, a talisman offers protection from the creature's power, with a figure of Isis serving this function in *The Mummy* instead of a crucifix.

This identification of the elements from which Balderston evolved the plot of *The Mummy* is not intended to disparage his achievement. Rather, it dramatizes the complex melding of materials which is at the heart of creativity. Certainly, the result is a work which transcends its sources and stands solidly on its own, a perfect blend of influences and a thoroughly unique entity.

Another sensibility, though, must also be credited with the success of *The Mummy*, that of its director, Karl Freund. However, any attempt to elucidate Freund's contribution, even in terms of visual style and pace, requires considerable speculation. This is because the shooting script, credited solely to Balderston, is highly detailed in its description of how events should be presented, cinematically. It includes extensive indications of editing and of camera movements. This in itself is noteworthy, but what is remarkable is the fact that—although some changes were made on the set and during post-production—all of the key creative decisions are represented in the script. Thus, the director had no major artistic problems to solve while shooting; he merely had to execute the already refined plans.

A perfect example is the scene in which Imhotep's mummy returns to life, which is an ideal case of visual discretion. The script's description of the scene closely matches its appearance in the finished film, including all of Freund's subtle camera movements, as well as the choice to avoid showing the mummy moving through the room. From a close shot of Norton reading the scroll, the camera moves to the mummy in its case, then back to Norton. The moment when life returns is shown in a close-up of the mummy's face as the eyelids open slightly, then the camera tilts down to the arms across the bandaged chest. A little later, only the mummy's hand is seen, reaching for the scroll. Finally, as Norton breaks into horrified laughter, the camera moves from him to show a trail of bandages moving through the door, up to the now-empty mummy case, then down to the casket which had contained the scroll.

Some minor details were changed during the filming: the "little blue flames" which the script describes as appearing on the ends of the scroll were omitted, as was the fact that the mummy's hand at first fumbles in its attempt to pick up the scroll; the movement of the mummy's arms replaces the sight of its chest

65

The Mummy's visual style is not typical of its contemporaries. Its use of moving camera, in particular, and the inevitable slow pace that results link it to Freund's background in the German film industry of the 1920s.

moving "as though the figure were drawing breath"; and Norton stands and backs against a wall, instead of remaining seated in a chair. However, everything of significance in this scene already existed in the screenplay.

This would, at first glance, suggest that Freund had virtually nothing to do with the visual style of *The Mummy*, that he merely carried out Balderston's instructions in the script. However, it is difficult—perhaps impossible—to imagine that this playwright and first-time scriptwriter could have possessed such a refined cinematic sense. If he did, he surely would have been in great demand, and yet aside from his adaptation of his own play *Berkeley Square* (1933), he did not receive another screen credit until 1935, and of his nineteen credits all but two (*The Mummy* and *Victory*, 1940) were written in collaboration with others.

It is equally difficult to imagine that Karl Freund would have defered so completely to a scriptwriter's filmic imagination, especially for his first film as

66

a director, with which he would doubtless have wanted to make a strong impression. This eminent cinematographer had, in Germany during the 1920s, been a major artistic collaborator on ten films directed by the renowned F. W. Murnau, as well as on Paul Wegener's *Der Golem* (*The Golem*, 1920), E. A. Dupont's *Variete* (*Variety*, 1925), and Fritz Lang's *Metropolis* (1927). In addition, he had helped write and film the documentary *Berlin—die Symphonie der Grossstadt* (*Berlin—The Symphony of a Great City*, 1926) and had supervised Bertold Viertel's direction of *Die Abenteuer eines Zehnmarkscheins* (*The Adventures of a Ten-mark Note*, 1926). After coming to the United States in 1929, he devised the poetic ending of Universal's *All Quiet on the Western Front* (1930) and, reportedly, had considerable influence on the direction of Tod Browning's *Dracula* (1931). His background and perspective were as much those of a filmmaker as of a photographic technician.

Is it possible that Freund had some degree of input while Balderston was writing *The Mummy*? Michael Brunas, John Brunas, and Tom Weaver, in *Universal Horrors* (p. 52), imply the opposite when they state that Freund "received the script on a Saturday in late September, 1932, spent the next day casting and screen-testing, and was all ready to begin shooting on Monday." This statement, however, may misrepresent the situation. In fact, on August 29 Universal officially announced Freund's assignment to direct what was then called *Imhotep*—one week before Balderston completed his sixth version of the screenplay, two weeks before the date of the seventh version (the shooting script), and about 21 days before shooting began during the week of September 19. That alone would have provided an opportunity for Freund to be involved in developing the script.

In addition, Freund had completed the photography of *Afraid to Talk* (Universal, 1932) earlier in August, so for about one month he was free to devote his attention to his directorial debut. Without further evidence, one cannot be certain of the nature or extent of Freund's contributions. However, it is more reasonable to assume that he participated than to assume that he stood aside and waited until the finished script was handed to him, and then modestly shot it as written. Certainly, Freund did develop a close working relationship with Balderston, for *Variety* reported on December 20 that Universal adopted a new system under which "a director is permitted to call the writer of his story to the set to assist in script revision," based on the fact that the system had "worked successfully on *The Mummy*." (p. 42)

The visual style of *The Mummy* is not typical of its contemporaries. Its use of moving camera, in particular, and the inevitable slow pace that results link it to Freund's background in the German film industry of the 1920s, which tended to linger on images to create what is known as *Stimmung*, a sense of the psychological or emotional atmosphere that hovers in the space around people and objects. The feeling which results is described by Lotte Eisner, in her book on

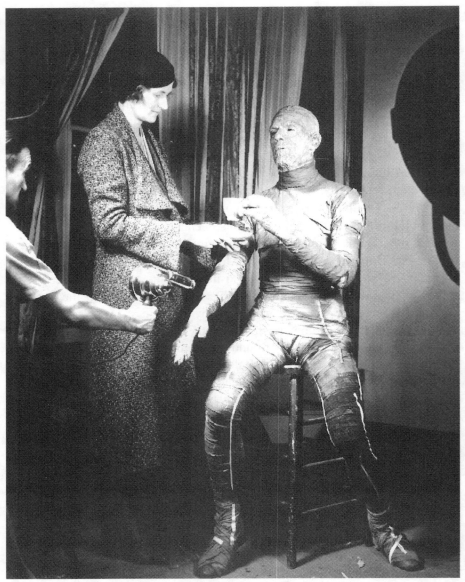

Karloff relaxes during filming with his wife Dorothy as Jack Pierce uses a dryer on his makeup.

German Expressionism, *The Haunted Screen* (p. 199), as "a kind of sorrowful nostalgia" and "languor coloured with desire, lust of body and soul," a description which readily applies to the resonant tone of *The Mummy*. To a viewer who expects facts and concrete details, someone whose sensibility is confined to the physical and tangible, a German filmmaker's willingness to devote time to cre-

68

ating *Stimmung* in his images will seem only like an intolerably slow pace, for action is deliberately rendered secondary to the imprecise and the unstated.

Freund photographed Murnau's innovative *Der letzte Mann* (*The Last Man*, a.k.a. *The Last Laugh*, 1924), which made extensive use of tracking and panning shots. Often, his camera follows a character from place to place, but at one point it moves with a night watchman's disembodied flashlight beam as it glides along the walls of a hotel's darkened corridor. A similar image appears in *Metropolis*, as a beam of light pursues the heroine through a tunnel, finally pinning her to the wall. Comparable uses of camera movement appear in *The Mummy*, which even has the camera follow the light cast by a guard's flashlight in the darkened museum, until it discovers Imhotep kneeling with the scroll. Such stylistic decisions surely link the film with Freund's earlier work, and yet the shooting script includes explicit descriptions of these shots.

Also Germanic in concept is the emphasis placed in *The Mummy* on the force of Imhotep's will, which can summon or kill across considerable distance. A good example can be seen in Murnau's *Nosferatu* (1922, photographed by Fritz Arno Wagner), in which similar intercutting evokes the fact that the heroine senses the vampire's approach and is drawn to watch for his ship's arrival. Another, more immediate, influence was probably a sequence in *Svengali* (Warner Bros., 1931), in which the title character (John Barrymore) summons Trilby (Marian Marsh) to him, as director Archie Mayo moves his camera from Svengali's face, across the city's rooftops, to Trilby's bedroom—an approach similar to the moment in *The Mummy* when the camera sweeps across Cairo to connect Imhotep to Helen.

The Mummy's screenplay was so faithfully followed by Freund during shooting that in only one major instance was its structure altered beforehand. In that, the scene of Imhotep's attack on Frank Whemple was moved to a position just before the film's climax at the museum, where it has greater dramatic impact; at the same time, in that scene the character of Frau Muller was replaced with that of the nurse who is tending Helen.

Otherwise, everything in the script seems to have been filmed, with omissions and changes only made during post-production. Prior to the climax, a total of twelve scenes were omitted, including two dialogue scenes between Frank and Helen (which develop their relationship, but do not advance the plot meaningfully) and two between Whemple and Muller (which are prematurely explicit about Imhotep's true nature).

A more significant omission is a lengthy scene in which Imhotep summons Helen to the museum, where the two discuss Anckesenamon's possessions on display there. In the script, this follows a scene of Helen promising to remain in her hotel room, and her visit to Imhotep's house and the scene by his pool occur the next day. By cutting the museum scene and its adjacent, shorter scenes—

leaving only the one in which Muller, in Frank's car, realizes that the scroll had not been burned—the filmmakers compress events so that Helen's departure from the hotel on this occasion turns into her later visit to Imhotep's house. Although one would certainly like to see that missing scene, its dialogue in the script is unnecessarily blunt about Helen's feeling of kinship to Anckesenamon and its presence would have dissipated the impact of her meeting with Imhotep at his house.

On November 15, *Variety* reported that *Imhotep*, now titled *The Mummy*, was in its ninth week of shooting. (p. 25) Four days later, *Universal Weekly* declared that the film, "being rushed to completion," was currently in the editing room. (pp. 5, 6) After less than two weeks, *The Mummy* was previewed, and the *Motion Picture Herald* published a review on December 3 which gave its length at 78 minutes. (p. 27) It was probably between this preview and the film's release on December 22 that another significant change was made.

Originally, at the pool in his house, Imhotep had shown Helen only Anckesenamon's death, her burial, and his interrupted attempt to revive her. Then, in the final sequence at the museum, he used a mirror to reflect her five prior lives as she sees herself reject a young gallant in 18th century France, bid farewell to 13th century crusaders, commit suicide in an 8th century Saxon stockade, become a Christian martyr in ancient Rome, and embrace Imhotep in the sanctuary of Isis. After that, he finally showed his own burial alive. Wisely, the extraneous material on Helen's lives was dropped and the footage of Imhotep's fate moved to the scene at the pool, so that the flashback tale is told all at once. This renders the film more compact, while making Imhotep's statement by the pool about his suffering for her more comprehensible. However, publicity materials continued to list in the cast two actors who appeared in the cut flashbacks, one of whom is even included in the film's cast list.

This and the other alterations are all so seamless that, without having the shooting script for comparison, one would never know they had occurred.

When Karloff began work on *The Mummy*, he had just left the chaotic shooting of *The Mask of Fu Manchu*, with its extensive re-writing of scenes during production. The actor must have found the process of filming *The Mummy* from its carefully pre-planned screenplay a thorough relief. Although it is not clear how much time he had to prepare for his role (scenes for *Fu Manchu* were still being shot while *The Mummy* was in production), Karloff seems to have slipped into the part effortlessly and he perfectly captures what the script describes as Imhotep's "slow dignity" and his "uncanny force and power." Here was a character as ideal for Karloff's voice, his body, and his aura as any would be until *The Body Snatcher* (1945). If one film and character and actor can embody the exotic, yet accessible, satisfactions of the classic horror film, then that film is *The Mummy* and that character is Imhotep and that actor is Boris Karloff.

CREDITS: Director: Karl Freund; Presented by Carl Laemmle; Producer: Carl Laemmle, Jr.; Screenplay: John L. Balderston; From a story by Nina Wilcox Putnam, Richard Schayer; Director of Photography: Charles Stumar; Film Editor: Milton Carruth; Art Director: Willy Pogany; Make-up: Jack P. Pierce; Special Effects: John P. Fulton; Music: James Dietrich, Heinz Roemheld, Michel Brusselmans; Main Titles Music from Tchaikovsky's *Swan Lake*; Released December 22, 1932 by Universal Pictures Corp.; 73 minutes

CAST: Boris Karloff...Imhotep, Zita Johann...Helen Grosvenor, David Manners...Frank Whemple, Arthur Byron...Sir Joseph Whemple, Edward Van Sloan...Doctor Muller, Bramwell Fletcher...Ralph Norton, Noble Johnson...The Nubian, Kathryn Byron...Frau Muller, Leonard Mudie...Professor Pearson, James Crane...The Pharaoh, Eddie Kane...Doctor, Tony Marlow...Inspector, and (in cut scenes) Henry Victor...The Saxon Warrior, Arnold Grey...Knight

Paul M. Jensen is the author of three books—*The Cinema of Fritz Lang* (1969), *Boris Karloff and His Films* (1974), and *The Men Who Made the Monsters* (1996)—and has contributed articles on film-related subjects *to Scarlet Street, Video Watchdog, Phantasma, Film Comment, Photon, Films in Review*, and *Variety*. Childhood exposure to *The Mummy*, as well as Howard Hawks's *Land of the Pharaohs* (1955), stirred an enduring fascination with Egypt, which resulted in three visits to that country (so far) and inspired the chapter in this volume. Mr. Jensen is currently completing his third decade teaching film appreciation and productions at the State University of New York at Oneonta.

THE OLD DARK HOUSE (1932)

by David J. Hogan

In the fall of 1932, Universal was rightfully excited about *The Old Dark House*, the second teaming of actor Boris Karloff and director James Whale, who had electrified audiences the year before with *Frankenstein*. In ballyhoo directed at exhibitors, the studio made extravagant claims for its new star, top-billed for the first time in his career: "The man who played the Monster in *Frankenstein* now transforms himself into the mad butler in *The Old Dark House*. A characterization that will make the world talk! Screen acting that lifts the screen to new heights!"

The studio's brand of sell was enthusiastic... and intentionally misleading. Although Karloff is effective as the mute, disfigured butler who serves a family of reclusive psychotics, his role (as in the J.B. Priestley novel, *Benighted*, upon which the film is based) is a supporting one. Karloff's natural presence—aided by a flattened nose, scruffy black beard, and facial scars devised by makeup artist Jack Pierce—is forceful and unnerving, and viewers are keenly aware of his presence even when he is not on the screen. Regardless, any capable, physically imposing character actor could have done justice to the role.

Morgan is merely a dark blot on a larger landscape of insanity. The primary drama plays out between aging Horace Femm (Ernest Thesiger) and a young visitor, Penderel (Melvyn Douglas, in a role originally slated for Russell Hopton). It is these two characters, one sunk in psychosis, the other struggling to avoid surrendering to despair, who keep the narrative chugging. Indeed, of the ten characters who appear in *The Old Dark House*, Morgan, although arguably the showiest, is the least well-developed. In the course of the film's 71 minutes, we learn little about him except that he is without speech, becomes violent when drunk, and (in a scene very nicely played by Karloff) has unexpected feelings of tenderness for the family pyromaniac, Saul Femm (Brember Wills). Although *The Old Dark House* has a printed preamble assuring viewers that the actor who plays Morgan is the same actor who played Frankenstein's Monster, the fact is that Universal was not taking full advantage of Karloff's talents. By restricting him to a mute role lacking the inherent sympathy of the Monster, the studio almost did Karloff (and itself) a disservice. The top billing that came with the part was a major step forward for Karloff, but the role itself was not.

Karloff in makeup not used in the final film.

For John Boynton Priestley (1894-1984), *The Old Dark House* was just one mark of success in what was to be an impressively long-lived career. Priestley was a prolific and quick-witted novelist, playwright, and essayist whose intro-spective sort of social satire suited the tastes of two generations of readers and theatergoers. Always respected by the intelligentsia, he gained broad popular acceptance throughout Britain via radio during World War II, and was a fixture on English television until his death.

Priestley's novels include *Angel Pavement* (1930), *They Walk in the City* (1936), and *Lost Empires* (1965). His most successful novel, *The Good Companions*, concerns eccentrics who run and perform in a touring music-hall company. The book was published in 1929 and was adapted for the screen in 1933. Priestley was comfortable with film, and wrote the screenplays for adaptations of two of his novels, *They Came to a City* (1945) and *Last Holiday* (1950); Priestley produced the latter film. Additionally, he wrote Charles Laughton's dialogue (at the actor's request) for Alfred Hitchcock's *Jamaica Inn* (1939).

Priestley adaptations scripted by others include *Laburnum Grove* (1941), *Somewhere in France* (1943), and *An Inspector Calls* (an Alastair Sim/Guy Hamilton project from Priestley's play, 1954). William Castle's 1963 version of *The Old Dark House* used the Priestley story merely as a springboard, and was an adaptation in name only.

Benighted was published in 1928. It is a grotesque, darkly allegorical novel of one family, the Femms, and the way in which the trauma of the Great War has fragmented it and ruined the spirits of its members. Horace Femm, sepulchral and arch, has become emotionally dead while his sister, Rebecca, has taken the opposite course, finding a perceived refuge in a private, highly charged world of religious fanaticism. Another sibling, Saul, is a mindless creature of destruction who seems to have absorbed all of the terrible animosities that raged across Europe from 1914 to 1918. The patriarch is Sir Roderick Femm, an aged man of normal moods who has nevertheless abrogated his responsibilities, passively turning his back on his middle-aged children and allowing them to descend into emotional disarray.

When the Femm home is visited by travelers seeking refuge from a rainstorm and incipient flood, the worst qualities of the individual family members come to the fore: The asocial Horace is a pathetic host and Rebecca is downright hostile, loudly berating lovely young Margaret Waverton for what Rebecca assumes are sins of the flesh. Sir Roderick sinks deeper into passivity, and Saul eventually explodes into horrific violence.

One of the visitors is a war veteran named Penderel, who has been emotionally scarred by his experiences. Outwardly cheeky and carefree, he struggles with a deep cynicism and a suspicion that frightens him badly: Nothing matters.

In key ways, Penderel is simpatico with the Femms. This is clear during a mordant toast he directs to God in reference to Horace and himself: "Behold two mortals whose hearts were fashioned for your service but who sit in a darkness within a darkness, homeless, lost, the black waters rising around them."

The bleakly metaphoric toast is apt, for the Femm household is an emotionally diseased place that causes another visitor, Philip Waverton, to remark on the "density of evil" that chokes the house.

Priestley delineates the menacing family butler, Morgan, as a force of nature whose fury is fueled by the storm outside. The elemental aspect of Morgan's character is only hinted at in the film version, in which Morgan is simply surly, lustful, and prone to outbursts of drunken violence.

As Priestley presents him, there is something innocent about Morgan. His psychosis is part of the natural world, and not a result of the insanity of war, that is, the works of man. Saul Femm, on the other hand, is very much a creation of an angry, rudderless society, and thus is infinitely more dangerous than Morgan. Saul's climactic escape from his upstairs room culminates in a terrible fight in which Penderel is killed.

The novel was not a popular success in Britain and its title was changed by its American publisher to the more commercial *The Old Dark House*. The book appealed to 25-year-old Carl Laemmle, Jr., Universal's production chief since April 1928 and known somewhat derisively on the lot and around town as "Junior." Even today, some accounts of Universal are dismissive of the younger Laemmle, suggesting that he was a cipher who lacked the intellect and temperament to run a movie studio. In truth, Laemmle was a young man of taste and sharp ambition, and if he made a mistake in his tenure, it was his eagerness to make expensive, "prestige" productions intended to elevate Universal's standing in the industry.

The first big pictures made under Laemmle's regime—*Broadway* (1929), *Show Boat* (1929), and *All Quiet on the Western Front* (1930)—were pricey but scored big at the box office. When the Depression took hold early in 1930, Laemmle showed laudable prescience; he instinctively realized that things were going to be bad for a long time and scaled back his budgets accordingly. When Universal posted a not unexpected $2.2 million loss for 1930, Laemmle resolved that 1931 and subsequent years would be better. He fell back on formula pictures in familiar genres: serials, crime thrillers, small-scale musicals, weepies—and most significantly, horror films.

It was Laemmle's decision to film the stage version of *Dracula*, to film Mary Shelley's *Frankenstein*, and to exploit the horror genre (which had already proved itself abroad, notably in Germany) as vigorously as the market would allow. These are the pictures that "made" Universal, that kept it afloat during the Depression, and that gave it an identifiable, commercially viable persona. Movie fans owe much to "Junior."

That the younger Laemmle's decision to return to big films in 1935 led to his professional undoing a year later is regrettable, but of no relevance to us here. For as long as he bet the farm on horror, he was a genius. And so was a British director named James Whale.

The Old Dark House **set was serious and faintly formal.**

A slender, waspishly handsome man, Whale (1886-1957) carried himself as well as he dressed. With only three films to his credit by 1932, he already was noted in Hollywood for his sophisticated sensibilities, dramatic visual style, and sardonic sense of humor. Most important in that one-industry town is that Whale, who came to Hollywood in 1930 to direct the film version of *Journey's End*, a play he had directed on Broadway, delivered big box office, and seemed an ideal choice to helm *The Old Dark House*, particularly since the studio was prepared to reunite him with Karloff.

Whale was attracted to Priestley's *Benighted*, less for the novel's philosophical overtones than for the possibility the book afforded for unrestrained lunacy. Laemmle approved Whale's request for the book and assigned journeyman screenwriter Benn Levy, a friend of Whale, to the script.

After shooting began, playwright R.C. Sherriff came onto the set to contribute dialogue. A onetime insurance adjuster who developed into a heavyweight writer, Sherriff was the original writer of *Journey's End* and the scripter of *All Quiet on the Western Front* (1930). Later film credits include *Goodbye Mr. Chips* (1939), *Odd Man Out* (1947), *Quartet* (1949), *No Highway in the Sky* (1951), and *The Night My Number Came Up* (1955).

The Old Dark House was the second teaming of Karloff and James Whale.

Benn Levy almost certainly took his cues from the director, fashioning a script designed to take advantage of the eccentric nature of the distinctly Anglo cast put together by Whale. Sherriff's emphatic, off-kilter dialogue added a queasy sauciness that is matched by no horror film of the period other than Whale's *Bride of Frankenstein* (1935).

Production began at Universal City in the middle of April 1932 and wrapped a month later on a set that was serious and faintly formal. Despite the small cast and confined setting, Whale was determined to make *The Old Dark House* ferociously cinematic. He believed in extensive rehearsal, during which he worked closely with the actors and his gifted director of photography, Arthur Edeson (1891-1971). A master of mood, Edeson was among the best cinematographers of his era, and shot some of Hollywood's greatest films: *Robin Hood* (1923), *The Thief of Bagdad* (1924), *The Lost World* (1925), *All Quiet on the Western Front* (1930), *Frankenstein* (1931), *The Invisible Man* (1933), *Mutiny on the Bounty* (1935), *Each Dawn I Die* (1939), *The Maltese Falcon* (1941), *Sergeant York* (1941), *Casablanca* (1942), and *The Mask of Dimitrios* (1944).

Once the camera rolled, Whale expected cast and crew to be prepared and to do things his way. Co-star Gloria Stuart remembered him as generally thoughtful and courteous. He generated no tension on the set, but never allowed any doubt that what was happening was serious business. "Once in a while," Stuart recalled, "if someone angered [Whale] or opposed him—said 'Yes' and then did it their own way—he was very swift to notice and point it out, sometimes with an unkind word. There was never any yelling, though; simply an intellectual retort."

Whale was undoubtedly mindful of Karloff's growing popularity. The two of them had achieved something tremendous with *Frankenstein*, and both were quickly climbing the ladder of Hollywood success. For Karloff (1887-1969), the impact of *Frankenstein* and the star billing in *The Old Dark House* were sweet payoffs for years of struggle and obscurity. Like many actors, he had labored at odd jobs until, in 1919, he came to Hollywood. He had more than 80 bit parts until finally establishing himself as a character actor of modest import in 1931 with his seventh-billed role as a convict in Howard Hawks's *The Criminal Code*. He had another good role in Mervyn LeRoy's *Five Star Final* (1931), and was spotted by Whale in the Universal commissary while doing a fourth-billed part in Christy Cabanne's *Graft* (1931). Whale suggested that Karloff test for the part of Frankenstein's Monster and—well, you know what happened next.

Whale, like Karloff a Briton who came from modest origins, appreciated Karloff's unique physical qualities but considered him a minor talent whom he freely worked like a dog during the filming of *Frankenstein*. More inexplicable still is that Whale expressed disdain for the gentlemanly, always-prepared Boris, calling him "a coal-heaver, a truck driver." If Gloria Stuart's recollections are accurate, that sort of mean-spiritedness never manifested itself on the set, but the fact that Whale could make such remarks at all suggests a pointed self-consciousness about his own beginnings, his acquired fondness for high art, and, perhaps, his homosexual lifestyle, which he cultivated at a time when the proclivity was frowned upon within the closed doors of Hollywood society, and that could have ruined his career and life should it become public. Undeniably, though, Whale's taste and eccentricities elevated him as a filmmaker; his best films are unique and clearly identifiable as Whale projects.

The Old Dark House follows the broad outline of *Benighted*. As suggested earlier, the film does away with much of Priestley's subtext (although Melvyn Douglas's Penderel is very much a member of the Lost Generation; early in the film he describes himself as "war generation, slightly soiled... a study in the bittersweet, the man with the twisted smile").

In hands less capable than Whale's, the film could have been a plodder little different from *The Bat* (1926) or numerous other "clutching hand" thrillers that were staples of the silent and early sound eras. But the Whale touch, combined with a powerhouse cast, Sherriff's delightfully rancid dialogue, and Edeson's cinematography, make for a picture that has vigor and a special weirdness.

The film begins in the darkness of a howling rainstorm in Wales (complete with a dramatic mudslide) that forces separate groups of travelers to take refuge at an isolated mountain estate. Following a creepy establishing shot of the gloomy mansion as seen from the struggling car carrying Penderel (Douglas) and a young couple, Philip and Margaret Waverton (Raymond Massey and Gloria Stuart), Penderel gaily remarks, "Wouldn't it be dramatic if the people inside were dead, all stretched out with lights all around them!"

Well, he's close. The gaunt and ashen Horace Femm (Thesiger) invites the group inside with great reluctance, muttering, "You will have to stay here. The misfortune is yours, not ours!"

Sister Rebecca (Eva Moore) is an even less congenial host: "No beds!" she shrills at the visitors. "You can't have beds!"

Rebecca and Margaret hit it off badly right away, through no fault of Margaret's. As the graceful younger woman changes from her wet clothing in an upstairs bedroom, the squat, puffy Rebecca regards her with unconcealed hatred. Then, her memory jogged, Rebecca recalls her sister, Rachel, who died at 21: "She was a wicked one," she exclaims. "Handsome and wild as a hawk. All the young men used to follow her about, with her red lips and her big eyes and her white neck. But that didn't save her!" Rachel, it seems, injured her back after falling from her horse and spent the remainder of her days in agony in the very room in which Rebecca and Margaret now stand. "She used to cry out to me to kill her, but I'd tell her to turn to the Lord. She didn't. She was godless to the last!"

At this, Rebecca takes careful stock of the lissome Margaret, by now stripped down to her satin slip and stockings. Rebecca fingers the slip maliciously. "That's fine stuff," she pronounces, "but it'll rot." Then, in one of the film's most awful moments, she plants her palm on the naked flesh of Margaret's upper chest. "That's finer stuff, still, but it'll rot, too—in time." Margaret recoils, horrified.

The Old Dark House **did not cause the stir that** *Frankenstein* **had created.**

The preceding is brilliantly staged and edited, alternating between two-shots of the women, closeups on their faces, and extreme closeups of reflections of Rebecca's features as they are contorted by the imperfect glass of the bedroom's vanity mirror. When Rebecca exits the room, Clarence Kolster's editing becomes rapid and disorienting as the shaken Margaret replays the scene in her mind, Rebecca's face alternating with quick cuts to something only we can see: the brutish visage of the butler Morgan (Karloff), who spies on Rebecca in her *déshabillé*.

Dinner with the Femms is a hoot, as Horace eats (and offers) as little food as possible, while Rebecca fills her plate and attacks it like a starving Rottweiler. Morgan, serving, eyes Margaret with undisguised lust.

The unexpected arrival of two more travelers, Sir William Porterhouse (Charles Laughton) and his mistress, Gladys Perkins (Lillian Bond), strains an already tenuous situation, particularly as Porterhouse is a loudly robust sort who immediately makes himself at home, apparently unconcerned by Horace's confused protest and Rebecca's withering disapproval.

81

Interpersonal relationships inside the house deteriorate further. Morgan retreats to the kitchen and becomes drunk, and smashes his fist through a pane of glass in a futile attempt to grab Gladys. Soon after, Horace is inexplicably terrified when Rebecca orders him to retrieve an oil lamp from an upstairs landing. Waverton fetches the lamp himself, noticing a double-bolted bedroom door and a plate of half-eaten food on a nearby table.

Downstairs, Margaret indulges in a moment of whimsy, standing before a crackling fire and enjoying the shadow she casts on the wall. She pirouettes, makes shadow animals with her hands, then freezes, horrified, when Rebecca's inky shadow suddenly emerges from her own. Rebecca regards her for a moment, quickly touches Margaret's breast, and scuttles off. It's a wonderfully unnerving moment.

Enter Morgan, by now blind drunk and anxious to rape Margaret. He chases her about the house until challenged by Waverton, who manages to knock him cold.

In a bedroom upstairs, the Wavertons find Sir Roderick Femm (John [Elspeth] Dudgeon), a frail, bedridden wisp of 102. He is weak but lucid, and warns his visitors that the Femms are terribly ill: "Madness came. We are all touched with it a little, you see. Except me." He adds that "the real danger isn't Morgan, but Saul. He just wants to destroy, to kill. Poor Saul."

Whale's intense buildup to Saul's entrance prepares us for some Brobdingnagian fiend, but no: When Saul (Wills) peers around the wall at the head of the stairs, we see a small man of middle age, dumpy and mousy, hesitant of speech and very nervous. He pleads with Penderel, telling him he's being kept a prisoner by his siblings, and that Rachel died at the hands of her brother and sister. Penderel listens sympathetically, and when he momentarily turns away, the camera lingers on Saul's face. Slowly, like the blooming of some hideous flower, Saul's head tilts and his expression shifts, the eyes becoming hooded and predatory, the mouth curling in a mirthless smile. Penderel has been snookered.

Saul plucks a dagger from the rubble left by Morgan's outburst, and—viewed from an overhead camera—engages Penderel in a sort of choreographed dance, Saul backing away, blade in hand, the alarmed Penderel compelled to follow.

"Are you interested in flame?" Saul asks mildly. "I've made a study of flame.... Flames are really knives. Sharp and cold, my friend."

The physical struggle that follows is shocking, as Penderel, a large man in his prime, is overpowered by the stunted Saul. An instant later, Saul is cackling happily and torching the curtains. Penderel and Saul now take a fatal-looking fall from a high landing onto the floor below. Fortunately, help arrives in time. Saul is killed, the fire extinguished, and Penderel (in the film's major departure from Priestley's plot) revives. Morgan, conscious again, is suddenly calm, despondent over Saul's death.

The film's final scene is a marvelous joke: In the bright sun of morning, Horace stands in the doorway as the frazzled guests depart. "Goodbye," he says cheerily. "So happy to have met you."

The Old Dark House is a giddy celebration of insanity, an exercise in what radio frightmaster Arch Oboler later termed "sick horror." The film's influence on popular culture may be inestimable: Consider Oboler's own *Lights Out* radio program, the *New Yorker* cartoons of Charles Addams, EC horror comics written by Al Feldstein and illustrated by the spidery pen of Graham Ingels, the films of John Waters, the fiction of Stephen King, David Lynch's *Twin Peaks*. There is a lot of Whale's film in all of these.

Clearly, it was the grotesque possibilities of the story that interested Whale most keenly. The film's exposition of the romance that develops (with unconvincing rapidity) between Penderel and Gladys is perfunctory, pat, and, to modern eyes, rather humorous. But it does provide the film with a "happy ending," which is what audiences expected in 1932.

Audiences also wanted star power, and *The Old Dark House* obliged with a stellar "supporting" cast that easily overshadows top-billed Karloff. Like Penderel, Melvyn Douglas (1901-81) served in the Great War, as a medic. He made his Broadway debut in 1928 and came to Hollywood in 1931 to repeat his stage triumph in the film version of *Tonight or Never*. For the remainder of his life Douglas was one of the most respected of Hollywood stars, an "actor's actor" who made an effective transition from romantic leading man to incisive character lead. During the first portion of his long screen career Douglas appeared in such hits as *Annie Oakley* (1935), *Captains Courageous* (1937), *Ninotchka* (1939), and *Mr. Blandings Builds His Dream House* (1948). He returned to Broadway in 1951 and did not film again until *Billy Budd* eleven years later.

Other later films include *Hud* (memorable as Paul Newman's disappointed father, 1963), *The Candidate* (1972), and *Being There* (Academy Award, Best Supporting Actor, 1979). Douglas's last was *Ghost Story* (1980).

Douglas brings to Penderel engaging charm and good looks, mixed with a melancholy cynicism that makes him appealingly vulnerable rather than annoying. His scenes with pretty Lillian Bond, though burdened with sappily romantic dialogue, certainly helped his ascension to the top rank of romantic leading men.

For British-born Charles Laughton (1899-1962), life was a perpetual conflict between his art, his homosexuality, and his tragically low self-esteem. Another veteran of World War I who was drawn to the stage, he made his professional debut in London in 1926. He met an eccentric, gifted young actress named Elsa Lanchester early in his stage career and married her in 1929. He and Lanchester came to Broadway in 1931 to appear together in a production of *Payment Deferred*. Laughton had made film shorts and a few features in England beginning in 1928. According to Lanchester, he initially "suffered agonies in controlling his [stage-like] gestures." Quickly, though, Laughton mastered film technique.

Laughton's long Hollywood career began in 1932 with *Devil in the Deep*. From the start, Laughton (like Whale) was enchanted by the sun and color of Los Angeles, qualities in marked contrast to the frequent dreariness of England.

Laughton's mind was always active. He was a knowledgeable collector of pre-Columbian sculpture, a curious man who experimented freely with peyote, and a lover of nature who was terribly self-conscious about his looks (the unfailingly coarse Tallulah Bankhead took perverse delight in loudly pronouncing him "ugly"). Abuse of that sort probably led to Laughton's later suicide attempts and, after he turned 40, frequent liaisons with young male prostitutes. Through it all, Lanchester remained loyal, understanding, and concerned.

Laughton enjoyed numerous triumphs and accolades following *Devil in the Deep*, displaying an impressive range via a remarkable variety of roles. Gifted with a stirring, resonant voice, he could be evil, humorous, pompous, and serious, as the roles demanded. Key Laughton films include *Island of Lost Souls* (as the sadistic Dr. Moreau. 1932), *The Private Life of Henry VIII* (perfectly cast as Henry; Academy Award, Best Actor, 1935), *Ruggles of Red Gap* (1935), *Mutiny on the Bounty* (as Bligh, 1935), *Rembrandt* (1936), *The Hunchback of Notre Dame* (deeply affecting as Quasimodo, 1939), *It Started with Eve* (a delicious comic role, 1941), and *Forever and a Day* (as one of an enormous ensemble cast, 1943). Laughton remained a major figure to the end of his life, with starring roles and meaty supporting parts in *The Man on the Eiffel Tower* (1950), *Abbott and Costello Meet Captain Kidd* (as Kidd, in one of the most unlikely team-ups of the fifties, 1952), *Hobson's Choice* (1954), *Witness for the Prosecution* (1958), *Spartacus* (as Gracchus, 1960), and *Advise and Consent* (his last, 1962).

Laughton worked frequently on radio and television, and directed just one film, the (now) universally respected gem called *The Night of the Hunter* (1955). It is a stylish, highly disturbing mix of stagecraft and pure cinema starring Robert Mitchum as a self-styled preacher whose avocation is the murder of emotionally defenseless women. The film's commercial failure was a major disappointment to Laughton, and put an end to what might have been a highly significant directorial career.

Laughton appeared in *The Old Dark House* at the urging of co-scripter Benn W. Levy. His interpretation of Porterhouse, the loud, rich lout from Lancashire, is considerably more subtle than it may first appear, for although Porterhouse knows he's not in love with Gladys, he feels genuine tenderness

The Old Dark House **is a giddy celebration of insanity. Karloff's role, although a supporting one, is forceful and unnerving.**

for her and a palpable sense of loss when she declares her love for Penderel. Porterhouse has known loss before, as he reveals in an unguarded recollection of his long-dead wife, "a Manchester girl, pretty as paint." She died, he believes, because of the shame of a social snub. It was her death that caused Porterhouse to turn all of his considerable energies to the pursuit of money and the power that comes with it.

Off the set, Laughton was mildly disturbed by Whale's flamboyant private life and the director's love of money and other material things. Neither Laughton nor Elsa felt comfortable in Whale's gaudy Italianate home.

To a generation of filmgoers, tall, lean Raymond Massey (1896-1983) is remembered as Abraham Lincoln, whom Massey played in the stage and screen versions of *Abe Lincoln in Illinois* (film, 1940). But by that time the Canadian-born star had been a stage actor for 18 years and was an 11-year veteran of motion pictures. An imposing physical presence, Massey was a versatile character actor who ranged freely along the emotional scale. His best-known films

85

include *Things to Come* (1936), *The Prisoner of Zenda* (1937), *Santa Fe Trail* (as John Brown, 1940), *Desperate Journey* (1942), *Arsenic and Old Lace* (as the murderous Jonathan Brewster, filmed 1941, released 1944), *Stairway to Heaven* (1946), *The Fountainhead* (1949), *East of Eden* (1955), and *MacKenna's Gold* (his last, 1969).

From 1961 to 1966 Massey found small-screen fame as Dr. Gillespie to Richard Chamberlain's *Dr. Kildare*. Massey served with the Canadian army in both world wars and was wounded during both conflicts. Two of his children, Anna and Daniel, became successful stage and screen actors.

Massey does a workmanlike job as Waverton; he's amusingly irritable early in the film when rainwater drips from the top of his touring car onto the back of his neck, and appropriately protective of his wife when events inside the house get out of hand. Surprisingly, Massey never saw the finished film and dismissed his role as "colorless" and "juvenile."

The screen career of lovely Gloria Stuart (born 1910) was regrettably brief, beginning in 1932 and concluding with her retirement in 1946. Along the way she became one of Universal's most important leading ladies of the thirties (Paramount had battled Universal for the right to sign her). Slender, expressive, and blessed with an intelligent sort of beauty, Stuart made strong impressions in *The Invisible Man* (1933), *Sweepings* (1933), *Roman Scandals* (1933), *Gold Diggers of 1935* (1935), and in a pair of Shirley Temple vehicles, *Poor Little Rich Girl* (1936) and *Rebecca of Sunnybrook Farm* (1938). Following her retirement, Stuart became a successful painter.

Stuart's beauty was a major factor behind her casting as Margaret Waverton, yet she brought sophistication and intelligence to the role. Margaret is well-bred but has enough spunk to appeal to Depression-era audiences.

Gaunt Ernest Thesiger (1879-1961) is best-known as the loony Dr. Pretorius in Whale's *Bride of Frankenstein*, a great film that afforded the British character star a plum role. His screen career began in Britain in 1918. Over time he was firmly established as an eccentric thanks to roles in *The Ghoul* (1933), *The Man Who Could Work Miracles* (1936), *They Drive By Night* (chilling as a demented crime buff, 1939), *Henry V* (as the Duke of Beri, 1944), *Caesar and Cleopatra* (as Theodotus, 1945), *Quartet* (1948), and *The Man in the White Suit* (as the absurdly avaricious head of Britain's textile cartel, 1953).

Like many of the other stars of *The Old Dark House*, Thesiger worked in high-profile pictures until his death. Later projects include *The Robe* (as Tiberius, 1953), *The Horse's Mouth* (1958), *Sons and Lovers* (1960), and his last, *The Roman Spring of Mrs. Stone* (1961).

If anyone in the impressive cast of *The Old Dark House* steals scene after scene, it's Thesiger, whose Horace Femm is at once funny and completely creepy. Cadaverous and representative of the absolute worst in British hospitality, Horace is nevertheless a creature of musty dignity. When he intones "Have a po-ta-to" to the guests at dinner, you're impressed by his attempt at civility even as you're appalled by his clumsiness. Other moments are even better, as when Horace blithely tosses a bouquet into the blazing fireplace after offhandedly explaining, "My sister was on the point of arranging these flowers." Later, when he offers his guests gin, apologizing because it's the only alcohol in the house, he pauses and adds with just a hint of childlike slyness, "I like gin."

Vivacious Lillian Bond (1910-91) was a British stage actress who never made much of an impression on Hollywood studio executives. Following her film debut in *Just a Gigolo* (1931), she worked steadily throughout the thirties but returned to the theater by about 1940. Other films include *When Strangers Marry* (1933), *China Seas* (1935), *The Westerner* (1940), *The Picture of Dorian Gray* (1945), *The Maze* (1953), *Man in the Attic* (a Jack the Ripper thriller, 1954), and *Pirates of Tripoli* (1955).

Although a relative novice during the shoot of *The Old Dark House*, Bond is charming as Gladys, and off the set happily conducted herself like a real star, piloting a fabulous automobile from one function to another with her mother inevitably in tow.

The Old Dark House was the first American film of British stage actress Eva Moore (1870-1955). Her first picture was *The Law Divine* (1920); other credits include *Of Human Bondage* (1946) and *The Bandit of Sherwood Forest* (1946). Spiteful and perpetually squinting as Rebecca, she embodies the dangerous final evolution of undisciplined religious fervor; she lives for nothing but food and the scolding of sinners.

The small, mild-looking British stage actor Brember Wills (1883-1948) was a clever choice to play Saul Femm. The characterization is one of the creepiest and most cunning in the long history of horror cinema. (The Saul of Priestley's novel is not nearly so clever.) Wills also worked in *Unfinished Symphony* (1935).

Finally, another veteran of the British stage, Elspeth Dudgeon (1871-1955), was cast as the aged Roderick Femm because, as Whale's friend David Lewis recalled, "she looked a thousand." Fitted with snowy false whiskers (and billed as John Dudgeon), the actress brought a disturbing and oddly funny androgyny to the part.

The Old Dark House was Dudgeon's first film; she also appeared in *The Moonstone* (1934), *Becky Sharp* (1935), *The Prince and the Pauper* (1937), *Sh! The Octopus* (1937), *Pride and Prejudice* (1940), *The Canterville Ghost* (with Charles Laughton, 1944), *The Paradine Case* (1948), and her last, *Lust for Gold* (1949).

The Old Dark House was Universal's Halloween release for 1932. Although the picture turned a profit, it was not as successful as the studio had hoped, and certainly did not cause a stir akin to that raised by the previous Whale-Karloff teaming, *Frankenstein*.

Reviews were mixed. Britain's *Film Weekly* was indisposed to the horror genre and began its notice by saying, "The vexed question of the horror film again rears its ugly head... with the arrival this week-end of the latest James Whale-Boris Karloff excursion into the realms of the unnatural." The critic apparently liked the film against his or her will, complimenting "as fine a company of players as one could wish to see in any picture," and noting "new and welcome restraint" in Whale's handling of bizarre material.

Mordaunt Hall of the *New York Times* focused on the film's performances ("Karloff," he said, "leaves no stone unturned to make this character thoroughly disturbing"), and noted that Whale "again proves his ability."

Harrison's Reports felt the film had "everything to send chills up one's spine.... The second half is tensely exciting. The situation showing the madman [Saul], at first gentle, and then murderous... holds the audience in tense suspense...."

A semi-literate reviewer with the trade paper *Variety,* oblivious to Whale's sense of humor, labeled the picture "somewhat inane." The writer objected to the bedroom scene featuring the half-dressed Gloria Stuart, then appeared to backpedal: "Still, if there wasn't the s.a. [sex appeal] angle, mebbe Morgan wouldn't get all hot and bothered as he did. And maybe there'd been no picture as a result, and mebbe that was a good idea, too."

Universal re-released *The Old Dark House* in the late forties and early fifties, before the rights to J.B. Priestley's *Benighted* reverted to the author, who sold the book to Columbia for the aforementioned "remake" by producer-director William Castle. No longer in possession of the story, Universal allowed prints of *The Old Dark House* to sit, ignored and apparently valueless, in the studio vault.

By a fortuitous happenstance, Curtis Harrington had come to Universal as a contract director in 1967. A devoted film buff as well as a filmmaker, Harrington immediately set to badgering the head of the editorial department about the whereabouts of the old Universal material. The original nitrate negative of *The Old Dark House* was subsequently located at the studio's New York facility, but the first reel had suffered irreparable deterioration. Fortunately, a lavender (fine grain) protection print survived intact. Thrilled, Harrington contacted the Library of Congress, New York's Museum of Modern Art, Eastman House in Rochester, and other film-preservation organizations. James Card of Eastman House was quick to respond and a new print was struck, although with the stipulation that it was for preservation and scholarship only, and could not be put to commercial use.

"Eventually," Harrington recalled for David Del Valle in 1996, "they made four or five beautiful 35mm copies—one for Eastman House, one for the Museum of Modern Art, one for the American Film Institute in Washington, and one for Universal Studios. Those are the only extant copies that I know of."

Poor-quality bootleg copies began to circulate on video in the early nineties, and a fair-quality print subsequently aired on the American Movie Classics cable-television network. The film is now available on videocassette from Kino Video and on laserdisc from Image Entertainment; the latter includes a commentary track by Whale biographer James Curtis and an on-camera interview with Curtis Harrington.

Today, critics and historians recognize *The Old Dark House* as a small masterpiece of wit and terror, and one of the finest Universal horror thrillers. Pauline Kael, doyenné of American film critics, called it "a wonderful deadpan takeoff of horror plays" that is "witty, perverse, and creepy."

Seattle Times critic John Hartl pronounced it "simply one of the most entertaining movies of the early 1930s," and Leonard Maltin's authoritative *Movie and Video Guide* awarded it three-and-a-half stars, calling it "outstanding" and "[a] real gem."

Better, more challenging roles would follow for Boris Karloff. Although Morgan was not an artistic triumph for him, his presence adds significantly to the appeal and commercial value of this quirky, almost-lost milestone of film history.

CREDITS: Producer: Carl Laemmle, Jr.; Director: James Whale; Screenplay: Benn W. Levy, from the novel *Benighted* by J.B. Priestley; Additional Dialogue: R.C. Sherriff; Cinematographer: Arthur Edeson; Art Director: Charles D. Hall; Editor: Clarence Kolster; Music: Bernhard Kaun; Makeup: Jack Pierce; Assistant Director: Joseph A. McDonough; Sound Recorder: William Hedgcock; Running Time: 71 minutes; A Universal Release presented by Carl Laemmle; Released October 20, 1932

CAST: Boris Karloff...Morgan, Melvyn Douglas...Penderel, Charles Laughton...Sir William Porterhouse, Lillian Bond...Gladys Perkins, Ernest Thesiger...Horace Femm, Eva Moore...Rebecca Femm, Raymond Massey...Philip Waverton, Gloria Stuart...Margaret Waverton, John (Elspeth) Dudgeon...Sir Roderick Femm, Brember Wills...Saul Femm

Sources: "Curtis Harrington on James Whale" by David Del Valle, *Films in Review*, January/February 1996; *Elsa Lanchester, Herself* by Elsa Lanchester, St. Martin's Press, 1983; *Hollywood Cauldron* by Gregory William Mank, McFarland, 1994; *James Whale* by James Curtis, Scarecrow, 1982; *Karloff* by Denis Gifford, Curtis Books, 1973; Kino Video

THE BLACK CAT
(1934)
by Dennis Fischer

Few films are as decidedly odd and yet so well-regarded as Edgar G. Ulmer's production of *The Black Cat*. The film earns its spurs as a cult classic if it had done no more than provide an effective teaming of the titans of terror, Karloff and Lugosi, and of all the films pairing those two fine actors, *The Black Cat* comes the closest in providing equally substantial parts.

However, there is much more to the film than that. Perhaps one of its oddest attributes is that, in many ways, it seems as if Karloff and Lugosi were given each other's roles. Obviously, the titans of terror were still getting established, but in the film Karloff is playing what would typically be a Bela Lugosi role... that of a brilliant but ruthless man, devoid of morals and devoted to evil, who will stop at nothing to get his way. Lugosi's distinction was his ability to portray living embodiments of pure evil.

On the other hand, Lugosi is playing the typical Karloff role. Karloff's distinction was the touch of pathos and of humanity that he brought to his greatest horror roles. No matter how many murders the Frankenstein Monster commits, Karloff's Monster remains a sympathetic figure, searching for light and kindness in a world which spurns him and shows him only fear and hatred.

Other great Karloff roles are suffused with this tinge of vulnerability and humanity—the resurrectionist Gray's pity for a crippled girl; *Bedlam*'s Master Sims' self-loathing toadying; the tortured dead men of *The Walking Dead* and *The Ghoul*; Karloff's tortured physicians in *The Haunted Strangler* and *Corridors of Blood* who only wanted to better mankind; his aspiring inventors of *The Devil Commands* and *The Sorcerers* entering into experiments which get beyond their control. One of Karloff's greatest gifts was his ability to evoke empathy, but none of his creations are as purely evil as Hjalmar Poelzig, with the possible exception of the fiendish Dr. Fu Manchu, and even he is prompted to his schemes by the oppressive British regime which dominated his country.

The truth is *The Black Cat* was drastically altered and reconceived during its brief retake session. Originally, director Edgar G. Ulmer's story and Peter Ruric's script based on it offered the public two fiends for the price of one. Lugosi's Werdegast was originally meant to have been driven mad by the sight of his dead wife, unleashing a torrent of lust in the man so that he vies for Joan Alison, not to save her as in the final film, but to take her sexually for himself.

91

However, Lugosi himself was campaigning for more benign characterizations and the front office was aghast at Ulmer's perversity, however slyly hinted at, and in the process the story was refashioned after a frantic recutting period which only added to the confusion, leaving behind only confusing hints of its original intentions.

The Black Cat was created as an efficient little programmer by Universal. It was shot in 19 days on a budget of $95,745 (including overhead and retakes), making it one of the most inexpensive of the Universal horror films of the '30s.

The Black Cat was for its time (and remains) pretty daring, what with its intimations of necrophilia, perversity, sadism, and Satanism, not to mention that the character Karloff portrays is a brilliant engineer who betrays his comrades, causing the deaths of thousands of men, who abducts the wife and daughter of a former friend, telling them that the man died while he was languishing in prison, who murders and embalms the wife and other women, marries the daughter, presides over a devil cult, and finally kills the daughter and prepares her for embalming as well, before he is skinned alive and then dynamited to death. All this while the new Production Code was coming into effect to trim down the perversity of Hollywood product.

Although it sometimes railed against it, Hollywood supported the Production Code for the simple reason that they felt it was better to have their own censor than to leave Hollywood films at the mercy of a series of censors across the country. It was a way to assure the public that its concerns about the content of motion pictures was being addressed, and while additional censorship did sometimes occur, it proved remarkably effective.

When queried on eroticism in fantasy films in 1965, director Edgar G. Ulmer responded, "It's perhaps the hardest thing to handle because one can easily fall into sexual aberrations. I am a little afraid to go in that direction because it can easily become vulgar."

The film originated in early 1932 when a copy of Edgar Allan Poe's tale "The Black Cat" came across the desk of Universal story editor Richard Schayer, who decided that the tale of an alcoholic brute walling up his wife and cat in a cellar seemed too trite and unsavory for a feature.

This version of *The Black Cat* never passed the treatment stage. Obviously, very few elements of this story ended up in the final version, but it was seriously intended as a Karloff project and was to have been directed by E.A. Dupont after the studio gave up on producing either *Bluebeard* or *The Wizard* with Karloff.

Meanwhile, on April 3, 1933, the financially strapped studio was forced to shut down temporarily while Karloff flew to England to appear in *The Ghoul*.

In December of 1933, Junior Laemmle hired Edgar G. Ulmer to write *Love Life of a Crooner* for Edward Buzzell to direct. Ulmer had been a designer for Max Reinhardt at the age of 19 and was a set builder on scores of German silent

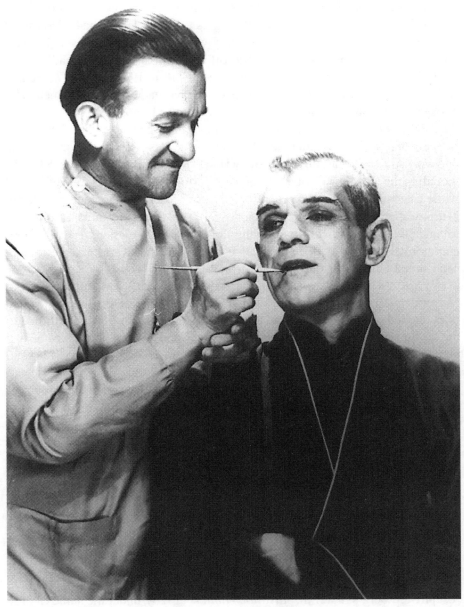

Jack Pierce's makeup helped Karloff portray his character of Poelzig as the most sadistic of men.

films in the twenties, before moving to America and Universal, where he worked on *The Phantom of the Opera* among other films. Famed German director Murnau hired Ulmer to serve as assistant art director on all of Murnau's American films.

When *Crooner* fizzled, Ulmer was assigned to work on the sets of Frank Borzage's *Little Man, What Now?*, the rights to which Ulmer had encouraged Laemmle to buy. However, what he really wanted to work on was a German-style horror film which would star Karloff and Lugosi. Universal had considered teaming their horror stars for *The Suicide Club* in 1931 and for *The Return of Frankenstein* in 1933, but the former was never made and *Return* metamorphosed into the later *Bride of Frankenstein* without Lugosi.

Ulmer's idea caught Laemmle's enthusiasm, especially when Ulmer explained that he would need a mere $9,000 for the sets—the plans for which he had worked out with art director Danny Hall. The cast would only cost $17,350 including the fees for Karloff and Lugosi. (Karloff was paid a flat rate of $7,500 while Lugosi took home a weekly paycheck of $1,000). Stage manager Martin Murphy approved an estimated budget of $91,125. Seeing a quick profit for the financially troubled institution, Laemmle, Jr. gave his blessing provided (for commercial reasons) Ulmer retain Poe's title and that Karloff agree to star. That suited Ulmer just fine.

While on the set of *The Golem*, Ulmer heard *Golem* author Gustav Meyerinck tell a grisly anecdote about the French fortress Doumont which had been shelled by the Germans and about a sinister commander who returned to the scene of the crime. *The Golem*'s designer and Ulmer's boss was a man named Hans Poelzig, whose name was transformed to Hjalmar Poelzig and given to Karloff as the sinister commander of Fort Marmaros.

The character for Karloff's antagonist was also suggested by infamous occultist Alestair Crowley, whose novel *Moonchild* was badly adapted into an awful low-budget feature starring John Carradine and Victor Buono in 1972. Crowley was a self-described "most evil man who ever lived" who led a devil-worshiping cult and practiced black magic.

For the character of Dr. Vitus Werdegast, Ulmer, perhaps inspired by *Dr. Caligari*, created the ironic character of a brilliant psychiatrist who not only suffers from hysterical cat phobia but who ends up practically insane. Ulmer finished his outline for the film on February 6, 1934.

George Carrol Sims, who was born in Des Moines, Iowa, in 1902, took the pen names Peter Ruric and Paul Cain. At the age of 21, he was an art decorator in Los Angeles and he worked as a production assistant two years later on Joseph Sternberg's first film, *Salvation Hunters* (1925), under the name George Ruric. It was he who suggested to Myrna Williams that her name should only have three syllables and so she became Myrna Loy.

In 1931, Ruric began writing stories for *Black Mask* magazine, where he specialized in writing the hardest hard-boiled stories of them all under the name Paul Cain. He lived in New York City with actress Gertrude Michael before returning to Hollywood to write the Cary Grant film *Gambling Ship,* which was based on a series of stories Ruric had written about a violent gunman named

Gerry Kells. Shortly afterward, he wrote his only novel, *Fast One*, before Ulmer selected him as the screenwriter for *The Black Cat*.

Relatives described Ruric during this time as a blond, bearded member of the Malibu Beach crowd, taken to wearing ascot scarves.

Ruric completed the script in only two weeks, handing it in on February 19, 1934, and it is likely that he identified with the character of Peter Alison, who describes himself in the film as the "world's greatest writer... of unimportant books." Universal's bland leading man, David Manners, was selected to play Peter Alison, while Jacqueline Wells, who had just finished playing the sister on Paramount's lavish version of *Alice in Wonderland*, played Joan, named after Ulmer's first wife.

A few months later, Ruric would abandon Hollywood and sail for Europe with his mother. He later returned to Hollywood in 1939 and resumed his career without much success. He married a cigarette girl named Virginia and persuaded her to change her name to Mushel. On March 11, 1940, the bride was reported as having jumped out of the window of the couple's third-story Hollywood apartment after a drunken quarrel with her husband; however, she only sustained an injured arm. Mushel Ruric reported that Lugosi was a some-time visitor to their home. Ruric continued to drink and they continued to quarrel until they finally divorced in 1943.

Rumor has it that Ruric remarried and tried his hand at playwrighting, but without much success. When a collection of his stories entitled *Seven Slayers* was published in 1945, Ruric submitted a bizarre biography, describing himself as a professional gambler and Dadaist painter, and in a later sketch declared he was dividing his time "between three plays, a definitive work on the sexual implications of Oncidium Fuchsias, and Warner Brothers."

His final story, "The Tasting Machine," appeared in *Gourmet* magazine and has a young man trying to seduce a girl via semaphore while the title contraption performs cunnilingus on the moaning girl as her cook-lover tries to break the door down with an ax. It appears that over the years, Ruric lost none of his odd perversity.

He then relocated to Mallorca, Spain, for a few years, followed by a stint in North Africa, both havens for penniless writers, before returning to Hollywood to write for television in the late '50s. In 1966, he died of cancer.

Ulmer desperately needed Karloff to play Poelzig, though it apparently took some persuasion as Karloff didn't want to get typecast in horror roles having just enjoyed non-horror roles in *The House of Rothschild* and *The Lost Patrol*. However, he was intrigued that Ulmer had designed a special wardrobe for him which would give him an "out of this world appearance."

The final script was bound on February 27, 1934, and shooting began the next day. Originally, Ruric scripted an elaborate cathedral wedding for Peter and Joan, based on the prologue in Ulmer's draft, which were intended to em-

Behind the scenes of *The Black Cat*, Boris Karloff reads Jacqueline Wells' palm.

phasize Joan's status as a just-married maiden, and thus a suitably virgin sacrifice for the Satanic cult later in the film. Ulmer decided to discard this sequence, trimming the script's 333 scenes to 320.

Assisting Ulmer as script girl was Shirley Kasseler Alexander. She and Ulmer fell in love and were married a year later. She remained devoted to Ulmer and remained with him for the rest of his life. Shirley had been married to Max

Alexander, Carl Laemmle's nephew and an executive at the studio, before falling in love with Ulmer and marrying him a year later. As a consequence, Ulmer was effectively blackballed from the majors for the rest of his career, relegated to producing and directing poverty row productions with occasionally impressive results.

Ulmer was only paid $150 a week and was under the benignly neglectful supervision of E. M. Asher who was paid $2,000 as production supervisor, though he receives no credit on the film. Carl Laemmle, Jr. was called away to New York two weeks before production began to answer in court charges of salary gouging, while Carl, Sr. was away in Europe. (It is doubtful that Laemmle, Sr. would have approved the project if he had known about it.)

The film opens at a French railroad station (indicated by a "Sortie" sign) where the Orient Express is boarding and bakers are supplying the dining car with bread. Aboard are the newlyweds Peter (David Manners) and Joan Alison (Jacqueline Wells) bound for a honeymoon resort near Vizhegrad. The pair are obviously much in love.

Ulmer eliminated 23 scenes involving crossing the Czech border on the way to Bratislavia (the film still retains the couple's passports being checked as a way of introducing them) and he discarded several scenes with a maitre'd (who was played by Herman Bing, Murnau's assistant director on *Sunrise*) who tries to overwhelm the couple with his charm and his Chateaubriand.

Instead, he cuts right to the conductor apologizing for a mistake and asking the newlyweds to make room for a svelte and aristocratic gentleman, Dr. Vitus Werdegast (Lugosi), who removes his hat and addresses them.

"Do please forgive this intrusion. It is not necessary to make it seem so important. I can make myself very comfortable in this passageway."

Joan grabs Peter's arm in concern, but Peter kindly offers to share. Lugosi plays the part with tenderness and a wistful smile, but the action creates a palpable feeling that doom has entered the compartment with them, as when Lugosi looks over Joan appreciatively, and then up at a big valise that was stored overhead as it tips and almost falls on the young couple. Werdegast springs up to intercept it, catching it with Peter's help.

"I'm sorry I frightened you, darling," says Peter.

"It is, after all, better to be frightened than to be crushed," comments Werdegast with an amused smile.

The couple report that they are going by Gömbös, and Werdegast reports that he, too, is headed near there.

"For the sport?" Peter inquires.

Werdegast considers the implications, raises an eyebrow, considers what he is about to undertake in confronting his nemesis and says, "Perhaps. I go to visit an old friend." He then opens a shade and we see his reflection against the smoke billowing outside. He becomes the very incarnation of dark memory.

As the couple sleep, we hear the sounds of the Tchaikovsky's love theme from *Romeo and Juliet*. Werdegast looks longingly at the virginal bride and tenderly caresses Joan's beautiful locks, introducing the themes of sexual desire and sexual repression. Peter, who has yet to consummate his marriage, wakes and notices this unexpected gesture.

"I beg your indulgence my friend," Werdegast explains. "Eighteen years ago I left a girl... so like your lovely wife, to go to war. Kaiser and country, you know. She was my wife. Have you ever heard of Kurgaal? It is a prison below Omsk along Lake Bakail. Many men have gone there. Few have returned. I have returned. After fifteen years—*I* have returned."

Lugosi was originally to have struck his fist on the window sill at his last line, but with the forcefulness of his delivery, it was decided that such a gesture was unnecessary. His delivery certainly captures the pain and indomitable will of the man.

The train stops in a downpour, and the trio disembark. A bus driver carrying a Hotel Hungaria umbrella escorts them to his bus. Werdegast is joined by his servant Thamal (Harry Cording), whom Ulmer describes in his treatment as "an enormous Tibetan, slant-eyed, with the cold, impassive face of an evil Buddha." (Cording later appeared in *Son of Frankenstein*, *The Wolf Man*, and *The Ghost of Frankenstein*.) Ulmer intended to keep the character mute until the climax where he was supposed to shock the audience by calling out in pain— however, that notion was discarded and the figure remains mute throughout, though clearly not deaf.

The bus driver passes the time by providing commentary during the drive. "It is too bad about the rain," he says, "it's very unusual. This road was built by the Austrian army. All of this country was one of greatest battlefields of the war. Tens of thousands of men died here. The ravine down there was piled twelve deep with dead and wounded men. The little river below was swollen... red... a raging torrent of blood. The high hill yonder where Engineer Poelzig now lives was the site of Fort Marmaros. He built his home on its very foundations. Marmaros, the greatest graveyard in the world."

Throughout this recitation of horrors, the young couple sit uncomprehending while Lugosi magnificently registers his terrible memories of the events, closing his eyes and making it seem as if the vision of those horrible deaths were still fresh before him. Even Thamal gives a subtle reaction.

The bus suddenly skids off the road, through a wooden fence, and slides down into the ravine in Ulmer's $250 bus wreck scene in which we see a tree stump in silhouette printed over a falling miniature tree dissolving to the overturned bus (we never see a collision). The bus driver is killed instantly and Joan is rendered unconscious. It was Ulmer's intention that Thamal carry Joan as though she were a "sacrificial offering to a savage god," but though she will be presented to the satanic Poelzig later, this impression doesn't quite come off,

Poelzig has married Werdegast's daughter Karen (Lucille Lund). Unfortunately, most of Lund's scenes were cut from the final print.

though it is reminiscent of a scene from *The Golem*. Additionally, there was to be the first appearance by a black cat in this scene—Werdegast was to fling it against a rock after it licks blood from Joan's shoulder, but this was discarded. Instead, Thamal simply leaves carrying Joan with Werdegast and Peter following, carrying the luggage as they head up the hill to Poelzig's house (actually a matte painting by Russ Lawson which was photographed against rear-projected clouds by Jack Cosgrove for a total cost of $175).

Next, to the strains of Chopin's *Piano Prelude No. 2*, we're introduced to the fantastic interior of the house, Ulmer's $3,700 set, complete with large curving staircase, futuristic art deco touches, Bauhaus squares, Breuer chairs, and other touches. It suggests the future instead of the past. There is nothing comfortable or familiar here, underscoring the sense of unease that this sinister locale will give our protagonists.

After introducing the setting, Ulmer finally introduces his villain. (Karloff is shown only from behind at the organ at the opening of the film when his introductory credit is shown). A radio crackles to life and the Majordomo (Egon Brecher in a truly terrible toupee) intones, "Dr. Werdegast has arrived."

Poelzig (Karloff) is lying on the bed next to his wife Karen (Lucille Lund) and arises in profile like one of the undead at twilight. His rigidly straight back upon arising is also reminiscent of Max Schreck's Count Orlok in *Nosferatu*. We see him as a black shape in silhouette, employing slow, deliberate movements as if he were a sleepwalker like Cesare in *The Cabinet of Dr. Caligari*.

In an interview with Peter Bogdanovich which initially appeared in *Film Culture* and later was reprinted in *Kings of the Bs*, Ulmer commented about his star: "Karloff was a very charming man....Very charming. And he never took himself seriously. My biggest job was to keep him in the part, because he laughed at himself...

"One of the nicest scenes I had with him, he lies in bed next to the daughter of Lugosi, and the young couple rings down at the door, and he gets up, and you see him the first time in costume, in that modernistic set... He got into bed, we got ready to shoot, and he got up, he turned to the camera, after he put his shoes on, and said, 'Boo!' Every time I had him come in by the door, he would open the door and say, 'Here comes the heavy....' He was a very, very lovely man...

"Yes, a very fine actor. Five star. As you know, he lisped—but the way he used that lisp—he knew exactly how to overcome the handicap."

We get our first clear glimpse of Poelzig when he opens a door to the strains of an orchestrated version of Liszt's *Piano Sonata in B Minor*. He wears white-lined black pajamas over a black outfit and stares at the sleeping Joan who has been spread out on one of the beds in what will be her bedroom. John Mescall's camera moves towards him twice, once for a facial close-up immediately followed by a medium shot that dollies forward to catch Poelzig's eyes glancing right to Werdegast who now enters the frame.

"It has been a long time, Hjalmar. The years have been kind to you," says Werdegast while Poelzig glances once more towards Joan. Taking the glance as a question, Werdegast responds, "An accident on the road below. Mr. and Mrs. Alison will go on to Gömbös. Mrs. Alison is slightly injured. I look the liberty of bringing them here."

Poelzig's eyes continue to get drawn back to the figure of Joan. Karloff keeps his body unnaturally still, making him seem as one entranced, struck still by Joan's beauty. Finally, he nods slightly to the others and opens the door, gesturing Werdegast to go into the corridor, but he can't resist stealing another peak at Joan before he goes.

In this film, Karloff alters his acting style. He relies more on his sheer presence to bring his scenes off rather than indulging in distracting bits of business. As a consequence, his Poelzig appears to be a concentrated individual, very intense and lustful.

Once in Werdegast's study, the good doctor immediately charges, "You sold Marmaros to the Russians. Scuttled away in the night and left us to die. Is it to be wondered that you should choose this place to build your house? The masterpiece of construction—built upon the ruins of the masterpiece of destruction—the masterpiece of murder. The murderer of 10,000 men returns to the place of his crime.

"Those who died were fortunate. I was taken prisoner—to Kurgaal, where the soul is killed, slowly. Fifteen years I've rotted in the darkness, waited. Not to kill you—to kill your soul—slowly. Where is my wife? And my daughter?" The psychically scarred psychiatrist reveals that he has been pursuing Poelzig from continent to continent, having been to America, Spain, and South America before discovering that Poelzig had returned to Marmaros.

"Vitus, you are mad," responds Poelzig darkly as he rises threateningly, but his demeanor completely changes to one of cordiality when he perceives the presence of Peter Alison and offers him a drink. Peter helps underscore the theme of things not appearing as they seem when he espies what looks to be a one-handed clock, until Poelzig moves the hand to another position and reveals it to be a radio from which a snippet of Schubert's *Unfinished Symphony* blares and continues to underscore the scene.

As Werdegast offers a toast to Peter's wife and to love, a black cat makes its appearance. Werdegast drops his glass in shock, grabs a knife lying on a nearby table, and hurls it into the offscreen cat, killing it. Overcome, he covers his face and almost swoons.

Poelzig smiles at this sign of weakness on the part of his adversary. As if the cat had transformed into her, Joan now makes her appearance. "You are frightened, Doctor?" she inquires with a peculiar smile, then turns to Poelzig and addresses him, "You are our host."

"At your service, Madame," responds Poelzig at his most gentlemanly as he kisses Joan's hand. "You must be indulgent of Dr. Werdegast's weakness. He is the unfortunate victim of one of the commoner phobias, but in an extreme form. He has an intense and all-consuming horror—of cats."

Joan gives off a feline, predatory feeling as she slinks over to her husband and gives him a very passionate kiss. The sexual display brings out a silent but intense reaction in Poelzig as he grasps tightly the arm of a naked statuette at the sight, indicating his intense desire for the woman which he has effectively repressed for the moment.

According to Ulmer's treatment, the black cat represents the seed and spirit of all evil, which at the moment of death passes from the cat to Joan, turning her into the living incarnation of evil itself. Her chaste beauty supposedly takes on a sensual, faintly animalistic contour. When she wakes later, she remembers nothing of this experience, her memory blanked out after the car crash.

101

Werdegast tries to reassure Peter with his own explanation for Joan's behavior: "It is perhaps the narcotic. I have seen it affect certain people very oddly. One cannot be sure. Sometimes these cases take strange forms. The victim becomes in a sense mediumistic, a vehicle for all the intangible forces around her." Why Dr. Werdegast would have administered such a narcotic in such circumstances remains a mystery.

"Sounds like a lot of supernatural baloney to me," responds Peter.

"Superstition, perhaps…. Baloney, perhaps not," intones Lugosi in dead earnest. "There are many things under the sun," making a reference to Hamlet's admonition to Horatio.

"I will show you your rooms," offers Poelzig.

Peter still hasn't recovered from the previous scene. "Strange about the cat. Joan seemed so curiously affected when you killed it."

"That was coincidence, I think," responds Werdegast. "However, certain ancient books say that the black cat is the living embodiment of evil. At death, that evil enters into the nearest living thing. It is…."

"The black cat does *not* die," interrupts Poelzig pleasantly. "These same books, if I'm not mistaken, teach that the black cat is deathless—deathless as evil. It is the origin of the common superstition of the cat with nine lives." Opening the door, he instructs, "You will sleep here, Vitus."

Oddities pile up. Peter should not be surprised his wife would be affected when Werdegast unexpectedly kills a cat before her eyes. It's also strange that Werdegast would administer a narcotic that would render Joan open to intangible forces when he will continually harp on the atmosphere of death surrounding Marmaros. Karloff subtly indicates animosity towards Werdegast while maintaining a polite façade in front of the Alisons, though his gentility seems more British than the Austrian background of his character would indicate.

During retakes, a scene of Karloff stroking a black cat—it is left ambiguous whether this is a different feline or the return of the one Werdegast had killed earlier—while walking through the gun room/cellar of his mansion, was inserted. Here we see a series of women suspended in glass coffins, one of whom is portrayed by Lucille Lund to represent Werdegast's late wife, accompanied by Heinz Roemhold's orchestration of Liszt's *Piano Sonata in B Minor* in 5/4 time.

Ulmer's treatment indicates that as part of his Satanic rites, Poelzig, as the earthly incarnation of Satan, rapes and then murders his female sacrificial victims at the climax of the rite, and these necrophiliac displays represent his victims since his return to Marmaros. (Originally, the film had simply dissolved from Karloff's feet pacing the hallway to the clock near his bed).

Poelzig enters Peter's room expecting to find Vitus, saying, "Now, Vitus, we have something to settle, we two," surprising Peter in his bed. Werdegast opens the door from the adjoining room, asking Poelzig if he is looking for him

Karloff as Poelzig portrays a brilliant but ruthless man devoid of morals and devoted to evil.

and inquiring after his wife. The pair go downstairs, and strangely, a quick, "Wait here," that Werdegast gives Thamal is dubbed by somebody other than Lugosi.

As they enter the entrance to the downstairs gun turrets, Werdegast comments, "I can still sense death in the air."

"There is still death in the air." returns Poelzig. The pair enter the chart room where, framed against a looming glass chart, Werdegast's wife appears before them in her glass tomb. Poelzig throws a switch which illuminates her features while Karloff looks up at her adoringly, wistfully as one of his most prized "possessions."

"You see, Vitus?" he says very tenderly, "I have cared for her tenderly and well. You will find her almost as beautiful as when you last saw her. She died… two years after the war."

"How?" cries Werdegast, his heart breaking.

"Of pneumonia." (Karloff blinks at this lie). "She was never strong, you know."

"And the child? Our daughter?"

"Dead," Poelzig responds. (The script's original line was "She died—at birth," suggesting that Poelzig abducted Werdegast's wife when she was pregnant, though how Werdegast could know the gender of his child before birth before the days of amniocentesis isn't clear. Wisely, Ulmer decided to remove this additional perversity).

"And why she… why she like *this*?"

"Is she not beautiful?" says Poelzig, apparently oblivious to the effect this sight is having on Werdegast. "I wanted to have her beauty—always. I loved her too, Vitus." Here Karloff gives a touching hint of Poelzig's own sense of loss, Hjalmar's most (and almost only) sympathetic moment in the film.

"Lies! All lies! (The lines in italics were scripted but cut). You killed her *to save her youth and beauty for your own monstrous end!* You killed her as I'm about to kill you," screams Werdegast, pulling his Luger only to be frightened out of his wits by the appearance of a black cat that causes him to startle and fall back into the glass chart. Obviously, Werdegast has had a profound shock, from the sight of both his dead, preserved wife and the cat itself. He has undergone a change of heart, going from wanting to kill Poelzig's soul to threatening Poelzig's life.

However, this is the point in the film where in the original version Werdegast was to be overcome by pure evil and resolve to fill the void in his life by murdering Poelzig and abducting Joan for himself. This is why his servant Thamal takes his fist and knocks Peter unconscious later in the film. Also, Werdegast was not at the Satanic ceremony as an observer, but was originally the one who welcomed the Satanists into Poelzig's abode while Poelzig was donning his ceremonial robes. When Werdegast releases Joan from the cross, it was his original intention to drag her upstairs and rape her, not rescue her as in the final film. The original ending was to have been much more horrifyingly graphic as well.

What does follow the scene is one of John Mescall's best camera dollies, an extended POV shot from Poelzig's point of view as he leads Werdegast up a

104

spiral staircase back to the house. Accompanying this magnificent, fluid, al- most floating camera move is the moody allegretto from Beethoven's *7th Symphony* and one of Karloff's best monologues, beautifully delivered by the master himself:

"Come, Vitus, are we men or are we children? Of what use are all those melodramatic gestures? You say your soul was killed, and that you have been dead all these years. And what of me? Did we not both die here in Marmaros, fifteen years ago? Are we any the less victims of the war than those whose bodies were torn asunder? Are we not both—the living dead? And now you come to me playing at being an avenging angel, childishly thirsting for my blood. We understand each other too well. We know too much of life. We shall play a little game, Vitus. A game of death, if you like. But under any circumstances, we shall have to wait until these people are gone, until we are alone. Until tomorrow."

Mescall would have an erratic career as a cinematographer, partly due to his alcoholism. He did some of his best work with James Whale on *Bride of Frankenstein, Show Boat,* and *The Road Back.* After the mid-'40s, he worked less, specializing in trick photography. His subsequent work includes *Davy Crockett, Indian Scout* , and Roger Corman's *Not of This Earth.*

Karloff then has a scene with Karen, Werdegast's daughter, whose performance was drastically altered in recutting to being the somnambulistic one we see. He passes his hand over her face in a gesture at once caressing and apparently a hypnotic trigger; with the change of a camera angle, her eyes go from open to shut and she does not consciously hear what Poelzig says to her. He tells her, "You are not to leave your room tomorrow. You are the very core and meaning of my life. No one shall take you from me, not even Vitus. Not even your *father.*"

A scene was inserted during reshooting of the silent, impassive Thamal removing a knife from his sleeve while Werdegast tells him, "Not yet, Thamal, put that away. We will bide our time. Other lives are involved. This whole place is so undermined with dynamite that the slightest mistake by one of us could cause the destruction of all. Until I tell you different, you are his servant, not mine."

While this helps explain Thamal's later actions against Peter, it does nothing to explain where Werdegast got his intelligence about the dynamite, though it does clue the audience to its presence. Of course, why Poelzig would want to be able to self-destruct his own house is left to the imagination as well.

In his bedroom, Poelzig picks up a book and reads a chapter entitled "Rites of Lucifer," which begins as follows: "In the night, in the dark of the moon, the High Priest assembles his disciples for the sacrifice. The chosen maiden…" (The book was originally to have been of Ibsen's play *When We Dead Awaken,* in which a sculptor creates a statue in the image of his lover, echoing the idea of

Karloff romancing Karen, who is the image of Karloff's previous lover and her mother, but this idea was altered during filming.)

There was a comic scene cut where Peter has breakfast and insults the servants in the house when he realizes that they can't understand what he is saying. Instead, the film resumes with Joan awakening and Werdegast coming in to examine Joan's dressing on her shoulder in the morning. Joan has returned to her normal self.

Joan inquires after her husband and is informed that he is at breakfast. As Poelzig is leaving, he leers so openly at Joan that it causes her to close her nightgown. Shots of Lugosi leering as well were eliminated during re-editing.

Next comes the famous chess game scene. According to Ulmer's treatment, "We imply that Joan's fate does not revolve upon the chess game. Rather, that it is a symbol of a deeper game—the game of life and death." However, the film contravenes this intention by clearly making Joan's fate rest on the outcome of Werdegast and Poelzig's game.

The game originally ended in a stalemate, with Poelzig commenting, "We are evenly matched, Vitus. The advantage moves back and forth like a pendulum!" However, new material was contrived to more clearly spell out the intentions of the altered version.

"Don't pretend, Hjalmar. There was nothing spiritual in your eyes when you looked at that girl. You plan to keep her here!"

Poelzig's fondles the breasts of his queen to underscore his sexual intentions as he responds, "Perhaps."

"I intend to let her go!"

"Is that a challenge, Vitus?"

"Yes, if you dare fight it out alone!"

"Do you dare play chess with me for her?"

"Yes, I will even play you chess for her—provided if I win, they are free to go."

"You won't win, Vitus," predicts Poelzig accurately.

Peter and Joan have a brief love scene where Joan expresses her dislike of "Pigs-low," as she designates Poelzig, and the pair decide to depart immediately. They descend and are interrupted by an odd comic relief scene in which two gendarmes of differing nationalities appear to investigate the bus crash, bicker with each other (perhaps meant to underscore the Austrian-Hungarian animosity in the film except that Armetta is clearly Italian), and they urge the couple to honeymoon in either Gömbös or Pisthyan while a variation of Liszt's *The Rakoczy March* underscores the comic intent of the scene.

Peter is intent on leaving after the officers have left. He tries to make a polite adieu, but Poelzig brusquely interrupts him with "I beg your pardon, but do you play chess? If you don't mind, I think we'll go on with our game." Poelzig surprises Werdegast by claiming that moving Joan is against the advice

Poelzig and Werdegast (Bela Lugosi) play chess for the life of Joan.

of the good doctor. The majordomo returns to inform them that Poelzig's car is out of commission, and then when Peter wishes to phone the hotel to send a car, that the phone is dead.

"You hear that, Vitus," reacts Poelzig with a smile, "The phone is dead. *Even* the phone is dead!" underscoring again the prevalent atmosphere of death and hopelessness that surrounds the characters.

Poelzig achieves checkmate and says so, but the front office was concerned that uninformed cinema-goers might not understand what that meant, so they had the line, "You lose, Vitus," dubbed on afterwards by someone who doesn't remotely sound like Karloff.

Peter is about ready to walk to Vizhegrad with his wife when Thamal smashes his head before carrying Joan, who faints, upstairs to her room where Poelzig locks her in. Thamal then descends and locks the unconscious writer in a rotating room. Poelzig celebrates by playing Bach's *Toccata and Fugue in D Minor,* a piece destined to become a horror film cliché.

Werdegast takes the key from the chess table and goes to Joan's room to warn her that she is to play an important part in a Satanic ritual. In the original version of the scene, he was to have told her that she was very beautiful, and when she asks what they have done to Peter, responds, "That is hard to say! Herr Poelzig has strange and effective ways of disposing of people who get in his way!"

Joan naturally accuses him: "Your servant struck him down. You are his accomplice!" Werdegast was to try to molest her originally, but instead footage was added where Lugosi tells her that Poelzig is a mad beast who murdered Vitus' wife and child, that he must wait his time and until then do Poelzig's bidding, that Poelzig is the priest of a Satanic cult and intends her to play an important part in his ritual, ending his exhortations with, "Be brave. It is your only chance."

Poelzig takes the key for Joan's room from Werdegast. Meanwhile, upstairs in Joan's room, first a black cat and then Karen, who disobeys Poelzig's injunction, enters Joan's room.

While Karen only appears in a few brief scenes, Lucille Lund was recalled for three and a half days of retakes between March 25 and March 28. The entire 5 1/2 days only cost $6,500, when the film was reconstructed. Ulmer initially wanted Karen to resemble a Siamese cat, but this concept was ultimately rejected. Still, the part as originally scripted and no doubt filmed had Karen as a miserable prisoner of Poelzig's power, one who is aware of her husband's abhorrent excesses.

However, in reconceiving the character as a virtual sleepwalker unaware of the degenerate activity her husband is involved with, Karen's emotional moments were pared away. The lines below in italics were trimmed from the scene where she meets Joan.

"You are new here, aren't you?" Karen was to have said.

"What do you mean?" replied Joan.

"I have not been out of this house since I was brought here nine years ago. In that time, many women, young and beautiful like you, have come."

"Who are you?"

"I am Karen—Madame Poelzig."

"Karen? Not Karen Werdegast?"

"You know my name? My father died in prison during the war. Herr Poelzig married my mother."

"You are his wife?" There is the sound of door chimes. *"What's that?'*

Karen was to laugh as an evil look entered her eye as she said, *"Your wedding bells, my dear! Another bride for the devil! Another offering to the gods for my master! Prepare!"*

Instead of the door chiming, Karen now responds, "Yes," to which Joan exclaims, "Karen, listen, your father is not dead. He's here. Here in this very house. He's come for you. Karen, don't you understand me? Your father has come for you."

108

Poelzig enters and corners her with a black cat under his arm, and sends Karen back to her bedroom with a glance. He locks Joan's door and enters Karen's bedroom from which we hear her screaming, "No, Hjalmar! Please!" before a loud scream erupts. Later, we discover that he has killed this woman who was "the core and meaning of his life" rather than risk losing her to Werdegast.

Poelzig dons his ceremonial robes and pentagram, and looks up at a stormy, windy sky while his Satanists converge downstairs. An organist (John Carradine, who is only shown from an overhead shot looking down on top of his head and his hands on the keyboard) plays Bach's adagio from the *Toccata and Fugue in C Major*. Joan is taken by the cultists to the altar where, upon seeing Werdegast in the audience, she faints against an inverted cross on a dais before a podium to which Poelzig ascends and begins reciting in Latin.

While the Satanists in the film appear very ordinary, Ulmer initially wanted them to be "as aberrant as possible," and included descriptions of a dwarf and a woman named Frau Goering who was to be given a Hitlerian mustache.

What Karloff is actually chanting in Latin translates fairly innocuously: "With a grain of salt, the brave may fall but cannot yield. The wolf changes its skin, but not its mind. Great is the truth and it shall prevail. That which I admit I do not know I cannot lose. The loss that is lost is not lost at all. Every madman thinks everyone is crazy. He who repents is almost innocent."

During the ceremony, a female cultist cries out (Ulmer indicated in his treatment that she was experiencing an orgasm, but there is no hint of that in the final film), which proves enough of a distraction for Werdegast and Thamal to abduct Joan from the sacrificial altar. (To rape her in the original script, to save her in the final film.)

Meanwhile, Peter revives in the revolving room and uses a match to find the light switch. He then manipulates the controls to turn the room to an opening, but it's locked. He then tries another opening, behind which proves to be the majordomo with gun in hand preparing to kill him. The pair grapple on the floor and the majordomo manages to knock the hapless writer out.

Joan, Werdegast, and Thamal descend the spiral stair with Werdegast assuring her that he only wishes to save her and knows of a way out. They are interrupted by the appearance of the majordomo who shoots Thamal. The wounded Thamal breaks the majordomo's neck with a karate chop. Joan reveals that Werdegast's daughter is alive and married to Poelzig, much to Werdegast's shock and dismay. The majordomo dies before Werdegast can find out from him where his daughter Karen is.

As Poelzig dashes downstairs after them, Werdegast finds his daughter dead under a sheet on a table in the embalming room. (Originally, she was to have been suspended on the same rack he skins Hjalmar from, which completes the task of driving him utterly mad.) The pair grapple each other with Poelzig seeming to get the upper hand, but the wounded Thamal enters the room, shuts the gate, and then assists his master in overcoming the engineer and fettering him to the embalming rack before expiring himself.

Karloff's grimaces in this fight scene and when he is restrained clearly recall his performance as the monster in *Frankenstein*. Poelzig is strapped to his own embalming rack and, in an idea Ulmer borrowed from the German film *Behind the Door*, Werdegast announces his intentions to skin his adversary alive.

"Did you ever see an animal skinned, Hjalmar," he asks after selecting a knife and stripping the shirt away from Poelzig. "That's what I'm going to do to you." The original lines was to have been "Tear the *stinking, putrid skin* from your body, slowly, bit by bit." However, Lugosi had difficulty with the line which appears in the film as, "Flare the skin from your body. Slowly. Bit by bit."

The shadows of the action on the wall, suggestive of Lugosi giving Karloff a shave, and Karloff's hands writhing in their manacles while emitting a canine yelp are used to suggest the action.

Originally, Ulmer had planned something even more gruesome. He wanted Werdegast to split the scalp and pull the sheath of skin from over Poelzig's head and shoulders. With a superhuman effort, this partially skinned Poelzig was to struggle free from the rack and fall to the floor and, as a living hideous pulp of blood and putrid flesh, approach Joan as she grabs the key and runs to the door, and then turn with his last vestige of strength and crawl on his belly towards an insanely cackling Werdegast.

However, such gruesomeness would have to wait for the eighties explicitness of pictures such as Stuart Gordon's *Re-Animator.* As it was, *Variety* called the tamer final version "a truly horrible and nauseating piece of sadism."

Joan screams at this piece of sadism. "How does it feel to hang on your own embalming rack, Hjalmar?" inquires the vengeful Vitus. Meanwhile, Joan struggles to retrieve the key to the room from the dead Thamal's hand. Peter, having taken the majordomo's gun, discovers them locked in the room. Werdegast goes to assist, but from Peter's angle it looks as if she is struggling against him, and so he shoots the now sadistic psychiatrist.

"You poor fool," exclaims Werdegast with sorrow. "I only tried to help you. Now go. Please—*go!*" As the honeymooners flee, the wounded Werdegast pulls the self-destruct switch on the wall, intoning, "It's the red switch, isn't it Hjalmar? The red switch ignites the dynamite. Five minutes—Marmaros, you, and I, and your rotten cult will be no more. It has been a good game."

The mad game played out, the couple reach the road just as Marmaros explodes. A bus pulls up to drive them to safety. As an ultimate self-reflexive joke, Ulmer and Ruric scripted a bit where the bus driver would be none other than Ulmer himself who tells them, "I'm not going to Vizhegrad. I'm going to

CARL LAEMMLE
presents

KARLOFF and BELA LUGOSI

in EDGAR ALLAN POE'S

"The BLACK CAT"

with
DAVID MANNERS
JACQUELINE WELLS
LUCILLE LUND

Directed by
EDGAR G. ULMER

Produced by
CARL LAEMMLE, Jr.

A UNIVERSAL PICTURE

[Courtesy Ronald V. Borst/Hollywood Movie Posters]

a sanitarium to rest up after making *The Black Cat* in fourteen days! However, it will be a long walk. For you, I shall make an exception."

This outlandish comic ending was replaced with a more standard one in which the train-traveling couple receive a review of Peter's last novel, chiding him on his tendency to exceed the bounds of credibility, advising him to stick to real life, which naturally strikes the Alisons as extremely amusing.

Carl Laemmle hated the classic score Roemheld came up with for the film, but Laemmle Junior defended Ulmer and approved it for release after the retakes, re-editing, and scoring had been completed. Ulmer continued a tendency to insert classic music quotes in many of his subsequent poverty row productions, which include such low-cost classics as *Detour, Bluebeard, Strange Illusion* (a no budget reworking of *Hamlet*), *Ruthless, Naked Dawn* (a western variation of *Sunrise*), and *The Man From Planet X*.

The film earned a $140,000 profit for Universal during its first run. It appeared ten months after its U.S. release in Great Britain under the title *House of Doom*, and after giving the censor fits, had its Satanic subplot significantly altered so that there were now sinister references to a cult of sun worshipers (!).

In 1968, two brief snippets from the film featuring Karloff and Lugosi were inserted into the Monkees' film *Head*, scripted by director Bob Rafelson and Jack Nicholson, a colorful but incoherent '60's mélange that promotes a prefabricated product but protests the war and commercialism.

The look of Karloff's villain was copied by Walter Hill for Willem Dafoe's villain in *Streets of Fire* (1984). The shot of Karloff arising from his bed was imitated by Jeremy Irons for his Oscar-winning role as suspected wife-slayer Claus von Bülow in *Reversal of Fortune* (1990), directed by Barbet Schroeder. Both are evidence that *The Black Cat* exerts an influence that is felt even to the present day.

We remember the film for many reasons. It is an elliptically suggestive, compact work which compresses many outré suggestions into its minimal running time and yet has been created with definite panache and style. Part of that derives from Karloff's low-key performance which perfectly counterpoints Lugosi's more histrionic one. It was a definite milestone in Karloff's career as it allowed him to essay his most overtly evil part, albeit still one with human dimensions. Poelzig expresses definite feelings of pain and loss however abhorrent we might find him to be otherwise.

Karloff's performance gives hints of amusement while retaining its sinister qualities, something which the actor achieved with a great deal of finesse in future roles which combined Karloff's penchant for humor and horror. He also relaxes on screen and allows his sheer presence to ably carry this memorable horror excursion to its explosive climax. His Poelzig maintains an outward, civilized exterior, capable of playing the accommodating host to the Alisons, but he is also shown to be a master manipulator of men and a malodorous traitor and deceiver of others, ruthlessly intent on achieving his maleficent schemes regardless of any social constraints.

No other master of the macabre could bring to the role what Karloff does in terms of malignant cruelty and practiced malevolence and yet remain an interesting character who never careens over into camp or ham. While the master of Marmaros was only one of Karloff's many masterful dramatic interpretations, it remains one of his best, abetted by one of co-star Lugosi's finest performances as well. It will no doubt haunt horror aficionados for decades to come.

CREDITS: Director: Edgar G. Ulmer; Production Supervisor: E.M. Asher; Screenplay: Peter Ruric (based on a story by Edgar G. Ulmer and Peter Ruric, suggested by *The Black Cat* by Edgar Allan Poe); Camera: John J. Mescall; Art Director: Charles D. Hall; Music Director: Heinz Roemheld; Editor: Ray Curtiss; Assistant Directors: W.J. Reiter, Sam Weisenthal; Continuity: Tom Kilpatrick; Script Clerk: Moree Herring; Script Girl: Shirley Kassel; Camera Operator: King Gray; Makeup: Jack P. Pierce; Special Effects: John P. Fulton. Released May 7, 1934 by Universal Pictures. Running time: 65 minutes

CAST: Karloff...Hjalmar Poelzig, Bela Lugosi...Dr. Vitus Werdegast, David Manners...Peter Alison, Jacqueline Wells (aka Julie Bishop)...Joan Alison, Lucille Lund...Karen, Egon Brecher...The Majordomo, Harry Cording...Thamal, Albert Conti...The Lieutenant, Henry Armetta...The Sergeant, Anna Duncan...Maid, Herman Bing...Car Steward, George Davis...Bus Driver, Conductor...Andre Cheron, Train Steward...Luis Alberni, Alphonse Martell...Porter, Tony Marlow...Patrolman, Paul Weigel...Station Master, Albert Polet...Waiter, Rodney Hildebrand...Brakeman, Virginia Ainsworth, Michael Mark, Symona Boniface, Paul Panzer, Lois January, King Baggot, Peggy Terry...Satanists, John Carradine...Man Playing Organ

(The author would like to acknowledge the invaluable assistance of Mushel Ruric, Gregory William Mank's book *Karloff and Lugosi* and especially Paul Mandell's article in the October 1984 issue of *American Cinematographer* in the writing of this article.)

THE LOST PATROL
(1934)
by Gregory William Mank

> Madman! Strangest of the fearless
> warriors troop is SANDERS, whose frenzied
> religious zeal changes to hopelessly insane
> ravings, as one by one the lives of the men are
> snuffed out by an invisible enemy!
> —from RKO's souvenir program for
> *The Lost Patrol* (1934)

Circa 1971, John Carradine was a guest on *The Dick Cavett Show*. He was regaling Cavett and the audience with tales of his legendary friendship with John Barrymore—which led to the mention of Lionel Barrymore.

"I never cared for Lionel," said Cavett. "He was so *hammy*."

"I think," said Carradine, his face lighting up in a smile, "that was a point in *his favor*!"

Naturally, John Carradine would have agreed. "I am a *Ham*!" he'd proudly proclaimed in 1945. "And the ham in an actor is what makes him interesting. The word is an insult only when it's used by an outsider—among actors, it's a very high compliment, indeed..."

Personally, I agree. There's something glorious about an actor (a fine actor) playing a juicy role (and one that *allows* for overacting) with thespic abandon. "Refreshingly underplayed" has long been the critical cliché I love to hate (indeed, many actors lack the energy and/or imagination to do anything but underplay!). It's odd (to me) to hear many people protest what they consider to be overacting; it's like an epicure who despises restaurants where they give you too much food, or a sports fan who hates a baseball game where the final score is 15-14.

Thus, in the horror genre, it's always perplexing to me to hear so many writers lament what they consider to be overacting. A case in point: Vincent Price was a beloved Superstar of Horror, but even his most ardent fans patronizingly carp about his "hammy" performances. (Presumably they don't realize that it was probably this ham, which Price always served with such spice and humor, that originally made them Vincent Price fans in the first place!)

As this raving madman goes baroquely berserk, Karloff has an actor's feast day.

I guess that many critics find "overacting" intimidating—feeling the actor is showing off, or waving his talent in their faces, or simply having too much fun.

There are only two actors in Horror Films who perennially get away with overplaying: John Barrymore and Bela Lugosi. In the case of Barrymore, audiences accept his excesses (wonderful excesses!) in *Dr. Jekyll and Mr. Hyde*, *Svengali*, and *The Mad Genius* as part of his own mad genius, a byproduct of his demonic, self-destructive nature. As for Lugosi... well, I have a theory: Bela's professional, marital, financial, alcohol, drug problems were so overwhelming that modern day critics feel they can cut him a break, employ lagesse, and let him ham. (Also, he's great fun to watch!)

Anyway, as a devoted fan of King of Horror Boris Karloff, with a self-confessed weakness for overacting, I have a special affection for *The Lost Patrol,* John Ford's classic 1934 melodrama of soldiers facing death in the Mesopotamia desert. It features Karloff's notoriously over-the-top portrayal of Sanders, the religious lunatic.

Boris *is* a spectacle.

As this raving madman, going baroquely berserk as Arabs pick off his companions at a desert oasis, Karloff has an actor's feast day: he (in alphabetical order) cackles, eyeballs, gasps, gyrates, leers, pouts, screams, shrieks, and twists, all leading up to a mad death scene in which Boris marches, in Old Testament rags and staff, up a sand dune to meet his Maker in a hail of Arab gunfire—the Max Steiner music blasting away.

It's a showboat performance that makes Lugosi's Monogram Mad Doctors look like Michael J. Pollard.

And yet—miraculously—amidst this histrionic sideshow, Boris captures the soul of the maniac.

Sanders is a key performance in the Karloff canon. Coming after the actor's Big Parade of Horror Hits (*Frankenstein, The Old Dark House, The Mask of Fu Manchu, The Mummy*), *The Lost Patrol* was a major, mainstream box office hit/critical triumph; it was directed by John Ford, on the brink of his own Golden Age; and it proved Boris Karloff was a Top Character Star—not just a Sensation of Horror. As such, its impact on the future of his career was dynamic. Yet even some of the most devout Karloff fans feel obliged to attack or make excuses for the Sanders performance. Even Denis Gifford, a champion of Karloff and author of the 1973 *Karloff: The Man, the Monster, the Movies* writes that Boris acts "atrociously" in *The Lost Patrol.*

A little retrospect re: Karloff and *The Lost Patrol* is in order. It's a classic film, and says a lot about Boris Karloff—Movie Star *and* Actor.

TENSE AND SUSPENSEFUL DESERT WAR DRAMA
AIDED BY GOOD PERFORMANCES
AND ACE DIRECTION

Smacking of *Beau Geste,* and packing plenty of general human interest even though it hasn't a woman in the cast, this war story ranks as one of the best of its kind. It depicts, as an incident of the World War, the fate of a British patrol lost in the Mesopotamian desert where the bewildered soldiers are at the mercy of Arabian sharpshooters whom they cannot see but who pop off the squad one by one until only the sergeant, Victor McLaglen, is left. Then, coming out in the open a little to soon, the Arabs are mowed down with a machine gun by the avenging McLaglen just as a rescue company arrives. It is a gripping story... McLaglen turns in a corking performance as the sergeant, and other outstanding roles are those of Reginald Denny as a soldier of fortune, Boris Karloff as a religious fanatic and Wallace Ford as the last man killed.

—*Film Daily* review, April 9, 1934

Thank you, *Film Daily;* that's all the plot synopsis we really need for *The Lost Patrol.* That settled, we can move onto other areas:

The Significance of Karloff's casting: After Karloff came home to Hollywood following a merry trip to England to star as *The Ghoul* (1933), Universal played nasty games with their top star. In early 1933, the studio had refused to honor the contract and advance Boris' weekly salary from $750 to $1,000; he had accepted it, with the proviso that he got the full pay jump ($1,250) come the next option date (June 1). Universal promised—then reneged.

As *Variety* put it, "...Karloff walked."

Even a hypochondriacal, father-dominated screwball like Junior Laemmle quickly realized that his studio had made a mistake. Come July, and Karloff signed a new Universal Star Contract that provided the desired salary *plus* the right to work at other studios. On August 2, 1933, Harriet Parsons reported in her syndicated LA *Examiner* column:

Radio has signed Boris Karloff for a big role in *Patrol,* that much-discussed desert epic with lots of sand and no women. You'll remember I told you Karloff is free to make as many outside pictures as he wants before he starts his new Universal contract September 1. Karloff plays a religious fanatic and won't be as grotesquely greasepainted as usual. In fact, the Radio makeup man says it won't be any trouble at all to make him up as a crazy man. (Now what does he mean by that?)

All Hollywood took note that Universal's Star Bogeyman (who was also winning notice for his crusading work for the Screen Actors Guild) had defied

The Lost Patrol **is filled with John Ford's poetry as a filmmaker.**

Universal, won his war against the studio, and had copped a major outside role to boot—for a top producer and director. The producer: Merian C. Cooper, who had produced RKO's mega-hit of 1933, *King Kong*. The director: John Ford, who already had directed such films as *The Iron Horse* (1924), *Men Without Women* (1930), *Arrowsmith* (1931), and *Flesh* (1932). So the prestige Karloff won via his job in *The Lost Patrol* made an impact not only on Universal, but on the film industry, too. And, by the way: *The Lost Patrol* would provide Boris a top salary. For his visit to RKO, Karloff would collect $4,000 weekly.

The Shooting: Karloff, always upbeat, loved the adventure of shooting *The Lost Patrol* amidst the sand dunes and 130-degree heat of Arizona's Buttercup Valley. Robert C. Roman wrote in his profile of Karloff in *Films In Review* (Aug./Sept. 1964):

> Karloff says he learned a lot from Ford
> and that the entire company—Victor McLaglen,
> Wallace Ford, Reginald Denny, Alan Hale, J. M.
> Kerrigan et al.—was "wonderful to work with.
> Vic was just as he seemed on the screen, a big,
> good-natured guy living life to the full."

The company took a train to Yuma on August 30, 1933; at 6:30 the next morning,

119

they were on location in Buttercup Valley. (Some other films shot there: the 1926 and 1939 *Beau Geste;* 1936's *The Garden of Allah;* 1983's *The Return of the Jedi.*) *The Lost Patrol* company nicknamed the oasis set (with its little Arabian "mosque," pool, and 50 fake palm trees) "Abdullah Alley." In the *Daily Variety* Fiftieth Anniversary Issue (1983), Jerry Webb wrote of his experiences as a script supervisor on *The Lost Patrol* location:

> The fully air-conditioned Army tents— you rolled the canvas sides up for air—had wooden floors to protect us from Sidewinders and Vinegar Roos. The mess hall was a large open-sided tent with net sides. The half-a-dozen showers were outdoors and naked. Fortunately, the six holer latrine was downwind from the camp... The bugle sounded at 4:30 a.m., breakfast was at 5, shooting started at 6:30 with Mr. Ford and Winnie (Harold) Wenstrom, the cameraman, taking advantage of the long shadows on the dunes...

Sandstorms attacked; crew members collapsed in the 130-degree heat; machinery broke down in the hellish conditions; actors became ill. In an excellent retrospect on *The Lost Patrol,* published in the anthology *The Cinema of Adventure, Romance and Terror,* the book's editor, George E. Turner, wrote:

> Heat, sand, wind and frustration were eroding the nerves of a mostly good-natured group of men. Arguments and fights became everyday occurrences. Wallace Ford pummeled a cook who had refused to serve a black laborer. McLaglen's sometimes nasty practical jokes soon ceased to be amusing. Some of the actors were behaving very much like the characters they were portraying, a situation the director used to advantage.

Some historians have conjectured that Karloff's hysteria as Sanders might have been not so much an acting choice as a result of sunstroke; but apparently he stayed healthy and had a terrific time. Ford made sure the company got relaxation, as the cast and crew would take off each night for Yuma or Alcadones or Calexico to hit the cantinas.

The Film: From its opening shot—a soldier falling dead from his horse, victim of a sniper's bullet, his horse turning to look forlornly at the body—*The Lost Patrol* is filled with Ford's poetry as a filmmaker. The script (by legendary Ford collaborator Dudley Nichols) is chocked with the favorite Ford theme of people coping with danger and almost certain death—a theme Ford crystallized

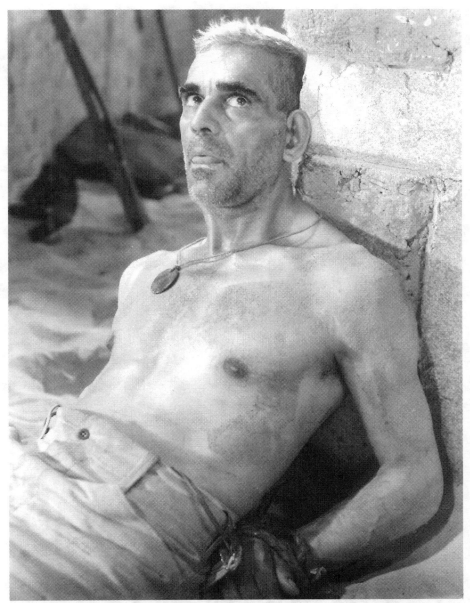

Some historians have conjectured that Karloff's hysteria as Sanders might have been not so much an acting choice as a result of sunstroke.

in *Stagecoach* (1939). Cinematographer Harold Wenstrom beautifully captures the mystery of the desert, making the locale seem as eerie and lonely as the moon.

Ford offers a grab-bag of characters—the stalwart Sergeant (Victor McLaglen, a last-minute replacement for Richard Dix, and playing the part his

Boris has the look of an anguished lost soul burning in a Renaissance painting of Hell.

brother, Cyril McLaglen, had played in the British 1929 version, *Patrol*); ex-vaudeville comic Morelli (Wallace Ford); playboy Brown (Reginald Denny); comic Cockney Hale (Billy Bevan)—all vivid (and economically characterized in comparison of Karloff's Sanders). Considering the plot, much of the color in the movie comes via the various death scenes: Bevan toppling from his lookout perch atop a palm tree with a bullet in his head; Alan Hale's Cook and Paul Hanson's Mackay (after a futile try to steal away and get help) returning to the oasis with their bodies strapped to their horses; J. M. Kerrigan's veteran soldier Quincannon, shot down as he makes one last valiant, vengeful charge. Of course, Karloff gets the wildest death scene of all—but more on that later.

The Lost Patrol also offers a grimly comic episode. When only McLaglen, Karloff, and Ford are left, a British biplane flies over the oasis. The trio go crazy with joy, waving to the young pilot (Howard Wilson). They think he'll fly back and send help. Instead, to their horror, the fool lands the plane—right in the line of the Arab snipers.

"Hello!" waves the pilot, as if he's making an entrance into the drawing room of a Noel Coward comedy.

"Get back!" scream the soldiers, waving madly, but the fool pilot jauntily struts across the dunes, in his short pants, riding crop in hand, thinking the boys are just jubilant to welcome him to Abdullah Alley. A shot...

"I say!" says the pilot—and drops dead.

Karloff goes nuts; "...You killed him!" he screams at McLaglen; "He came in answer to my prayers, for me!" and he attacks the sergeant with a rifle butt. The scene plays like a sly satire on British "cool" and stands out in the stark film.

By the end of the movie, only McLaglen is left, and he goes berserk—finally releasing all his stiff upper-lip reserve as he roars and bellows and madly aims a machine-gun (taken from the plane, which the men had burned in hopes the flames would signal help) at approaching Arabs. There's something sickly satisfying in this violent (and "racist," no doubt, in some viewers' eyes) scene, as we see our hero gleefully and vengefully mowing down the enemy, bragging of his victory to his buried comrades. As George Turner wrote:

> Major (Frank) Baker, who had been on hand throughout as technical advisor, was pressed into service to portray the leader of the Arabs gunned down by McLaglen. McLaglen at the time was gloriously drunk, which was exactly the way Ford wanted him, the better to convey the Sergeant's maniacal jubilation at his one moment of triumph. Baker was horrified when real bullets began kicking up the sand around him. The live ammunition was being fired by an expert marksman stationed off-scene while McLaglen, bellowing and staggering, was firing blanks...

A cavalry has seen the flames of the burning plane; they arrive when it's all over (naturally). The officer (Frank Baker again, in a different costume!) demands that McLaglen present his men. And McLaglen forlornly, unforgettably, points to the sabres, marking the men's graves. Max Steiner's music swells with *Auld Lang Syne* and the rescuing platoon rides off across the dunes, McLaglen's presumably composed Sergeant among them.

Karloff's performance: Like the performance or not, there's no denying it: as Sanders, Boris is a volcano. First of all, there's his "look" in the film. Skinny, gaunt to the bone, Boris resembles a cathedral gargoyle in some shots; in others, he has the look of an anguished lost soul burning in a Renaissance painting of Hell. (It probably was precisely the "look" that Ford, with his Catholic influences, wanted.) And Boris's acting blazes away. His first big scene comes early, as he insists on a prayer at the funeral for the dead officer. "Almighty Father... Earth to earth, ashes to ashes, dust to dust...!" Karloff prays so fervently that McLaglen tersely cuts him off. From there the performance grows increasingly crazy. One of my favorite moments comes after the troupe reaches the oasis, and Boris reflects on Mesopotamia, telling Quincannon:

"If you'd read your Bible, instead of hanging around canteens and native quarters, you'd know that Mesopotamia—this, this very spot you're standing on, this very minute—is the actual Garden of Eden!"

A lunatic smile lights Karloff's face; it's a wonderfully theatrical moment.

Later, by the pool, Karloff has a highlight as he demands of Brown, the playboy: "Oh, Brown, I *implore* you... You must have faith!" Boris twists and turns as if in need of an exorcist. There's much more: his mad face as he morbidly counts down the list of dead men... his crazy cackle as (finally tied up in the mosque), he frees himself of his bonds...

It's Karloff's Death Scene, however, that's tops. McLaglen's Sergeant and Ford's Morelli stare in horror—and, through their eyes, we see the escaping, gloriously crazy Sanders, his skeletal figure festooned in Biblical sackcloth, holding a makeshift cross staff—scaling a sand dune as Max Steiner's score passionately wails away. Throughout *The Lost Patrol,* Karloff's Sanders has been trying to save the men's souls; now, this mad, would-be Savior carries his own cross, up to his own Cavalry of Arab gunfire. For 1934 audiences, the episode must have been truly spine-chilling. (Odd, isn't it: Boris Karloff, Hollywood's top Horror Star, ironically served as a Christ symbol in two movies two years in a row: as Sanders in *The Lost Patrol* in 1934, and as the Monster, crucified in the forest, in James Whale's *Bride Of Frankenstein* in 1935.) Yes— it's a flamboyant, almost endearingly hammy performance. Yet this rich, full-blooded portrayal has a heart. The look of hurt on Karloff's face, e.g., when Denny mocks his faith, is unforgettably sad. This is truly a lost soul, and Boris has captured and delivered all of his insanity and pathos.

As always—Karloff transcends.

The Film's Success: On January 27, 1934, Karloff proudly promoted *The Lost Patrol* on radio's *Hollywood on the Air.* "HEARTS THAT BURN FOR WOMEN ON THE BURNING SANDS OF HELL!" proclaimed RKO. The film opened on Friday night, March 30, 1934 at the Rialto Theatre, New York City. The *World-Telegram* reported:

> *The Lost Patrol,* at the Rialto, is almost a great film and certainly one of the finest that has come out of Hollywood. It has depth, remarkably complete characterizations, moments of strong animal excitement, picturesque figures of enlisted men, banded but helpless against death and excitement that will cause you to hold your breath... You will not see better impersonations hereabouts than those of Messres. Victor McLaglen, Boris Karloff, Reginald Denny, Wallace Ford, J. M. Kerrigan and the others in the cast of *The Lost Patrol,* or better direction than that of Mr. Ford.

There had been fear at RKO that *The Lost Patrol* was too grim (the *New York News* critic praised it as "the most effective horror film I've ever seen"); the *London Times* also wondered about the film's box office power:

> Mr. John Ford, the director, has made little effort to spare the feelings of his audience... Mr. McLaglen and Mr. Boris Karloff, as the religious fanatic who tries desperately to save the souls of his comrades, are outstanding in a good cast, but the film has probably been produced with too much realism to be everybody's idea of entertainment.

In fact, *The Lost Patrol* turned out to be a critical *and* box office success. The film made the "Ten Best" List of the National Board of Review (#6) and the *New York Times (#8);* the $254,000 production grossed $750,000, becoming one of 1934's top-grossing films. Max Steiner won an Academy nomination for Best Musical Score (losing to Louis Silvers for Columbia's *One Night of Love).* The film's success paved the way for Ford to direct *The Informer* (1935) for RKO, and win his first Best Director Oscar. (*The Informer* would also win a Best Actor Oscar for Victor McLaglen.)

How did Karloff fare with the critics? As the aforementioned reviews show, he won his share of laurels for *The Lost Patrol.* Over the years, however, the performance has become increasingly controversial. "Depending upon the spectator's response," wrote George Turner, "(Karloff's) is either the best or the worst acting in the show." "All the old ham came out," wrote Denis Gifford in *Karloff: The Man, The Monster, The Movies.* Personally, I agree with Richard Combs, who wrote in *Monthly Film Bulletin:*

> In a generally solid ensemble cast, the honors probably go to Boris Karloff as the religious zealot, sliding insidiously from wheedling nag to raging fanatic and finding the means to stage his exit into the desert with some style, dressed like an Old Testament prophet, complete with staff.

The Significance: In final analysis, *The Lost Patrol* was a bonanza for Boris Karloff. It "legitimized" him as a major Character Star (as did 20th Century's *House of Rothschild,* which Boris did right after *The Lost Patrol,* as the anti-Semitic Baron). To most 1934 audiences (and, probably, to some today), Karloff's wild emoting as Sanders must have seemed to be Great Acting, and the star went back to Universal for such Horror triumphs as *The Black Cat* and *Bride of Frankenstein* with new prestige and assurance. The respect he won via *The Lost Patrol* would be vital to his longevity as a movie star. When the Horror Movie "Limbo" came-a-calling in the late 1930s, producers would remember *The Lost Patrol;* Bela Lugosi had no such credit.

Also, the Sanders performance nicely shatters the old cliché that Karloff always underplayed, Lugosi always overplayed. In fact, Karloff's most emotional performances—the Monster in *Frankenstein* and *Bride of Frankenstein,* Rukh in *The Invisible Ray,* Dr. Laurience in *The Man Who Changed His Mind,* and Sanders—are all played with considerably more face-making/vocal trickery/ body language than some of the key Lugosi performances. Throughout his career, Karloff could and would adjust the pitch of his acting to suit the role.

Once again, however, *The Lost Patrol* shows why Boris Karloff was not only the King of Horror, but an Irreplaceable Actor as well. Whatever "ham" Boris gives to Sanders, he captures the soul of the character. In his eyes, we see a man who not only sees his God, but his Satan as well; and once again, through the brilliance of Boris Karloff, melodrama becomes true tragedy.

Epilogue: As for "overacting"...in 1985, I played "Prof." Harold Hill in *The Music Man* at the Towsontowne Dinner Theatre in Baltimore (my third time in the role). It was set for a 12-week run and we were hoping for good reviews to make it as successful an engagement as possible.

Well, "Critics Night" came and we all acted as if the next 12 weeks' paychecks depended on it. I humbly note that the reviews were almost unanimously very good; in fact, "The Critics Love Us... And So Will You!" became the advertising tag that summer. But it's not a perfect world, and there was one pan, in which the critic attacked the basic production—and yours truly. "Gregory Mank works too hard at playing Harold Hill," wrote the critic.

I thought of Boris Karloff in *The Lost Patrol*—and smiled.

CREDITS: Executive Producer: Merian C. Cooper; Director: John Ford; Associate Producer: Cliff Reid; Screen Play: Dudley Nichols; Adaptation: Garrett Fort; from the story *Patrol,* by Philip MacDonald; Cinematographer: Harold Wenstrom; Art Directors: Van Nest Polglase and Sidney Ullman; Musical Director: Max Steiner; Sound Recorders: Clem Portman, P. J. Faulkner; Editor: Paul Weatherwax; Process Photography: Vernon L. Walker; Makeup Artist: Carl Axcelle; Music Recorder: Murray Spivack; Assistant Director: Argyle Nelson; Unit Managers: Wallace Fox, John B. Burch; Wardrobe: Sandeen; Technical Advisors: Major Frank Baker, Jamiel Hasson; Pilot: Garland Lincoln; RCA Recording; Running Time: 73 minutes; (Current prints, edited, run 66 minutes.); Released by RKO Radio

A remake of *Patrol* (British Instructional Pictures, 1929), which had starred Cyril McLaglen; Cyril's brother, Victor, played the starring role in the RKO film. Remade by RKO as the western *Badlands* (1939), and (unofficially) by MGM as *Bataan* (1943).

Filmed in Buttercup Valley, Arizona, August 31-September 22, 1933; rear projection shots made at RKO Studios, Hollywood, September 28, 1933; Original budget: $227,703.22; Final cost: $254,000; Opened at the Rialto Theatre, New York City, March 30, 1934

CAST: Victor McLaglen...The Sergeant, Boris Karloff...Sanders, Wallace Ford...Morelli, Reginald Denny...Brown, J. M. Kerrigan...Quincannon, Billy Bevan...Hale, Alan Hale...Cook, Brandon Hurst...Bell, Douglas Walton...Pearson, Sam Stein...Abelson, Howard Wilson...Aviator, Paul Hanson...MacKay, Noville Clarke...Officer, Major Frank Baker...Arab

Gregory William Mank is the author of the books *It's Alive! The Classic Cinema Saga of Frankenstein; The Hollywood Hissables; Karloff and Lugosi;* and *Hollywood Cauldron.* Greg is currently completing a book on Actresses in Melodramas, as well as a book on Dwight Frye (along with Jim Coughlin and Dwight David Frye). Greg is a high school English teacher in Baltimore City, which makes him a very brave man.

THE BLACK ROOM
(1935)

by Don G. Smith

In 1936, Boris Karloff referred to *The Black Room* as "my favorite picture so far." Consider for a moment that he had already done *Frankenstein, The Old Dark House, The Mummy, The Ghoul, The Black Cat*, and *Bride of Frankenstein*. Though actors are sometimes not the best judges of their own work, I believe Boris Karloff was right. In fact, I would rate Karloff's performance in *The Black Room* the best of his career, followed closely by *Bride of Frankenstein, Frankenstein*, and *The Body Snatcher*. While the screenplays, cinematography, and direction of *Bride of Frankenstein, Frankenstein*, and *The Body Snatcher* probably outshine those of *The Black Room*, I would argue that Karloff's performance in the latter film is nevertheless his best.

So what makes *The Black Room* so good, and why is Karloff so good in it? First, *The Black Room* is an artistically rendered film of contrasts, of thesis and antithesis: the obvious contrast being good vs. evil represented by the twins, and the other being the contrast of nobility vs. peasantry inherent in class conflict. Second, Karloff provides a performance replete with the nuances of personality necessary for successfully bringing off a demanding dual role performance. Let us examine these elements, along with the artistic elements that make *The Black Room* a classic film.

In Hungary in the late eighteenth century, twins are born to the house of Berghman. There is no celebration, however. Since the family began with a set of twins, the younger of whom killed the older "in the black room," legend has it that if male twins are born again, the house will end as it began, with the younger killing the older in "the black room." The bitterness of being second to inherit, plus the misfortune of being born with a paralyzed right arm, could tempt the younger brother to fulfill the prophecy. To evade the prophecy, the father has the black room sealed with bricks. Twenty years later, when the father dies, Gregor, the older twin, becomes baron, and younger brother Anton moves from the house of Berghman. Gregor is a tyrant, however, and the peasants whom he oppresses want to kill or depose him. He is also reputedly responsible for the disappearance of certain wives and daughters of the village. With the peasants threatening rebellion, Gregor asks Anton to return to the

129

In this scene director Neill and cinematographer Siegler introduce a recurrent motif, that of the mirror image.

house of Berghman. When Anton returns we can contrast Gregor and Anton, both played by Boris Karloff. As the wicked Gregor, Karloff speaks in a slightly deeper, gruffer voice. His hair is mussed, and there is a hardness in his eyes. As Anton, Karloff, is gregarious, polite, and jovial, especially in the scene in which he first arrives in the village and takes a seat in the inn.

Colonel Hassel transports Anton by coach to the house of Berghman. There, Anton meets Thea, the colonel's daughter. As Gregor, Anton, and Colonel Hassel sit and listen (and as Lt. Lussan, Thea's sweetheart, stands), Thea accompanies herself on the harp while singing:

"Love is like music,

Beautiful music, to my heart."

Gregor is entranced, and Anton likes what he hears and sees. All the while, Mashka, a peasant girl, serves as waitress. She has designs on Gregor and resents his attention to Thea.

In Gregor's room, later in the evening, Mashka plays the harp for Gregor and sings "Love is like music" as he peels and eats a pear. At this point, director

Roy Willian Neill and cinematographer Allen G. Siegler introduce a recurrent motif, that of the mirror image. In *A Dictionary of Symbols*, J. E. Cirlot writes that, among other things, the mirror, "like the echo... stands for twins (thesis and antithesis)...." Therefore, on the most obvious level, the mirror symbolizes the thesis and antithesis of the twins Gregor and Anton. In the harp scene, as Mashka plays and sings, a large mirror reflects her image. According to Cirlot, the mirror also symbolizes "the world as a state of discontinuity affected by the laws of change and substitution." In this scene, Mashka attempts to substitute for Thea in Gregor's affections, playing and singing the same song that Thea did earlier (a mirror image). The laws of change are at work, however, as Gregor has already decided that Thea will substitute for Mashka, requiring Mashka's departure. When she finishes singing, Mashka approaches Gregor, whose attentions are completely focused on the pear he is eating. This leads to the best dialogue in the film (or shall we say monologues, since the two speakers are not really listening to each other?):

> Mashka: Don't I play as well as she does? Didn't you listen? Don't you want me to kiss you?
>
> Gregor: A pear is the best fruit.
>
> Mashka: Every time you see her, you want rid of me.
>
> Gregor: Lots of juice in a pear.
>
> Mashka: Well, I won't be gotten rid of so easy. Do you hear what I say?
>
> Gregor: Adam should have chosen a pear.
>
> Mashka: You've got it all planned, haven't you? You're going to marry her and make her your wife—your baroness.
>
> Gregor: I like the feel of a pear. And when you're through with it... [he tosses the core aside].
>
> Mashka: You're not going to marry her. I'll put a stop to it.
>
> Gregor: [unconcerned] You will? How?

In dialogue stressing the theme of thesis and antithesis inherent in class conflict, Gregor points out that no one will blame him for choosing Colonel Hassel's daughter over a peasant girl. Mashka, in defense (or offense) tells Gregor that she knows the other entrance to the black room, and that she has seen him carry heavy things there late at night. With this threat of blackmail, Mashka suddenly has Gregor's full attention, though his attention in this case means death for her. He rises, backs her down, and ends her life with the knife he used to peel the pear. All the while, the mirror reflects the image, reinforcing

Unfortunately Mashka (Katherine De Mille) finally gains Gregor's (Karloff) full attention.

the message that the pear reflects Mashka. As Gregor did with the pear, he enjoyed Mashka's feel, sucked her juice, "peeled her," and tossed her aside.

The film's major conflicts have been apparent all along. Good vs. evil is evinced in the contrasting personalities (thesis and antithesis) of Anton and Gregor. Class conflicts have been embodied by the subservient, angry villagers and by Mashka vs. Gregor. An auxiliary class conflict is Lt. Lussan vs. Gregor. It is, after all, the class standing of Gregor and Anton that allow them to maneuver a marriage with a young woman already in love with someone else.

With Mashka's disappearance and the discovery of her scarf outside Gregor's room, the villagers decide to depose Gregor. Gregor cunningly agrees to renounce his title in favor of Anton, all the while planning to kill him and continue as baron in the guise of his popular brother. Before his expected departure, Gregor shows Anton the secret way into the black room. There, he wipes clean a section of the shiny onyx wall and looks at his own reflection. As Cirlot writes in his *Dictionary of Symbols*, "Again, [the mirror's] close relationship to the moon is demonstrated by the fact that among the primitives it was seen as a symbol of the multiplicity of the soul: of its mobility and its ability to adapt itself to those objects which 'visit' it and retain its 'interest.'" Gregor's peering into the wall in the black room is symbolic of his ability to adapt to the objects that visit him. He is attracted to Thea (as he was once attracted to Mashka), yet he knows Thea does not love him (who does, or could?), and he knows that peasant unrest requires his departure. He adapts to the situation by killing Mashka and by planning to kill and take the place of his brother. Gregor's soul is as dark as the moon and can only shine in his brother's reflected light.

Gregor cranks open a trap door covering a pit, revealing to Anton the bodies of those he deposited there. Picking up the knife that killed Mashka, Anton inquires with indignation tempered by credulity if the horrors he has heard about Gregor are true. At first Anton cannot believe Gregor is indeed the fiend he is accused of being, but just as the truth fully dawns upon him, Gregor pushes Anton into the pit. There he lies, vowing revenge with his last words—the knife in his paralyzed hand pointing skyward. Gregor cranks down the door, engulfing Anton in the darkness of death.

Thea is reflected in glass as rain pours down. Then, she and Lt. Lussan are mirrored in glass as they watch two reflected music box miniatures. As Thea points out, the man and lady in the music box symbolize them. The glass, acting as mirror, drives home the point.

Unfortunately for Thea and Lt. Lussan, Colonel Hassel agrees to a marriage between Thea and the man he thinks is Anton. In speaking to Gregor, the impostor, Colonel Hassel reinforces Gregor's suspicions that the Colonel never liked him and always hoped his daughter would never marry him. Of course, Colonel Hassel is pleased to give his consent upon learning that he is giving his daughter to "Anton" and not to Gregor.

To Karloff's credit, he not only plays a dual role, but he also plays one person in that dual role playing the other! As such Karloff's Gregor does not just adopt Anton's hair style, voice, etc., and repeat his performance as Anton. Rather, as Gregor's Anton, Karloff's voice sometimes assumes a dark irony missing in the voice of Anton. At times a slight grimace plays about his face as he utters words as Anton that he finds repellent. As Scott Allen Nollen writes in *Boris Karloff*:

> "Required to create two separate characters with disparate personalities, ...[Karloff] attempted to imbue each of them with subtlety and restraint, ensuring that one was not too evil and the other too kind. Appearing in the sequences that feature Gregor masquerading as Anton, he carefully merges these two persons, ...in effect, portraying three characters in the film."

When Lt. Lussan hears that "Anton" has asked for Thea's hand, he threatens Colonel Hassel if the latter consents to the marriage. After warning the lieutenant that he is out of line, Colonel Hassel does agree to give his daughter to "Anton." But when Gregor has to use his right arm to sign the agreement, the Colonel, whom Gregor has sent for a spot of liquor, sees the subterfuge in a mirror. Again a mirror plays a central part in the proceedings, in this instance by reflecting the truth and by reinforcing the thesis and antithesis represented by the twins.

When Colonel Hassel confronts Gregor with his discovery, Gregor kills him and arranges for Lt. Lussan to take the blame. Before discovering the Colonel's body, the maid primps before a mirror. The mirror in this instance, reflects the silliness of a peasant taking on airs, reinforcing the theme of class conflict. After the Colonel's body is found, a trial ensues, and the judge condemns the lieutenant to death by firing squad. Everything is as Gregor wants it. He quickly stresses to Thea that their marriage was her father's last wish, convincing her to marry him.

On the day of the marriage, Gregor stands before a mirror and practices being Anton, reminding himself that he must never use his right arm again. Again, the mirror stands for the thesis and antithesis represented by the twins.

Problems arise when Anton's dog, sensing that Gregor is not his real master, mercilessly barks at the impostor. "Drown him; poison him," Gregor tells a shocked servant. "Do anything, but get rid of him." All the while, Gregor attempts to restrain his anger as he thinks Anton would do. The tell-tale tension, however, plays about his rigid mouth. Gregor wants to play Anton, but his acting skills (unlike Karloff's) are lacking.

When Gregor emerges from his carriage at the wedding, the peasants shower him with flowers, forcing a smile of acknowledgment to cover his hatred for the lowly crowd. Again, Karloff injects just the right amount of Gregor into his portrayal of Gregor's Anton to make the switch believable.

Before the minister can pronounce Gregor and Thea man and wife, Anton's dog attacks the impostor. Under this assault, Gregor forgets himself for a moment and raises his "paralyzed arm" in defense. Immediately, the cry goes out that Anton is actually Gregor, the man who must have killed Colonel Hassel. Gregor retreats by carriage to the house of Berghman and hides in the black room. The dog, who has followed from the church, tips off the peasants that Gregor has availed himself of a secret passage. The peasants search and find the hidden aperture, after which the dog rushes in and attacks Gregor, causing him to tumble into the pit. The peasants crowd in and gaze into the pit, where Gregor lies impaled on the knife held by his dead brother. "The older brother killed by the younger," someone says. "The prophecy is fulfilled." And so ends *The Black Room*, Boris Karloff's greatest thespian achievement.

Of possible interest to trivial pursuitists, 1935 was the year that Hollywood "saw double." In 1935, three actors who would end their careers as horror film legends appeared in pictures playing dual roles. Commodore Films starred Lon

Boris Karloff provides a performance replete with the nuances of personality necessary for successfully bringing off a demanding dual role.

Chaney, Jr. in a dual role in *A Scream in the Night*, Imperial/Cameo featured Bela Lugosi in a dual role in *Murder by Television*, and, of course, Columbia showcased Boris Karloff in *The Black Room*. Of the three, Karloff undoubtedly takes top acting honors for *The Black Room*, a film that surely ranks among the top five or six films of horror's golden era.

Of course, one could protest that in 1935 Lon Chaney, Jr. was still learning his craft. Though aided with makeup resembling that used by his famous father in *The Road to Mandalay*, young Lon nevertheless turns in an unmemorable performance in an unmemorable film. Unlike Chaney, Bela Lugosi was no fledgling actor in 1935. Though he shared the mantle of horror film king with Boris Karloff, *Murder by Television* is a stagy, uninteresting, low budget production that requires little of Lugosi in a rather unbelievable dual role. Though Chaney and Lugosi were at a disadvantage, Karloff turns in a performance that those actors at their best could probably never duplicate.

When *The Black Room* was released, it and Karloff garnered positive reviews: "For once in a while Boris Karloff appears with no enormity of disguise

135

and, in consequence, he is able to thrill even more effectively in this inge-niously devised story of fratricide. He differentiates well between the twin broth-ers and gives a sound performance...." (*Kinematograph Weekly*)

"...Everything eerie has been injected into the picture... Roy William Neill has directed as well as possible a ...obvious story ...kudos must go to Al Siegler for his beautiful camera work and to the makeup man... The double exposures of Karloff in dual character are exceptionally fine and Neill has handled these episodes with finesse. As for Karloff, he is his usual self, in practically every sequence..." (*Variety*)

Members of the Screen Actors Guild were also suitably impressed with Karloff's performance in *The Black Room*. On the evening of February 22, 1936, the Screen Actors Guild and Screen Writers Guild held their Third An-nual Ball at the Biltmore Hotel. Among the celebrants was Bela Lugosi, one of the Screen Actor's Guilds thirty-nine Advisory Board members. At the ball, the Screen Actors Guild awarded Boris Karloff, their assistant secretary, a "first honorable mention" for the month of August for his performance in *The Black Room*. Tying for best performance were Henry Fonda in *The Farmer Takes a Wife* and Will Rogers in *Steamboat 'Round the Bend*.

Since *The Black Room*'s release, critics have continued to praise it:

"In the dual-role, Karloff differentiated admirably between the two broth-ers and was equally effective as villain and hero... elaborate settings and good photography helped to make this picture successful...." (Peter Underwood, *Karloff*, 1972)

"Some suspense in one of the better minor thrillers of the mid-thirties...." (Donald C. Willis, *Horror and Science Fiction Films*, 1972)

"Superficially, at least, it is almost as stylish a production as James Whale's films for Universal, and Columbia never again did anything quite like it... Karloff turns in an excellent performance, and the editing in his dual role scenes is particularly neat. The musical themes throughout are first rate, interestingly speeded-up in the climactic reel, and transformed from macabre mysterioso motifs into all-out agitato music.... [Director Neill] was stronger on pace and movement than on atmospherics, but in *The Black Room* he manages both with distinction. (William K. Everson, *Classics of the Horror Film*, 1972)

"A heavily stylized period piece, more gothic melodrama than pure horror movie... Karloff's performance is outstanding throughout, particularly in the subtle mime sequence in which the bad twin carefully rehearses his transfor-mation into the brother he has killed." (*The Overlook Film Encyclopedia: Hor-ror*, 1994, a revised edition of *The Horror Film Encyclopedia*, 1986)

"[The] central performances are complemented by the brooding, expres-sionistic visual style of Neill and Siegler. Whereas a mobile camera explores the vast corridors of Castle De Berghman, scenes situated in the family grave-yard are deliberately unrealistic and claustrophobic, featuring medium long shots and close-ups filmed on a studio soundstage. The 'dead' look of the cemetery is also offset by the open spaces of the village set, in which hundreds of peasants celebrate on 'Anton' and Thea's wedding day. Recalling a similar scene in *Frankenstein*, the liveliness of this image contrasts sharply with the gloomy world of Gregor." (Scott Allen Nollen, *Boris Karloff*, 1991)

While I agree with all of the above, I want to particularly second William K. Everson's praise for the music, which I consider a major strength. The main theme is dark and heavy, the music accompanying the action scenes is appropriately exciting, and the dreamy "Love is Like Music," though its lyrics are only mediocre, is one of the most beautiful melodies ever to grace a horror film.

In 1955, Columbia re-released *The Black Room* and *The Face Behind the Mask* (1941, directed by Robert Florey, starring Peter Lorre) as a double feature. Of course, ads read "Karloff and Peter Lorre Double Chill-Bill Stars."

Among the catch lines for *The Black Room* were:

"Karloff Reveals... What the Grave Conceals!"

"Master of the House of Horror!"

"Dead or Alive... He Could Kill!"

At this writing, *The Black Room* occasionally plays on television and is available on video for new generations of film fans. Here, indeed, is a classic film and a career-topping performance that deserve to be remembered.

CREDITS: Director: Roy William Neill; Producer: Robert North; Screenplay: Henry Myers and Arthur Strawn, based on a story by Arthur Strawn; Cinematographer: Allen G. Siegler; Editor: Richard Cahoon; Art Director: Stephen Goosson; Musical Director: Louis Silvers; Costume Director: Murray Mayer

CAST: Boris Karloff...Baron Gregor De Berghman/Anton De Berghman, Marian Marsh...Thea Hassel, Robert Allen....Lieutenant Albert Lussan, Thurston Hall...Colonel Hassel, Katherine De Mille...Mashka, John Buckler... Beran, Henry Kolker...Baron Frederick De Berghman

BRIDE OF FRANKENSTEIN (1935)

by Gary J. Svehla

Perhaps James Whale's *Bride of Frankenstein*, the brightest bud on Universal's ungodly tree of horror classics, is in reality a much more personal statement by James Whale than most film critics care to admit. In article after article the film is referred to as a horror classic, a dark comedy, a fairy tale from hell, and an eccentric art house flick before the era of such a misnomer. Granted, *Bride of Frankenstein* is all of these things, plus more! James Whale, an admitted homosexual and Hollywood eccentric, became, for a brief period in Hollywood history, one of the most exciting mainstream directors to ever helm mass-marketed movies. When the Laemmles lost Universal Pictures, the more money-oriented new regime completely discarded Whale for less eccentric and more predictable directors, thus the studio's *Son of Frankenstein*, released in 1939, overpowered its audience by virtue of its all-star cast, highly budgeted and intricate sets, and thrill-a-minute (yet highly predictable) script—it never overwhelmed by virtue of its personalized artistic vision, created by pedestrian director Rowland V. Lee.

James Whale completely turned the tables around on his long-in-the-wings sequel to 1931's *Frankenstein*; while the original vision was one of solemnity portraying man's punishment for daring to tamper in God's domain, the 1935 sequel dared to be grotesque, horrifying, outright humorous, eccentric, and ultimately unsettling. Instead of recreating the film's original mood or reprising the same themes in the same ways (the only sure way to make a "safe" sequel), James Whale decided to flex his artistic muscles and make a sequel which is reverent to the original vision yet original and cutting edge, both by 1930s' standards and today's. Whale delivered a moneymaker to Universal and a personal vision of the artist as Outcast when he made *Bride of Frankenstein*, and my intent in returning to this, one of the most critically exposed movies in horror history, is to try to explore Whale's artistic vision and tell why he molded the sequel in the manner in which he did.

Already stated, James Whale was a Hollywood eccentric, able to admit publicly to a homosexual life-style in the far more conservative decade of the thirties. Yet, his artistic vision was always one of the Outsider, no matter how many elaborate Hollywood parties he hosted. By the 1940s his movie-making career was over, and he became a has-been only a decade after his triumphant debut on the silver screen. By the late fifties, alone and forgotten, Whale (by most accounts) took his own life, drowning in the swimming pool of his Hollywood home.

Bride of Frankenstein celebrates the maverick, the rebel, the outsider, the creative being who dares to counter the mainstream culture and its confining morality, no matter what the personal cost. The movie contrasts the image of the Outsider to the Conformist and tries to show the fate of those poor unfortunates who play the game of life by their own rules, bucking the system and finally being destroyed, "blown to atoms," because of these beliefs and lifestyles.

Bride's monster narrative is prefaced by a brief introduction detailing Lord Byron, Percy Shelley, and Mary Shelley holed up in a Gothic mansion during a tremendous thunder storm. Byron and Shelley represent the socially outcast Romantic Poets, a literary group in England which generally existed from 1780-1830. These poets sang the praises of nature and longed for a time before the industrial age, before pollution, before the Modern World raped and marred the inherent beauty of nature. The Romantics turned away from the values of the Age of Reason and turned toward what they perceived as a more daring, individual, and imaginative approach to both literature and life. Most of the Romantics died early in their youth and were considered social misfits who rebelled against the mores of their current society. The wife of one such poet wrote the novel *Frankenstein*, and only part of the story, she admits, was told in the original Universal movie. "There's more," and there lies the mechanism of a sequel.

James Whale, truer to his artistic vision than to history, embodies these three outsiders as being energetic, passionate, and totally self-centered. Bryon, in love with the sound of his own voice, looks out at the storm declaring it the "crudest, savage exhibition of nature" that ever beset "we elegant three." Placing his own importance at the center of the universe, Bryon states, "I'd like to think that an irate Jehovah were pointing those arrows of lighting directly at my head—England's greatest sinner." And his enthusiasm shows him to be most proud of such a declaration. And he describes his friend's wife, Mary, as an angel. However, the ambivalent nature of Mary is quickly juxtaposed: her frail, angelic presence being described as the writer of a book which *chilled* Bryon's blood. This ambiguity of images becomes a major focal point of *Bride of Frankenstein*. Bemoaning the fact that her novel has yet to be published, Mary coyly declares "It will be published... I think." To which her husband Shelley adds, "Then, darling, you will have much to answer for!"

This brief sequence creates the microcosm which the remainder of the film symbolically illustrates. Here the head-strong artists, the rebels with both a cause and a clue, attack the conservative morality of their day and realize there will be a price to pay for living the lifestyle they choose to live, outside of the

Dr. Pretorius (Ernest Thesiger) becomes the playful rebel who bathes in his hedonistic lifestyle.

accepted ways of society. Hollywood director James Whale most likely identified with his vision of Lord Bryon, England's greatest sinner, a man who reveled in his sins and was proud of them.

Bride of Frankenstein pits the Outsider (Frankenstein's Monster, the Bride, the Gravediggers, Dr. Pretorius, the Blind Hermit, the Gypsies) against those Conformist Forces of Society (Elizabeth, the Burgomaster, Minnie the Maid, Maria's grief-stricken parents), with Colin Clive's Dr. Frankenstein clearly being caught in the middle. While he may appear to be an exemplary example of the Outsider upon first view, by the conclusion of the movie, he has joined the ranks of the other side, and this internal psychological war which is being waged becomes a dramatic center of the movie.

First, let us explore the Outsiders, the true heroes in James Whale's universe. Dr. Pretorius, the manipulative philosopher/scientist, needs Henry's knowledge and active help to continue his experiments. His appearance at Henry's home, after dark, as the winds of a tremendous thunder storm are brewing, is prefaced by wife Elizabeth's speech warning him of the dangers to be: "It's the devil who prompts you... insane desire... it comes, a figure like death, as if to take you away from me." At that instant a foreboding knock sounds at the door—Pretorius has arrived. Described by Minnie as a "queer old gentleman" here on "a secret grave matter," Pretorius at first lures Henry to his "humble abode" using curiosity to seduce him into resuming his experiments. Pretorius tells Henry to "leave the charnel house," that he "grew from seed" his experiments as nature intended. Interestingly enough, one of his miniature people is the Devil ("Do I flatter myself?" he asks), cast in Pretorius' own image, furthering the imagery in Elizabeth's original entrance speech. As the oddball, frizzy-haired madman mutters, "...life might be so much more amazing if we were all devils—and no nonsense about angels and being good." In not-so-subtle symbolic terms, Pretorius becomes the playful rebel who bathes in his hedonistic lifestyle, the rebel who finds goodness and God dull, and evil and the Devil stimulating.

Karl (a masterful Dwight Frye performance), the more interesting of the two graverobbing assistants of Pretorius, looks to the good doctor for handouts of silver coins for doing the doctor "favors." When he is told to go to "the Accident Hospital" to find a young victim of "sudden death," he gleefully exits singing a macabre tune about stabbing a victim to death, before he stalks the lonely London streets to claim such a "fresh" victim. After later stealing the corpse of "the Bride" to be, a young woman aged 19 years three months, Karl feels living outside the law is becoming too risky. To his gravedigging companion he chimes, "If there's much more like this, whatja say, pal, we give ourselves up and let them hang us. This is no life for murderers!" As illustrated here, even criminals long to be part of the dominant society and do not enjoy being Outsiders.

The Blind Hermit, not evil in any sense, also becomes a symbol of living outside society's confines, in his case by choice. However, the loneliness of living a solitary life in a cabin in the woods wears thin. When the monster comes along, the Hermit is delighted. "You're welcome, my friend... whoever you are. If you're in trouble, perhaps I can help you!" The Hermit and Monster bond when the Hermit discovers, "Perhaps you're afflicted too—I cannot see and you cannot speak... I shall look after you and you will comfort me." The Hermit, tears welling within his blank eyes, prays to God, thanking Him for sending a friend. He later admits, "It's bad to be alone." In other words, the Hermit represents all those miscalculating Outsiders who regret their solitary state and secretly wish to be part of society again. Interesting enough, during the pivotal "lesson" sequence whereby the Hermit teaches the Monster that bread and wine are "good" and that smoking is also "good," the Monster, who has been badly burned, growls at the match which lights the cigar. The Hermit convinces the Monster that smoking is pleasurable and allows the artificial human to puff away on the cigar, which he readily enjoys. However, the ambiguity of fire as both friend and foe is reiterated again when the two woodsmen

The Blind Hermit (O. P. Heggie) becomes a symbol of living outside society's confines.

invade the sanctity of the forest retreat and warn the Hermit against the Monster, soon setting his cabin on fire, thus illustrating both the good and bad aspects of fire. Here again, the ambiguity theme appears.

Of course Boris Karloff's Monster becomes the primary focus of James Whale's vision of the beloved Outsider. Naive, awkward, and childlike (remember, in Don Smith's accompanying chapter in this book, he sees Karloff's Monster in *Frankenstein* as being symbolic of a child; I would like to further that metaphor by viewing the Monster in *Bride* as having reached adolescence), the Monster, constantly evolving and growing, is learning, as a child, to think more like an adult. The look on the Monster's face as he listens to the blissful violin music played by his friend the Hermit suddenly changes upon the arrival of the two woodsmen. Even before they see the Monster, Karloff's face registers both all-knowing depression and anger with the realization that his idyllic world is crashing down because of these unwelcome invaders. The absolutely brilliant performance by Karloff is nicely encapsulated in the Hermit sequence. His childlike joy at puffing on the cigar, slurping up the wine, and declaring all this oral pleasure to be "good," is stark, so vital, so alive. The tears slowly

The Monster's evolution to adolescence is accompanied by his movement from the egocentric to the outwardly social.

pouring from Karloff's heavily made-up eyes as the Hermit prays, thanking God for a friend, are so sensitively rendered that the audience suddenly realizes that this God-forsaken creature actually does have a human heart, if not perhaps even a soul, as the scene fades to black the crucifix remains illuminated. Again, the ambiguity theme returns as Karloff's Monster is revealed to have a human underbelly with the Monster's unholiness constantly being compared to the religious martyrdom of Christ (another Outsider). Karloff's joy of music as he bops to the rhythmic sounds, his arms bouncing back and forth, becomes a pivotal image of the Monster's humanity. Mimicked five decades later by Tim Burton in *Edward Scissorhands*, Karloff's Monster, though seen as a monstrous outcast of society, still exudes more humanity and joy of life than many of his surrounding *human* beings.

But the Monster's evolution to adolescence is accompanied by his movement from the egocentric to the outwardly social: the realization, taught him by the Hermit, that being alone is bad and that friends are good. Sensitive and intelligent enough to realize he is one of a kind, a patch-quilt reject of human-

144

ity, he demands that Victor create a mate for him, a woman! As Pretorius manipulates the Monster, he tells him, "Woman, *friend* for you." And Karloff responds, "Yes, friend, like *me*!" "You're wise in your generation," Pretorius declares, to which the Monster longingly wonders aloud, "Women... Friend... Wife." His needs have matured in a brief few moments, but like the antisocial artistic rebel, this Outsider wants an Outsider Mate so the two of them can live outside society's conservative mores. In James Whale's vision and Karloff's performance, we have encapsulated the image of the Outsider as Monster, a sensitive and childlike outcast, someone feared and hated by the dominant culture, but a creature with compassion, sensitivity, and humor. True, his actions are sometimes antisocial and destructive, for he does brutally murder little Maria's parents at the film's beginning, silently stirring in the dark waters below the windmill, growling, aggressively attacking, strangling, drowning, and flinging still-living bodies below to their death. No, Karloff's Monster may be naive and childlike, but he is *never* innocent, for he has been corrupted by all of humanity's imperfections, becoming a mirror of his very flawed human maker, a creature damned by the Creator. Yet he is still a reprobate who tries to rise above, an antisocial Outcast still worthy of the audience's sympathies. For in his corruption we can see ourselves. And Karloff's performance, perhaps the best of his stellar career, becomes so much more than simply a portrayal of a Monster made from cadavers. Karloff represents the corrupted human soul—like the concept of "original sin," the Monster is born into perversity he knows not of—trying to regain its purity and perpetual state of bliss.

The final major image of the Outsider is the Bride herself, she being of the same "cut" as Karloff, she who is intended to be the Monster's friend and mate. But unfortunately, this hell-spawn only has eyes for the heaven-spawned Henry Frankenstein, violently rejecting the Monster. In such a pathetic universe as ours, even victims of artificially created life can not find comfort in each other: these unfortunate beings, the Monster and the Bride, are destined to be alone, unable to find comfort in each other, let alone within themselves. The Bride's hissed rejection and her panicked screaming only emphasize her misreading of her place in the universe and of the Monster's intentions. Too bad that these birds of a feather cannot flock together, their inability to "couple" resulting in the film's explosive climax.

On the other extreme, examining those examples of Conformists to Society, we first and foremost have Elizabeth (Valerie Hobson), the virginal bride to whom is delivered the half-dead corpse of her husband on her wedding night. She damns his experimentation, tries to protect Henry from the wily Dr. Pretorius (even telling him that he is not welcome in their home), and refuses to leave the soon-to-be-destroyed castle laboratory at the film's end without her husband Henry. She is symbolic of Society's Ideal of husband and wife living together in mutual harmony, both contributing to the well-being of society. With the death of Henry's father, she will be the Baroness Frankenstein and her respect of wielding such political clout within her community makes her a pivotal force of conformity. However, while Elizabeth is faithful and devoted, she is somewhat of a fuddy-duddy, a "wing-clipper" whose goal is to impede the creativity and life's work of her husband. She is much too concerned with what society will think.

Minnie the Maid, the delightful Una O'Connor, primarily delivers comic relief. After the brutal slaying of Maria's parents, the Monster confronts the frightened servant who, instead of being savagely murdered (what the audience expects), instead mugs for the camera and gets away while milking the audience for a laugh or two (what the audience does not expect). But more so than simply delivering comic relief, she delivers conformity for the well-being of the community. Her first line of dialogue to the Burgomaster is, "You better cross yourself," alluding to the fact that conformity to religious faith will be our salvation from the monsters of society. Maybe, after she runs to Frankenstein's home after facing the Monster, she proclaims, all in the best interest of public safety, "The Monster's alive. It ain't turned to a skeleton at all." When she is called "an old fool" and her insight rejected, she then defiantly offers, "I wash my hands of it—let them all be murdered in their beds." Her role, as she sees is, is the "mouthpiece" of public safety and she views her brave run to the Henry's home to be heroic, a feat worthy of public praise. When she does not get her reinforcement, she turns briefly against society by wishing "them" all be murdered in their beds—all because of the village's failure to heed her advice and warning. Thus, she serves the community only when it kowtows to her, not a heroic act at all.

The pompous Burgomaster (E. E. Clive), he who always says the right things to the people at the right times (a true politico, if ever there were one born in this village), becomes the glue who holds the community together: he is a combination mayor, police chief, judge, and wizened ruler. But ultimately, he is revealed to be hot air and bluster. "You may thank your lucky stars they sent for me to safeguard life and property," the Burgomaster boasts at the windmill, the scene of the supposed Monster's death. When the Monster is found to be alive, the Burgomaster promptly does the right thing by assembling a "posse" to capture the fiend, and when Karloff is cornered in the rocky woods above, the Burgomaster calmly yells for the mob to "tie his feet first," which apparently is not heeded by the animated mob. In frustration he declares, "I get no cooperation at all!" But after the Monster is returned to the village, locked up in stocks in the dungeon below, and finally breaks loose to escape, the old Burgomaster is poised outside the jail, quietly beaming at himself for the good work he has done, crying out condescending comments like, "Just an escaped lunatic, nothing to fear," when suddenly the Monster's rampaging figure is seen. Quietly, the Burgomaster registers shock and slowly starts shoving his

The pompous Burgomaster (E. E. Clive) is revealed to be hot air and bluster.

way out of harm's way, pushing people away so *he* can he safe from the Monster's clutches. Certainly the arrogance and pretension of the titular community leader is not heroic nor praiseworthy in any way.

Maria's parents, another symbol of the community responding to loss and pain, only appear momentarily to be the Monster's first victims. Their grief has turned to hatred with Hans, the father, declaring, "I want to see with my own eyes... blackened bones." But his pain is the community's pain, for if the current saying is true, that it takes an entire village to raise one child, then one child's death grieves *all* the community. So the parent's presence represents the grieving component of the entire social order.

While the audience supposedly is meant to identify with all these community symbols and forces of Conformity, the movie goes out of its way to show the pettiness of Minnie the Maid, the pompous pretense of the Burgomaster, the blandness of Elizabeth, Henry's colorless wife, and the futility of Maria's grieving parents. On the other hand, the film's most distinctive characters are the misfits and outcasts—the crazed Karl, the eccentric Dr. Pretorious who holds a picnic atop a casket, the "dead" Monster who holds more humanity in his cold heart than any number of normal citizens. Even in one brief sequence, the Monster finds comfort and warmth amid the Gypsy camp, certainly Europe's most notorious Outsider community! Thus, in Whale's vision, the Outsider is to be admired, even if admittedly flawed, and while these misfits might be guilty of minor or major criminal acts, they are depicted as being never less than interesting, something for which the Conformity characters strive.

But finally, what of Henry, the Monster-Creator, the manically depressed explorer of a new world of gods and monsters; which side of the fence does he fall?

Surprisingly, as stated earlier, even though he appears to be the archetype Outsider, in *Bride of Frankenstein*'s scheme of things, he becomes one of the Conformists at the film's conclusion. Let's see just why.

From the movie's start, Henry has been torn between devotion to Elizabeth and everything that means (taking the marriage vows, assuming his position as Baron, becoming a pillar of the community, conforming to society's mores, etc.) and his devotion to science, exploring those domains which rightfully belong to God, areas that man is not meant to traverse. His devotion to the artificial creation of life is easily understood by examining his relationship to the Monster (challenging God's power and authority, daring to break moral and criminal codes, daring to go too far!). What shall it be: his devotion to Elizabeth (his wife, his love) or the Monster (his creation, his art, his work). For most of the movie Elizabeth is losing the battle. Her objection to Pretorious is ignored and the boys seem to be spending more time together than husband and wife.

Henry has been agonized by his blasphemous work. "I've been cursed for delving into the mysterious of life—perhaps death is sacred, and I profaned it... give to the world the secret God is so jealous of... think of the Power... I might have bred a race..." Interestingly, in his antisocial activity of creating life Henry does conceive of breeding a race of artificial humans, in other words, a *society* of Monsters, not just a solitary *one*. Even his ideal society is not one of Burgomasters and grieving parents and dutiful wives, but one populated by life created from dead corpses. And Pretorious also shares a similar societal vision:

148

"to create a race of humans here on Earth!" Dr. Pretorius' twisted world vision also includes creating a *race* of humans, not one or two solitary ones. As both scientists rebel against society, they envision themselves as Creators, as Gods, of new societies of monsters and miniature people. Pretorius appeals to Henry's moral code to ensare the obsessed scientist to do his bidding: "You are responsible for all those murders (referring to the murders committed by the Monster). There are penalties to pay for killing people!" Granting credit where credit is due, Pretorius admits to Henry, "I have created life in God's own image." Henry calls this aberrant science "black magic."

But Henry still refuses to become further involved in creating races of monsters, relishing his new (safe) life with Elizabeth. Pretorius has one last method: to have the Monster kidnap Elizabeth and hold her for ransom until Henry agrees to help Pretorius create a woman, a mate for the Monster. Henry's love and dedication to Elizabeth is the only lever Pretorius can utilize to make Henry do his bidding and continue their ungodly work together. And for Elizabeth's well-being, Henry agrees.

Even the image of the watch tower, the unholy laboratory where these experiments will be conducted, is isolated and alone. Colin Clive, whining and obsessing to the high heavens, screams, "I can work better *alone*." And alone he does work, the Monster ruthlessly driving the frayed and drained scientist onward without granting him any time to rest. At the end, when the Bride rejects her groom and Elizabeth breaks free to save her husband from his work, she becomes the catalyst who saves *both* their lives. Henry frantically yells "Get back, get back" as the Monster luckily finds that lever which will blow them all to atoms, Henry's concern clearly shown for his wife. However, she refuses to leave without him. The Monster, seeing in Henry and Elizabeth what he so longs to have in his own life, yells to Pretorius, "You stay... we belong dead!" realizing the tragedy of their mutual existence. "You go!" he yells to Henry and his bride. Thus, the Monster and Pretorius and all the experiments go up in smoke and flame, and Henry and Elizabeth escape, truly as husband and wife, ready to partake their position as Conformists to Society and no longer antisocial rebels who buck the system. Their reward for Conformity—survival amidst a society of bland, dutiful characters.

Perhaps director James Whale saw the ambiguity in all of this. While he could surely identify with Karloff's character as the Monster, Whale could even more so identify with the ambivalence of Henry Frankenstein, the rebel at heart who ultimately must choose to be on society's side, to play the game by the community's standards. For no matter how artistic and eccentric James Whale happened to be, no matter how far outside of the community mores Whale dared to be, finally, for his career, Whale had to conform to certain dictates of both communities (in his private life and in his public Universal director's life) and do just what the antisocial Henry Frankenstein finally did: turn from being the enthusiastic Outcast and surrender to Conformity.

Perhaps in Whale's vision, the wonderful performance of Boris Karloff in portraying the Monster as the single-minded, dedicated, compassionate judge and executioner (his dominant role at movie's end)—note the ambiguity of having the Monster Outcast become *moral* judge, decreer of life and death— became the character he most admired in this strange managerie of horror. While the wishy-washy Henry had to literally sell out, or at least, to sell himself short, the Monster, cursed by his blasphemous creation and fate, represented the degeneration of human compassion and love, those qualities missing in a world strangely perverted, longingly uncaring, and finally quite empty. Perhaps the Monster became the hero of the story, a martyr who in many ways emulated the director's own life. Maybe James Whale identified with Henry Frankenstein because both had to conform, to a certain extent, in order to survive. But perhaps James Whale most *admired* the Monster, for in that characterization he saw, though twisted and distorted, the real human thread of humanity and compassion that he himself admired in his beloved vision of the Outsider. Perhaps the Monster became James Whale's very own role model (remember, *both* ultimately gave in to their self-destructive impulses), in an offbeat, eccentric sort of way.

CREDITS: Producer: Carl Laemmle, Jr.; Director: James Whale; Screenplay: William Hurlbut from an adaptation by William Hurlbut & John L. Balderston, suggested by the novel by Mary Shelley; Director of Photography: John J. Mescall; Music: Franz Waxman; Musical Director: Mischa Bakaleinikoff; Film Editor: Ted Kent; Art Director: Charles D. Hall; Special Photographic Effects: John P. Fulton and David Horsley; Makeup: Jack P. Pierce; Electrical Effects: Kenneth Strickfaden; Released May 6, 1935 by Universal Pictures; Running Time: 75 minutes

CAST: Boris Karloff...the Monster, Colin Clive...Henry Frankenstein, Valerie Hobson...Elizabeth Frankenstein, Ernest Thesiger...Dr. Pretorius, Elsa Lanchester...Mary Shelley/The Monster's Mate, Una O'Connor...Minnie, E. E. Clive...the Burgomaster, O. P. Heggie...the Hermit, Gavin Gordon...Lord Byron, Douglas Walton...Percy Shelley, Dwight Frye...Karl, Lucien Prival...Albert, Reginald Barlow...Hans, Mary Gordon...Han's Wife, Anne Darling...Shepherdess, Ted Billings...Ludwig, Neil Fitzgerald...Rudy, John Carradine, Robert Adair, John Curtis, Frank Terry...Hunters, Walter Brennan

Gary J. Svehla created his first publishing venture at the ripe old age of 13, *Gore Creatures*. 33 years later he is still publishing the magazine, now *Midnight Marquee*, as well as overseeing Midnight Marquee Press. Gary teaches high school English at North County High School in Glen Burnie, Maryland. He has contributed to *Movie Club,* and *Midnight Marquee,* as well as *Midnight Marquee Actors Series: Bela Lugosi* and *Cinematic Hauntings.*

THE MAN WHO CHANGED HIS MIND
(1936)

by Gregory William Mank

"Think of it! I offer you eternal youth! Eternal loveliness!"
—Boris Karloff to Anna Lee in *The Man Who Changed His Mind (1936)*.

Take Boris Karloff, vintage 1936. Cast him as a gloriously Mad Doctor, with a shock of white hair, a chain-smoking habit—and enough raging emotions to have intimidated Shakespeare.

Add Anna Lee, one of horror's most attractive and spirited heroines, destined to spar brilliantly with Boris again in Val Lewton's 1946 *Bedlam*.

Provide a clever story by John L. Balderston, whose name appeared on the writing credits of *Dracula, Frankenstein, The Mummy, Mark of the Vampire, Bride of Frankenstein,* and *Mad Love*.

Engage Robert Stevenson, future prolific director for Walt Disney, to bring the brew to a boil.

The result: *The Man Who Changed His Mind,* one of the two British pictures that Hollywood star Karloff made in his native England in 1936. (The other: the not-so-fortunate *Juggernaut.*) Offbeat, original, spiced with dark comedy, this terrific little melodrama offers (in my opinion) Karloff's finest Mad Doctor portrayal, acted during what's widely considered his most creatively rich (1931 to 1936) era. It's a very underrated (and, due to the scarcity of prints, under-seen) film, ripe for full revival—and a showcase for the irreplaceable talents of its star.

"He's arrived in England with a couple of monkeys and claims he's discovering the human soul!"
—Dick Haslewood (John Loder), describing Dr. Laurience (Boris Karloff) in *The Man Who Changed His Mind*.

Dr. Laurience discovers a way to transfer the "mind contact" of one living brain to another. He experiments

153

on chimpanzees, changing a docile animal to a vicious one, and now determines to experiment upon human beings. His assistant is Clare Wyatt, a pretty young doctor, who loves Dick, the son of Lord Haslewood, a pompous newspaper proprietor. Haslewood sees good publicity value in Laurience and persuades him to use his own private laboratory for experimentation, but soon drops Laurience when he fails to break down the skepticism of the leading scientists of the day. Humiliation turns Laurience's brain and out of revenge he transfers Haslewood's "mind contact" to the crippled body of the bitter paralytic, Clayton. After a short time, while both men die, Laurience develops an overwhelming desire for Clare, and realizing he is too old to win her, transfers his "mind contact" to that of handsome Dick. Unhappily, while in Dick's body, he meets with a fatal accident, but before he dies, Clare is able to operate and restore her lover's mind to his own body.

—Synopsis for *The Man Who Changed His Mind* from Denis Gifford's book, *Karloff: The Man, The Monster, The Movies* (Curtis Books, 1973).

Background: 1935 had been a triumphant year for Boris Karloff. It all began at Universal with his magnificent reprisal of the Monster in James Whale's *Bride* of *Frankenstein*. He followed in *The Raven* with Lugosi, at his home lot, then visited Columbia for his virtuoso performance as the Good and Evil twins of *The Black Room*. He rejoined Lugosi at Universal for *The Invisible Ray* (released in 1936), and managed to squeeze in *The Walking Dead* (also a 1936 release) for Warner's, completing his work there at 2:30 a.m. on December 21, 1935—just in time to relax for the Yuletide holidays.

Meanwhile, Boris had contracted with London's Gaumont-British Gainsborough Studios for a "vehicle" and a $30,000 guarantee. However, as

Anna Lee remembers Boris being very kind to the chimps even though they were smelly.

anti-horror factions bristled, Gainsborough apparently had second thoughts about a Karloff frightfest. *The Hollywood Reporter* ran this notice (1/13/36):

> Due to the Middlesex County Council restrictions of horror pics, which when enforced next month will keep children out of theatres when such films are played, G-B has withdrawn its plan to make a thriller with Boris Karloff. Karloff was to have come here under a contract guaranteeing him $30,000. Cable negotiations are now on between G-B and Karloff for a cash settlement on the pact.

The Reporter followed up 1/21/36:

> Failing to settle its 1-picture contract with Boris Karloff,

> Gaumont-British has decided to bring
> the player to London to do another type
> story instead of the horror film for
> which he was signed.

Karloff's very aggressive agent, Myron Selznick, made sure he still was guaranteed his $30,000—and managed to sign his client to a new 3-picture deal with Universal (and sweetened his Warner Bros. contract) as Boris sailed for London.

There, Boris indeed found "another type story."

The Film: *The Man Who Changed His Mind* has so many happy surprises, so many delightful touches that one hardly knows where to begin to list them.

So, "Ladies First."

First of all, a salute to Anna Lee, who co-stars with Boris as attractive, blonde, and brilliant scientist Dr. Clare Wyatt. Miss Lee is so pretty, so vivacious that she instantly pulls a viewer into the story. (She was wed at the time to the director, Robert Stevenson, who stages the melodrama cleverly and with fine melodramatic punch.) Her chemistry with Karloff (as it would be in *Bedlam*) is terrific. In 1991, Anna Lee, on a day off from her role as "Lila Quartermaine" on ABC's *General Hospital,* sat in her West Hollywood house and talked with me about "Dear Boris":

> Boris—a dear man! We both loved
> poetry, and apparently we both loved
> the same poems. We'd have a sort of
> "poetry jam." We'd say a poem—he'd
> say one line, and I'd say the second line;
> he'd say the third line—we'd go on
> until we ran out! I remember one..."The
> Children's Hour"—I'd say:
>
> "Between the dark and the
> daylight, when the light is beginning
> to lower,"
>
> And then Boris would *boom* out,
>
> "Comes a pause in the day's
> occupation, which is called The
> Children's Hour."
>
> "We used to go on for hours and
> hours, with little poems that we
> remembered—ones I hoped he *hadn't*
> remembered, but he always did! A
> *lovely* man!"

Here's a blonde horror heroine who never swoons; in fact, the brave and gallant lady saves the day, controlling the climactic laboratory experiment

Donald Calthrop is both funny and eerie as Clayton, the mad doctor's crippled, cynical familiar.

that saves John Loder (a fine, relaxed, and clever leading man) and defeats Karloff's madness. Anna Lee's performance in *The Man Who Changed His Mind* is a fine forecast of her brave, crusading (and brunette!) Nell Bowen in *Bedlam,* in which she and Karloff created a shower of dramatic sparks (onscreen; offscreen, they still enjoyed their "poetry jams"). She certainly rates as the "Female Lib" heroine of Horror's Golden Age.

The supporting cast is excellent. Donald Calthrop is both funny and eerie (*a la* Dwight Frye) as Clayton, the Mad Doctor's crippled, cynical familiar. "Most of me is dead," sneers Calthrop to Anna Lee from his wheelchair. "The rest of me is damned. Laurience manages to keep the residue alive." He also has one of the great lines of 1930s horror, as he queries of Miss Lee:

"I wonder which revolts you most—my miserable body, or my perverted mind!"

Frank Cellier, as pompous ass publisher Haslewood, is delightful, especially in the sequence in which Karloff switches the minds of Clayton and Haslewood; Cellier must evoke Calthrop's weasely, bitter personality in his hearty, well-fed

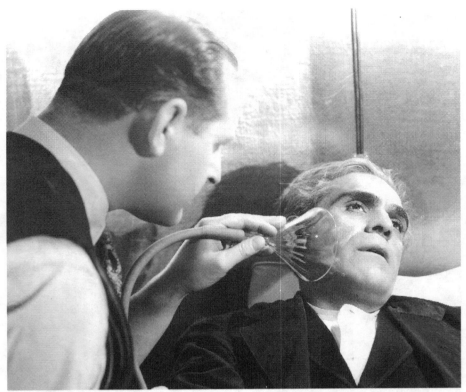
Dr. Laurience is one of Boris's finest performances.

body, and the result is wonderful character acting. Lyn Harding, who had played Moriarty in the British The *Speckled Band* (1931) and *The Triumph* of *Sherlock Holmes* (1935), has a brief but memorable part as Prof. Holloway, who humiliates Karloff at the scientific soiree. The actors have great material to work with; one suspects the honors belong to John L. Balderston, who provided the story (but not the screenplay). The early episode in which a superstitious driver takes Anna Lee to Karloff's "sinister manor house" almost plays like a spoof of Dwight Frye's ride to Borgo Pass in *Dracula*. (Baldertson had just stuffed MGM's *Mad Love* with "in-jokes" based on horror films, and one expects this was his mischief at play again.) The laboratory sequences are a bit modest (particularly coming the year after *Bride of Frankenstein*!), but director Stevenson directs them with style, employing the same quick-cutting that Whale had used in the creation of Elsa Lanchester's "Bride."

It's a slick, fascinating film, loaded with talent—but the real treat, of course, is the star.

Karloff's Performance: Dr. Laurience is one of Boris's finest performances, and the emotions he stuffs into this little 63-minute film are almost miraculous.

There's Boris's introduction, as Anna Lee enters his laboratory. He looks up dramatically, smoking the first of many, many cigarettes he drags on throughout the movie; he gently approaches the heroine, sees the fear in her eyes, and says:

> You're thinking that I'm changed.
> You're right—I am changed. (Looking
> in a mirror.) The leading surgeon in
> Genoa. The greatest authority upon the
> human brain—until I told them
> something about their own brains! (To
> Clare) They said I am mad. Look at me!
> (With a strange smile) Am I mad?

Stock lines, a familiar scenario, but Karloff reads them as if they were Shakespeare's poetry, and the odd smile with which he asks Miss Lee, "Am I mad?" is heartbreaking.

There's a laboratory episode in which Boris conducts the "mind-swapping" on the chimpanzees (as crippled Clayton accompanies at the piano!). Karloff escorts in a comical ape, sporting a lab smock. Anna Lee laughs at the sight, and in a delightful moment, Mad Doctor Karloff laughs too—flashing a merry smile, and showing the doctor's (and, one expects, Boris's!) affection for the chimp. By the way, Anna Lee recalls that it wasn't very easy to warm up to these particular apes:

> They were rather smelly. I had the
> dressing   room   next   to   the
> chimpanzees—and   I   remember
> suffering! Boris was very kind to them,
> but I don't think he was great friends
> with them, like he would have been to
> a dog or a horse. Very smelly!

Boris barnstorms where the script calls for it; "You fools!" he shrieks in his big scene before the scoffing scientific society (effectively seated in a laboratory tier room, *a la* the opening of Fredric March's *Dr. Jekyll and Mr. Hyde*). His revenge on Lord Haslewood is played with properly Machievellian leers. But perhaps most memorable is his growing, obsessive, tragic love for Clare, and his bizarre boast to her:

> This new power—I can share it
> only with you, for you alone are worthy
> to receive it... I could take a new body,
> a young body, and keep my own brain!
> And you too! You won't always be
> young. When you grow old, I could

give you a young body! Think of it! I offer you eternal youth! Eternal loveliness!

The dialogue (reminiscent of Lionel Atwill's speech to Fay Wray in 1933's *Mystery of the Wax Museum*) was already a bit "stock" by 1936. Yet Karloff plays the lines with a fresh, dramatic glee—like a crazy, lovesick poet (and with a little spark of lechery!). Anna Lee walks out on him in her Molyneux dress and 1936 high heels, but Karloff has scored with the audience, registering (as London's *The Cinema* put it) "appeal and repulsion"; he has our sympathy.

Of course, Karloff must go the "mad dog" route, just as he would do in his slick (but far less quirky and eccentric) "Mad Doctor" series at Columbia. He kills Clayton as Haslewood, leaves clues that he (Laurience) did it—then races to trade bodies with Dick. He's wonderfully scary as he smiles madly at the hero, the gaunt Karloff face bathed in eerie light, ranting:

"I killed him in his study an hour ago. And I left plenty of evidence to prove that Laurience is the murderer. But by the time the police get here, you will be *Laurience!*"

The transformation is completed; Loder does a clever little impersonation of Karloff's walk (and lights a cigarette!); he smashes a vial, planning for the fumes to kill the hero (now in Karloff's body). Karloff falls from a window while escaping the fumes. In a great novelty for the era, it's heroine to the rescue; Miss Lee works the mad miracle in the lab, assisted by her friend Dr. Gratton (Cecil Parker), returning the minds (and, as delicately but definitely hinted in the film, the souls) to their original bodies.

And we see Karloff's death scene. Broken, repentant, he says to the leading lady:

"Clare. Please forgive me. You were right. The human mind is sacred... Destroy all this... Promise me?"

"I promise," says Clare.

And, in a final closeup, Karloff's dying Dr. Laurience once again gives his heartbreaking smile.

THE END

The Impact: Karloff stayed on in London, signing for *Juggernaut* and having a jolly summer in his native England. He came home to Hollywood in September, and *The Man Who Changed His Mind* eventually followed him to the States, previewing at the Rialto Theatre in New York City the night of December 14, 1936. There was a new US title—*The Man Who Lived Again.* "Mr. Karloff Haunts the Rialto," headlined the *New York Times* review, which regretted Karloff never tried out his mind-swapping experiment on Shirley Temple and Mae West. *Variety* reported:

Moving his baby-scaring tricks to London, Boris Karloff has been induced to spread horror in the midst of very English surroundings in a tenderly entertaining concoction called *The Man Who Lived Again.* The box office potentialities are fair. Gaumont-British has followed the most tried and true formulae of Hollywood producers in turning out spinechillers but there is no mistake that this one comes from British workshops. The accents of the cast members, outside of Karloff, are very limey and the way "laboratory" is pronounced throughout may have some of the American schoolchildren wondering...

Aside from its apparent prejudice against British films, *Variety* allowed, "The idea is screwy but it serves to equip Karloff with the sort of thing he likes to do and usually does well."

While *Variety* attacked *The Man Who Changed His Mind* as a rip-off of Hollywood horror films, it was actually the opposite; indeed, many later Hollywood horrors seemed to take *their* cue from it. Karloff's aforementioned Mad Doctor series for Columbia (1939-1942) certainly owes much to the 1936 film; Universal's Karloff & Lugosi *Black Friday* (1940), with Curt Siodmak's brain-swapping script, seems a not-too-distant relative to the British movie. And Universal's *House of Frankenstein* (1944), with Karloff madly plotting brain transplants, and hunchback J. Carrol Naish pining for his own brain to be popped into Lon Chaney's "big and strong" body, makes one wonder if someone ran off a print of *The Man Who Changed His Mind* while brainstorming the script.

Meanwhile, *The Man Who Changed His Mind/The Man Who Lived Again* resurfaced in the 1940s under the new title of *Dr. Maniac* and even made the rounds in later years as *Brain Snatcher.* Oddly, for a film that played so long under assorted titles, *The Man Who Changed His Mind* is forlorn today. Sinister Cinema, Greg Luce's excellent video mail order company, offers the film, noting, "Our video master comes directly from the only known 16mm print in North America." As Sinister Cinema also writes,

This could very well be Karloff's best performance as a mad scientist, and the film must certainly rank as one of the best horror films of the 1930s...

[Courtesy Ronald V. Borst/Hollywood Movie Posters]
US poster for *The Man Who Changed His Mind*

Dynamite lab scenes, great script,
excellent acting... Don't miss it!

Elsewhere in the catalogue, Sinister Cinema notes, "Boris does in this role what Bela did in his role as Dr. Vollin in *The Raven*.. He lets it all hang out..."

More eccentric than the Columbia series, more original than the later Universals, and, of course, light years away from the Monogram and PRC mad scientist yarns in creativity and intelligence, *The Man Who Changed His Mind* has it all, even daring to tamper (as do the most sublime of horror films) with the soul. And the soul of this movie is Boris Karloff. Kind to animals, chain-smoking, passionate in his research, frightening and touching in his dream of "eternal youth," lovesick, vengeful, half (and later totally) mad, and, at his death, wise and repentant, Karloff again shows his genius.

"He was a very well-loved man," says Anna Lee of Boris Karloff.

And he'll forever be a well-loved star.

CREDITS: Producer: Michael Balcon; Director: Robert Stevenson; Screenplay: L. Du Garde Peach and Sidney Gilliat (from a story by John L. Balderston); Cinematographer: Jack Cox; Editors: R.E. Dearing and Alfred Roomer; Art Director: Vetchinsky; Makeup: Roy Ashton; Dresses: Molyneux; Musical Direction: Louis Levy; Recordist: W. Salter; Filmed at Gaumont-British/ Gainsborough, London; Running time: 63 minutes; Alternate titles: *The Man Who Lived Again; Dr. Maniac; Brain Snatcher;* US release (as *The Man Who Lived Again)*: Rialto Theatre, New York City, December 14, 1936

CAST: Boris Karloff...Dr. Laurience, Anna Lee...Dr. Clare Wyatt, John Loder...Dick Haslewood, Frank Cellier...Lord Haslewood, Donald Calthrop...Clayton, Cecil Parker...Dr. Gratton, Lyn Harding...Professor Holloway

THE WALKING DEAD (1936)
by Bryan Senn

Sh-h-h-h! Karloff is coming... Karloff, King of Horror, in his most grue-some masterpiece, "The Walking Dead"! See how a dead man comes back to the land of the living to avenge his own death! Watch how science brings an electro-cuted man back to half-life by means of the famous Lindbergh heart. See Karloff in *"The Walking Dead"*! He'll make your flesh creep! He'll make your hair rise!
—radio spot for *The Walking Dead*.

By 1935, Boris Karloff had become a highly-paid box-office draw, sought after by many studios and producers eager to cash in on the actor's popularity. Among them was Warner Bros., who enticed Karloff to appear in five of their productions in as many years (*The Walking Dead* [1936], *West of Shanghai* [1937], *The Invisible Menace* [1938], *Devil's Island* [1940] and *British Intelligence* [1940]). Karloff hadn't worked on the Warner lot since 1931 when, as a relatively unknown bit-player, he won small roles in four Warner Bros. productions that year, including *Five Star Final* and *The Mad Genius*.

Though only one of Karloff's five subsequent starring Warner Bros. vehicles was a horror film (and of the four non-horrors only *West of Shanghai* proved at all memorable), Karloff's return to Jack Warner's domain proved a triumphant one if only due to his inaugural assignment. Filmed during December 1935 and January 1936, *The Walking Dead* is an often overlooked classic (perhaps due to its present unavailability on video) that frequently gets unfairly lumped in with Karloff's "Mad Doctor" and "Back-from-the-Dead" films (*The Man They Could Not Hang*, 1939; *Before I Hang*, 1940; etc.). These later horror entries are basically low-budget potboilers, albeit with a touch more class than most of their contemporaries. It is a mistake, however, to dismiss *The Walking Dead* as simply another knot in Karloff's long string of "Mad Monster Movies," for it is a well-crafted, superbly acted film that works on several levels and imparts its message with sensitivity rather than shock.

John Elman* (Boris Karloff), a mild-mannered musician, has just been released from prison after serving 10 years for second degree murder. "It was my wife," he explains. "I struck a man, but I didn't mean to kill him." Elman has been dealt a rather harsh hand by the deck of fate and now only wishes to find a job and resume what is left of his life. Unfortunately for him, he's taken in by four powerful (and ostensibly "respectable") racketeers who frame him for the murder of an honest judge who caused trouble for them.

Elman is convicted and sentenced to die. On the eve of the execution, two witnesses who can clear Elman, Jimmy (Warren Hull) and Nancy (Marguerite Churchill), finally overcome their fear of the racketeers and come forward—but it is too late and Elman is put to death in the electric chair.

Jimmy and Nancy both work for an eminent researcher named Dr. Beaumont (Edmund Gwenn). Beaumont, who'd been working on the reanimation of dead animals, performs an experimental procedure on Elman's body and brings him back to life. Elman has changed, though, and is only the shell of the man he once was. He has very little memory and is almost an invalid. However, at certain times he gains some mysterious access to knowledge denied him in life—namely, the identities of his hidden enemies, those who had secretly framed him. "I'm positive Elman has some knowledge not given to him by Man," declares Dr. Beaumont.

One by one Elman confronts his enemies. Elman's very presence unnerves each of the racketeers, and their own guilt and terror lead them to their deaths. One man (the group's hitman) falls backwards in fright and shoots himself with his own gun; another runs into the path of an oncoming train; a third backs through an upper story window.

Finally, Elman retreats to a cemetery. "I belong here," he says quietly. The two remaining racketeers follow him there and shoot him, but receive their just reward when their fleeing car careens off the road and crashes into a power pole—sending them to their own impromptu electric chair.

As Elman lies dying (for the second—and final—time), Dr. Beaumont questions him: "John, look at me, try to remember, you must.... Try John, try; that's why I brought you back from death... Tell me, what is death?" Suddenly, everything seems to become clear to Elman. "I think I can," he says. "After the shock I seemed to feel peace and—and—" and he dies, taking his mysterious knowledge with him as he rejoins his Maker. As Elman had said earlier, "The Lord our God is a jealous God."

In 1932, during the filming of *Doctor X*, director Michael Curtiz remarked (in his trademark broken English) that "we are not here to preaching with pictures, to take political sides or bring a great message; we are here to entertain." This certainly sums up the exciting, spine-tingling gems of entertainment he created in *Doctor X* and its follow-up feature, *Mystery of the Wax Museum* (1933). With *The Walking Dead*, however, Curtiz had a much more meaningful script upon which to build, and while he succeeded in achieving his primary goal of entertaining, the film also manages to effectively "take political sides" and "bring a great message."

The collaborative efforts of screenwriters Ewart Adamson, Peter Milne, Robert Andrews, and Lillie Hayward resulted in a very strong and literate script

Elman (Karloff), even after he is brought back to life and sets out to bring retribution to the guilty, is no monster.

which possesses a greater thematic depth than most. The confirmation of an afterlife, the revelation that the guilty *will* be punished, and the assurance that there is indeed a God watching over us, ready to take a hand, touch some very real and basic human needs. The screenwriters exploit these needs in order to draw the viewer into their story. They deliver the goods in the end, for the film's message is one of reassurance and as such is rather appealing and, ultimately, satisfying. (Warners seemed afraid that theater managers might take their picture too lightly and so warned exhibitors that "The film ends on a very somber note—and leaves an audience in no mood for jocularity. So don't follow this film with anything having a too-gay opening. Sharp change from a tense drama to comedy might not blend well.")

Also appealing is the character of John Elman. He is a likable but rather naive man who trusts people and the system but is betrayed by them. It's easy

As Elman, Boris presents a striking figure: cadaverous cheeks, half-veiled eyes, a streak of white in his hair, his left arm turned up tight at his side.

to empathize with Elman, because most of us have been taken advantage of at one time or another (though, it is hoped, not to the extent of Elman's case!). The sympathy engendered by Elman's plight gives each viewer an emotional stake in the proceedings and draws them into the story. In the end, Elman (and, through him, the audience) receives assistance from, and finds solace in, a higher court than the fallible American judicial system.

Elman is always a sympathetic figure. Even after he's brought back to life and sets out to bring retribution to the guilty, he is no monster; he's merely an innocent victim who, through some preternatural power, has become an instrument of justice. He never actually kills the racketeers; he merely confronts them with their guilt and lets their own consciences press them on to their deaths. This is an important distinction, one that separates him from—and sets him above—his enemies, for he could never intentionally kill as they did, even if in his case it might be justified. (Ewart Adamson and Joseph Field's original story for *The Walking Dead* [dated November 19, 1935] painted Elman in a drastically different light than the gentle being seen in the finished film. Ac-

168

cording to the original treatment, "Dopey" Elman is "a nervous wreck" due to drug and alcohol addictions. Even worse, after his resurrection Elman "is a repulsive, vicious thing without the power of speech, which makes one recoil in horror." Thankfully, subsequent script revisions turned this vicious monster into a sensitive man.)

The story's topicality provides food for thought—and made for good PR copy as well. *"Film Revives Controversy Over Capital Punishment"* read the headline in a Warner Bros. publicity piece: *"Members of Cast of 'The Walking Dead' Divided in Opinion."* According to the article, both Karloff and Barton MacLane were against the Death Penalty, but their enlightened viewpoint was not shared by the remainder of the cast. Henry O'Neill, Marguerite Churchill, Warren Hull, Edmund Gwenn, and Ricardo Cortez were all in favor (though Cortez limited it to men over 45, since "men over 45 haven't a chance to reform"). Director Michael Curtiz was "on the fence," believing "people should not be killed to pay a debt to society unless they have definitely committed a cold blooded, premeditated murder."

Beyond intellectual arguments over capital punishment, Warner Brothers ran into a bit of legal difficulty over their *Walking Dead* script. According to *The Hollywood Reporter* (October 3, 1936), a writer named Ferdinand Voteur charged that *The Walking Dead* plagiarized his story "Resurrection Morning." The studio answered that the film's four screenwriters concocted their screenplay from yet another script by Ewart Adamson and Joseph Fields. Nothing further seems to have come of Voteur's accusation.

"He is modest and retiring, not at all 'spooky' in his habits—Reads much and understandingly—Likes to travel—Has his greatest film role in *'The Walking Dead'*..." (Warner Bros. "Star Silhouette" profile of Boris Karloff)

For *The Walking Dead*, Warner Bros. signed Boris Karloff to a one-picture contract at a princely $3,750 per week. Out of the $217,000 spent to make the film, the actor's salary may very well have been the best $18,700 investment Warners made, for Karloff's performance here is among his best. His pleading at the trial, for instance, is heartbreaking: "You can't kill me for something I didn't do I tell you, you can't, you can't!" Later, as he's about to be executed, we see his despair turn to bitterness. When the Warden offers him a last request, Karloff's sardonic reply is, "Take away my life and grant me a favor in return—now that's what I call a *bargain*." This momentary rancor is never directed at an individual, however; it is simply a bitter stab at his unjust circumstance—and it doesn't last long. The actor's natural soft-spokenness and humanity shines through his performance, and no animosity or baseness is allowed to creep into the character. A kindness and innate belief in his fellow

169

man shines through Karloff's eyes. Throughout the film Karloff inspires sympathy and the audience is behind him one-hundred percent.

Warners played up the actor's well-known gentility and sensitivity in their publicity. One press release recounted that "Boris Karloff, who scares others in films, got the shivers himself during the production of the Warner Bros. picture, *The Walking Dead*. He stood watching the film crew build a prison set. The death row tier of cells had been completed and the workmen were busy assembling various pieces of furniture and electrical apparatus. Finished, the workmen stepped back, and a huge black ominous chair was revealed—the 'hot seat' in which Karloff was soon to be electrocuted for film purposes. The chair was too much like grim reality. Karloff gasped and shivered, then turned and went away from there. 'It made the chills run up and down my spine,' he said."

After Elman's miraculous revival from the dead, Karloff presents a striking figure: cadaverous cheeks, half-veiled eyes, a streak of white in his hair, his left arm turned up tight at his side. His movements are slow and at first glance he puts forth an image of frailty. At the same time, however, his inexorable advancing gait and determined voice give an impression of strength and undeniable power. Karloff's body language is superb. For the remainder of the film, Karloff delivers few lines of dialogue and instead develops his character with the subtle facial expressions and insightful physical acting that brought him stardom in the first place with *Frankenstein*.

Director Michael Curtiz utilized much of the skill and expertise on *The Walking Dead* that would later bring him such acclaim for classics such as *Angels With Dirty Faces* (1938) and *The Sea Wolf* (1941), and an Oscar for *Casablanca* (1942). Few directors are as adept at drawing their audiences into the action as the Hungarian-born Curtiz.

Curtiz consistently places objects and people in the foreground of a shot to create three dimensional images which hold one's visual interest and perfectly complement the story and actions unfolding onscreen. Curtiz' varied use of unusual camera angles is equally outstanding. In the memorable sequence in which Elman takes the long walk to the electric chair, the camera creates a moving tableau of sadness. The camera angle makes it appear that Karloff is walking at an upward slant, symbolizing his impending ascent to the heavenly beyond. This sequence, which normally could be a very tense and suspenseful moment, attains a very different mood, one that is not at all frightening but more like the feeling of a sad but peaceful passing. From a slightly off-kilter angle we see the shadows of bars on the wall and a slowly rotating fan overhead. The camera moves in as Karloff swallows and raises his head upwards. In a low, soft voice he says, "He'll believe me." (In England, the British Censor excised Karloff's death cell scenes so as not to portray execution by electric chair—a practice considered barbaric in the British Isles. Consequently, on

Elman's pleading at the trial is heartbreaking: "You can't kill me for something I didn't do, I tell you, you can't, you can't!"

British prints the story cuts from Karloff's "long walk" from his cell to his appearance as a corpse in Dr. Beaumont's lab.) After Elman is revived from the dead—and has become the instrument of justice—Curtiz photographs him exclusively from a low angle, as if he were a deity looking down in judgment. (To "heighten" the effect even more, Karloff was given lifts. "According to prison authorities," reported the film's pressbook," a man 'grows' an inch or two after taking the 'jolt' in the electric chair. It was necessary to increase Karloff's stature four inches to produce the effect.") Concurrently, the racketeers are usually viewed from a higher camera position so they appear smaller and not as powerful as Elman. All of these cinematic tools, combined with Karloff's ability to evoke sympathy and pathos, contribute to the dramatic impact of the scenes.

Michael Curtiz directed nearly one hundred films for Warner Bros., including two previous horror classics, *Doctor X* and *Mystery of the Wax Museum*. Curtiz, an established Warners 'A' director, commanded a hefty $17,660 fee for

Boris Karloff, Edmund Gwenn, H. G. Wells, and Jack Warner on the set of *The Walking Dead.*

directing *The Walking Dead*—a salary nearly equal to that of his high-priced star! By all accounts, Curtiz was quite an outspoken character and Warners' publicity department was never slow to take advantage: "When Michael Curtiz... saw Karloff for the first time in the ghastly yellow-and-green make-up he uses in portraying a man who's just got out of his grave, he said: 'Swell! Now I'll tell you of another job you can have. Go out and haunt the houses of those tenants of mine who are not paying their rent!'"

Curtiz had worked with Boris Karloff once before, on the John Barrymore vehicle *The Mad Genius*. At that time (before *Frankenstein* had launched Boris into the limelight), Karloff was little more than a bit player and Curtiz cast him in the small role of a drunken Russian. When reunited on *The Walking Dead*, Curtiz told the now-famous actor why he'd won the brief part in *The Mad Genius*: "The reason I called you in," explained the director, "was because I thought you actually were a Russian. Your name certainly sounded Russian! When you came in you seemed so anxious to get the job that I decided to let you have it!"

Along with Curtiz, much of the credit for the technical superiority of *The Walking Dead* must go to Hal Mohr, the film's ace cinematographer. This highly

172

skilled craftsman, fresh from his Oscar-winning work a year earlier on *A Midsummer Night's Dream* (1935), plays an integral part in the dreamlike visual quality of *The Walking Dead*. (Interestingly enough, Mohr was not even *nominated* for *A Midsummer Night's Dream* but won on a write-in vote, becoming the only person to ever win an Oscar in that fashion. After Mohr's surprise victory, the Academy changed the rules so that no one could vote for anyone other than the official nominees.) A standout feature in *The Walking Dead* is Mohr's use of low-key lighting from the side, which effectively highlights the emotional changes in the characters. Mohr occasionally shifts the lighting emphasis from the side to the front, thus emphasizing a new understanding on the part of a character or underscoring the fear in the faces of Elman's adversaries. A key example of these subtle but effective changes in lighting occurs at the climax, when Karloff describes his experience in the heavenly realm. Just as Elman utters his last words, the lighting shifts from the side to the front, illuminating his entire face. This subtle change, combined with a very soft focus, suggests an awareness of a supreme force at work and also conveys a sense that Elman himself has been absolved and can finally rest in peace and wholeness.

The Walking Dead was cinematographer Hal Mohr's only Golden Age horror film, though he photographed two genre entries in the 1940s: the lavish 1943 Claude Rains remake of *Phantom of the Opera* (for which Mohr won another Oscar) and the tepid *Phantom* follow-up, *The Climax* (1944; again starring Boris Karloff). Mohr also shot such varied classics as *Destry Rides Again* (1939) and *The Wild One* (1954). Sadly, the talented director of photography finished up his illustrious career shooting no-budget sci-fi features like *Creation of the Humanoids* (1962) and *The Bamboo Saucer* (1968; his final film as cinematographer).

The Walking Dead simply looks good, thanks in no small part to art director Hugh Retiker's efforts. Apart from successfully melding grittily realistic big city street sets with quietly atmospheric graveyard settings, Retiker also secured some laboratory equipment for *The Walking Dead* that was of a more authentic nature than the usual "Mad Medico" apparatus seen in films of the time. Several experimental devices in the picture were based on innovative medical inventions, including the "Lindbergh Heart" (a mechanical circulating system designed by famed flyer Charles A. Lindbergh and Nobel Prize winner Dr. Alexis Carrel) and a motor-controlled, tilting operating table utilized by Dr. Robert E. Cornish in his experiments in the reanimation of dead dogs. According to the film's pressbook, "the studio built a working model [of the Lindbergh Heart] from blue-prints sent from the Rockefeller Institute." The pressbook also claimed that "this is the first time either of these reanimating mechanisms have been shown on the screen." (Obviously, Warners' PR department conveniently ignored [or simply hadn't seen] Universal's *Life Returns* released a year

[Courtesy Ronald V. Borst/Hollywood Movie Posters]

earlier, a banal boy-and-his-dog tale built around actual footage of Cornish's famous "dead dog" experiment conducted on May 22, 1934 at the University of Southern California.)

The sequence which employed these devices—Elman's resurrection scene—was not an easy one to shoot for Karloff. If a studio press release can be believed, it took twelve tries before everything went right: "The call for action was heard and the actor played his part. Something went wrong—a light flickered out, necessitating another take. Again and again Karloff rose from the dead only to be told that some important object in the scene was not recorded properly." After eight grueling hours, Curtiz was finally satisfied. Karloff, however, was a bit the worse for wear. After see-sawing up and down for hours on end, strapped to the tilting table, the actor could not bring himself to eat his dinner. Worse, he returned later that evening to play a scene "and had to eat, for the benefit of the cameras, six hot dogs smeared with mustard and drink six cups of coffee. He got them down, but they refused to stay."

Though a superb film, *The Walking Dead* is not without its flaws. It did not, for example, escape the seemingly obligatory unfunny comedy relief so often deemed necessary for "horror" pictures in the 1930s. This time it comes in the form of an annoying character named Betcha, the lead racketeer's dim-wit driver, who tries to wager on just about anything (including Elman's conviction). This coarse, unsuccessful comedy is so out of step with the serious, weighty tone of the film that it becomes a jarring intrusion rather than a smooth relief from tension.

Also, though the script is well-fashioned (ill-placed wagering excepted), it possesses one troublesome area: the characters of Jimmy and Nancy (the intended audience identification figures) are too sketchily drawn. We don't really know *why* they didn't come forward until the eleventh hour (other than base cowardice), and their feelings are never fully explored. When the pair finally do present themselves (too late, of course), it happens in an abrupt manner. There is no build-up revealing their change of heart (or acquisition of courage), no scenes of moral torment or conscience wrestling—just bam!—they're suddenly in Beaumont's office pleading with the doctor to help them stop the execution. In many films, this injudicious use of plot expediency would easily slide by, but *The Walking Dead*'s generally superior level of writing makes the lapse both noticeable and disappointing.

Reviews at the time were mixed, though most came out on the positive side. The *Motion Picture Herald* (March 7, 1936) seemed pleased that "although the picture is up to previous Karloff efforts, the desired result is obtained without outright shocking.... The production values are excellent, especially those laboratory scenes during which the dead man is brought back to life."

Variety's "Odec," however (March 4, 1936), was unimpressed by this Warner Bros. foray into the realm of the macabre: "Those with a yen for shockers will get limited satisfaction from the story that has been wrapped around Boris Karloff's initial stalking piece under the Warner Bros. banner. The director and the supporting cast try hard to give some semblance of credibility to the trite and pseudo-scientific vaporings of the writers, but the best they can produce is something that moves swiftly enough but contains little of sustained interest.

Karloff will have to be sold on past performances. *The Living Dead* [sic] lets him down badly on opportunities."

Britain's *Kinematograph Weekly* (April 30, 1936) saw some merit in the production, calling it a "High voltage melodrama linking gangsterdom with the supernatural through the macabre histrionics of Boris Karloff," and stated that "this picture hands out holding entertainment for the masses, those who never tire at nibbling at the eerie.... Boris Karloff gives a human and sympathetic performance in the fantastic role of Ellman [sic]; acting ability rather than grotesque make-up invests his portrayal with conviction."

The *New York Times'* Frank S. Nugent (March 2, 1936) noted that "there is no denying that [Karloff] makes an impressive zombie. With a blaze of white streaking his hair, with sunken mournful eyes, hollow cheeks and a passion for Sindling's 'Rustles of Spring,' Karloff is something to haunt your sleep at nights. We didn't even dare laugh when he sat down to play the piano...'"

Most recent assessments recognize the picture's quality. Leslie Halliwell called *The Walking Dead* "a smoothly made movie... all impressionist shadows in the best Michael Curtiz manner" (*The Dead That Walk*, 1988). Phil Hardy, in *The Encyclopedia of Science Fiction Movies* (1984), noted that "though the plot is little but a clever variant on the revenge-inspired gangster films Warners were churning out, Curtiz's slick direction and Mohr's expressionistic lighting make this outing far superior to Karloff's other films of this period." Scott Allen Nollen (in *Boris Karloff*, 1991) dubbed the film "an engaging sixty-five minutes of understated cinema." In his *Classics of the Horror Film* (1974), William K. Everson stated, "In many ways, *The Walking Dead* is one of Karloff's most interesting and satisfying films" and called it "an underrated Karloff vehicle [that is] far more intelligent, thoughtful, and directorially stylish than its rather sensational title and misleading, gruesome trailer would lead one to expect." One of the very few derogatory opinions came from Donald C. Willis (*Horror and Science Fiction Films: A Checklist*, 1972) who called the film "badly written, weakly directed." (Of course, this is the same writer who labeled Karloff's *Frankenstein* "one of those you-know-it's-a-classic-because-it's-dull films"!)

It was not only the poverty-row outfits that came up with outlandish selling slants for their pictures; even a studio as prestigious as Warner Bros. could generate some downright bizarre promotional suggestions: "Think you can hold a screening at the morgue?" asked *The Walking Dead*'s pressbook. Or how about this angle: "Newspapers have been devoting considerable space to doctors who are conducting experiments on bringing dogs back to life after asphyxiation. If there's a local medico who ever conducted such an experiment or would be likely to try it, hop around to see him and see if he'll cooperate by working it—with proportionate tie-in for film." Imagine: Bring Rover to the Roxy on Friday to be gassed and restored to life at intermission!

A few minor faults (and wild promotional ploys) aside, *The Walking Dead* remains one of the most sensitive and least appreciated films from horror cinema's "Golden Age," and one that features a subtle, sympathetic performance that confirms Boris Karloff's standing as that decade's greatest genre contributor.

CREDITS: Producer: Lou Edelman; Director: Michael Curtiz; Screenplay: Ewart Adamson, Peter Milne, Robert Andrews, and Lillie Hayward; Cinematographer: Hal Mohr, A.S.C.; Art Director: Hugh Reticker; Editor: Thomas Pratt; Dialogue Director: Irving Rapper; Gowns: Orry-Kelly; Release Date: February 29, 1936; Running Time: 66 minutes; Warner Brothers

CAST: Boris Karloff...John Elman, Ricardo Cortez...Nolan, Edmund Gwenn...Dr. Beaumont, Marguerite Churchill...Nancy, Warren Hull...Jimmy, Barton MacLane...Loder, Henry O'Neill...Werner, Joseph King...Judge Shaw, Addison Richards...Prison Warden, Paul Harvey...Blackstone, Robert Strange...Merritt, Joseph Sawyer..."Trigger", Eddie Acuff...Betcha, Kenneth Harlan...Stephen Martin, Miki Morita...Sako, Ruth Robinson...Mrs. Shaw

  * The spelling of the character name Elman has been a source of some debate. The opening credits list the spelling as Elman while during the film a newspaper lists the spelling as Ellman. According to Greg Mank, in the script the Karloff character is merely refereed to as "Creepy!"

Bryan Senn is the author of *Golden Horrors: An Illustrated Critical Filmography, 1931-1939* (McFarland, 1996) and co-author of *Fantastic Cinema Subject Guide* (McFarland, 1992) as well as contributing chapters to *Midnight Marquee Actors Series: Bela Lugosi* and *Cinematic Hauntings*. He is currently working on *Drums of Terror: Voodoo in the Cinema* for Mid Mar Press. Bryan lives with wife Gina and son Dominic in Washington state.

[Courtesy Ronald V. Borst/Hollywood Movie Posters]

CHARLIE CHAN
AT THE OPERA
(1937)

by John Soister

I'm not quite sure how it came about, but the popular perception still seems to be that the first and greatest horror cycle stopped on a dime sometime in May, 1936, with the release of *Dracula's Daughter.* As an old Universal man from way back, I'm grateful for the impression that this is so, as it reflects the extent to which the more discriminating (read: older) fans have come to associate classic horror films with the House That Carl Built. Impressions apart, however, this just is not true.

Now, the last Golden Age Universal chiller to be enriched by the Karloff presence (and the Lugosi mystique) was *The Invisible Ray,* which shone upon screens everywhere in mid-January of that most damnable of years. Although a carefully monitored, purposefully understated science-fiction opus, *Ray* couldn't abate the snapping and snarling which had characterized the British reaction to Hollywood's becoming carried away with this horror business. As it had been an earlier Boris/Bela bogey-fest, *The Raven,* which had taken things that fateful one step too far, this more subdued effort by the Laemmle Bully Boys might well have been regarded as an act of contrition. Alas! The less sensational nature of Lambert Hillyer's piece did nothing to placate the Brits who, along with America and the rest of the overseas market, opted to follow a loftier path and forego base and common thrills.

Neither of the Twin Titans of Terror would have much to look forward to at Universal City until 1939's *Son of Frankenstein,* which would rejoin them *con brio* and would jump start the second great horror cycle. In the interim, Mr. Karloff would scoot past the guard at the front gate only once—in April, 1937—when he would play Foxy Grandpa in the studio's hymn to inveterate tinkers everywhere, *Night Key.* Mr. Lugosi had had *his* only post *Ray* appearance not quite a year earlier than his rival when he had added a pittance to his bank account (and less than nothing to his reputation) with *Postal Inspector.*

Bela Lugosi's struggles during the horror cinema's dormant period have been well documented elsewhere. The quirk that few people appreciate is that, in various ways, the Briton and the Hungarian were more like two peas in a pod than two ships passing in the night. Both actors owed their fame to the horror genre, both essayed numerous memorable portrayals within that genre, both were reduced to foraging outside their usual haunts when hard times developed, and both recreated their most celebrated roles to great acclaim when horror films came back into vogue. The ultimate cosmic injustice lay not in the men themselves, but in their stars. Almost from the moment their signature roles were unveiled before an eager and receptive public, Bela had always but *always* gotten a royal screwing, while Boris had came up smelling like a rose with equal regularity.

By blurring your eyes slightly, you can see that the two actors had run a parallel track which was far more ironic and insidious than any of the generalizations outlined above. Not long after each man had taken the movie world by storm, he drew a line in the sand and challenged the powers that were to recognize that—By Thunder!—he was his own man. In an era when blind obedience was the industry norm, both Bela and Boris stood up to the studio chiefs; however, the bogies' similar actions brought on wildly *dissimilar* reactions.

In retrospect, the worst thing Bela Lugosi ever did (professionally) was to turn his back on Universal when Junior was prepared to put all the studio's eggs—*and* the then-premier horror star—into a basket marked *Frankenstein*. The Hungarian actor, ever notorious for his pride, made some concessions and briefly went along for the ride before standing up for himself. The upshot was that Junior then saw to it that Bela was relegated to second-banana status and was never again sole menace in a company feature. Nor was anything found for him at Universal during the lean years cited above, when he was reduced to walking the streets, hat in hand, in search of whatever dreary projects he could find to keep the Lugosis in their home and off the front page.

In retrospect, the *best* thing Boris Karloff ever did (professionally) was to turn his back on Universal when, following the release of *The Mummy,* Uncle Carl had proved reticent at honoring either his word or his check. The British actor had always had both pride *and* integrity and, thanks to his sticking to his guns when Laemmle balked at agreed-upon terms, soon came to have a virtual *carte blanche* to freelance at other studios. It was during his "hiatus" from Universal in the early thirties that Karloff worked for such brilliant technicians as John Ford *(The Lost Patrol)* and with such stellar personalities as George Arliss (*The House of Rothschild*). Studios like RKO Radio and United Artists profited by Karloff's presence in decidedly non-horrific roles, and the lesson was not lost on the other majors, either. Came those same lean years, Boris Karloff was always gainfully employed.

After *Dracula's Daughter,* when hen's teeth were supposedly more readily available than genre pictures, the Briton with the soulful eyes and legendary backbone found himself in one of the best, ever. Before anyone thought to tell

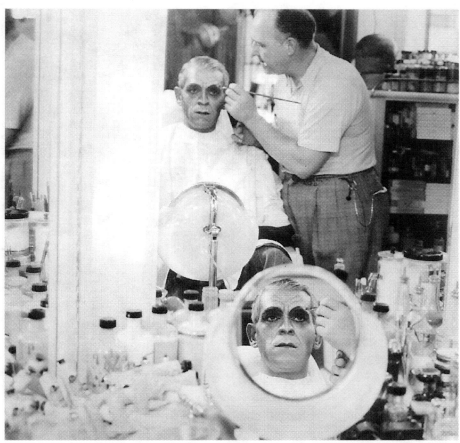

Karloff was enticed to add his unique flair to one of the world's most popular film series, Charlie Chan.

Warner Brothers that the horror film had died, the traditional home to mugs and molls had cranked out a doozy: *The Walking Dead.* One of the earliest of those reputedly non-existent "gray area" spookers not only demonstrated a strong kinship to the classic features which had preceded it, but also stood head and shoulders above the lion's share of the related product that would follow in its wake. With his John Elman resembling a kinder, gentler Frankenstein's Monster, Karloff lumbered after pathos and, under the direction of the prolific Michael Curtiz, succeeded in wringing tears where tradition had once called for necks.

The same British who had railed loudly against the actor's *Hollywood* genre output wasted no time in summoning him back to England to indulge in a couple of nobler, homespun thrillers, *The Man Who Changed His Mind* and *Juggernaut* (both 1936). (Yeah, I know that Gaumont-British initially got cold feet at the thought of their native son's lumbering where angels now dared to tread, but if the English are renowned for anything other than their straight-laced

181

Warner Oland and Boris Karloff glance over their script on the set of *Charlie Chan at the Opera.*

determination, it's for their insistence on value for money.) Karloff gratefully accepted the invitation to return home—his second such trip within five years—and gave the otherwise pedestrian efforts an imprimatur by his presence. Both films had their moments, but the former lost its clever edge when cloddishly retitled *The Man Who Lived Again* in the States, and neither made enough money outside the UK to warrant another invitation.

On his return from his beloved England, Karloff was enticed to add his unique flair to one of the world's most popular film series. Another of those "gray-area" treasures, *Charlie Chan at the Opera* marked the first (and last) time that the horror legend would darken the sound-stages of 20th Century-Fox, a surprising fact considering that the Karloff name above the title assured the Chan entry not only of outstanding revenues at the box-office but also of the sort of popular acclaim which has endured to this day. Boris *had* appeared in inconsequential roles in a couple of features for Fox Studios (20th Century-Fox in an embryonic stage), and the first of these appearances had been in a Charlie Chan film.

Actually, *Behind That Curtain* was anything but a typical Charlie Chan film for the simple reason that, prior to Warner Oland's total identification with the Chinese detective, there *were* no "typical" Charlie Chan films. Karloff's was the first adventure of the Honolulu-based sleuth to be shot in (partial) sound, but E. L. Park, the British actor assigned to essay the oriental detective, found his role nearly as minuscule as Boris's. (Karloff received billing as a "Soudanese Servant," which may not have meant a hell of a lot, but he *was* billed *above* Mr. Park.) Neither of the silent films which preceded *Behind That Curtain* gave much shrift to their Chans, and neither of the actors to be stuck with the part—the films in question offered them nothing in terms of artistic challenge and necessitated only limited screen time—can have counted the experience among his favorites.

(Both the screen's original Charlie Chan and his successor were bona fide Orientals. George Kuwa, a Japanese, introduced the Chinese criminologist to the screen in *The House Without a Key* [1926], a relatively faithful adaptation of Earl Derr Biggers' source novel, although messaged enough to fit the awkward confines of a ten chapter serial. Charlie next saw the carbon arc in *The Chinese Parrot,* adapted from the eponymous Biggers' original. This film had been directed by Paul Leni, surely among the genre's most creative lights, and had featured one of the silent screen's great eccentrics, Kamiyama Sojin, as Chan. Emaciated, sardonic, and possessed of an incredibly arch sense of humor, the Japanese magician-cum-actor had stolen every scene he had shared with Douglas Fairbanks in the American star's breath-taking *Thief of Baghdad* [1924], and, according to extant reviews, had pretty much returned to the scene of the crime in *Parrot.* Sadly, neither the Leni mystery nor the Pathe chapterplay have survived the years.)

Most folks catching *Charlie Chan at the Opera* during its first-run must have suspected mightily that Karloff was little more than a high-priced red herring, and their suspicions were, of course, correct. The call was an easy one; after all, the *other* monster man, Mr. Lugosi, had pretty much filled the same shoes (but not the same *bill*—Bela had been listed below Mr. Oland) in an earlier installment *(The Black Camel,* 1931). (For the record, it reads *Warner Oland* vs. *Boris Karloff* above the title here.) Making it even easier was the realization that screenwriters Scott Darling and Charles Belden really only had two viable alternatives from which to draw: 1) have the Briton skulk and lurk and glower, only to be ultimately found innocent of wrongdoing, or 2) ditto, ditto, ditto, but see him nailed as the heavy in the much-anticipated wrap-up. (Actually, two *other* avenues were at least possible: a) have the actor portray the most harmless of souls before being unmasked as the mystery killer, or b) have him do the milquetoast routine throughout and remain thus at the finale. Since no American mogul in his right mind would exploit the potent Karloff persona [or pay the healthy Karloff fee] without receiving at the very least a

Charlie Chan at the Opera **is arguably the most popular title in the durable series, and it wouldn't be impertinent to give a good bit of the credit to Boris Karloff.**

good shot of the actor's trademark malevolence, these "options" never got full play.)

As Boris' proving to be the psychotic killer would have been akin to having the butler actually *do* it, Darling and Belden took the only course still open to them and merrily slapped on the vermilion. Nevertheless, knowing that Gravelle would finally be absolved of every little thing didn't really make the armchair sleuthing easier for regular mystery fans; the cast was stuffed with popular character players who had forged rock-steady careers embodying guilt—or feigning innocence.

For Charlie Chan-atics, unraveling the solution to the mystery was of minor importance; after all, the series rarely succeeded in confounding its die-hard followers all the way to the end. More enjoyable were the bits of procedure which the great detective would follow religiously, no matter the enigma at hand. His pithy aphorisms—straight out of fortune cookies—came to be cherished parts of the patented Chan shtick. (One of my favorites: "Mind like parachute; only function when open.") More times than not, Charlie would set a trap for the killer, only to see his carefully laid plans gang a-gley due to the exuberant interference of his Number One Son, Lee (Keye Luke). The most enjoyable Chan tradition was also the most predictable. As the film unreeled toward its denouement, Charlie inevitably assembled the cast and, with every suspicious puss in the movie within finger-pointing distance, would usually finagle an admission of guilt on the flimsiest of circumstantial evidence.

Karloff is Gravelle, former leading baritone of the San Marco Opera Company and current inmate at the Rockland State Sanitarium. The singer has been hammering away at the asylum's baby grand for seven years now without knowing so much as who he is or how he got there. A newspaper photo of Lilli Rochelle, a prima donna returning to Los Angeles in triumph after an extended absence, puts him back on the wobbly road to total recall.

Grinding the picture under his heel, Gravelle overpowers the attendant and makes for the big city.

The newspapers follow the fugitive's progress, and the *L.A. Star* blares *Report Madman in Los Angeles,* a headline which can be taken several ways, none of them complimentary. The cops are disgusted with phony leads, there's only the sketchiest of descriptions to go on ("The asylum never takes any [pictures]," complains Sergeant Kelly [William Demarest]), and the only clue—that torn and heel-imprinted newspaper—has naturally flummoxed the police. It looks like a case for Charlie Chan.

Chan (Mr. Oland) agrees to help Inspector Regan (Guy Usher) with the investigation, especially after he's invited to do so by Lilli Rochelle (Margaret Irving) herself; the diva has stopped by the inspector's office (accompanied by fellow singer and rumored paramour, Enrico Barelli [Gregory Gaye]) to demand protection from a death threat which she found in a large basket of flowers. Regan promises a thorough search of the opera house and a highly visible police presence at the performance that night. Kelly promises nothing but makes the authorities' position clear on another matter when he grumbles, "I don't like that guy, Barelli. I think he uses perfume."

Charlie follows up the obvious lead and seeks out the floral shop whence came the bouquet and the threatening note. He discovers that while Mme. Barelli—Enrico's wife—received flowers that day, Mme. Lilli did not. He also discovers Number One Son, Lee (Keye Luke), who passes on an opportunity to send a nosegay to a young Chinese beauty in order to help his Pop.

At the theater later, things are jumping. Lee is working undercover as a supernumerary in that night's opera, *Carnival.* Kelly is acidly giving the gate to Kitty (Charlotte Henry) and Phil (Thomas Beck), a young couple insistent upon seeing Mme. Lilli "on a private matter." Angry words between Barelli and Mr. Whitely—Mme. Lilli's husband—are overheard by everyone with ears, and that includes the baritone's humiliated wife. Returning to her dressing room, the company's second soprano is confronted by Gravelle, who vows that he will sing his greatest role—Mephisto in *Carnival*—that very night. Mention of the role jars the lunatic's mind; he remembers flames... a theater in flames... and his being locked in his dressing room by his wife and Barelli and left to die!

The arrival of Charlie Chan spurs Gravelle's disappearance, and the oriental sleuth catches Mme. Barelli in what he perceives to be a lie. The soprano had claimed not to have received flowers from anyone, but a charred note and florist's tissue in her wastepaper basket make this statement suspect. Several doors away, Gravelle visits a cowed Barelli, who whines that he was not to blame for that deadly fire some fourteen years earlier. A stagehand's knock summons the baritone for his entrance, but it is a masked and cloaked Gravelle who saunters onto the stage. During his duet with Mme. Lili, Gravelle draws his dagger and apparently murders the prima donna in front of a capacity house. 'Tis all part of the show.

When the actor carrying the prostrate Mme. Lilli offstage cannot rouse her, however, all hell breaks loose. Kelly and a couple of uniforms chase Mephisto back to Barelli's room while Whitely hefts his wife's inert form back to hers. Breaking down the dressing room door, the cops find Barelli dead, stabbed through the heart; as Chan points out, the murder had taken place some time earlier, as the blood has already begun to congeal. Kelly climbs through a trapdoor found in the alcove ceiling and almost immediately falls through some weakened floorboards, landing in Mme. Lilli's dressing room; he witnesses a very nervous Phil trying to take a powder. Whitely returns, discovers that his wife has also been fatally stabbed and inadvertently helps the murderer's cause by handling the murder weapon—Mephisto's dagger—which he spots in a nearby vase of flowers.

Charlie assembles the principals and gives Phil the chance to reveal that Kitty is Mme. Lilli's daughter, and that the young couple were only trying to ask the diva's permission to wed. Kitty cries that her mother had spent her whole life distancing herself from her child and had refused to consent to the marriage, as she had feared an adverse public reaction to her having a grown daughter. The pay-off comes when the frazzled Kitty tells Chan that her father "died in a theater fire when I was four years old. He was an opera singer." Chan finds a newspaper clipping on the old opera house fire—it has occurred in Chicago, in 1923—and has Lee ask the *L.A. Bulletin* to obtain a wire photo of Gravelle. In a flash, Charlie is looking at an 8x10 glossy and maintains, mystifyingly, that "Many things now clear." The mad baritone has meantime come upon Kitty, closeted alone in a dressing room. Discomfiting the young

Peter Lorre visits his friend Boris Karloff on the set of *Charlie Chan at the Opera*.

girl no end, Gravelle begins to noodle a lullaby on a convenient piano. After squirming tearfully through more than a few moments of the singer's impassioned but vague questions, the distraught Kitty rather sensibly faints. Chan shows up not long after and plays mind games with Gravelle, convincing him to don his Mephisto costume once again and recreate that night's triumph onstage.

No one—and that includes both the members of the company and the police—understands just what is going on, but a game Mme. Barelli stands in for the fallen prima donna, and the big duet starts anew. Once that dagger begins to wend its way out of its scabbard, however, a rifle-toting cop plugs Gravelle and brings Charlie's dangerous experiment to a screeching halt.

The theater stage is emptied, but the dramatic stage is chock-a-block as Chan begins the traditional, climactic unveiling of the killer. Both murders had been committed with Barelli's dirk. Gravelle was clearly carrying only one knife, explains Charlie, and that one still has a protective coating of oil on its blade. As no bloodstains were found on his Mephisto costume, he couldn't have lugged the second dagger around on his person. "Also, madman would not use Barelli's knife, having one of his own in his scabbard. Method devised by real murderer born in rational mind..."

At first, things look pretty dim for Whitely. The widower confesses to nabbing the flowers from Mme. Barelli's room; he had re-sent them, along with the death threat, to his own wife. "I only wanted to frighten her away from Barelli," he offers. Too, Whitely had rather conveniently come upon the murder weapon and had destroyed crucial evidence by obliterating any possible fingerprints. Nevertheless, the older man has an alibi for the few minutes in which both murders had been committed; he had been standing in the wings, in plain sight of the company and the police.

Not so Mme. Barelli. Under Charlie's pointed questions, the soprano's credibility and veneer of innocence fall away like the petals of a flower. "You are murderess!" Chan intones with finality. Mme. Barelli had come upon her husband, unconscious in his dressing room, while Gravelle was singing onstage. Overcome by a desire to revenge herself for years of humiliation, she stabbed her faithless partner with his own dagger. Having hidden the knife in her costume belt (which Chan produces—replete with bloodstains—on the spot), she was asked by Whitely to fetch smelling salts for his wife. "You're right," the diva confesses, "and I used [the knife] on Lilli when I came back with the smelling salts and found her alone."

The only remaining loose end seems to be Gravelle. "Your fella got a lucky break, Inspector," advises a doctor. "The bullet never reached the brain. In fact, it may relieve the condition that's been causing amnesia." Charlie paddles over to Kitty, and puts it to her: "Innocent man, unfortunately wounded by impetuous marksman, call for daughter not seen for many years. Would please take place of missing loved one for small moment? Perhaps save life. Please?"

Kitty, of course, does the right thing, and as the door closes behind her and the fallen Gravelle, Sergeant Kelly comes over to kiss and make up. "You're all right," Kelly beams, "just like chop suey—a mystery, but a swell dish!" Amid general glee and a venerable sight gag involving visors and helmets, Charlie and Lee head off to the Los Angeles waterfront and, from there, home to Honolulu.

Charlie Chan at the Opera is arguably the most popular title in the durable series, and it wouldn't be impertinent to give a good bit of the credit to Boris Karloff. As almost every genre feature to that point had drawn upon thunderstorms, madmen and glandular music—either singly or in tandem—to buoy up its particular charms, Fox was on safe ground when it decided to incorporate them all when it pitted its formidable Chinese cash-cow against Hollywood's preeminent goblin. Nor was it merely a case of an obvious tie-in with the actor's most notorious alter-ego, although an inside joke has Mr. Arnold, the stage manager (Maurice Cass), vowing to Kelly that "This opera's going on

It's fortunate that *Opera* had the Karloff magic working for it; as a mystery, the film is no great shakes.

tonight even if Frankenstein walks in." Whether sweeping through the corridors as the Devil incarnate or moving noiselessly about musty and little-known passageways, Karloff also clearly evokes images of the Phantom of the Opera.

In many ways, it's fortunate that *Opera* had the Karloff magic working for it; as a mystery, the film is no great shakes. Time-honored rules governing red herrings forbid anyone making overt threats, mucking up evidence, or exhibiting tendencies toward violent behavior from actually pulling the trigger or slipping in the shiv. Since insipid and forgettable Phil is exempted from serious consideration (an obviously innocent man's daughter would never love a scoundrel), and since Whitely has been *way* too openly hostile, that leaves Mme. Barelli as the only act in town.

The almost careless approach to some of the film's more sensitive elements compounds the felony. Phil and Kitty are two of the least well-defined juveniles to be found in pictures of this sort, and they spend most of their time edging around the periphery of the story. What's more, from the moment they're first seen arguing with Kelly, the two are treated cavalierly by the screenplay, and this denies the viewer any real shot at understanding or even getting to know the young couple.

What was doubtless meant to be a scene of heart-tugging emotion between father and daughter—Gravelle and Kitty reunited after long years of separation—also falls to pieces and becomes a study in pigheaded stupidity. Darling and Belden might have had the baritone take his daughter's hands in his own and quietly reveal that he had, in fact, survived the fire and has returned to her. Instead, the script forces Gravelle to fart around melodramatically in the hope that some forgotten musical cues or his overindulgent moans and gropes will cause the frightened girl to realize that this raving lunatic is her dear old Dad.

Another questionable bit comes near the end, when Charlie asks whether Kitty would stand in for the wounded man's daughter. "Much better that relationship not known until recovery certain," the sleuth avers. Why? The truth could only bolster Kitty's enthusiasm and happiness which would, in turn, only increase Gravelle's chances at full recovery. Again, the screenwriters' decision to keep the truth about the two characters close to the vest does nothing for the picture's depiction of realistic behavior. Darling and Belden may be able to recount a murderer's actions effectively, but their dealings with more mundane and readily identifiable reactions leave a great deal to be desired.

In fact, there are a couple of gaping holes in the plot line which diminish the film authors' reputations still further. As *Opera* takes place in 1937 (all Charlie Chans are contemporary mysteries), and the Chicago opera house fire occurred in September, 1923, some 14 years separate the two events. If Gravelle has been institutionalized for only half that period (Regan points out the escapee had been "a charity case for the last seven years"), where had he been and what in blazes had he been doing for the identical stretch *prior* to his "amnesia"?

Blowing credibility to bits is Kelly's insistence that Rockland State Sanitarium didn't take pictures of the man later identified as Gravelle. It would seem that both logically and legally (covering one's institutional ass, you know),

the *first* step to be taken when confronted with a man with no past is to circulate all the photos and pertinent data one can in an effort to reach his loved ones. Granted, the asylum's curious policy does help Gravelle get the dramatic ball rolling, but it certainly doesn't smack of anything like true-to-life SOP.

(Fairness alert! It may well be that director H. Bruce Humberstone had removed any business about photos from an early shooting script in order to indulge in his own pet practice; he loved to insert footage of the latest scientific breakthroughs in his Chan features. The story line of *Charlie Chan at the Race Track* had allowed the director a meticulous segment on photofinish equipment and electric-eyes, and *Charlie Chan at the Olympics—Opera's* successor— would include an extended look on the latest in radio transmitters. If, indeed, some first reel authenticity had had to be sacrificed so that expository footage on the transmission of wire photographs could be justified, my apologies to the shades of Messrs. Darling and Belden.)

Another gripe concerns Chan's arranging the reenactment of the crime. When the tried and true device—an all-time favorite of fictional clicks—is properly executed, the results infallibly trip up the murderer, whose movements the second time around fail to jibe with his/her original steps. In *Opera,* the murderess is forced by Chan to undertake a *different* role than she had had during her commission of the crimes. As these circumstances *cannot* lead to any kind of valid deductions, the whole exercise does little other than endanger

Gravelle's life. For once, a discomfited Chan *deserves* the heat he takes from an exasperated Kelly: "Egg Foo Yung, the guy that pulls rabbits out of his hat, sending a woman out there to let a guy stick a knife in her!"

As it turns out, the beginning of the end for Mme. Barelli *is* marked by her absence during the crucial time being noted by Mr. Arnold. The stage manager's recollection, however, has absolutely nothing to do with the woman's singing opposite the heady Gravelle in the reenactment and only emphasizes how futile and dangerous Chan's experiment really was. The screenwriters try to fob off another detective-genre *no-no* on their audience by having a critical piece of the action—Whitely's requesting that Mme. Barelli run to find smelling salts—take place off-camera and without the cognizance of the viewer. One doesn't at all mind being "had" by mysteries which set down rules and then follow them, but having the solution require information never proffered in the first place is dirty pool.

People easily offended by ethnic jokes will likewise take offense at Sergeant Kelly's facile name-calling. The crusty cop refers to Chan as *Chop Suey* before the Chinese detective even shows his face and later tags him as *Egg Foo Yung* at least twice. A sight gag which must have had a portion of the 1937 audience in stitches involves Kelly chasing a costumed Lee Chan into a group of similarly clad extras. "It's one of these guys, and I can pick him out," the sergeant barks to a harness bull. "He's a Chinese." The gag's pay-off—*all* of the extras are Chinese (Charlie identifies the men as "honorable fraternity brothers of worthy son, incognito")—must have been as transparent to first-time ticket-holders as it was 20 minutes ago. Sometimes the pervasive nostalgia we feel for simpler times clouds the less-than-sensitive sentiments that characterized them.

Despite all the grousing, *Charlie Chan at the Opera* is a happy, inter-genre marriage. The oriental policeman had ventured into climes more properly associated with Mr. Karloff when he had detected among the pyramids in *Charlie Chan in Egypt* (1935). As expected, ancient superstitions, forbidden tombs, dusty mummies, and sarcophagi made one forget stock footage and the illogic of a Honolulu lawman operating on the banks of the Nile. Drawing on his experiences as Fu Manchu and an earlier appearance that same year as a lycanthrope in *Werewolf of London*, Warner Oland took his marginal dealings with the supernatural in stride.

Not for a moment suspected of being the villain by anyone who'd seen even one of these pictures, Karloff's macabre maniac enlivened a world many movie-goers had regarded as high-hat and uninteresting (the opera) and imbued the recherché art-form with more readily understood passions. In 1944, the Briton would star in yet another tale of madness and murder in the opera house: Universal's bloated, Technicolor disappointment, *The Climax*. For all the relative opulence of the George Waggner overproduction, Karloff's menace would pale beside his earlier, black-and-white, scenery-chewing, lip-synching lunatic, Gravelle.

An enjoyable entry in both the adventure series devoted to the eponymous sleuth and in the unofficial *Mysterious Goings-on in the Theater* sub-genre, *Charlie Chan at the Opera* is required viewing for fans of Boris Karloff, fans of Warner Oland, and for all those folks who felt that the Fat Lady had indeed sung back in May of 1936.

CREDITS: Associate Producer: John Stone; Director: H. Bruce Humberstone; Screenplay: Scott Darling and Charles Belden; From an original story by Bess Meredyth; Based on the character, Charlie Chan, created by Earl Derr Biggers; Original musical composition, *Carnival,* Oscar Levant; Libretto: William Kernell; Orchestrations: Charles Maxwell; Musical Director: Samuel Kaylin; Art Director: Duncan Cramer and Lewis Creber; Photographer: Lucien Androit; Assistant Director: Sol Michaels; Film Editor: Alex Troffey; Sound: George Leverett and Harry M. Leonard; Costumes: Herschel; Released January 8, 1937 by Twentieth Century-Fox; 67 minutes

CAST: Warner Oland...Charlie Chan, Boris Karloff...Gravelle, Keye Luke...Lee Chan, Margaret Irving...Lilli Rochelle, Guy Usher...Inspector Regan, William Demarest...Sergeant Kelly, Gregory Gaye...Enrico Barelli, Nedda Harrigan...Mme. Barelli, Frank Conroy...Mr. Whitely, Charlotte Henry...Kitty Gravelle, Thomas Beck...Phil Childers, Maurice Cass...Mr. Arnold, Tom McGuire...Morris, Fred Kelsey...Dugan, Lee Shumway...Sanitarium Guard, Emmett Vogan...Smitty, Joan Woodbury, Stanley Blystone, Selmer Jackson

John Soister has been enjoying the films and personality of Boris Karloff for over 45 years now, but has only been writing about them (and other, related topics) for two. Actually, he *used* to write about these things during the sixties—the "Golden Age" of fanzines—but he's much better at it now. Then again, that's purely a matter of opinion. By day, a teacher of modern and classical languages, John is usually asleep at night. In his spare time, he is whipping up a book on Universal's horror canon, as a housewife "whips up" an omelet.

WEST OF SHANGHAI
(1937)
THE INVISIBLE MENACE
(1938)
DEVIL'S ISLAND
(1939/40)
BRITISH INTELLIGENCE
(1940)

by Tom Weaver

The place was Hollywood, the year was 1937 and the horror genre was extinct, hounded out of existence by the yowls of censors, civic organizations and women's clubs. No individual felt the pinch more than Bela Lugosi, so completely typecast that other sorts of movies were out of the question. The "prevailing wisdom" has always been that Hollywood closed its studio gates to Poor Bela during this 1937-38 period while they continued to make room for Dear Boris, the more-versatile, "better-liked" actor. Was this the case—or was it just dumb luck that prevented Karloff from sharing Lugosi's unhappy fate?

First, a bit of "horror ban history"...

The winds of change swept first through England, where new restrictions on horror films kept children out of theaters where such films were played. Karloff had a $30,000 deal with Gaumont-British to shoot a thriller in England, but in January, 1936, it was announced that Gaumont-British had canceled the picture and was negotiating with Karloff via cable, attempting to reach a cash settlement. In other words, the company preferred paying off the screen's chief creep to having him in one of their movies. Failing to come to terms, G-B brought him to London to star in a different type of story than the horror film for which he was signed; the new film, the witty *The Man Who Changed His Mind*, relied on the thrills and humor of a mind-switching experiment. (When the producers were charged with plagiarism in 1939, the associate producer testified in court that the picture made no profit.) At the same time, Universal—also acutely aware of the growing backlash against undue horror—decided to pay off Lugosi rather than allow him to play a promised part in *Dracula's Daughter*. Lugosi took the money and ran.

On February 19, 1936, Karloff inked a new deal with Warner Brothers, the studio where he had recently starred in the chiller *The Walking Dead*. One wonders if the studio was banking on a sooner-than-later resurgence in the popularity of horror when they signed the actor; it took over a year for them to finally place him in a picture, as though they were waiting for something to happen. Universal didn't know what to do with Karloff, either; they bought a *Cosmopolitan* magazine story as a Karloff-starrer, but the actor was absent from the movie made from it (*Love Letters of a Star*, 1936). While Universal *and* Warner Brothers tried to figure out how to use their (now undesired?) contractee Karloff, he turned up in a red herring role opposite Warner Oland in 20th Century-Fox's *Charlie Chan at the Opera* (1936). On September 23, 1936, after searching for months for a non-horror vehicle for Karloff, Universal decided upon *Night Key* and ordered a revision of the script that had already been written. Karloff played the near-sighted, grandfatherly inventor of a new-fangled burglar alarm in this flyweight, C-grade comedy-drama.

"Boris Karloff is now going to be a nice man who captures murderers and crooks," *The Hollywood Reporter* disclosed on October 1. "Universal has decided to transform its horror star into a detective character and is hunting for a suitable story to introduce him in the dick role. If such a part can't be found, the studio will make Karloff into a G-man, politician or any role other than a horror one."

It should have been obvious to industry insiders that many of the jobs Karloff and Lugosi were given during this period were merely the ass-end of multiple-picture deals made during better days (prior to the horror ban). Once those contracts were fulfilled, the presence of the two horror stars on those lots was no longer required. Even Universal, despite its staunch "promise" of continuing employment for Karloff, featured him in only one movie (*Night Key*) during the *three-year* stretch between October, 1935, and November, 1938—and probably used him in *Night Key* only because they were contractually bound to use him in *some*thing. (As usual, Karloff was luckier than Lugosi, having more picture commitments "hanging fire" than his rival when the boom was lowered on horror flicks.)

There's a general consensus among aficionados that Karloff was still a desirable actor in 1937-38 and that Lugosi wasn't; it's no doubt based on a comparison of their filmographies. In that two-year period, Karloff worked in *Night Key*, *West of Shanghai*, *The Invisible Menace*, *Devil's Island* and *Mr. Wong, Detective* while Lugosi appeared only in the serial *SOS Coast Guard*. But if we want to nit-pick and be argumentative and esoteric (my specialty!), let's agree that Lugosi's 1936 Universal film *Postal Inspector* (made just prior to the period we're talking about) "cancels out" Karloff's *Night Key* and that Lugosi's

Fang was among Karloff's first comic film roles and is certainly one of his best.

Poverty Row *SOS Coast Guard* "cancels out" Karloff's Poverty Row *Wong*. *Now* all that's left Karloff-wise are the three Warner Brothers movies—commitments left over from a contract signed when Warners probably still hoped to place him in horror movies. All of these Warners films—plus the fourth, *British Intelligence*—were cheapies cranked out by Bryan Foy, the studio's indefatigable "Keeper of the B's." This is *sheer speculation*, but I'd be willing to bet that the Brothers Warner rued the day they signed up Dear Boris, and they decided that placing him in these economical, low-profile second features was the quickest, most painless way to honor the contract and have done with him. (It's interesting, and not too surprising, that no studio wanted either Lugosi *or* Karloff cluttering up their bigger, better films, even in small parts.) Without the Warners deal, Karloff probably would have been every bit the dead duck Lugosi was during the years of the horror ban.

West of Shanghai, the first of the four Karloff-Warners under discussion here, was derived "FROM A PLAY BY PORTER EMERSON BROWNE" according to the opening credits (spelled out in exotic calligraphy over artwork of a Chinese dragon, accompanied by Oriental music). It's clear that Warners

197

Despite its plot absurdities, *West of Shanghai* is the best of these four Karloff pictures for Warners.

didn't want audiences to know that the unspecified play was actually Browne's famous Western "The Bad Man," the story of kind-hearted Mexican bandit Pancho Lopez—already filmed as *The Bad Man* in 1923 and 1930, the latter version starring Walter Huston. With the Sino-Japanese war monopolizing headlines in 1937, Browne's tale was transposed to China and the star role (played by Karloff) became that of bandit general Wu Yen Fang, the "White Tiger" of Northern China. With John Farrow directing from a script by Crane Wilbur, production began on March 8, 1937.

"China is a vast country with far-flung borders. To the north, beyond the reach of steel rails, is a region sparsely inhabited but rich in oil and mineral deposits. An area very difficult to police! In *every* country, such a frontier has its adventurers, and China is no exception. With their followers, in uniforms made to look as much as possible like those of regular troops, men with illusions of military grandeur assume false military titles, and ape the manners of high-ranking officers. The career of such a bandit is a short one, for the efficient Chinese government soon runs him to earth."

This narration having "set the stage" (and given away the ending!), *West of Shanghai* begins with Americans Gordon Creed (Ricardo Cortez), Myron Galt (Douglas Wood) and his daughter Lola (Sheila Bromley) boarding the Suiyuan train en route to the northern province where Jim Hallet (Gordon Oliver) has made a fabulous oil strike. (Even though the movie appears to have a contemporary setting, the then-current real-life Sino-Japanese war plays no part in it.) The unscrupulous Galt, who loaned Hallet the money to begin drilling, now intends to foreclose, and the even *more* unscrupulous Creed intends to get there first and offer Hallet $50,000 for a partnership. The three travelers share a compartment with Chow Fu-shan (Vladimir Sokoloff), a Chinese general who is stabbed and killed in his sleep during a brief blackout. General Mu (Tetsu Komai) suspects Creed, Galt and Lola until Mu's men locate the actual killer (Eddie Lee)—one of the spies of Wu Yen Fang, the infamous bandit general. The spy is caught and executed.

Proceeding by mule train, the Americans make their way to Hallet's base at Sha-Ho-Shen, where—by one of those amazing coincidences that seem to exist only in B movies—Creed's estranged wife Jane (Beverly Roberts) happens to work as an apprentice missionary. Jane and Hallet are in love, but romance is prevented by the fact that Jane doesn't believe in divorce. Fang and his marauders swoop down on the walled town and take over, setting up headquarters in Mr. Abernathy's (Gordon Hart) mission and imprisoning the Americans.

Fang speaks pidgin-English, uses American slang, is corrupt but personable and enjoys, between massacres, being a do-gooder. He remembers that when he was a coolie, Hallet saved his life, so he tears up Galt's foreclosure note, "relieves" Creed of his $50,000 and offers it to Mr. Abernathy. When the roguish Creed foments a rebellion, Fang (who has taken an interest in Hallet and Jane's frustrated romance) uses that as an excuse to kill him, thereby enabling Hallet and Jane to eventually marry. General Mu and his troops take back the town, Fang surrenders and bravely faces Mu's firing squad.

Despite its plot absurdities, *West of Shanghai* is the best of these four Karloff-Warners. Like Walter Huston in *The Bad Man* seven years before, Karloff carries the show; Wu Yen Fang may be the scourge of Northern China and the killer of thousands of men, but he's a charming and even-handed mass murderer, and his aspirations toward being a Robin Hood and even a Cupid are endearing. (Karloff turns every "r" into an "l" as called for in the script, which is filled with phonetic spellings like "Evelything all light!" and "We dlink, my fliends.") It would take more effort than this author is willing to expend to find out whether Karloff's best lines came from Browne's play or from the pen of *West of Shanghai* screenwriter Crane Wilbur, but the droll delivery and the expert timing can unquestionably be credited to Karloff; Fang was among his first comic film roles and is certainly one of his best. Perhaps his shining moment comes when Beverly Roberts asks, "How did a coolie so soon become the great General Fang?" and Karloff off-handedly explains his rise through the ranks of the rebel army: "One day, the captain is killed. *I* become captain. Next day the major. *I* am major. By and by, the colonel. *I* become colonel." He then adds, in a confidential, parenthetical tone, "I kill the general myself!" Whether proposing a toast to himself, congratulating himself on leading the "mos' dang best army China" or indulging in a self-infatuated "I am Fang!", Karloff gives the sort of winning performance you don't find in many other Karloffilms.[1]

"...Boris Karloff admirably acquits himself as a comedian in *West of Shanghai*," wrote *The New York Times'* reviewer. "With infinite gallantry and urbanity, Mr. Karloff plays a Mongolized version of [*The Bad Man*]—a lovable, charming and ridiculous Chinese war lord. ...[I]t is the subtly comical work of Mr. Karloff, the nice inflections, the war-lordly economy of gesturing, which gives to *West of Shanghai* its modest value as a comic-melodramatic, if not, perhaps, as a strictly contemporary document." *Harrison's Reports* agreed that the film's chief virtue "lies in the performance given by Boris Karloff; he makes the part both sinister and comical."

"He's genial and good-natured and—despite the fact that he does a little killing now and then—a rather likable fellow on the whole," reported the *Brooklyn Daily Eagle*; *The New York Sun* concurred that Karloff had "a sense of humor and a surprising quality of gratitude." England's *Kinematograph Weekly* opined, "Boris Karloff has a difficult role to play as the big-hearted Wu Fang, but he surmounts all histrionic obstacles. His performance has strength and fascination."

Saddled with non-flashy, stereotypical parts, the other performers simply can't compete with the blustery, engaging Karloff. Ricardo Cortez (previously seen opposite Karloff in *The Walking Dead*) is appropriately unsavory as the slick financier, glib and surface-charming but also condescending and manipulative. (From the script: "[Creed] is a type frequently met within the outlands of China, sharp shooters in finance who are out for no good but their own.") Cortez plays him as such a smug scoundrel that the only suspense felt when Karloff climactically levels his gun at him is that he *won't* fire. None of "the young people" (Beverly Roberts, Gordon Oliver, Sheila Bromley) are particularly memorable, but Richard Loo gives an effective deadpan performance as

Cheng, a Chinese-American gangster who speaks Oxford English and who now (as bodyguard to Karloff) has taught the war lord gangland slang. Vladimir Sokoloff, a Russian playing a Chinese, makes his minutes on-screen count in his minor role as Chow Fu-shan, and Tetsu Komai (the dog-man M'ling in *Island of Lost Souls*) is suitably ruthless as the general on Fang's trail.

John Farrow was newly-married to actress Maureen O'Sullivan (but not yet the father of Mia Farrow) when he directed *West of Shanghai* in March, 1937. The unspoiled California scenery and the hordes of Chinese extras provide his film with picturesque backdrops; Farrow and photographer L. W. O'Connell offer a lengthy tracking shot through a train, a point-of-view shot (Karloff's) of the climactic firing squad execution and other nice visual touches which enhance the 65-minute proceedings.

Most of the reviews "exposed" *West of Shanghai* as a Chinese revamp of *The Bad Man*. *Variety* cited Karloff's performance as the renegade ("His work is distinguished for the character he cuts, his makeup being excellent, and for the lightness of touch the actor is able to give the interpretation...") but branded the movie itself a "slow-moving, poorly produced B." The *New York World-Telegram* and *Harrison's Reports* more or less agreed; the former complained, "While [Karloff] does a good job in the role, the film is at best a feeble blend of melodrama and comedy," and the latter chimed in: "There is not much to recommend in this one." *The New York Sun* was more generous (and, in my opinion, closer to the mark): "There's melodrama [in *West of Shanghai*], plenty of it, and, for an inexpensive film, not bad melodrama." For everyone, however, the big "surprise" in *West of Shanghai* was Karloff, who for "probably the first time in his career reveals a sense of humor—a quite pleasant way of being droll" (*The New York Post*). Karloff does just that in *West of Shanghai*, making it one of his very *best* "forgotten" (or, at least, "overlooked") films.[2]

•   •   •   •   •

The mixed critical reaction to *West of Shanghai* didn't deter Bryan Foy from re-teaming Karloff with director Farrow and screenwriter Crane Wilbur on another B, *The Invisible Menace*. The problem with this new Karloffilm was that the menace was just slightly more invisible than suspense, pacing and entertainment values. While *West of Shanghai* ranks with some of Karloff's most under-appreciated films, *Invisible Menace* sizes up as one of his worst from the '30s. With a running time of 54 minutes, it's perhaps Karloff's shortest-ever film, and yet it seems endless.

A 1937 Broadway play by Ralph Spencer Zink, "Without Warning," furnished writer Wilbur with his starting point for this mild mystery. Soldier Eddie Pratt (Eddie Craven) smuggles his new wife Sally (Marie Wilson) onto the government arsenal on foggy Powder Island, and the two search for a lonely spot to spend their wedding night. Amidst the shadows of the Experimental Building, the young scatterbrains discover the mutilated corpse of Reilly, an ordnance expert tortured to death with bayonet jabs. Sally's scream brings a Private (William Haade) a-running, the Private calls the Lieutenant (Regis Toomey), the Lieutenant calls the Colonel (Henry Kolker) and the Colonel phones an intelligence officer (Cy Kendall) who flies in from Washington by seaplane to help unravel the mystery.

Evidence indicates that Reilly was a gunrunner while the wandering finger of suspicion points to Jevries (Karloff), a saturnine construction supervisor. The intelligence officer remembers that, years before in Haiti, Jevries was a drunkard who abused native workers, embezzled government money and went to jail. (Even though the intelligence officer is telling the story, the accompanying flashbacks show that Jevries was framed for embezzlement by the real thief—Reilly—who also stole Jevries' wife.) The intelligence officer shoves and slaps and punches Jevries around at every opportunity, but he doesn't confess to the new crime.

Lots of "little things" happen to keep interest up: A hand grenade, set to explode upon handling, is discovered... a packing crate is pushed from a loft, nearly crushing the investigators... a rifle barrel occasionally pokes through an opening and fires at someone or something. Whenever the picture builds up a tiny head of steam, however, newlyweds Eddie and Sally are inflicted upon us once again for more "comic relief." (Eddie's such a sissified, squeaky little dork, you never get the impression he'd know what to do if he ever *did* manage to get Sally alone!)

The Lieutenant tells Jevries that he thinks he's being railroaded and will help him escape. This tips off Jevries that the Lieutenant is the killer, and he quietly summons the intelligence officer. Using Sally as a shield, the Lieutenant tries to shoot his way out, plugging Jevries. But the intelligence officer and other soldiers move in and the Lieutenant is shot and killed. (The Lieutenant was the gunrunner, and Reilly wanted to be cut in. Instead, he got cut *up*.) Apologies are made to the wounded Jevries, and the Colonel gives Eddie and Sally a tent of their own. It's seen in the fade-out shot, with poker-faced soldiers standing guard outside it while a bugler plays "Reveille" ("I can't get 'em up, I can't get 'em up...").

The Invisible Menace is a depressingly minor movie, with Karloff wasted as the pinkest of red herrings. Sporting glasses, a head of white hair and an unattractive close-cut haircut, he's a gloomy presence hanging around the edges of scenes, continually being ordered around by the Colonel (and later slapped around by the intelligence officer). Since the character is so put-upon, so high on everybody's list of suspects, and since Karloff is playing the role, even the greenest of armchair sleuths knows instinctively that he can't be the killer.

That's the funny thing about *Invisible Menace*, however. People who watch too much TV know that in a movie of this sort and of this vintage, a man in military uniform *never* turns out to be the killer; that leaves Jevries (Karloff)

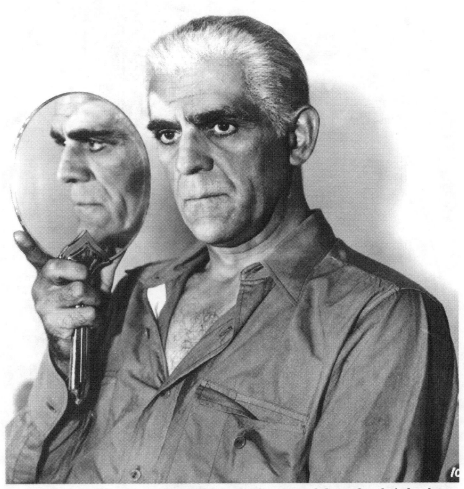

In *The Invisible Menace* **Karloff fans don't get much bang for their buck.**

and a doctor (played by Charles Trowbridge), the only two characters dressed in civvies. And yet at the end, the killer *does* turn out to be a soldier—the Lieutenant—who was also a gunrunner. The murdered soldier was a gunrunner *and* an embezzler *and* a perjurer. The intelligence officer is a brute who repeatedly tries to beat a confession out of the innocent Jevries. Soldiers who witness these beatings promise to testify that Jevries wasn't touched. Army investigators send the wrong man up the river for ten years. Jevries is a drunk, a brutalizer of men and a convicted embezzler who, after merely changing his name, has been given a top job on a high-security army base. The "comic relief" is a moronic pansy of a soldier who brings a girl onto the base to have intercourse with her. The other privates we see are drinkers and dumb clucks. Without wishing to sound like we're hinting at a subversive undercurrent, it

203

The Invisible Menace **wastes Karloff as the pinkest of red herrings.**

seems that *some*body involved in the writing of *Invisible Menace* had no love for Uncle Sam or This Man's Army. One wonders if the script was submitted to the military for approval (scripts involving the armed forces usually were); it doesn't seem likely that any army official would look kindly upon the fact that nearly every uniformed character in *The Invisible Menace* is a nincompoop, a sadist, a gunrunner, or a killer.

Karloff fans don't get much bang for their buck: For most of the movie he simply alternates between shadowy background figure and punching bag. His best scenes are found in the Haiti flashbacks (he's a punching bag there, too!) and at the end, when he turns "hero" for about 15 seconds before being shot by Regis Toomey. (The script features a different ending in which Jevries goes armed into his face-off with the Lieutenant. Jevries shoots and kills the Lieutenant but is fatally wounded himself. "At least—I've made good at something—!" he smiles moments before he dies.)

The supporting cast is better than *West of Shanghai*'s, but once again there just aren't any good roles to be had. Marie Wilson specialized in this sort of "dumb blonde" role, most conspicuously as "My Friend Irma" in movies and on TV. (Her *Invisible Menace* part was first assigned to Jane Wyman.) The familiar faces of Toomey, Henry Kolker, Eddie Acuff, Frank Faylen and John Harron drift through the darkness and the dullness, peeking out from under private/lieutenant/colonel hats. Badly miscast is Cy Kendall as the intelligence officer. A specialist at playing slimy, triple-chinned ganglords, he can't be taken seriously here as the U.S. government's top sleuth (even though his investigative tactics are not too different from the strong-arm methods he employed in his crime films). Dressed in evening clothes and talking about his guest of honor status at a Washington soiree, the actor looks no more "in his element" than a gorilla squeezed into a suit of armor. (A bit of trivia: Kendall played Charlie Chan on radio, and was briefly a contender for the role of the *movie* Chan after Warner Oland's death in 1938.)

The cards, of course, were stacked high against *The Invisible Menace* right from the start, since it's the sort of mystery tale where each act of mayhem can be committed only by unseen hands and/or in the dark. The whole story takes place at night, in the fog, and even when characters are inside buildings, they often don't turn on the lights. Characters tote lanterns from the site of one mishap to another, always too late for them (or *us*) to catch a glimpse of anyone in the act; the mutilated body of Reilly is kept off-camera while characters wince at it in horror, the audience having been deemed too queasy to be allowed a peek. Toss in the depressing, un-funny comic hijinks of Eddie Craven (a carry-over from the cast of the play) and Marie Wilson, and *The Invisible Menace* crosses into the category of "negative entertainment." Just as bad is *Invisible Menace*'s 1943 remake *Murder on the Waterfront*, but at least *that* ran only *49* minutes. (In the remake, John Loder played the "Karloff role.")

Variety was right to call *Invisible Menace* "undistinguished," wrong to suggest that Marie Wilson "should have been injected in more scenes to relieve the monotony of seeing so many and so much of army uniforms." Rose Pelswick of the *New York Journal-American* reported that "...Mr. Karloff is neither invisible nor menacing in this picture. Customers who settle down expecting to be scared will find themselves feeling sorry for him." The *New York Daily News*' Wanda Hale gave it two stars but complained, "Boris Karloff can make a murder picture mysterious but he can't make it good if the plot is as unreasonable as that of *The Invisible Menace.*" *The New York Post* enjoyed the movie much more than any of the rival papers' reviewers: "Mr. Karloff is a most maligned gentleman in the picture, and unless you suspect him, you'll feel mighty sorry for the poor fellow. He has such a nice English accent. ...John Farrow directed swiftly and with a good sense of the spooky and the comic."

• • • • •

Karloff's next Warners movie also had an island setting: *Devil's Island.* A rocky real-life islet off the Atlantic coast of French Guiana, the "island of dread" was part of the notorious French penal settlement; its most famous prisoner was Alfred Dreyfus, the French army officer unjustly condemned for treason, who arrived in 1895. The island was occasionally featured in movies throughout the 1920s and '30s, perhaps most notably Goldwyn's *Condemned* (1929) with Ronald Colman and Ann Harding and *The Life of Emile Zola* (1937), the multi-Oscared tale of Zola's (Paul Muni) crusade to free the unjustly-exiled Dreyfus (Joseph Schildkraut). (Horror fans may want to add to this list Tod Browning's 1936 fantasy *The Devil-Doll.*)

In 1936, Rene Benoit was one of five prisoners who escaped from Devil's Island—but the only one of the five to make his escape good. Benoit wrote a book, "Dry Guillotine," which became a non-fiction best-seller. Transportation of prisoners to French penal colonies was abolished by a decree of June 17, 1938; Bryan Foy, well-known for his passion for topicality, outdid even himself by getting *Devil's Island* into production just days after that date. France admonished Warners not to make the movie but the studio, which had a well-deserved reputation for timely and socially-conscious pictures, fearlessly forged ahead. Dramatically, however, *Devil's Island* never strays far from the beaten path of the genre; the plot is slightly similar to that of *Condemned* (revolving around a prisoner, the iron-handed warden, and the warden's wife). The circumstances leading to protagonist Karloff's incarceration seem to be patterned after the story of John Wilkes Booth and Dr. Mudd, recently dramatized in 20th Century-Fox's 1936 *The Prisoner of Shark Island.*

A written foreword advises viewers that *Devil's Island* is "of purely fictional material" and that it pictures a time "now past." Political revolutionary Gustave LeBrun (Stuart Holmes) is condemned to banishment and forced labor on Devil's Island, but his friends rescue him from the train delivering him to the port of embarkation. When LeBrun is wounded in the getaway, his friends pay a call on Dr. Charles Gaudet (Karloff), a famous French brain surgeon and friend to LeBrun. (Karloff sports a mustache and a curly black mop of hair *à la The Invisible Ray.*) Answering the call of duty, Gaudet rushes to the cellar where the dying LeBrun is hidden, and refuses to leave his patient even when the police begin to close in. Gaudet soon finds himself in the prisoner's dock at the Palais de Justice, charged with aiding and abetting. The trial is short, Gaudet's sentence long. Gaudet makes an impassioned speech before he's led away; the camera tilts up to the French motto LIBERTE, EGALITE, FRATERNITE on the wall above the head of the court president.

Shorn of his mustache, Gaudet arrives on Devil's Island and is assigned to timber cutting. Conditions are dehumanizing, the guards are sadistic and the warden, Colonel Lucien (James Stephenson), is a martinet guilty of graft, of brutality, and of being not-nice to his good-hearted wife Madame Lucien (Nedda Harrigan). (Funny how the fiends who run B-movie penal colonies always manage to have compassionate, disapproving wives!) Gaudet is on hand when the Luciens' little daughter Collette (Rolla Gourvitch) is thrown from a runaway carriage, sustaining a brain injury. A prisoner revolt breaks out but is just as quickly put down, and Gaudet is among the men sentenced to die for their part in the rebellion. But Collette's condition worsens and Colonel Lucien, who wants Gaudet to operate, is forced to agree to the convict's demand that he (Gaudet) and the other condemned men be spared. Collette's life is saved but Gaudet soon finds himself a prisoner in one of the dreaded "pits" (in-ground cages).

Madame Lucien has the right appreciative attitude, however, and she makes arrangements for Gaudet and others to attempt an escape. Gaudet and his pals, fleeing in an open boat across the Atlantic, eventually run out of gas and, worse luck, get picked up by a ship bound (where else?) for Devil's Island. Colonel Lucien realizes that Gaudet now Knows Too Much about the brutal and corrupt conditions on the island and orders his execution; Gaudet is placed under the guillotine. But another revolt breaks out at the proverbial last moment, and one prisoner sticks a rifle under the descending blade, saving Gaudet's life. The honest and principled new minister of colonies (Robert Warwick), brought to the island by Madame Lucien, now makes a timely entrance, and the jig is up for Colonel Lucien. Improved conditions are promised and Gaudet receives his pardon.

Despite *Devil's Island*'s meliorative foreword and the Pollyanna finish, the French government expressed outrage over the film. Warners considered shooting retakes in order to smooth things over, but by December, 1938, it was being announced in the trades that the studio had rejected that idea and was now planning to release *Devil's Island* in the United States regardless of all foreign opposition. In the pages of *The Hollywood Reporter*, an executive who refused to be named said regarding foreign distribution, "We will consider the foreign angle later. We have not definitely decided to release it on the other side, and in order to do it, we may or may not reshoot some sequences for that purpose." *The Reporter* reviewed the film on December 31: "The most creditable thing about the picture is that it moves fast due to the good direction of William Clemens, who wastes no time in dragging out the horror and tortures, and also to the excellent casting. Boris Karloff, in a sympathetic role, is very acceptable."

The continuing protests of French consular attachés in this country caused Warners to recall *Devil's Island* on the eve of its February, 1939, New York premiere. The situation continued to escalate, culminating in a startling headline which stretched across the entire front page of the April 6, 1939, *Hollywood Reporter*: **FRANCE BANS WARNERS PIX**.

Carrying a Paris dateline, the accompanying article began, "The threatened ban of Warners pictures as a result of the partial American release of *Devil's Island* became a reality yesterday when orders were issued refusing all releasing permits to any Warners pictures for a period of two months. An official, high in the Government, who asked that his name not be linked with the story, stated, 'We warned Warners not to make the picture, and after we found they had disregarded this warning, we told them that should the picture be given exhibition any place in the world we would be compelled to retaliate through some restrictions on their distribution in France. This order is our answer, and it proves we meant what we said.'" According to the article, the Warners home office confirmed that it was asked by the French government not to make *Devil's Island*, but when France announced it was going to do away with the penal colony, Warners felt a picture depicting it would not be offensive. The next day's *Reporter* carried a front-page item revealing that *Devil's Island* had been taken off the programs of several Quebec theaters after the French general consul protested its showing.

(*Karloff: The Man, The Monster, The Movies* by Denis Gifford, *The Films of Boris Karloff* by Richard Bojarski and other sources assert that the French *were* able to bring enough pressure on Warner Bros. that the studio cut some sequences and reshot and added others. This author has found nothing to substantiate those claims; the estimable "American Film Institute Catalog" makes no mention of cuts or retakes, and the December 1938 *Hollywood Reporter* review seems to match the film perfectly.)

This tempest, unfortunately, leads viewers to expect in *Devil's Island* a courageous exposé, done in the fabled no-holds-barred Warners tradition. It's an efficient, well-paced B-movie, make no mistake about that, but by and large it gets by on the same sort of standard melodramatics that you find in movies like, say, *Island of Doomed Men* (1940) and other run-of-the-reel B's with exotic prison settings.

Karloff does a good job as the unjustly condemned surgeon, perhaps enjoying his best moment when he rails against the French justice system in the moments following the pronouncing of his sentence. The character arrives on Devil's Island with a chip on his shoulder, however, and his big mouth gets him into a lot of trouble that you or I could have easily (and gratefully) avoided; you begin to get the impression that the renowned head doctor might have a screw or two loose himself. He ably takes charge during the ocean-going escape attempt, thinking ahead and maintaining discipline even after it's discovered

In *Devil's Island* Karloff does a good job as the unjustly condemned surgeon.

that the gasoline barrels are actually filled with water. But these clichéd scenes of Karloff and Friends weathering the perils of a rear-projected Atlantic underline viewers' growing suspicion that *Devil's Island* is essentially a commonplace second feature and not the revealing "social document" that the well-reported trans-oceanic feudin' and fightin' may have led them to hope for. (According to Bojarski's *Films of Karloff*, producer Foy first slated George Raft to star, but it's awfully tough to imagine Raft playing—or even being *asked* to play—a French brain surgeon.)

Female lead Nedda Harrigan (Madame Lucien) rubbed elbows with the horror greats early and often, playing a comic relief maid in the stage *Dracula* opposite Bela Lugosi and then acting with Karloff in *Charlie Chan at the Opera* and *Devil's Island.* Married to actor Walter Connolly when she made *Devil's Island*, she became a widow in 1940 and then the wife of playwright Joshua Logan in 1945. Widowed again, she died in 1989. Three years away from *his* untimely death, British-born stage actor James Stephenson fills the bill adequately in the colorless role of the self-serving warden; Stephenson's Colonel Lucien is reminiscent of Raymond Massey's island governor in Goldwyn's *The Hurricane* (1937), another movie from which *Devil's Island*'s writers may have taken some plot pointers. The supporting cast is dotted with lots of great "I-know-that-face-but-what's-his-*name?*" character actors, among them Edward Keane, Robert Warwick, Pedro de Cordoba, John Harmon, George Lloyd, Leonard Mudie, Egon Brecher, Frank Reicher, Harry Cording and John Hamilton. Adia Kuznetzoff, the Festival singer in *Frankenstein Meets the Wolf Man*, gets fourth-billing and perhaps his best screen role as a prisoner who goes to the guillotine for killing an abusive guard.

By waiting until the war in Europe intensified, Warners was finally able to release *Devil's Island* in 1940 without ruffling many (or *any*) further French feathers. "The picture most likely will gain some boxoffice benefit from the publicity attendant to its withdrawal," *Variety*'s Char predicted, "but intrinsically it is just another meller of the dreaded isle down in the Caribbean. ...The story is of the most obvious character and in some respects overdrawn." *The New York Times* was in accord: "[T]he drama is savagely realistic. It is only when the convicts make the traditional break for freedom that the tension abates... Mr. Karloff contributes a sterling characterization." *The New York Post* sniped, "It is being touted as an 'uncensored' version. But there is nothing in it that could startle a well-protected child of seven or give pause even to a censor. ...This picture sort of reminds you of a secondhand Dreyfus case with the politics out and only the suffering left. It's not quite enough."

After all the indignation expressed by the French government, they rescinded their promise to abolish the real Devil's Island and in fact resumed sending prisoners there; the last unfortunates didn't leave until 1953. The island was later promoted as a winter resort and today has a growing tourist trade.

• • • • •

By the time Warners was starting to plan their next Karloff movie, Universal had just released *Son of Frankenstein* (1939); that third Monster movie was doing the biggest box office business in the history of horror pictures in its key city openings, with holdovers being chalked up on every playdate. It now made perfect sense for Warners to place Karloff at the head of the cast of a new

In *British Intelligence,* Karloff as the unctuous servant/spy limps around, hangs up coats, leers at people, and consorts with the milkman (Clarence Derwent).

horror opus, and for a brief time in January, 1939, they were announcing that he would top-line *Dark Tower*, a "horror special" for the Bryan Foy unit. In mid-February the studio was mulling between *Dark Tower* and *The Return of Doctor X* for Karloff. Then, just weeks later, the final decision was made and production began on Warners' newest Karloff vehicle: *Enemy Agent*, a cheap, confusing potboiler about British Intelligence operations in World War I!

This last Warners-Karloffilm, released as *British Intelligence*, is the worst of these four, so of course this *had* to be the one to fall into the public domain and become available on pre-record and laser disc. Like *West of Shanghai* and *The Invisible Menace*, it too was based on a play, "Three Faces East" by Anthony Paul Kelly. (Kelly's play had already been filmed twice, in 1925 and 1930, the latter a Warner Brothers production with Constance Bennett and Erich von Stroheim.) *British Intelligence* reduces the play to near-total incomprehensibility; it's the *Kiss Me Deadly* of Boris Karloff movies. All you have to do to end your sleepless nights is to curl up with *British Intelligence*, which will induce unconsciousness as a welcome relief.

During World War I, British Intelligence is confounded at every turn by the mysterious Franz Strendler, a German spy so elusive that no one knows what he looks like. Frank Bennett (Bruce Lester), an English pilot, is assigned to pick up a British spy operating behind German lines. (When an officer asks Frank if he really wants to accept this dangerous mission, he pipes up, "Of course, sir. Democracy and all that, you know!" The dialogue never gets much better than this.) Overhearing the entire conversation is a gardener (his face unseen) who, of course, turns out to be Strendler; he alerts the Germans and Frank's plane is shot down. The flier recuperates in a field hospital where he falls in love with his nurse Helene (Margaret Lindsay).

Helene is next seen in Berlin: She's a German spy (gasp!), and she's assigned to infiltrate the London home of Cabinet minister Arthur Bennett (Holmes Herbert). Posing as Frances Hautry, an escapee from a German internment camp, she is welcomed as a houseguest by the Bennetts and their servant Valdar (Karloff). Valdar, another victim of German cruelty, has a bayonet scar on his face, a French accent, a limp, poor posture and an even poorer grasp of the English language ("Please to come in!"). But Valdar later turns out to be Schiller, another servant of the Fatherland; the first thing he does is lecture Frances on the importance of always calling him Valdar:

VALDAR: Even when we talk like this, *always* I r-r-remain
Valdar the ser-r-rvant! The only way to be someone you
ar-r-re not is to be that per-r-rson always, even in the
pr-r-resence of fr-r-riends!
FRANCES: But tell me, Schiller...
VALDAR: *Valdar*!!

By now, of course, since Karloff is playing the role, we begin to suspect that Valdar, who is really Schiller, is *really* really Strendler. But later, alone in an office with Bennett and British Intelligence chief Yeats (Leonard Mudie), Valdar straightens up and loses the limp and the accent, and you realize he's an English spy masquerading as a German spy masquerading as a French servant. But then again, maybe he's a German spy masquerading as an English spy masquerading as a German spy masquerading as a French servant. Come to think of it, maybe Frances isn't what *she* appears to be, either. The movie goes on and on and *on* in this vein, and you just know that everyone involved knew that the story made no sense. You feel your blood pressure rising.

Frank, the flier Frances/Helene nursed back to health, turns out to be the son of Arthur Bennett (a billion-to-one shot!); he comes home and recognizes Frances, a new plot development which goes nowhere.

While a secret meeting of all the Cabinet ministers is taking place in the Bennett home, Valdar pulls a gun on Frances and leads her down into the cellar, where he lays his cards on the table: He's not an English spy after all, he's Strendler, a German spy posing as an English spy posing as a German spy posing as a French servant. Satisfied that Frances is loyal to Germany, he plants a time bomb to destroy the house and the cabinet ministers. But Frances turns out to be an English spy posing as a German spy (etc., etc.) and *she* now springs into action, siccing the minions of the law on Valdar. The time bomb is tossed out a window onto the lawn, where its puny detonation makes a hole just a tad bigger than the average New York City pothole. As German zeppelins begin bombing London, Valdar flees to his nearby spy headquarters, which is blown to bits by one of the German bombs.

More than one printed synopsis states that the ending finds Margaret Lindsay and Bruce Lester stopping Karloff by sacrificing their own lives, which is wrong; Lindsay gets off without a scratch, and Lester isn't in *any* of the final scenes. Denis Gifford writes that Lindsay is shot. Richard Bojarski calls the master spy ("Strendler") "Schiller" and the A.F.I. book calls him "Shindler." *Variety*'s review mixes up "Schiller" and "Strendler," and says Karloff is shot down while fleeing arrest. Doesn't *any*body watch the movies they review??

This complicated story of plots, counterplots, anti-counterplots, double, triple and quadruple agents makes for one of the all-time worst Karloff movies. Like *The Invisible Menace*, it's a film that makes every character look bad: The British operatives can't prevent a Cabinet minister from filling his home and office with German spies. The Germans, not to be outdone, go to great lengths to plant a tiny time bomb grossly inadequate to its task of blowing up a large house, and later bomb their own London hideout. Even though Margaret Lindsay turns out to be a British agent at the end, we've seen her help Karloff steal secret papers which enabled the Germans to bomb a giant munitions dump and kill all the workers. The more you try to analyze the plot, the screwier and dumber it gets; you *know* that no one in the real British Intelligence service read and okayed *this* script. (As the fighting in Europe escalated in the late 1930s, Warners movies were constantly beating the war drums; even a pirate picture like Errol Flynn's *The Sea Hawk* managed to slip in a "let's-get-over-there-and-fight!" message. *British Intelligence* features so many thinly veiled references to Hitler, it's difficult to keep in mind that the movie is about the *first* World War, not the *second*.)

It's tough to derive any pleasure from Karloff's performance as the unctuous servant/spy; he limps around, hangs up coats, leers at people and consorts with the milkman (another German agent), speaking the whole time in that bogus French accent; without knowing if he's a good or a bad guy, you aren't sure whether to root for or against him. "Valdar" has a deep facial scar, a gruesome makeup undoubtedly inspired by Erich von Stroheim's forehead scar in *Three Faces East*, the earlier Warners version of the Anthony Paul Kelly play. But since von Stroheim's scar was *real*, the result of a fencing accident, Karloff's seems to be poking fun at von Stroheim's misfortune. (If the *British Intelligence* team had remembered the big real-life cyst on the back of von

With *British Intelligence* in the can, Karloff's deal with Warners was at an end.

Stroheim's fuzzy head, Karloff might have had *that*, too!) Warners' decision to give him the lead in *British Intelligence* during the onset of a new horror boom can only be described as bizarre; even Monogram had enough smarts to re-move Karloff from the shiny wigs of the *Mr. Wong* series and re-route him into a horror flick, *The Ape*.

Margaret Lindsay gives a good performance as the female espionage agent, but both she and Karloff seem to switch allegiances so many times that the film becomes totally exasperating. The stiffness of the British supporting players' upper lips is matched only by their acting; this is the sort of stuffy, outdated movie where people wear tuxedos when lounging in their own homes at midnight. If the English were really like this, the sun would have set on the British Empire long before it actually did.

The dedicated scrounger, determined to get at least a few laughs out of the proceedings, might be amused by the ancient, fast-motion clips of trench warfare which kick off the movie, or by the silly grab-bag of clips seen during the climactic blitz-bombing of London (negatively printed shots of bombs falling from a zeppelin, detonations intercut with footage of a giant street brawl— even a shot of an exploding storefront lifted from *The Public Enemy*!). Despite Valdar's angry lecture, Frances never *does* stop calling him Schiller. The dialogue is embarrassingly bad ("England's lost a good man in Thompson!"), and so were most of the reviews. One of the few places it was praised was *Variety*, but Wear's synopsis is so filled with errors that it's obvious he didn't watch all (or any!) of the movie. He writes that Karloff has no grotesque makeup, calls the spy chieftain "Schiller" instead of "Strendler," misses the whole point of the finale and says that Karloff is shot while escaping. According to Wear, the film is "exciting," the plot "fairly logical," and he praises director Terry Morse, who "has incorporated plenty of suspense and has stressed action rather than verbiage." We suspect that Wear received a check from *Variety and* from Warner Brothers.

The Motion Picture Exhibitor called *British Intelligence* an "over-complicated meller. ...Even Adolph Hitler appears in it, in the person of a bit player, who is supposed to the Fuehrer when he was just a clumsy corporal in the German army. The scene is ludicrous despite the fact that it was meant to be prophetic." (More than one review mentioned Hitler's cameo appearance, but it's in no print of *British Intelligence* I've ever seen.) According to *The Hollywood Reporter*, "The story was written with an apparent attempt to cram every possible angle which could be connected with a spy film into the alloted footage. Opening with a series of battle montages, several of which are becoming very familiar, the film gets to work immediately to make the audience properly confused. ...Terry Morse directed with a sure hand in handling the avalanche of plot."

With *British Intelligence* in the can, Karloff's deal with Warners was at an end. One interesting final note: He never worked in a Warner Brothers film again.

•　　•　　•　　•　　•

Within a few months of *Son of Frankenstein*'s release, nearly all of the studios had horror movies back on their drawing boards, and both Boris and

In *British Intelligence*, Valdar has a deep facial scar undoubtedly inspired by Erich von Stroheim's forehead scar in *Three Faces East*.

Bela Lugosi could look forward—at least temporarily—to steadier employment. Karloff, of course, got better horror roles than Lugosi did, and he even starred in his own Broadway play, *Arsenic and Old Lace*. He was highly effective in some of the Columbia "Mad Doctor" movies, merrily spoofed himself in *The Boogie Man Will Get You* and gave the screen performances of a lifetime in Val Lewton's *The Body Snatcher* and *Bedlam*. After turning its back on him in 1937 and '38, all Hollywood once again loved Boris Karloff...

...Until horror went back out of vogue in 1946, that is. The studio gates again slammed shut on Karloff, and whenever the sixtyish British actor wasn't playing small parts as American Indians, he could be found up the creek with Lugosi again.

1 No makeup man is credited, but according to the *New York Post* review, Perc Westmore was responsible for Karloff's Chinese features.

2 The rights to *The Bad Man* were purchased by MGM and it was made again under that title four years later, with Wallace Beery as the Mexican outlaw with the heart of gold and Ronald Reagan as the young man he befriends.

West of Shanghai
CREDITS: Warners, 1937; Associate Producer: Bryan Foy; Director: John Farrow; Screenplay: Crane Wilbur; Based on the Play "The Bad Man" by Porter Emerson Browne; Photography: Lu [L. W.] O'Connell; Art Director: Max Parker; Editor: Frank Dewar; Gowns: Howard Shoup; Technical Advisor: Tommy Gubbins; Dialogue Director: Jo Graham; Assistant Director: Marshall Hageman; Pre-release titles: *Warlord*, *China Bandit*, *The Adventures of Chang* and *Cornered*; 65 minutes

CAST: Boris Karloff...Wu Yen Fang, Beverly Roberts...Jane Creed, Ricardo Cortez...Gordon Creed, Gordon Oliver...Jim Hallet, Sheila Bromley...Lola Galt, Vladimir Sokoloff...Gen. Chow Fu-shan, Gordon Hart...Dr. Abernathy, Richard Loo...Mr. Cheng, Chester Gan...Kung Nui, Luke Chan...Chan, Selmer Jackson...Hemingway, James B. Leong...Pao, Tetsu Komai...Mu, Eddie Lee...Wang Chung, Maurice Liu...Conductor, Mia Ichioka...Hua Mei, Douglas Wood...Myron Galt, Paul Fung...Station Master, Frank Tang...Chinese Merchant, Bruce Wong...Steward, Sam Tong...Messenger, Tom Ung...Military Aide, Daro Meya...Chinese Officer

The Invisible Menace
CREDITS: Warners, 1938; Associate Producer: Bryan Foy; Director: John Farrow; Screenplay: Crane Wilbur; Based on the Play "Without Warning" by Ralph Spencer Zink; Photography: L. Wm. [L. W.] O'Connell; Art Director: Stanley Fleischer; Editor: Harold McLernon; Dialogue Director: Harry

Seymour; Gowns: Howard Shoup; Assistant Director: Elmer Decker; Sound: Leslie G. Hewitt; Pre-Release Title: *Without Warning*; 54 minutes

CAST: Boris Karloff...Jevries, Marie Wilson...Sally Pratt, Eddie Craven...Eddie Pratt, Regis Toomey...Lieutenant Matthews, Henry Kolker...Colonel Hackett, Cy Kendall...Colonel Bob Rogers, Charles Trowbridge...Dr. Brooks, Eddie Acuff...Corporal Sanger, Frank Faylen...Private of the Guard, Phyllis Barry...Aline Dolman, Harlan Tucker...Reilly, William Haade...Private Ferris, John Ridgely...Private Innes, Jack Mower...Sergeant Peterson, Anderson Lawlor...Private Abbott, John Harron...Private Murphy

Devil's Island
CREDITS: Warners, 1939/40; Associate Producer: Bryan Foy; Director: William Clemens; Screenplay: Kenneth Gamet and Don Ryan; Story: Anthony Coldewey and Raymond L. Schrock; Photography: George Barnes; Editor: Frank Magee; Art Director: Max Parker; Technical Adviser: Louis Van Den Ecker; Sound: Robert B. Lee; Dialogue Director: John Langan; Assistant Director: Arthur Lueker; 62 minutes

CAST: Boris Karloff...Dr. Charles Gaudet, Nedda Harrigan...Madame Lucien, James Stephenson...Colonel Armand Lucien, Adia Kuznetzoff...Pierre, Rolla Gourvitch...Collette, Will Stanton...Bobo, Edward Keane...Dr. Duval, Robert Warwick...Demonpre, Pedro de Cordoba...Marcal, Tom Wilson...Emil, John Harmon...Andre, Richard Bond...Georges, Earl Gunn...Leon, Sidney Bracy...Soupy, George Lloyd...Dogface, Charles Richman...Governor Beaufort, Stuart Holmes...Gustave LeBrun, Leonard Mudie...Advocate General, Egon Brecher...Debriac, Frank Reicher...President of Assize Court, Alan Bridge...Captain of Guards, Ben Hendricks...Sergeant of Guards, Earl Smith...Servant, Harry Cording, Galan Galt, Frank S. Hagney, Douglas Williams, Henry Otho, Stanley King, James Blaine, Dick Rich, Sol Gorss, Don Turner...Guards, Alonzo Price...Captain Fearreau, Walter Soderling...Waggoner, Glen Cavender, Cliff Saum...Gendarmes, Davison Clark...Captain of Gendarmes, Nat Carr...Court Clerk, Paul Panzer...Jury Foreman, Neil Clisby...Jules, Jack Mower...Sergeant, Lawrence Grant...First Official, Theodor von Eltz...Second Official, Earl Dwire...Priest, Eddie Foster...Supply Clerk, Dick Botiller...Pilot, Francis Sayles...Boatman, Billy McClain...Servant, Jack Wise...Convict, John Hamilton...Captain of Convict Ship, Jack Richardson

British Intelligence
CREDITS: Warners, 1940; Associate Producer: Mark Hellinger; Producer: Bryan Foy; Director: Terry Morse; Screenplay: Lee Katz; Based on the Play "Three Faces East" by Anthony Paul Kelly; Photography: Sid Hickox; Art Di-

rector: Hugh Reticker; Editor: Thomas Pratt; Gowns: Howard Shoup; Music Director: H. Roemheld; Sound Recorder: Stanley Jones; Dialogue Director: John Langan; Assistant Director: Elmer Decker; Shooting Title and British Release Title: *Enemy Agent*; Also known as *Secret Enemy*; 61 minutes

CAST: Boris Karloff...Valdar, Margaret Lindsay...Helene von Lorbeer [also known as Frances Hautry], Bruce Lester...Frank Bennett, Leonard Mudie...Colonel James Yeats, Holmes Herbert...Arthur Bennett, Austin Fairman...George, Maris Wrixon...Dorothy, Winifred Harris...Mrs. Bennett, Lester Matthews...Henry Thompson, John Graham Spacy...Crichton, Clarence Derwent...Milkman, Louise Brien...Miss Risdon, Frederick Vogeding...Kugler, Carlos de Valdez...Von Ritter, Frederick Giermann...Kurtz, Willy Kaufman...German Corporal, Frank Mayo...Brixton, Stuart Holmes...Luchow, Sidney Bracy...Crowder, Jack Mower...Morton, Leonard Willey...Captain Stuart, Morton Lowry...Lieutenant Borden, Evan Thomas...Major Andrews, Lawrence Grant...Brigadier General, Denis d'Auburn...Captain Lanark, Craufurd Kent...Commander Phelps, Carl Harbaugh...German Soldier, Ferdinand Schumann-Heink, Joseph De Stefani...German Officers, Jack Richardson, Bob Stevenson...Cockney Soldiers, Glen Cavender...Under Officer Pfalz, Henry Von Zynda...German, Hans Schumm...German Senior Officer, Arno Frey...German Junior Officer, Gordon Hart...Doctor, John Sutton...Officer, Leyland Hodgson...Lord Sudbury, David Thursby...Mysterious Man, Paul Panzer...Peasant

Tom Weaver is the prolific curmudgeon of film commentary. He has written *Universal Horrors* (along with John and Michael Brunas) and *Poverty Row Horrors!*, and has had over 130 of his interviews compiled into six individual books, including *Monsters, Mutants and Heavenly Creatures* from Mid Mar Press. He contributes to *Fangoria, Midnight Marquee, Starlog, Cult Movies, Comics Scene, Videoscope, Movie Club*, and *Monsters from the Vault,* as well as many other film publications.

Boris Karloff
MGM CORP. D · OC · 8 · N · 7

THE MAN THEY COULD NOT HANG (1939)
THE MAN WITH NINE LIVES (1940)
BEFORE I HANG (1940)

by Michael Brunas

What has become part and parcel of the Boris Karloff story is an almost Pollyanna-like inclination of his co-workers when recalling the great horror star. No doubt Karloff was a lovely man and testimonies of his great kindness, his resolute professionalism, as well as his gentle nature are legion. Matters concerning his professional judgment, a common pitfall of many an actor associated with the genre, can, however occasionally, cause a ripple in his almost impossibly peerless reputation.

A case in point was in a 1977 interview with Zita Johann. The actress who as Princess Anck-es-en-amon was alternately swooned and terrified by darkly romantic Karloff in *The Mummy* was not one given to fulsomeness and tempered her praise of her co-star with one stinging observation. As reported by Delbert Winans in *Midnight Marquee* #26, Johann opined: "He was one of the nicest people in the world; a gentleman in every sense of the word.... In my opinion he did something I could never do; he sold out. He became a vehicle.... I don't think he wanted to 'sell out' at first, but money talks and everyone becomes frightened."

Karloff, at least publicly, would undoubtedly disagree. Karloff always prided himself as being a working actor. Any yearnings he may have had to test his mettle in the classical repertory or more "upscale" roles never penetrated his public facade. As Karloff stated, and stated often, typecasting was about the best thing that could happen to an actor in the Hollywood system. Living by his own words, the actor remained comfortably employed for almost four decades after his breakthrough performance in *Frankenstein*.

Karloff may have been tagged a typecasted actor but the narrowness of range which the term suggests rarely affected him. Western stars invariably deliver the same performance every time out; actors identified with gangster roles or light comedy, however gifted, often trade heavily on their personalities. Karloff, however, took dramatic opportunities where he found them and in the process became the great character actor of horror movies. Curiously, when straying from the horror niche to more "prestigious" Hollywood fare, the results were often disappointing. His familiar lisp served him poorly in tough guy roles such as *Scarface*, he was little more than a cigar store Indian in De Mille's *Unconquered*, and red herring parts in *Lured* and *The Secret Life of Walter Mitty* were obvious bores.

In contrast, his horror roles such as The Monster, Cabman Gray, and Imhotep were multi-dimensional characterizations. Like a virtuoso, Karloff plunged into his work demonstrating dedication, imagination, and an artisan's skill. At least when the scripts were good ones.

Which brings us to Karloff's trio of "mad scientist" thrillers produced by Columbia between 1939 and 1940 and directed by Nick Grindé. It's a corner of Karloff's career rarely ventured into by habitués of highbrow cinema. Unlike Columbia's well-regarded *The Devil Commands*, which was directed by Edward Dmytryk, even the most sympathetic Karloff chroniclers tend to shrug off *The Man They Could Not Hang, The Man With Nine Lives*, and *Before I Hang* as tired variations of the same theme.

The films were a fulfillment of a 5-movie deal Karloff made in 1939. It was a typical bread-and-butter contract which assured him of star billing but gave few illusions as to the quality of the films themselves. At the time the studio was scrambling to upgrade its "Gower Gulch" reputation, an embarrassing reminder of the days when Columbia's production roster leaned heavily towards cheap westerns. By the late thirties Columbia had dusted off its cowpoke image into what Edward Dmytryk described as "a grade-B studio with pretensions." And B films were exactly what Columbia had in mind for their new star contractee. Karloff's vehicles allowed no budgetary allocations for special make-up or effects, utilized mostly standing sets, and limited recruitment of his co-stars to studio contract players. What Columbia *did* play up was the Karloff name to attract audiences. Unlike his arch-rival Bela Lugosi who could barely keep his dignity afloat in the near-degrading fare he was forced to accept, Karloff was never humiliated when slipping below grade B status and even rose to deliver crisp, inspired performances.

The production team, which remained fairly intact through the run of Karloff's contract, made up the creative core of his Columbia assignments. Nick Grindé, who was just starting a long stint at the studio after working at Warners and MGMs B-units, filled the directorial slot. The principal writer was Karl Brown, another B specialist who regularly cranked out such Hollywood fodder as *Tarzan Escapes* and Tod Browning's *Fast Workers*. (Brown's only real fame, ironically, came late in life when he penned his reminiscences of D.W. Griffith with whom he worked as a camera assistant and jack-of-all-

The Man They Could Not Hang's **courtroom scene gave Karloff one of his better showcases.**

trades during the silent days. Said Floyd W. Martin in *The International Dictionary of Films and Filmmakers* [St. James Press, 1993], "Had not Brown had good notes and recollections and had been encouraged to publish them, he would probably be almost forgotten today.")

Heading up the Karloff unit was producer Wallace MacDonald who seemed himself a character out of a grade B movie script. Edward Bernds, who worked under the yoke of MacDonald first as a sound man and later as a full-fledged director, tells of MacDonald's unorthodox rise in the Columbia organization:

"Wally MacDonald became a producer under strange circumstances. Columbia provided a living for Harry and Jack Cohn's younger brother. They made him handle insurance purchases so he got commissions on all the insurance that Columbia bought. The only thing was that he wasn't very sharp. When Irving Briskin sent a western troupe to Arizona, Cohn forgot to buy workers' compensation. At the time MacDonald was an actor, kind of a Columbia regular. While on location, Wally's horse fell on him and broke his hip. He really could have sued Columbia for a lot of money. The story I heard, and I have no reason not to believe it, was that Columbia bought him off by making him a producer. Which must have cost Columbia millions through the years because Wally was a very destructive producer.

"He produced several pictures which I directed and he was maddening. He always wanted to prove he was smarter than his writers and directors. I don't know how you would rate the movies that he produced, but in my opinion, he could only louse up anything he had anything to do with."

Mr. Bernds' dismal appraisal not withstanding, it should be said that the first of MacDonald's Karloff films was not only the best, it established the format for the entire series. *The Man They Could Not Hang* certainly didn't warrant much attention when it was first released, so similar was it to Karloff vehicles of the recent past. But *The Man They Could Not Hang* has aged well and while it still lacks originality, its bromides bristle with confidence and Karloff's performance could hardly be better.

Karloff stars as the earnest Dr. Henryk Savaard, whose madcap theory to revolutionize surgery seems destined to run afoul of authorities. By first gassing patients to death and then reviving them by means of a mechanical glass heart, Savaard believes he has found the perfect anesthetic. An obliging young medical assistant (Stanley Brown) volunteers to become a human guinea pig in the experiment over the frantic objections of his fiancee (Ann Doran) ("But, Bob, you are going to *die*!" she pleads to her handsome young jock who fatuously retorts, "That sounds a lot tougher than it actually is.") Predictably, the experiment is interrupted by the police but Savaard's claim that he could bring young Bob back to life leaves the windbag coroner and the yokel police lieutenant unconvinced. Stone-faced, the simpatico scientist is charged with murder.

As the film launched Karloff's contract, the writers were eager to please the star and checkered the script with several fine monologues. The courtroom scene gave Karloff one of his better showcases. Taking the stand, Savaard valiantly tries to vindicate himself with a bravura defense of his research. It's the obvious highpoint of the script and Karloff seizes the moment with an impassioned, flawlessly delivered speech that would have taxed even the most seasoned actor. (Hardcore Bela Lugosi fans find it fashionable to take potshots at Karloff, championing the exotic villainy of the Hungarian's Count Dracula or Murder Legendre of *White Zombie*. But there is much to be said for Karloff's commanding presence and even the staunchest Lugosi fanatic must cringe at the prospect of the heavily-accented star coping with such lengthy passages of intricate dialogue.)

Savaard's guilty verdict is assured but he goes to the gallows realizing vengeance is at hand. A faithful assistant uses the mechanical heart to resurrect the scientist who embarks on a campaign of terror. Anonymously summoning to

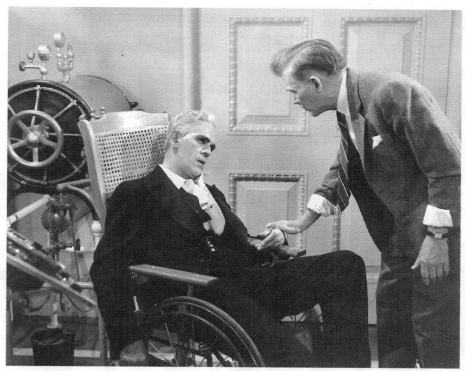

The Man They Could Not Hang is a trifle too restrained in keeping with the rigidly enforced Production Code regulations.

his home the jurists and others who condemned him, he proceeds to kill them one by one. Savaard's daughter (Lorna Gray) stumbles on the scene and is electrocuted by one of the mad scientist's booby traps while trying to free her father's captives. Savaard is shot while rushing to his daughter's aid but manages to use his life-giving apparatus one last time before expiring.

The Man They Could Not Hang doesn't add much to the standardized mad scientist formula but succeeds as a swiftly paced thriller that works up a fine head of steam to its _Ten Little Indians_ climax. Despite the carnage of the last act (Karloff kills off the jury foreman by means of a rigged telephone that sends a poison needle into his brain), the film is a trifle too restrained in keeping with rigidly enforced Production Code regulations. The script, at least, has a few sound ideas in its head in spite of being written by the same Karl Brown who penned the humiliating _The Ape Man_ for Lugosi a short time later. The film can be read as a melodramatic tract on unchecked scientific progress and takes on, however crudely, the theme of arrogance of power. Virtually every character of authority in the film is shown unsympathetically and, in the end, even Savaard becomes a monster who sheds his humanitarian ideals the moment he gains the upper hand.

The Man With Nine Lives presents Karloff as Leon Kravaal, a darker, more austere figure; his mustache and goatee suggest a devil without a pitchfork.

Unlike Karloff's Warner Brothers contract which kept him far afield from
the horror genre, Columbia had no such designs for the star as his next vehicle
would attest. Announced alternately as *The Man Who Wouldn't Die* and *The
Man Without a Face* (an obviously bogus title), it was finally released as *The
Man With Nine Lives*. The film was little more than an eager re-shuffling of the
plot of *The Man They Could Not Hang* and is easily the weakest of Karloff's
Nick Grindé-directed assignments.

A departure from the dapper, silver-haired Henryk Savaard, Karloff's Leon
Kravaal seems a darker, more austere figure; his mustache and goatee suggesting a devil without a pitchfork. Whatever the cosmetics, it is plain Kravaal is
simply Savaard redux, facing familiar situations and familiar adversaries.

The film opens as Dr. Tim Mason (Roger Pryor) demonstrates "frozen
therapy," a cancer treatment that was attracting attention at the time. Mason
admits that the treatment which involves freezing the victim into a suspended
animation-like state was actually pioneered by one Leon Kravaal, an obscure
physician who vanished years before.

226

Hoping to trace the mysterious doctor, Mason and his fiancee nurse, Judy Blair (Jo Ann Sayers), arrive at the lakeside community where the scientist practiced. From the onset, the film strikes the right note of intrigue amid the isolated rustic locales and the gratifyingly sinister banter concerning Kravaal's weed-infested homestead. Paddling to their destination by canoe, Mason and Judy find that the Kravaal residence doesn't live up to anyone's expectations of a haunted house but Pryor and Sayers are capable enough players to keep the mysterioso mood engaged. The outdoorsy respite is cut short as the film settles into the dinginess of Kravaal's subterranean laboratory and never seems to get out of it.

It is here that the couple find the frozen bodies of Kravaal and a few local lawmen who years before tried to apprehend the scientist only to unwittingly become part of his experiment. Mason restores the men to consciousness but by now the film gets bogged down by the wild contrivances of the script. Kravaal sets out to test his theories using his guests as guinea pigs. In the end, Judy becomes the subject for Kravaal's last experiment when state troopers arrive, killing the scientist in a hail of bullets. Mason revives Judy for a happy ending.

Karloff does the most with his role in spite of the built-in limitations of the script. Being kept offscreen for the first couple of reels may have been intended to give him a "big build-up." But thanks to the pedestrian writing, not only doesn't it come off, the film practically stops in its tracks just when it should be shifting into high gear. The confined sets combined with Grindé's inability to provide any visual interest gives *The Man With Nine Lives* a dreary claustrophobia worthy of the worst of Monogram. Typical of most B movies of its vintage, shooting involved working the cast and crew long into the night, many hours of which were spent in the same Los Angeles ice house which was used by Frank Capra to recreate the frozen Himalayan tundra in *Lost Horizon*. The discomfort and unpleasant shooting conditions seem to have seeped to the core of the movie, making it a rather dispiriting hour or so entertainment.

Before I Hang proved to be a worthier vehicle which placed Karloff back on familiar terrain. The picture can't be said to be on a par with *The Man They Could Not Hang*, but it leaves *The Man With Nine Lives* in the dust as a film of legitimate interest. Unfortunately, both circumstance and the talent involved have played the film a bad hand. Robert D. Andrews' perfunctory script nudges it out of its potential sleeper status and the movie was released too early to qualify as a "horror noir," a classification which it could rightfully claim as its own. *Before I Hang* is a film which is rarely investigated except for Karloff completists although it is a noteworthy example of the B film.

Karloff plays Dr. John Garth, an aging medical researcher whose effort to perfect a fountain of youth serum is interrupted when he is convicted in the mercy killing of one of his patients. Garth is sentenced to the gallows (by Charles Trowbridge reprising his hanging judge role from *The Man They Could*

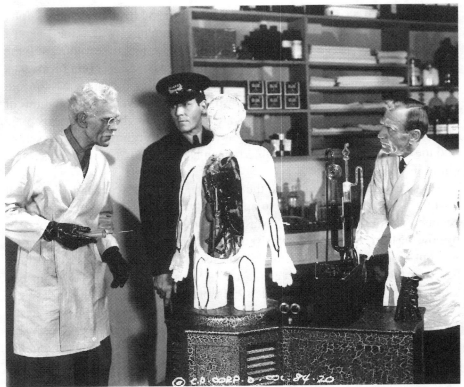

Before I Hang offers a good share of B movie thrills. The director and star overcome a sketchy plot to contribute exceptional work.

Not Hang) but spends his time on death row continuing his experiments with the assistance of the prison physician Dr. Howard (Edward Van Sloan). Finally perfecting his formula, Garth inoculates himself moments before his scheduled execution when word comes that his sentence has been commuted. Garth collapses, regaining consciousness to learn that the serum has rejuvenated him by twenty years.

The serum is deemed a miraculous success and the scientist is rewarded with a full pardon but his glory is short-lived. The blood used in preparation of the formula, taken from an executed killer, has triggered homicidal tendencies in Garth who becomes a deranged killer whenever he attempts to repeat the procedure. Dr. Howard is the first to die by Garth's hands and the death toll mounts impressively by the last reel. Faced with his crimes, Garth is shot during one of his homicidal lapses by a prison guard while turning himself over to the law.

At a glance, *Before I Hang* reveals a script mired in the mad scientist clichés that had become *de rigueur* for Karloff vehicles since *The Walking Dead*. The late William K. Everson found the film so redundant he disposed of it in a single sentence in *More Classics of the Horror Film* (Citadel Press, 1986) after granting modest coverage to the first two films in the series. Yet *Before I Hang* offers a good share of B movie thrills, and the director and star overcome the sketchy plot and boilerplate dialogue to contribute exceptional work.

Visually, it is perhaps the most stylish film of the lot and Grindé proves to have sound command of basic film noir technique. The scene in which Karloff garrotes Van Sloan, played with minimal dialogue, makes excellent use of low-keyed lighting, ominous musical cues, and stark, well-chosen camera angles to create a mood of almost palpable tension. Although this was long before the days when zoom lenses were common, Grindé uses a fast-tracking camera to create a wonderfully atmospheric effect when Karloff comes calling on his victims. In fact, the last half of the film is so dimly lit and fog shrouded that the wrap-up with the romantic leads (Evelyn Keyes and Bruce Bennett) in Karloff's sun-drenched study seems like part of another movie.

The film is graced by two strong performances in the roles of Karloff's victims: Edward Van Sloan in his last decent horror role and Pedro de Cordoba who lends a touching dignity to the part of an aging pianist. But it's still Karloff's show, offering the actor's subtlest work since Roy William Neill's *The Black Room*. In fact, the old Garth/young Garth part compares favorably with Karloff's bravura dual role in the Neill classic.

It was the kind of physical performance that the actor excelled in, using voice and body language as much as make-up. The frail, almost doddering, elder Garth rejuvenates into a tightly wound spring of nervous energy, pacing incessantly, seemingly energized by his own guilt. Karloff's transformation into a maniac is a skillfully worked-out bit of business starting with a rush of pressure from behind his neck, emblematic of the hanged killer whose blood flows in his veins. Fidgeting for a handkerchief which he furtively twists into a garrote, he dispatches his victims with a robotic single-mindedness of purpose. There's iciness in Karloff's young Garth but it is not the stiff villainy found in his by-the-numbers performances in *House of Frankenstein* or *Dick Tracy Meets Gruesome*. Rather, it is Karloff essaying a character torn between guilt and his obsession to leave a lasting gift to mankind.

Before I Hang marked the end of the Karloff- Grindé collaboration. Karloff went on to *The Devil Commands* which made hash of the William Sloane novel from which it was based (*The Edge of Running Water*) but was redeemed by the stylish direction of Edward Dmytryk. The actor finished up his Columbia commitment with *The Boogie Man Will Get You*, a desperate bid to recreate the homespun black humor of *Arsenic and Old Lace*. Despite the best efforts of the energetic players, the casting of Peter Lorre as a hick sheriff was the movie's funniest conceit.

Nick Grindé never graduated from programmer ranks and in later years seemed somewhat touchy about his work in Hollywood B-units. Writing in

The Penguin Film Review in 1946, he made a feisty defense of low-budget filmmaking in Hollywood. In a piece entitled "Pictures for Peanuts," he wrote: "A B picture isn't a big picture that just didn't grow up; it's exactly what it started out to be. It's the $22 suit in the clothing business, it's the hamburger of the butcher's shop, it's a seat in the bleachers. And there's a big market for *all* of them." But even Grindé's days in B picture days were numbered. He eventually went on to a busy if undistinguished television career.

By the time Karloff departed the Columbia lot, the mad scientist was one Hollywood mainstay that had seen better days. The classic line of the cruel fate that awaited any soul who dared to tamper in God's handiwork, or any of its endless variations, took its place among the more tepid of movie bromides. Who could have predicted that the mad scientist would come back with a vengeance so soon? Of course, it was the war that revitalized the formula, unleashing a newer, more twisted breed of scientific crazies who spewed their madness on the screen. Zombies, werewolves, human/animal hybrids, and other monstrosities of science weren't new but now they were created in laboratories manned by John Carradine, Lionel Atwill, and George Zucco. The films themselves were often outrageous, invariably fun on some level, but beneath the gimmickry and the greasepaint was something infinitely fearful. The cheap mad scientist movie began more and more to reflect the disturbing stories that began trickling out of Europe; stories recounting dark experiments being performed by Nazi scientists on their human captives. Compared to such sensationalistic fare, Boris Karloff's Columbia films seem like staid, even polite entertainments. Karloff's characters, despite their misguided zeal, hoped in the end to serve mankind, not to exploit it. The actor in later years remembered his Columbia vehicles with a grudging respect, recognizing the worthy themes disguised in a cloak of melodrama. When all is said and done, these films not only served their star commendably but the audiences as well.

The Man They Could Not Hang
CREDITS: Producer: Wallace MacDonald; Director: Nick Grindé; Screenplay: Karl Brown; Story: Leslie T. White and George W. Sayre; Director of Photography: Benjamin Kline; Music Director: Morris Stoloff; Film Editor: William Lyon; Art Director: Lionel Banks; A Columbia Picture; released August 17, 1939; running time 65 minutes

CAST: Boris Karloff...Dr. Henryk Savaard, Lorna Gray...Janet Savaard, Robert Wilcox...Scoop Foley, Roger Pryor...District Attorney Drake, Ann Doran...Betty Crawford, Charles Trowbridge...Judge Bowman, Don Beddoe...Lieutenant Shane, James Craig...Watkins, Stanley Brown...Bob Roberts, Joseph DeStefani...Dr. Stoddard, Byron Foulger...Lang, Dick Curtis...Kearney, John Tyrrell...Sutton, John Dilson...Editor

230

The Man With Nine Lives
CREDITS: Producer: Wallace MacDonald; Director: Nick Grindé; Screenplay: Karl Brown; Story: Harold Shumate; Director of Photography: Benjamin Kline; Film Editor: Al Clark; Art Director: Lionel Banks; Technical Advisor: Dr. Ralph S. Willard; A Columbia Picture; released April 18, 1940; running time 73 minutes; British title: *Behind the Door*

CAST: Boris Karloff...Dr. Leon Kravaal, Roger Pryor...Dr. Tim Mason, Jo Ann Sayers...Judith Blair, Stanley Brown...Bob Adams, John Dilson...John Hawthorne, Charles Trowbridge...Dr. Harvey, Byron Foulger...Dr. Bassett, Hal Taliaferro...Sheriff Stanton, Ernie Adams...Pete Daggett, Ivan Miller...Sheriff Haley, Lee Willard...Jasper Adams, Bruce Bennett...State Trooper

Before I Hang
CREDITS: Producer: Wallace MacDonald and Irving Briskin; Director: Nick Grindé; Screenplay: Robert D. Andrews; Story: Karl Brown and Robert D. Andrews; Director of Photography: Benjamin Klein; Music Director: Morris Stoloff; Film Editor: Charles Nelson; Art Director: Lionel Banks; a Columbia Picture; released September 17, 1940; running time 63 minutes

CAST: Boris Karloff...Dr. John Garth, Evelyn Keyes...Martha Garth, Bruce Bennett...Dr. Paul Ames, Edward Van Sloan...Dr. Ralph Howard, Don Beddoe...Captain McGraw, Ben Taggart...Warden Thompson, Pedro de Cordoba...Victor Sondini, Wright Kramer...George Wharton, Bertram Marburgh...Stephen Barclay, Frank Richards...Otto Kron, Robert Fiske...District Attorney, Kenneth MacDonald...Anson, Charles Trowbridge...Judge

With thanks to Edward Bernds and, as usual, to John Brunas and Tom Weaver.

Michael Brunas contributes to *Midnight Marquee, Movie Club*, and *Scarlet Street*. He is co-author, along with John Brunas and Tom Weaver, of *Universal Horrors* from McFarland.

BLACK FRIDAY (1940)
THE CLIMAX (1944)
HOUSE OF FRANENSTEIN (1944)

by Nathalie Yafet

Black Friday, The Climax, and *House of Frankenstein* are three films often grouped with *Voodoo Island, Frankenstein 1970*, and *The Strange Door* as featuring walk-through performances by Boris Karloff. Some of the more censorious critiques: "...labored and overly neurotic... completely one dimensional...." (*Boris Karloff*, Scott Allen Nollen); "... plumbs new depths of detachment... stolid... with an occasional touch of condescending hamminess...." (*Universal Horrors*, Michael Brunas, John Brunas and Tom Weaver). Not so; all three Universal films demonstrate just how much the actor could do even when burdened with weak supporting casts and uneven scripts.

Just imagine dear Boris having memory lapses, single-handedly wiping out seven people and Bela, sacrificing his friend for fortune's sake; this is the *Black Friday* that not only *might* have been but *should* have been. Stanley Ridges gives a *good* performance; it is not a *tour de force*. Ridges' gangster does provide some truly frightening moments, and his professor lends poignancy, but both are cliché-ridden and obvious. It is wrong to think that Boris Karloff could not have managed the dual role or the clinches. This is the same actor who loved and killed in *The Mummy*; who lusted and murdered in *The Black Room*.

Black Friday will always be painful to watch, knowing that it could have been one of the best Karloff/Lugosi films, with bravura roles for each. Instead, it is a Stanley Ridges film, co-starring Karloff with Lugosi thrown off to the side. Some things are unforgivable.

As Dr. Ernest Sovac (Karloff) walks the last mile (a familiar route for Boris Karloff), led by a minister solemnly intoning the Our Father, he does not look especially remorseful and seems much more concerned with getting his notes and records into the right hands. With effortless brilliance, Karloff outlines his character succinctly in the first few minutes of the film—ethics and morality playing second fiddle to science.

In *Black Friday* Karloff outlines his character succinctly in the first few minutes of the film—ethics and morality playing second fiddle to science.

In flashback, we see him exuding affability and easy charm when he picks up his friend, George Kingsley, and daughter Jean. The moment is breezy and relaxed (though somewhat marred by Ridges' need to show us what a cute old darling his professor is) which makes the closely following occurrence of gunfire and Kingsley's tragic accident even more shocking. Sovac worries as he rides in the back of the ambulance with his severely injured friend and the man who ran him down, Red Cannon. And yet, he cannot resist asking the gangster, "Some men were shooting at you; who were they?" A lesser actor could easily have glossed over this transitory dialogue, but Karloff uses it to prepare us for Sovac's descent. After the doctor learns that his friend is dying, he decides to transplant the Cannon brain to save Kingsley. His journal entry reveals his priorities, "...a chance to make a great scientific discovery and perhaps save my friend's life." The operation does save Kingsley but two detectives appear to question Sovac about the recently deceased Cannon. The unwholesome glimmer in Karloff's eyes at the mention of money is delightful.

Dr. Sovac starts in at once by cold-bloodedly urging the convalescing Kingsley to accompany him on a jaunt to New York City, Red Cannon's old

234

stomping grounds. They check in at the Midtown Hotel, Cannon's hideout, and visit the club where his former girlfriend sings. Although outwardly concerned with his friend, Sovac scrutinizes him constantly—like a cat watching a bird. Boris Karloff is top notch as he mercilessly probes away at poor George with scarcely contained intensity. Back at the hotel, the exhausted man collapses and Sovac prompts, "Red—Red Cannon," giving his poor friend no peace. Karloff's smugly satisfied smile when Cannon re-emerges is masterful. After the dominant Cannon murders Devore (a rival gangster), he returns to the hotel, awakening as Kingsley.

Margaret Kingsley and Jean Sovac arrive and Sovac unceremoniously shoves them out of the room when Cannon unexpectedly appears. Karloff easily dominates Ridges in the ensuing confrontation, deflecting Cannon's threats with a bigger one, "How'd you like to be George Kingsley for good?" He tells him that he witnessed a murder committed by Cannon. Then Sovac checkmates with, "I can make you forget you ever were Red Cannon.... From now on you'll do exactly as I say!" After Cannon agrees to share the money with him, Karloff's Sovac smirks victoriously. (His sly facial innuendo throughout enlivens *Black Friday* tremendously.)

Jean returns and determinedly questions her father until he admits what he has done. When she objects because Cannon is "a gangster and a murderer," Sovac shouts, "All right, but in the meantime I've proved what I always knew to be true—transplanted human brain cells will live and function. What a triumph! Think of it!" Boris Karloff and Anne Gwynne interact beautifully, allowing each other space to shine. Karloff is exceptional when he rationalizes his grotesque experiment. Jean wins this showdown by pointing out that Sovac could be imprisoned for performing an illegal operation. Thus pressed, he reluctantly consents to take George back to Newcastle in the morning.

Everything is going along swimmingly until Kingsley hears a siren while in the classroom and, again, we see Red Cannon. He finds Jean, demands the money, and tries to kill her. Sovac shoots Kingsley to save his daughter, dropping the gun in anguish. Ironically, we feel more for the calculating doctor than the dying professor at the finish, due to Karloff's exquisitely expressive face and body language.

The Climax is a film that gave me a new appreciation for the fast forward button on my remote. Excruciating, interminable production numbers, wandering storyline, strained humor, and some execrable acting makes this one of the worst overall 1940s' Boris Karloff movies. Susanna Foster, barely tolerable in small doses, is omnipresent here, Turhan Bey makes us squirm, and boy King, Scotty Beckett, is a not-so-distant cousin to Donnie Dunagan. Some saving graces: June Vincent, as the ill-fated Marcellina, is first rate; Thomas Gomez is convincing as general manager, Count Seebruck; Jane Farrar, as Jarmila, displays the same endearing bitchiness as she did in *Phantom of the*

Boris Karloff manages to maintain his concentration and dignity, not an easy task in such a muddle as *The Climax*.

Opera; William Edmunds, in the tiny role of Leon the doorman, puts some of the stars to shame with his lean, finely crafted acting; and Gale Sondergaard adds her brooding Luise. However, the ultimate savior of this mess is the man most often blamed for its failure, Boris Karloff. Relegated to secondary status, Boris Karloff's Dr. Fredrick Hohner, inarguably one of his least likable characters, is, nevertheless, focused and intense throughout. He provides us with *The Climax*'s only truly humorous moment when Angela comments about his medical paraphernalia as being "...rather frightening," and, Hohner, not missing a beat, dryly replies, "I know exactly what you mean. I feel the same way when I go to the dentist." Here is a man who was losing his reason long before he murdered his sweetheart, whose justification for his heinous deed is that he has only destroyed the thing that divided them—her voice. Granted, Dr. Hohner is insane, obsessed, and selfish, but that is how the character is written and Boris Karloff turns in a fascinating performance against nearly insurmountable odds. He wins our sympathy in the flashback scene because it is almost impossible to hate someone who loves so much; sick though he is. His line reading of, "I can't bear the thought that any man can hear you sing for him, feast his eyes on you— just for the price of a ticket," is flawless, particularly the abruptly angry pronunciation of "ticket." He is chilling, yet surprisingly moving, as he gathers the dead Marcellina in his arms, crooning, "We'll always be together now..." He uses his silent film experience to good effect as he enters Marcellina's dressing room, looks slowly around as if expecting to see her there, then sits, physically and emotionally worn out with macabre memories.

Moments later, Hohner hears a voice like Marcellina's singing an aria from *The Magic Voice* and discovers Angela and Franz. He informs the young soprano, "That music is sacred, sacred to the memory of Marcellina," and with restrained fury, saves the scene from drowning in the cloying excesses of Bey and Foster. (Why wasn't Peter Coe cast in the role of Franz?)

Persuading Angela to visit his office with the ploy of a post-performance throat examination, he displays his treasured souvenirs from Marcellina's operatic roles. Holding the pearls that Marcellina wore the night she "disappeared," he slowly winds them around Angela's neck, while mesmerizing her with the silky seductiveness of his voice. Karloff's musical rendering of, "Rest my dear; restore those tired and broken nerves. Drive out all fear and weariness. Chase away the shadowy forms that exhaust our emotions..." is hauntingly hypnotic. This is an actor who knew exactly how much honey to put on the bullet. Then, with consummate skill, he checks the trance and is again the genial house physician. Next day Angela's voice breaks during rehearsal and Dr. Hohner is all concern. While conferring with Count Seebruck, a sinister something flickers over his face for an instant and, extending his hand to her, proves himself an utterly irresistible menace.

He also does not give up easily. As Angela readies for a command performance of *The Magic Voice*, Dr. Hohner enters and, inches away from her, murmurs soothingly, "I've come to help you, my dear. It's cruel of them to do this to you..." Karloff in dark profile and Foster bent backwards in fear are a grim tableau reminiscent of Chaney, Sr. and Mary Philbin in the original *Phantom of the Opera*. Back at his office, the crazed doctor prepares to sever the singer's vocal cords and diabolically mutters, "This time I'll silence it forever." After Franz and Carl rescue the confused girl so that she can make her entrance, Carl stays with Dr. Hohner and guards him at gunpoint. His heroism is short-lived. Supremely stupid Carl relaxes his watch for a moment to exult, "Sing, Angela," and is instantly knocked out by the far more intelligent villain. Dr. Hohner then tries to leave and, when he sees police coming, runs to Marcellina's crypt where he burns to death. Such a haphazard ending is senseless, but Boris Karloff still manages to maintain his concentration and dignity; not an easy task in such a muddle.

From the first jolting appearance of Dr. Gustav Niemann harshly demanding his chalk to the last sight of his startled eyes as he sinks in the quicksand—

Boris Karloff's underrated performance is the thread that ties *House of Franken-stein* together.

Boris Karloff's underrated performance is the thread that ties *House of Fran-kenstein* together. Without him, its series of vignettes would be confusing and purposeless. Immediately following his near strangulation of the prison guard, Niemann cordially asks Daniel, his hunchbacked cell mate, "...shall we go on with our work," as innocently as if he were offering him a cup of tea rather than illustrating the transfer of a man's brain into the skull of a dog. The transition is seamless. An auspicious thunderstorm facilitates their escape into the night where they hook up with Professor Lampini's "Chamber of Horrors." The subsequent scene of cheer and good fellowship ends abruptly when Daniel murders their host. A highlight of this segment is the duet-like recitation of the Dracula legend by Boris Karloff and George Zucco as they relish each grisly detail.

After Daniel kills both Lampini and his driver, *House of Frankenstein* as-sumes the character of a travelogue as the companions, both freshly shaved and sporting new duds, continue on in the "Chamber of Horrors" wagon. Their ride through the seemingly idyllic bucolic paradise in the bright sunshine is a startling contrast to their conversation. Daniel is fearful and thinks they should hide but Niemann is confident that they will not be discovered and is eager to pursue Hussman, Strauss and Ullman. He punctuates his line, "Free to move on towards those—for whom I have unloving memories," magnificently, with slightly lowered voice, rolling enunciation, and stresses on the liquid and nasal consonants.

Later, at his first gig, the false Lampini appears nattily dressed in top hat, tailcoat, cravat and vest. He treats the gaping audience to his own unique spin on the words—"Ladies and gentlemen, the actual skeleton of Count Dracula, the vampire," dramatically throwing back his head and raising his malevolent eyebrows on the word, "vampire." Burgomaster Hussman accents this with his, "Rubbish, sheer rubbish," landing right on the end of the word, "vampire." Hussman suspicions that "Professor Lampini" looks strangely familiar and Niemann, with deadly eloquence replies, "Perhaps you will remember later, Herr Burgomaster." Backstage, the doctor pulls the stake from the skeleton's heart and gets a nasty surprise when the vampire himself rematerializes and tries to hypnotize him. Despite Dracula's supernatural abilities, Niemann retains the upper hand and bargains with the undead creature to eliminate Hussman in exchange for protection. Boris Karloff's powerfully upraised arm holding the stake that threatens John Carradine's sleek vampire makes for an indelible image.

Critics often bestow best of show honors to J. Carrol Naish for his pathetic, lovelorn Daniel, but I believe that Karloff's incisive Dr. Niemann is the winner here. Naish is genuinely affecting, but has a tendency to overact. When he strangles Lampini and attacks Fejos, he holds his arms out in an exaggerated, cartoonish gesture that is much more ridiculous than it is horrifying. He also overdoes the self-pity routine, very nearly beating Larry Talbot at his own game. Karloff, on the other hand, maintains his man on a mission focus throughout, nobly resisting being a generic mad scientist. Dr. Niemann wants two things: to revenge himself on those who betrayed him and, later, to experiment on the Frankenstein Monster. Anything else is annoying or superfluous. He proves he hasn't an ounce of romance when Daniel begs to take Ilonka with them and he grumbles, "All right, if it'll keep you in your right senses." Later on, he flippantly tells his gullible assistant, "...to please your little gypsy girl, friend Daniel, I'll make you an Adonis!"

On the other hand, Niemann can pour on the charm when necessary. After he and Daniel thaw the frozen Wolf Man and Frankenstein Monster, he uses his best bedside manner to coax the disgruntled Talbot into telling him where to locate Dr. Frankenstein's records. Karloff makes us believe that he will help the Wolf Man when we know he really couldn't care less. Back in the wagon, he looks uncannily like a harmless college professor reviewing his lecture notes.

Finally, the motley group arrives at the Doctor's old laboratory where he authoritatively orders his troops to get the place in shape. Now it is also time for Niemann and Daniel to pay calls on Strauss and Ullman, whom he reminds of his fifteen years spent in Neustadt Prison, rotting, "...in a stinking, slimy dungeon." (Spoken with not a trace of sibilantes!) Frank Reicher is right on target in the minuscule role of Ullman as he pleads for his life. The answer is another inimitably delivered line when Niemann says, "Kill my trusted old assistant? Why no (sliding down into a deep basso register for added emphasis), I'm going to repay you for betraying me," (exploding on the "p" in pay). The final scene with Daniel is a stunner as the latter begs for Talbot's body and Niemann cuts him off with a sharp, "No! Do you think I'd wreck the work of a lifetime because you're in love with a (disdainful pause) ...gypsy girl?"

It must have been a formidable challenge for this most endearing of actors to play the icily bitter Dr. Niemann, who reserves his only true tenderness for the Monster. He succeeded admirably.

Boris Karloff appeared in many vehicles unworthy of his time and far-ranging talents, but he never gave a bad performance in any of them; no matter how poorly written the role. He is the finest actor that horror films will ever know.

Black Friday
CREDITS: Producer: Burt Kelly; Director: Arthur Lubin; Screenplay: Curt Siodmak and Eric Taylor; Photography: Elwood Bredell; Art Director: Jack Otterson; Associate Art Director: Harold MacArthur; Film Editor: Philip Cahn; Musical Director: Hans J. Salter; Gowns: Vera West; Set Decorator: Russell A. Gausman; Sound Supervisor: Bernard B. Brown; Makeup: Jack P. Pierce; Special Effects: John P. Fulton; Technician: Charles Carroll; Running time: 70 minutes; Premiered March 21, 1940; Released: April 12, 1940

CAST: Boris Karloff...Dr. Ernest Sovac, Bela Lugosi...Eric Marnay, Stanley Ridges...Professor George Kingsley/Red Cannon, Anne Nagel...Sunny Rogers, Anne Gwynne...Jean Sovac, Virginia Brissac...Margaret Kingsley, Edmund MacDonald...Frank Miller, Paul Fix...William Kane, Murray Alper...Bellhop, Jack Mulhall...Bartender, Joe King...Chief of Police, John Kelly...Taxi Driver, James Craig...Reporter, Jerry Marlowe...Clerk

The Climax
CREDITS: Director and Producer: George Waggner; Executive Producer: Joseph Gershenson; Original Play: Edward J. Locke; Adaptation: Curt Siodmak; Directors of Photography: Hal Mohr and W. Howard Greene; Technicolor Color

Director: Natalie Kalmus; Musical Score and Director: Edward Ward; Art Directors: John B. Goodman and Alexander Golitzen; Director of Sound: Bernard B. Brown; Technician: William Fox; Film Editor: Russell Schoengarth; Assistant Directors: Charles S. Gould and Harry O. Jones; Set Decorators: Russell A. Gausman and Ira S. Webb; Makeup: Jack P. Pierce; Costumes: Vera West; Dialogue Director: Gene Lewis; Special Effects: John P. Fulton, Running Time: 86 minutes; Released: October 20, 1944

CAST: Boris Karloff...Dr. Fredrick Hohner, Susanna Foster...Angela Klatt, Turhan Bey...Franz Munzer, Gale Sondergaard...Luise, Thomas Gomez...Count Seebruck, June Vincent...Marcellina, Ludwig Stossel...Carl Bauman, George Dolenz...Amato Roselli, Jane Farrar...Jarmila Vadek, Erno Verebes...Brunn, Lotte Stein...Mama Hinzl, Scotty Beckett...King, William Edmunds...Leon, Maxwell Hayes...King's Aide, Polly Bailey...Cleaning Woman

House of Frankenstein
CREDITS: Director: Erle C. Kenton; Producer: Paul Malvern; Executive Producer; Joseph Gershenson; Screenplay: Edward T. Lowe; Original Story: Curt Siodmak; Director of Photography: George Robinson; Special Photography: John P. Fulton; Camera Operator: Eddie Cohen; Special Effects: Carl Elmendorf; Film Editor: Philip Cahn; Assistant Director: William Tummel; Art Directors: John B. Goodman and Martin Obzina; Musical Director: Hans J. Salter; Set Decorators; Russell A. Gausman and Andrew J. Gilmore; Sound Director: Bernard B. Brown; Technician: William Hedgcock; Properties: Eddie Keys; Makeup: Jack P. Pierce; Gowns: Vera West; Running Time: 70 minutes; Released: December 15, 1944

CAST: Boris Karloff...Dr. Gustav Niemann, Lon Chaney...Lawrence Talbot/the Wolf Man, John Carradine...Baron Latos/Count Dracula, J. Carrol Naish...Daniel, Anne Gwynne...Rita Hussman, Peter Coe...Carl Hussman, Lionel Atwill...Inspector Arnz, George Zucco...Professor Bruno Lampini, Elena Verdugo...Ilonka, Sig Ruman...Burgomaster Hussman, William Edmunds...Fejos, Philip Van Zandt...Inspector Muller, Charles Miller...Toberman, Michael Mark...Frederick Strauss, Frank Reicher...Ullman, Glenn Strange...The Monster

Nathalie Yafet lives in New Jersey with her wonderful husband, Steven. Currently, they are directing the opera *Hansel and Gretel*, with Steven at the piano and Nathalie singing the Mother. She is also a member of her local Board of Education, which takes up an inordinate amount of her time. Nathalie has been a passionate Karloff fan since she was a little girl growing up in Oconomowoc, Wisconsin.

ARSENIC AND OLD LACE (1941)

by Gary D. Rhodes

"The funniest show of the season has arrived, and is here to stay. The name of the show is 'Arsenic and Old Lace.'"
—John O'Hara in the January 20, 1941 *Newsweek*

"I should say that Mr. Karloff is a real addition to our stage, in both taste and a kind of static power."
—Stark Young in the January 27, 1941 *New Republic*

"I killed him because he said I looked like Boris Karloff!"
—Boris Karloff as Jonathan Brewster in "Arsenic and Old Lace"

"'If someone—me, for instance—came up to you and said: 'Hey, the funniest show of the season has arrived, and it's about two dear old ladies who have poisoned twelve men and buried them in the cellar of their Brooklyn home and Boris Karloff is in it, running a sort of murder race with the old ladies,... and—' I don't think I'd get that far. I think you might walk away. But that's why I have to ask you to wait and hear out the explaining."

That's how John O'Hara's review of "Arsenic and Old Lace" begins in *Newsweek*. Horror and humor had mixed on Broadway before, but never with such tremendous success. O'Hara's point made clear the unlikely success of a bizarre black comedy. Attempting to relay the plot and explain its merits, however, became a difficulty.

"When I begged them at least to tell me the plot of 'Arsenic and Old Lace' so that I could plug it among my cronies in cafe society," investor Frank Sullivan joked in the January 21, 1941 *New York Times*, "they made a noise at me with their lips, [producer] Lindsay tripped me and [producer] Crouse pushed me downstairs."

The hit play itself covers the exploits of Abby and Martha Brewster, who begin offering elderberry wine laced with arsenic to male boarders. After one lonely, elderly man died naturally in their home, the two sisters noticed the peace that had come to him. Their desire to extend the same "peace" to others climbs to twelve murders. Into this mix comes returning nephew Jonathan, a criminal whose face has been altered by companion Dr. Einstein to look like that of Boris Karloff. Jonathan's murder count itself numbers twelve, which quickly causes a rivalry between aunts and nephew.

Added to the chaos is "Uncle Teddy," brother to Abby and Martha. Believing himself to be Teddy Roosevelt, he consistently blows his bugle, charges up the "San Juan Hill" staircase, and buries the murdered bodies—"yellow fever victims"—in the cellar. Drama critic Mortimer—Jonathan's brother and the final member of the household—helps stir the crazy brew as he tries to have Teddy committed, rid the home of Jonathan, and marry lovely Elaine Harper. The comedy-farce plays out in three acts, with a wonderful curtain call given by the "bodies" in the cellar.

The January 20, 1941 *Time* magazine wrote that author Joseph Kesselring's idea for "Arsenic" stemmed from "considering what would be the most unlikely thing his gentle grandmother might do." Kesselring himself had grown up in Manhattan, sang in the Church of the Epiphany, went to the Stuyvesant High School, and later taught at the Bethel Mennonite College in Newton, Kansas. The magazine also mentioned, "He has acted on the road and in Chicago, has written pulp stories, vaudeville sketches, two Broadway flops. His press agent Richard Maney swears that Mr. Kesselring has recently lived on 'herbs, wild berries, and pemmican.'"

First titling it "Bodies in Our Cellar," Kesselring penned "Arsenic" hoping Dorothy Stickney—producer Howard Lindsay's wife—would want to play one of the two demented sisters. Lindsay gave the script to Stickney, who found it amusing enough to pique her husband's interest. He wired partner Russel Crouse, who instructed him to purchase the tale. They were not only involved in other projects, but realized script revisions would be necessary. The initial draft was allegedly in bad taste, including a terrible smell emanating from the Brewster's cellar/graveyard. As a result of their input, Lindsay and Crouse eventually received royalties as co-authors. Kesselring's name alone appeared officially as playwright, with Lindsay and Crouse at times even denying they had helped. Cornelia Otis Skinner's *Life with Lindsay and Crouse* (Houghton, Mifflin, and Co., 1976), however, claims that the duo "all but rewrote everything, changing many of the situations and introducing some new characters."

Boris Karloff himself had been uneasy about appearing in the play. Crouse made a trek to Hollywood to convince him, with their first meeting a farce in itself. Crouse laughingly told one interviewer, "I went to his house to sign him up with a pen in one hand and a contract in the other. But when he opened the door, I took one look at that face. I let out a scream that curdled milk for miles around and started running."

In the September 20, 1941 *Collier's*, Henry Pringle's article "Gentle Monster" detailed a Hollywood luncheon that followed: "Those present... were Mr.

Karloff, Russel Crouse the playwright, and an actor's agent who was all poised to say 'No, that's not enough,' when the subject of salary came up. 'We've got a play in New York we'd like you to do,' said Mr. Crouse as the coffee was being served. 'No, I won't do it,' said Karloff. 'I think its presumptuous for motion-picture actors to try to star on Broadway.' The agent nearly fainted. Crouse scalded his throat by gulping his coffee. Such a reply had never been made before in the history of either Hollywood or Broadway."

The producer later spoke about the same meeting on a November 13, 1958 episode of *This Is Your Life* honoring Karloff: "As much as I was stuck with the check anyway, we just sat and talked and finally curiosity got the better of [Karloff] and [he] said, 'What's the play about?'" A review in *The New Republic* claimed Karloff only accepted "upon the assurance that there would be 'other parts equally as good.'" He also enjoyed the idea of spoofing himself. As Howard Lindsay added on *This is Your Life*, "This first luncheon led to another luncheon... a slightly more expensive luncheon. Yes... We had to pay [Karloff's] salary for four years, but they were four happy and pleasant years."

Collier's recounted Karloff's fright after the first rehearsal: "'I was terrible,' he telephoned his wife, still in Hollywood, later that night. 'I couldn't read the lines at all. I stammered and stuttered. I'm taking the plane back tonight.' Mrs. Karloff soothed her monstrous spouse and suggested that he try one more rehearsal. Boris did so. Crouse and Lindsay told him he was wonderful; they had known so on the previous day but had forgotten to say anything."

Anna Erskine—Crouse's secretary/production assistant during the New York run of "Arsenic"—wrote about both producers in a Sunday theater section of the *New York Herald Tribune*. Her article—entitled "The Office of 'The Beamish Ones,'" after a nickname Karloff gave the two—claimed: "They couldn't be more unlike. For instance Lindsay answers all his mail, including insurance and haberdashery advertisements. Crouse answers nothing, leaves everything on his desk except for precious odds and ends which he files in his pockets. Lindsay, being the more photographed, is easily identified by callers, so Crouse, tired of always having to say 'And I'm Russel Crouse,' has a carved name plate on his desk."

With Karloff signed on the dotted line and rehearsals underway, Lindsay and Crouse moved the play closer to production. After a Baltimore tryout, the play opened on January 10, 1941 at New York's Fulton Theater. The cast also included Allyn Joslyn as Mortimer, Josephine Hull as Abby, Jean Adair as Martha, and John Alexander as Uncle Teddy.

Crouse himself wrote about the Broadway opening in the April 3, 1944 *Life* magazine: "Late in the afternoon of January 10, 1941, a few hours before the curtain rose on the first New York performance of Joseph Kesselring's 'Arsenic and Old Lace,' Mr. Howard Lindsay, who is known as the charming member of the firm of Lindsay and Crouse, shook my trembling hand and said 'We have not long to wait. It is my studied conviction that we either have a very big hit or we both will be run out of town.' He vanished into the dusk [Obligations to another play kept Lindsay from attending opening night]. With a hasty glance over each shoulder I hurried home, instructed my man to lay out my running pants and took a hurried look through my dog-eared copy of the elder James' (Jesse, not Henry) *Possees, and How to Outwit Them.* Depressed at the calculation that I probably would not get my second wind until I had passed Sandusky, Ohio, but cheered in the hope that if I could reach the Linwood Boulevard Methodist Episcopal Church in Kansas City, of which I believe I am still a member, I could claim sanctuary, I set out for the theater."

When critics addressed the play in the January 11 New York papers, the praise was unanimous. The *Journal and American* called it "a crazy combination of homicide and nonsense, the sort of peculiar mixture you might get if you put Ed Wynn in 'The Murders in the Rue Morgue' or Bea Lillie in the 'House of Usher.' In the exact meaning of the words it is frightfully funny." To Burns Mantle at the *Daily News*, it was "swell farce, expertly staged, [and] brilliantly played." Brooks Atkinson at the *Times* even declared "...none of us will ever forget it."

For Richard Lockridge at the *Sun*, it was a "noisy, preposterous, incoherent joy." His extreme praise is particularly interesting, as he co-wrote the novel that became Owen Davis' mystery-comedy play "Mr. and Mrs. North." The latter opened only two days after "Arsenic," causing the inevitable comparisons and competition between the two.

The national media echoed with thunderous applause. On January 20, *Time* called the play "absolutely top farce." The February *Catholic World* claimed: "We doubt if cadavers and laughs have ever met more pleasantly than in this surprising melodrama whose originality is endangered as much by panegyric as by explanation."

The first wave of New York reviews also highly praised Karloff's own performance as well. The *Sun* announced that "Mr. Karloff, whose startling resemblance to Karloff is constantly being commented upon by the other characters, manages to be horrifying without really scaring the audience out of its laughter." For Brown at the *Post*, "Karloff is a bogeyman who could make gooseflesh, at any rate, out of a sow's ear." The *Journal and American* thought much the same, mentioning "Mr. Karloff has charge of most of the horror and he is overpoweringly sinister in a performance that would, I should think, scare the other actors out of their makeup."

Even the usually anti-horror film critic Richard Watts of the *Herald Tribune* admitted "A really expert performer, this Mr. Karloff." Strong but hesitant praise also came from Whipple at the *World-Telegram*: "Mr. Karloff's acting had more restraint than I had considered possible in light of the long

Boris Karloff received critical praise for his role of Jonathan Brewster in the stage production of "Arsenic and Old Lace."

series of film horrors he has conducted, and I thought him excellent in every respect." The *Post* even wondered if the actor "must at moments even frighten himself."

A few reviews, however, didn't go overboard in assessing him, sometimes even offering kinder words for others in the cast. The *New York Times* merely wrote that Karloff "moves quietly through plot and poison without resorting to trickeries...." The January 12 *New York Newspaper PM* noted that "Boris Karloff is all that Boris Karloff is known to be. But it is Jean Adair and Josephine Hull... who take top honors." Six days later, *The New Yorker* review echoed that sentiment: "Boris Karloff (in person) is theoretically the star of the evening, and does very well too, but Josephine Hull, as the older of the Brewster sisters, is my girl."

Echoing the overall praise of critics were the audiences that filled theater seats every evening. "Swift, dry, and satirical and exciting, 'Arsenic and Old Lace' kept the first-night audiences roaring with laughter," the initial *New York Times* review made clear. The *Daily News* even said one group of viewers "simply howled itself red in the face." With regard to the handful of patrons that didn't "get it," the press generally had fun. John Cecil Holm's "Note on What's Wrong" in the September 7 *New York Times* took issue with a few such persons:

"Anyway, this woman had two friends who were sitting in the seats behind her and they kept up a running conversation for several minutes. The one on my left wanted to know who Boris Kosseloff or Karoff was. They didn't know either, but one of them did take a shot in the dark and guess that he might be from the movies. Well, that was all right. A lot of people never get to the pictures, but I was a little startled when one of the two in back suggested that the next play they went to should be a comedy. That made me feel a little sheepish for laughing so hard."

Regardless of the few wondering who "Kosseloff" was, audiences loved his work. *Collier's* article remembered Boris' reaction to his tremendous success: "The critics raved about the show and the cast. A matinee was scheduled for the next afternoon and producers Crouse and Lindsay stopped in Karloff's dressing room to congratulate him. They knew, from sad experience, that most actors would demand more publicity or beef about some review; anyway, complain about something. 'What a break for me!' said Karloff. 'Think of it. A broken-down movie actor in a Broadway play.'"

Along with mentioning his "modest and intelligent" qualities, *Collier's* also explained the actor's impression on New York society: "What surprised the sophisticates of New York most about Karloff last winter was the high order of his intelligence and the wide variety of his knowledge, which came to light when he was a guest expert on [the radio program] *Information Please*. Karloff stumped even so brainy a literary man as Franklin P. Adams in identifying a Mother Goose rhyme. He was as quick as John Kieran in thinking up poems beginning with the words, 'It was....' He [also] showed familiarity with the works of Joseph Conrad."

Despite Karloff's success, the actor remained amiable to cast, crew, and his two bosses. The good-natured relationship between him and Crouse and Lind-

"Arsenic and Old Lace" signaled an interesting cultural moment for Karloff. The repeated use of the "I killed him because he said I look like Boris Karloff" dialogue takes Karloff and offers him as a significant image outside the context of film.

say found the trio teasing one another throughout the Broadway run. According to *Life with Lindsay and Crouse*, the producers often kidded the actor about

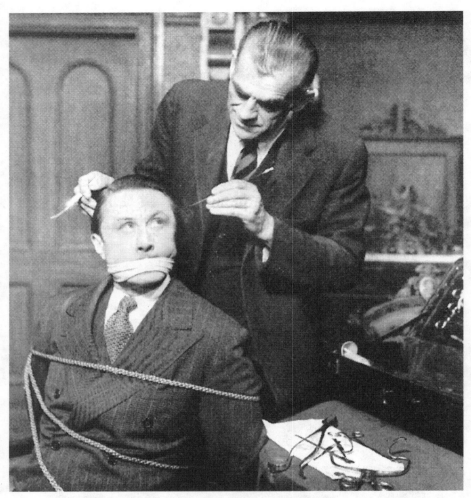

Echoing the overall praise of the critics were the audiences that filled theater seats every evening.

his $2,000 a week salary. Supposedly, Lindsay and Crouse once paid him that amount completely in nickels. Another day brought Karloff a new contract that listed a salary of $25 plus whatever the audience threw onto the stage. The actor jokingly threatened to quit unless he got a salary increase for makeup and powder. In return, the producers sent a kit containing "tooth powder, foot powder, baking powder, roach powder, gun powder, Seidlitz powder, and powdered eggs."

More than fun occurred during the show's run, however. A notice in the February 23, 1941 *New York Times* mentioned an almost incredible move for any theatrical hit. The management removed some thirty-two undesirable seats from the Fulton, "unthinkable along the Broadway pastures, especially when it affects the gross receipts of what is referred to as a 'smash hit.'" The loss of tickets had little impact in the long run, however. By March 24 of the following year, the *New York Times* announced that "Arsenic" had grossed just over $1,000,000 after 62 weeks and 501 performances.

The play's success even caused Lindsay and Crouse to increase the salaries of a few performers. Both also took turns sending humorous, joking notes to their investors. Some twenty-three backers had put money into "Arsenic," each realizing approximately $7,400 on each $583.34 invested for a 5/6th of one percent interest. These included longtime Broadway investor Howard Cullman, Gilbert W. Gabriel, and actress Nedda Harrigan, who had appeared in the 1927 stage version of "Dracula" with Bela Lugosi. Boris Karloff also ended up with a block of shares, which—thanks to Lindsay's and Crouse's kindness—passed into his hands just after the first wave of reviews.

Another investor, Frank Sullivan, enjoyed lampooning the play's success in the New York press. In a January 21, 1941 edition of the *Times*, he joked, "I really believe that the feeling of security an angel like me gets from owning a part of an actor like Boris Karloff is worth a dozen bottles of beef, iron, and wine, or six hours with a psychoanalyst." A few weeks later—on February 9— his next "Arsenic" article for the *Times* found him chiding Lindsay and Crouse for lack of proper payment on his investment:

"Naturally, I talked big and shot off my mouth somewhat after the opening of 'Arsenic and Old Lace,' for I, greenhorn that I am, expected that the auditor for Crouse & Lindsay Ltd. would be around the next morning and each morning thereafter with the milkman to leave a quart or two of $20 bills at my door. I even dreamed of such a happy period of chip supersaturation that I would be leaving an occasional note for the auditor say, 'Please leave only $1,000 this morning; haven't used yesterday's yet.' A sucker lives and learns. ...Someone is getting rich, though."

Beyond the play's economic success, however, it also blazed a few unique trails. For example, the May 18, 1942 *Newsweek* ran an article covering a particularly special May 10 performance of "Arsenic" at New York's Fulton. All of the actors were deaf-mutes, as were most of the 800-odd audience members. The fourteen cast members were part of the Dramatic Club at Gallaudet College in Washington DC, which at the time was "the country's only college for deaf-mutes." In fact, the magazine claimed it was the "first time any drama had been so publicly presented."

Along with impressive costumes and makeup, the evening's performance featured the players using luminous gloves to signal their lines during one scene when the light was out. Karloff, who was in the audience that night, was so delighted with their work that he personally sought out Eric Malzkuhn, the play's "Jonathan." After complimenting him in pantomime, Karloff led the entire company to the stage for a curtain call.

The original Broadway version finally closed on June 17, 1944, after a phenomenal 1,444 performances. At that time, only three plays—"Tobacco Road," "Abie's Irish Rose," and Lindsay and Crouse's "Life with Father"— had ran longer on Broadway. By its latter stages, however, "Arsenic" had undergone a few changes. The cast had some turnover and the show itself had moved from the Fulton to the Hudson. Boris himself followed closing night with six weeks of "Arsenic" on the road.

Due to the enormous success in New York, other versions had sprung up elsewhere in the country and world. By mid-'41, Erich von Stroheim appeared as Jonathan in a Chicago production of the play. He later took the role in a touring roadshow during the early forties, as did Bela Lugosi. Both received favorable notices and certainly must have offered unique interpretations of the role. At least a few critics even preferred Lugosi's performance to Karloff's. Furthermore, British critics gave strong nods to another non-Karloff version, which featured Edmund Willard as Jonathan. In fact, at 1,337 performances, it became the longest running American play on the London stage.

Yet another incarnation made headlines after taking Argentina by storm. One John Reinhardt obtained permission from Lindsay, Crouse, and Karloff to produce a version in Buenos Aires, then set about finding backers. For the role Jonathan, Reinhardt and fellow producer Luis Caesar Amadore found Ibanez Menta, who had portrayed Leroux's *The Phantom of the Opera* in Argentina. In fact, according to the February 1, 1942 *New York Times*, years before Menta "had taken lessons in makeup from the great Lon Chaney, [Reinhardt and Amadore] gave him a picture of Boris Karloff. In a few minutes he emerged as the mirror reflection of the horrific Mr. Karloff himself." The play itself became a tremendous hit, with the initial "three pessimists" [Lindsay, Crouse, and Karloff] "eating their words—but with pleasure." Subsequently, other non-Karloff versions surfaced in Stockholm and Göteburg in Sweden, Santiago in Chile, Lima in Peru, Melbourne and Sydney in Australia, and two cities in Uruguay.

In addition, Lindsay and Crouse were proud that an USO Camp Shows' production of "Arsenic" made a tour of some 96 camps and naval stations during World War II. Approximately 196,000 members of the armed forces saw the show. Moreover, the two producers defied Broadway tradition by releasing the rights for amateur production while the show was still running in New York. Rather than detract from the play's success, the amateur productions seemed to increase interest in it. In Seattle, for example, a professional roadshow version hit town as an amateur version simultaneously played the same city. Both quickly sold out.

Movie studios, of course, also took notice of the play's success. The screen rights eventually landed an advance of $175,000, with the film itself in production during 1941. Josephine Hull, Jean Adair, and John Alexander left Broad-

Despite Karloff's success, the actor remained amiable to cast and crew.

way to reprise their roles in the film, but Karloff stuck with the stage version. He remained forever saddened by not starring in the film, but never made Lindsay and Crouse aware of his feelings. To them, he had admirably remained on board the New York cast and helped keep it a success. In filling his cinematic shoes, the studio considered such actors as Bela Lugosi before signing Raymond Massey. In addition to the latter's Karloff-like makeup, the film's dialogue retains all references to Boris.

While not in the screen version, Karloff played Jonathan Brewster in at least two radio shows. The first was a 1946 *Screen Guild Players'* adaptation, which also featured Eddie Albert as Mortimer. In keeping with the program's policy, neither actor was paid. The *Screen Guild Players* acted as a charity, donating what would have been star salaries to the Motion Picture Relief Fund. More interesting, however, was a later version on *Best Plays*. Not only was the show—at sixty minutes—twice as long as the earlier adaptation, it captures more flavor of the original New York run. Along with Karloff, the cast found Jean Adair and Edgar Stehli reprising their Broadway roles.

Karloff also performed in a few TV versions of "Arsenic." The first adaptation—which included Josephine Hull as Abby—came on the *Ford Theater* in

Critics called "Arsenic and Old Lace" "a crazy combination of homicide and non-sense."

1949. Equally intriguing is a *Best of Broadway* broadcast of 1955, pairing Boris with Peter Lorre as Dr. Einstein. A January 12 *Variety* found the latter excellent, believing "Karloff and Lorre made the perfect murderous pair, relishing every line and turning them out beautifully."

His final television appearance in the role apparently came in a 1962 *Hallmark Hall of Fame* episode that included Tony Randall as Mortimer and Kesselring's original choice for a Brewster sister, Dorothy Stickney, as Abby. Though *Variety*'s review on February 7 was not particularly favorable to Stickney and Randall, Karloff received a decent nod. "In short," the trade regretted, "the wit and fantasy of the Kesselring original were swamped by earthbound actors."

Equally curious is Karloff's brief return to the stage in "Arsenic" for a 1957 Alaskan version. Shortly before, he had read that oil had been discovered in that state near some of his own land holdings. Wanting to find a way to pay his fare from England, Karloff offered to play in an amateur production of the play at the Anchorage Community College Workshop. Along with presenting Karloff a golden trowel as a sign of their affection, a representative of the Alaskan production related the following on the *This Is Your Life* salute: "From the very beginning, Boris became part of the group. Not a star... but just one of us. When he discovered we were trying to raise the funds to build our own theater, he turned over every penny of his percentage of the profits to our building fund."

More than being an important factor in Karloff's career, however, the play itself signaled an interesting cultural moment for the horror film star in general.

The repeated use of the "I killed him because he said I looked like Boris Karloff" dialogue takes Karloff and offers him as a significant image outside the context of film. However much icons like Karloff and Bela Lugosi are accepted today, such was uncommon in the thirties and forties outside of direct promotions for their films.

Prior to this, of course, horror elements had worked their way out of films and into other aspects of the media. Lon Chaney Sr., for example, had become a humorous, popular joke ("Don't step on that! It might be ...."), as well as immortalized in song (*The Hollywood Revue of 1929*'s "Lon Chaney's Gonna Get You If You Don't Watch Out"). As a reevaluation of his work has finally highlighted, however, Chaney was not essentially a horror film star. Even if he appeared in a handful of films classed in that genre, Chaney was not created or popularly confined by such movies and topics. Indeed, the very existence of a codified horror genre in 1920s' American cinema is arguable.

When the thirties' horror cycle took hold, it is true that the media enjoyed drawing on the images from those films. For example, the cartoon *Mickey's Gala Premiere* (1933) featured Dracula, Frankenstein's Monster, and Mr. Hyde. In conjunction with plays or films, various newspapers offered caricatures of Lugosi and Karloff. Certainly advertising for their films drew on their connection with the genre, offering either a tag like "Uncanny" for Karloff or practically making "Dracula" Lugosi's middle name. Together, Bela and Boris even sang "We're Horrible, Horrible Men" on radio's *Baker's Broadcast* of October 31, 1938.

Yet, generally in these cases—such as with the Mickey Mouse cartoon—the emphasis was not on the horror film *star* but rather the *image* offered by a specific film. Much the same could even be said of, say, the short subject *Hollywood on Parade* (1933) where a wax statue of Lugosi comes to life and meets Betty Boop. Even though the actor really is Lugosi, it is the image of cinema's Dracula that is stressed, even to the degree of "biting" Mae Questel, a real-life incarnation of Fleischer's cartoon star. And, when emphasis did move to the star in other cases, it was usually tied to the promotion of a specific film.

It seems of course that the dialogue referring to Karloff was in the play prior to the actor himself being signed for the initial Broadway run. Certainly—with the exception of Lugosi and von Stroheim's stabs at the role—the script's references to Karloff remained in subsequent, non-Karloff stage, television, and film versions. Indeed, this culturally-accepted iconography of Karloff himself (rather than, say, an image of the Frankenstein Monster) is what appears in such later works as the Dr. Seuss cartoon *How the Grinch Stole Christmas*.

As a result, the play represents more than simply a successful moment in Karloff's career or a door to Broadway that opened for him. "Arsenic and Old Lace" can also be seen as both an interesting and important recognition of a horror film star as a cultural icon. Beyond any advertisement for a film or generic "appearance" in a cartoon, Kesselring's play takes the Boris Karloff image itself and—without mention of specific films—places it as a recognizable and meaningful factor outside the parameters of cinema.

"Arsenic and Old Lace"—Opening night on Broadway:

CREDITS: Producers: Howard Lindsay and Russel Crouse; Playwright: Joseph Kesselring; Opening night: January 10, 1941 at the Fulton Theater in New York

CAST: .Josephine Hull...Abby Brewster, Wyrley Birch...Rev. Dr. Harper, John Alexander...Teddy Brewster, John Quigg...Officer Brophy, Bruce Gordon...Officer Klein, Jean Adair...Martha Brewster, Helen Brooks...Elaine Harper, Allyn Joslyn...Mortimer Brewster, Henry Herbert...Mr. Gibbs, Boris Karloff...Jonathan Brewster, Edgar Stehli...Dr. Einstein, Anthony Ross...Officer O'Hara, Victor Sutherland...Lieutenant Rooney, William Parke...Mr. Witherspoon

Radio versions with Boris Karloff:

Lady Esther Screen Guild Players—"Arsenic and Old Lace"

CREDITS: Producer-Director: Bill Lawrence; Adaptation: Bill Hampton [or Harry Kronman]; Music: Wilbur Hatch; Broadcast: November 25, 1946; Running time: 30 minutes; CBS circa 1944

CAST: Boris Karloff...Jonathan Brewster, Eddie Albert...Mortimer Brewster, Jane Morgan...Abby Brewster, Verna Felton...Martha Brewster.

Best Plays—"Arsenic and Old Lace"

CREDITS: Supervisor: William Welsh; Director: Edward King; Broadcast: circa 1952-53; Running time: 60 minutes; NBC

CAST: John Chapman...Host, Boris Karloff...Jonathan Brewster, Jean Adair...Martha Brewster, Donald Cook...Mortimer Brewster, Evelyn Varden...Abby Brewster, Edgar Stehli...Dr. Einstein

Television versions with Boris Karloff:

Ford Theatre—"Arsenic and Old Lace"

CREDITS: Producer: Garth Montgomery; Director: Marc Daniels; Sets: Samuel Leve; Music: Cy Feuer; Televised April 11, 1949; Running Time: 60 minutes; CBS

CAST: Josephine Hull...Abby Brewster, Ruth McDevitt...Martha Brewster, William Prince...Mortimer Brewster, Boris Karloff...Jonathan Brewster, Bert Freed...Teddy Brewster, Edgar Stehli...Dr. Einstein

Best of Broadway—"Arsenic and Old Lace"

CREDITS: Producer: Martin Manulis; Director: Herbert Bayard Swope, Jr.; Television Adaptation: Howard Lindsay and Russel Crouse; Televised on January 5, 1955; CBS

CAST: Helen Hayes...Abby Brewster, Billie Burke...Martha Brewster, John Alexander...Teddy Brewster, Boris Karloff...Jonathan Brewster, Orson Bean...Mortimer Brewster, Pat Breslin...Elaine Harper, Alan Tower...The Reverend Dr. Harper, Peter Lorre...Dr. Einstein, King Calder...Officer Brophy, Bruce Gordon...Officer Klein, Richard Bishop...Lt. Rooney, Edward Everett Horton...Mr. Witherspoon

Hallmark Hall of Fame—"Arsenic and Old Lace"
CREDITS: Producer and Director: George Schaefer; Television Adaptation: Robert Hartung; Televised in color on February 5, 1962; NBC

CAST: Dorothy Stickney...Abby Brewster, Mildred Natwick...Martha Brewster, Tom Bosley...Teddy Brewster, Boris Karloff...Jonathan Brewster, Tony Randall...Mortimer Brewster, Dody Heath...Elaine Harper, Farrell Pelly...The Reverend Dr. Harper, George Voskovec...Dr. Einstein, Dort Clark...Officer Brophy, Nathaniel Frey...Officer Klein, Alan MacAteer...Mr. Gibbs, Ralph Dunn...Lt. Rooney

Gary Don Rhodes is the author of *Lugosi: His Life in Film, on Stage, and in the Hearts of Horror Lovers* (McFarland, 1996). He has contributed to such film magazines as *Classic Images, The Big Reel, Filmfax,* and *Cult Movies.* His documentary films are released through such companies as VIEW Video of New York after PBS broadcasts. Rhodes also teaches at the University of Oklahoma, Department of English. He is currently co-authoring a book on Bela Lugosi's last years with Richard Sheffield, as well as penning a book-length analysis of the film *White Zombie* for Mid Mar Press.

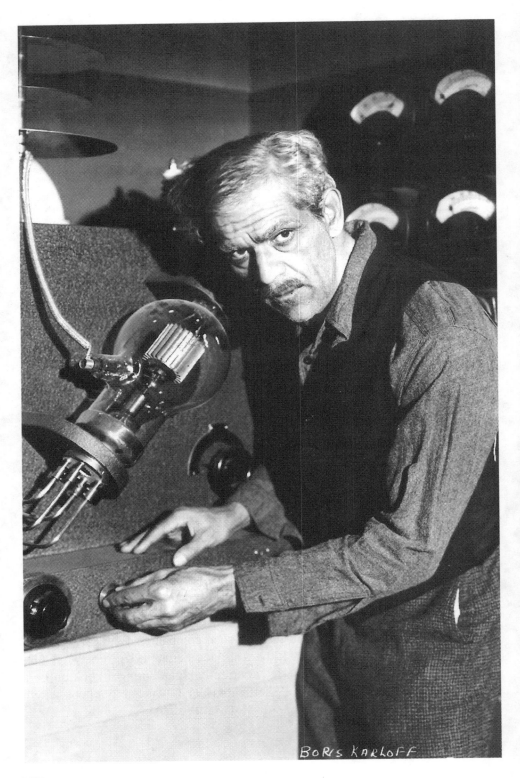

BORIS KARLOFF

THE DEVIL COMMANDS (1941)

by David H. Smith

"It is enough that there *is* a beyond." —George Bernard Shaw

"When the devil commands Karloff obeys...!" the one-sheet poster copy read for *The Devil Commands*. Some might say it was no satanic decree, but rather the imperium of pugnacious Harry Cohn (1891-1958), the president of Columbia Pictures. By all accounts the stereotypical old-style movie mogul, Cohn had cannily signed Karloff to a multi-picture contract in 1939 at the outset of the second great Hollywood horror movie boom, and reaped the profits from the "Mad Doctor" series of films that ensued.

Only a year after signing on, however, after completing three of the covenantal films, Karloff was offered the chance to flex his Thespian muscles in a dramatic personae other than the Hollywood assembly line of homogeneous mad scientists. Theatrical producers Howard Lindsay and Russel Crouse offered him the starring role in *Arsenic and Old Lace* on Broadway, a part Boris approached with much trepidation but eventually undertook to great acclaim. Still, there was that Columbia contract to honor, and Karloff, ever the professional, would never give a diminished performance no matter the impending opportunity

The Devil Commands became the final chapter of the serious Karloff/Columbia "Mad Doctor" series. The fifth film, the farcical *The Boogie Man Will Get You* (1942), fulfilled his Columbia contract with less than memorable results. Perhaps recognizing the qualitative decline of the first three entries directed by Nick Grindé (1893-1979), Cohn seemed to pull out some stops for the fourth. As Denis Gifford pointed out in *A Pictorial History of Horror Movies*, compared to those initial installments, the film "had better things for Karloff: a new director, Edward Dmytryk, and a good book as a basis." *The Devil Commands* truly delivers the goods.

Dr. Julian Blair (Boris Karloff) is the beloved head of the science department at Midland University. Assembling five distinguished colleagues in his laboratory one stormy night, Blair demonstrates his invention for them to prove that "the human brain gives off an impulse that can be recorded." He straps a bulky helmet contraption onto his assistant Dr. Richard Sayles (Richard Fiske)

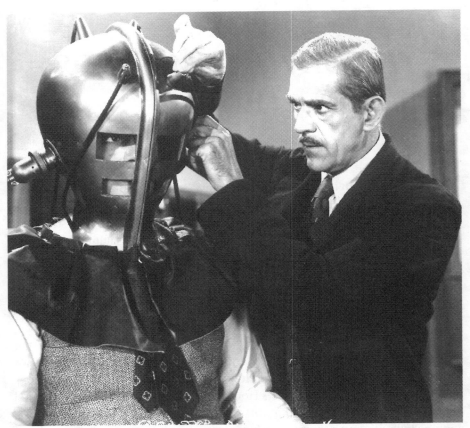

Dr. Blair (Karloff) demonstrates his invention to prove the human brain gives off an impulse that can be recorded.

and revs up the roomful of electrical equipment to which it is wired. With a crackling Jacob's ladder for effect, a mechanical pen traces a spiky path on a huge sheet of graph paper on the wall.

"Dr. Sayles' brain is sending out waves you see recorded on that chart, and whether he speaks or is silent, or even if he tries to hide what he was thinking with meaningless words, his true thoughts would be recorded on that chart," Blair explains. He shuts down the apparatus, and the convened brain trust check to make sure the young man feels no ill effect. When asked if such a chart could be made of anyone's thought patterns, Blair affirms, remarking "and each brain has its own wavelength, and they're as unlike as fingerprints."

Blair's wife Helen (Shirley Warde) comes into the lab from out of the rainy night with their thickskulled minion Karl (Ralph Penney) in tow. Treating her husband like the cliché absent-minded professor he is, Helen lovingly reminds him their daughter Anne is returning by train from a visit with friends in New York that evening, and that this is her twentieth birthday. Naturally, the jolly old scientists encourage their host to forgo further demonstration and fulfill his paternal duties.

Begging his wife's indulgence, Blair hooks his wife to the apparatus to make a comparative brain wave chart. The pen traces a different path, and Blair reveals to the scientists that the wave impulses of women are stronger and more regular than men's. The gathered men are convinced, and ask Blair about his plans for the device.

"Well," he modestly proposes, "eventually, conceivably, we may be able to record and read the thoughts of every human brain without a word being spoken." One scientist expresses doubt, but Blair convinces him by reminding him rather extraneously that, at one time, radio was impossible too.

"All this that you see is only the first step towards what I hope we can achieve," Blair elaborates. "It may take years, perhaps a lifetime. If science can unlock the human mind, can uncover the secrets of every human brain, well, that's a job worth doing, isn't it?" Helen sweetly reminds him of their rendezvous, so off they go.

Blair and his doting wife stop at a bakery to pick up a birthday cake ordered for their daughter. They are unable to find a parking place, so Blair ducks out into the driving rain while Helen drives around the block. Coming out of the bakery with the extremely altruistic owner carrying the pasteboard box, Blair hears the screech of tires and a sickening crash. Their car has been broadsided, and Helen dies in his arms.

After the funeral, the inconsolable Blair returns to his lab and absent-mindedly starts up the equipment for distraction from his grief. Amazingly, the mechanical pen begins to trace a chart identical to Helen's. Accompanied by Richard, daughter Anne (Amanda Duff) comes into the lab, wearing a raincoat and looking identical to her mother the night of her death. Blair is understandably taken aback, then gathers his thoughts to postulate his new theory. He tells the young couple that the graph is proof of life after death, and that Helen must be trying to reach him.

The assemblage of scientists reconvene to hear his hypothesis. "My wife passed through a change that we call death, but the impulse that spoke from her living brain that you saw me record on that chart did not die," Blair rationalizes. "If Helen could send me that message, and she did send it, then there must be a way to establish controlled and scientific communication between the living and the so-called dead."

The scientists express their doubts, but Blair tries to allay them. "Don't you see?" he says passionately "We hold in our hand the key that might unlock the door between us and those whom we call dead. If we can set humanity free from fear, if we can show people that those we love are not lost to us, if we can wipe out the horror, the superstition conjured up out of fear of darkness—"

One scientist interrupts, asking, "What if you do find the way to pierce the veil between us and them?"

Another continues, "And let the world of the dead back in upon the living?"

A third scientist says, "We don't know what evil may be lurking behind that veil, waiting to get through."

"What if you let loose on humanity something much more terrible than any fear that haunts us now?" the first doubting Thomas queries.

"But why should that happen?" Blair asks.

"I know one thing, Julian," the man responds with trite mad scientist movie moralizing. "There are things even human beings have no right to know."

Blair interjects, "There speaks fear, even from you."

"Call it fear if you want to," the man responds "I tell you, *you* must not go on with this."

"*Must not?*" Blair echoes indignantly. "Is there a wall beyond which science may not go?"

"This is not science," his colleague proclaims. Realizing his arguments have fallen on deaf ears, Blair dismisses them all from his lab. Lackey Karl, hovering in the background, at last makes his presence known by reassuring Blair of his belief in the hereafter. Karl has been visiting a spirit medium since his own mother died two years before, and urges Blair to join him for that evening's seance.

Once introduced to the spiritualist, Blanche Walters (Anne Revere), and participating in a brief seance, Blair proceeds to uncover all of the woman's showman gimmicks and debunk her claims of communication with the beyond. He remains puzzled, however, by the strong electric charge he felt during the ceremony. Though understandably miffed at her unmasking, Mrs. Walters states she cannot explain that aspect. Blair, intrigued by the amount of voltage the woman's brain seems to generate, is anxious to test her capacity in his lab and promises to pay her well for her time.

At the lab, Blair tests to see her generate electrical current, progressing so far as to pass 10,000 volts through her, causing a lightning bolt to pass between two metallic globes without ill effect. This familiar spark-gap device, pervasive to the fantastic cinema from *Metropolis* (1926) to *The Mask of Fu Manchu* (1932) and beyond, was actually developed by the Croatian-born inventor and electrical physicist Nikola Tesla (1856-1943). Delighted, Blair reveals to Mrs. Walters his plan to use her, by varying the hookup in his brain signal recording apparatus, as a receiving station for his late wife's thought waves. He hopes to learn to read the messages sent, and perhaps even bring back her voice. Avaricious Mrs. Walters sees the lucrative moneymaking potential, and readily agrees.

When their first efforts fail to yield results, Blair adds Karl to the circuit to boost the mental power running through the equipment. Sure enough, the pen

Dr. Blair is startled when his daughter Anne (Amanda Duff) comes into the lab looking identical to her mother.

starts to repeat Helen's singular pattern. Unfortunately, there is feedback from the tremendous power discharge that courses back into Karl's hookup, and the slowwitted galoot is nearly electrocuted, "which injures his nerve centers." Even as Blair and Mrs. Walters tend to him, Anne and Richard come to the lab door. Richard warns Blair the university board is considering action for his bizarre experiments. Mrs. Walters tells Blair they have to get away to continue his work in solitude, taking Karl with them.

Blair resigns from the school faculty, sells his home, and sends Anne away to New York, promising to write later "if he could." The scientist, the spiritualist, and their brain-damaged helpmate set up shop in a forlorn house in Barsham Harbor, Maine, on the New England coast. There they work in secret for two years. The townspeople begin to fear them for their reclusive ways. When a number of bodies begin to disappear from the cemetery, the sheriff (Kenneth MacDonald) figures there may be a connection and pays an official visit to the asocial household.

When Blair at last emerges from his lab at the beckoning of the tremulous housekeeper (Dorothy Adams), it is a far different Karloff than we have seen in the earlier scenes. No longer the natty and groomed scholar of before, Dr. Blair is now a stooped and disheveled milksop, at the beck and call of the austere Mrs. Walters. Scott Allen Nollen, in *Boris Karloff*, rightly proclaims "the degeneration of Karloff's character is one of many outstanding visual components" of *The Devil Commands*. Following her lead, Blair refuses to explain his line of experiments to the lawman, and has Karl escort him to the property gate.

The sheriff waits on the road to town for the housekeeper to leave for the night and asks her to check out the mysterious laboratory for him. The very next day, Blair accidentally leaves the lab door unlocked, and she manages to sneak in unnoticed. Blair remembers leaving the door unlocked and sends Karl to lock it, trapping her inside. There, in a supremely Grand Guignol moment, she sees the five stolen corpses mentioned by the sheriff seated around a table in a macabre merging of the supernatural seance and Blair's telepathic equipment. She accidentally activates the apparatus, which opens a cartoon vortex into the ether. The housekeeper is buffeted by the tornadic winds, the seated corpses, secured by harnesses, rock back and forth in the turbulence. Michael Weldon, in *The Psychotronic Encyclopedia of Film*, justifiably called this the film's "standout scene"; the late William K. Everson was just as perspicacious when he described it in *Classics of the Horror Film* as "a particularly strong and well done episode."

The housekeeper dies of fright. Realizing what has occurred, Mrs. Walters seeks to deflect blame from them by donning the woman's shoes and walking a path near a seaside cliff, leaving the sheriff and the widower (Walter Baldwin) to believe she fell to her doom going home for the evening. Anne and Richard arrive and talk to the sheriff. "My father had become a very strange man," Anne's stream-of-consciousness narration understates.

With another body to add to the circuit (as if moldering corpses provide any electrical impetus), Blair and Karl put on their safety harnesses while Mrs. Walters assumes her position as the medium. The equipment again creates a vortical passageway to the beyond, and a spooky otherworldly voice is heard to mutter "Julian." Mrs. Walters collapses from the strain even as the sheriff pounds on the door.

Blair turns off the tumultuous equipment, and emerges to embrace his daughter. When Richard and Anne wonder why none of her letters to Blair have been acknowledged, he realizes Mrs. Walters has been intercepting them, and promises to make amends and join them downstairs in a moment. Back in the lab, Blair discovers Mrs. Walters has died, while in town the citizens decide to rally and march toward the house.

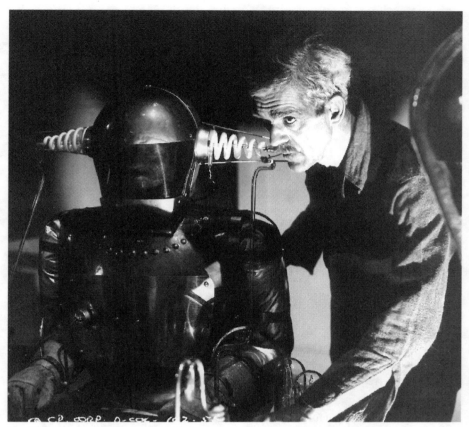

The biggest problem *The Devil Commands* has is overcoming grudges audiences harbor.

Richard comes into the lab and is mortified by the tableau. Blair argues that his work must continue because, after hearing the otherworldly voice, he has come to realize Anne's proximity is the key to success because her and her mother's "minds are in tune." The younger scientist is dead set against resuming the experiment with Anne's involvement, so Karl belts him unconscious. Assuming his most fatherly air, Blair hooks the intimidated Anne up to the apparatus and throws the switch.

The vortex opens and the beckoning voice is heard again. The townspeople break into the house and overwhelm Karl. The whirlwind increases its velocity, tearing the lab apart and sucking Blair into the ether. Richard manages to shut down the equipment and revive Anne amid the rubble. The whereabouts of her father are never discovered.

The biggest problem *The Devil Commands* has, as does any later entry in a film series, is overcoming the grudges audiences tend to harbor. Almost inevitably, sequels lack the something that made the initial foray so interesting

Karloff's performance is without a doubt a brilliant one.

and only try to imitate. This is not true one hundred percent of time, as witness *Bride of Frankenstein* (1935) and *Aliens* (1986), to name but two, that in many ways surpass their predecessors. And the only continuity the Columbia "Mad Doctor" series of films has is one of shared theme; the renegade scientist, forced by authorities or circumstance to work outside the mainstream, achieving success at too high a cost, and hoping the results will still be of value to humankind anyway.

This series stigma encroached on few of the reviews. Donald C. Willis, in *Horror and Science Fiction Films: A Checklist,* thought *The Devil Commands* was only "mediocre at best." The *Motion Picture Herald* found it "somewhat slow," but that it had "the necessary continuity to make it an interesting melodrama of horror and suspense "

A *Pictorial History of Science Fiction Films* author Jeff Rovin dismissed it as an "all-right mad-scientist film," but for sheer vitriol none can surpass "Char" in *Variety* who reviewed it upon original release obviously ignorant of the full title and of Karloff's Broadway role. "Exhibitors will have a word for [*The*] *Devil Commands*, but it can't be used in polite society," the critic deprecated. "It's something that required just nerve to produce. To put the film on the release schedule amounts to extreme bravery [and] billing the star as Boris 'Arsenic' Karloff. He's some kind of poison without doubt."

Such a vehement attack on the film and its star has been met and responded to many times over since. The sententious John Stanley, in his *Creature Features Movie Guide Strikes Again*, made especial mention of Karloff's "riveting performance," as well as citing the underrated Anne Revere's "cold, evil demeanor." Gene Wright, in *The Science Fiction Image*, noted, "Karloff is near his peak" in *The Devil Commands*, but never says what that pinnacle was. "Although the film's premise is pure abracadabra and the sets often look like Salvation Army rejects, the direction is stylish and first-rate and offers a number of unexpected *frissons*." Wright was more succinct in *Horrorshows,* saying, "Karloff is pure gold."

William K. Everson found the film a classic of its kind, "the least hackneyed" of the series, that still "plays chillingly well." Everson went on to discourse how *The Devil Commands* "is a classic example of how one good director, one good actor, and a basically good story can combine to produce something worthwhile." Phil Hardy, in *The Encyclopedia of Science Fiction Movies*, noted the director gave the images "a sadness that's unusual in such productions."

Canadian-born director Edward Dmytryk was raised in Los Angeles and became a cutter at Paramount in 1929 and a full editor in 1934. He directed his first film, *The Hawk*, in 1935, and earned contracts at Columbia (1940-1942) and at RKO (1942-1947). Aside from directing entries in the Falcon, Boston Blackie, and Lone Wolf film series, Dmytryk also freelanced at Universal for the goofy but beloved *Captive Wild Woman* in 1943.

Having joined the Communist Party in 1945, it was inevitable Dmytryk would be called before the House Committee on Un-American Activities which, two years later, had started to root out Communist sympathizers in Hollywood. The hearings turned into hideous spectacles that violated constitutional rights. Witnesses friendly to the red-hunters, like conservatives Robert Taylor (1911-1969) and Adolphe Menjou (1890-1963), railed against perceived radical elements in the industry. Some turned informers.

The hostile witnesses, the supposed subversives, refused to answer the committee's questions, and some launched into speeches before being cut off. Shortly afterward, the movie industry started the blacklist, which denied work to Communists and those suspected of leftist sympathies. Dmytryk, among the hostile witnesses known as "The Hollywood Ten," was charged with contempt of Congress and imprisoned. Dmytryk later became the only member of the Ten to become a friendly witness and name names.

In the early 1950s, Dmytryk was hired by producer Stanley Kramer to direct four films, the last being *The Caine Mutiny* (1954) that went on to be nominated for a Best Picture Oscar. He worked with a future luminary of the horror genre in 1955, directing Peter Cushing in *The End of the Affair*. Dmytryk also headed up the campy *Bluebeard* (1972) before becoming a professor of filmmaking at USC. In 1981, at the age of 73, his autobiography entitled *It's a Hell of a Life but Not a Bad Living* was published; he's written a number of other books since.

Karloff's co-stars run the gamut from sublime to innocuous to annoying. Anne Revere (1903-1990) was an experienced stage actress who went to Hollywood in 1940 for a decade's worth of fine supporting roles and won the Oscar for Best Supporting Actress in *National Velvet* (1944). Like Dmytryk, Revere was investigated by the HUAC and blacklisted by the film industry. She eventually returned to Broadway and, in a fine *lex talionis* on Tinseltown, won a Tony Award in 1960. As Mrs. Walters in *The Devil Commands*, Revere is the epitome of the clichéd turbaned "ice princess," supercilious, dominating the befuddled Blair with ease, her dark eyes glinting with greed. With a script that developed her character further, Revere could easily have outshone Karloff, and Mrs. Walters' ignominious death before the finale is a major failing of the film.

Nominal hero Richard Fiske is bland and ultimately forgettable, as is Amanda Duff as Karloff's daughter, though she gives her all with the lugubrious voice-over narration that nevertheless still sounds stilted and a bit silly. Kenneth MacDonald is likably authoritative and more astute than genre lawmen are wont to be, and Dorothy Adams is nicely terrified even as she putters domestically about the gloomy house and before her dervishilke death. But Ralph Penney rates right down there with Edward M. Hyans, Jr. of *Jungle Woman* (1944) fame for most annoying lummox in horror movies, failing to raise nary a hackle amidst all the low-key lighting when brain damage leaves him the ubiquitous hulking brute.

Forgiving its meaningless title, *The Devil Commands* was based on a book called *The Edge of Running Water* by William F. Sloane, published in 1939. Why at this stage of the Columbia series game a source novel (read: more expensive) was adapted rather than a wholly original screenplay procured is anyone's guess. The book, nowadays fairly rare and fairly expensive, told of a rising young psychologist in a remote farm house and his researches to communicate with the dead. One reviewer said of the book, "Cold chills and thrills combined in a most unusual item for those who crave a touch of the unknown, a bit of wrestling with things beyond human ken and footprints pointing to foul play." William K. Everson found the original novel "a minor masterpiece of subtle horror."

Ken Hanke made a thoughtful remark about the film in *A Critical Guide to Horror Film Series*. To him, it contains "finely crafted, full-blown horror that departs in many significant ways from its pussyfooting predecessors [in the

[Courtesy Ronald V. Borst/Hollywood Movie Posters]

Columbia "Mad Doctor" series]." He further stated *The Devil Commands* was "a small classic of its genre," and that it was "a distinctly unsettling film that manages not to cheat on its shocks, while still maintaining a sense of balance, believability, and, best of all, an obvious belief in the intelligence of its audience."

Karloff's performance is without a doubt a brilliant one. His disarming forgetfulness, timidly begging his wife's indulgence, and fretting over the dampness of her hair from the rain as he closes the cumbersome helmet (never mind Richard's pomade!) show the unspoken love that exists between a couple married for many years. Blair's grief over his wife and his mental torture at deceiving his housekeeper's husband are palpable. Karloff's only stumble, and it's a small one, comes when Anne, her features shrouded by her raincoat, comes into the lab, momentarily echoing an identical entrance scene with his wife earlier. Sly old Columbia reinforced the comparison by inserting Shirley Warde's entrance scene again (her features are visible), but the lack of ominous music and Karloff's too-quick realization of his mistake undo the fright factor.

Blair's original research is greeted by his colleagues with much *elan*, but the outsized helmet and roomful of equipment seem awfully unwieldy for something so reminiscent of an EEG. The electroencephalograph, similarly used for measuring and recording the electrical activity of the brain, was invented by German psychiatrist Hans Berger in 1929, and Blair's slow and clumsy mechanical pen seems antiquated even by 1941 standards. When you consider *The Devil Commands* is told in flashback from a point seven years after the death of Helen—the Barsham Harbor sequence two years later with Anne's narrative five years after that—Julian Blair's device seems all the more anachronous.

Adding human corpses to the circuit channeled by Mrs. Walters to increase her telepathic receiving capacity makes for a terrifically ghoulish *mise en scene*, but it is not remotely logical. The townspeople storm the house for no good reason other than to chew up a few seconds' running time, and thankfully no one brandishes a flaming torch or yammers about destroying monsters and protecting the womenfolk.

Interpolating straightforward mysticism with hard-core science fiction is a tack producers have tried only infrequently and with varying degrees of success, most often in the next decade. The atomic age, constrained filmmakers to marry the two genres with sporadically untoward results for jaded audiences' acceptance of werewolves, vampires, and zombies. But *The Devil Commands* shows a scientist readily accepting the idea of an afterlife, a decidedly supernatural precept, without trying to explain it away with the usual genre blather about parallel dimensions, alien worlds, and/or alternate planes of existence.

Coupled with Boris Karloff's earnest, believable portrait of a man whose physical health is overwhelmed by the research he has undertaken and his emotional well-being sundered by the people he has alternately embraced and (inadvertently) spurned, *The Devil Commands* is an adventurous foray into a genre marriage as happy as Julian and Helen's was.

CREDITS: Screen Play: Robert D. Andrews and Milton Gunzburg; Story: William Sloane; Director of Photography: Allen G. Siegler; Film Editor: Al Clark; Art Direction: Lionel Banks; Musical Director: Morris W. Stoloff; Special Effects: Phil Faulkner; Director: Edward Dmytryk; Copyright 1941 by Columbia Pictures Corporation; Running Time: 64 minutes; Released on February 3, 1941; Alternate Pre-release titles: *The Devil Says No* and *When The Devil Commands* [Note: Although credited with a basis story, William F. Sloane's contribution was actually the 1939 novel *The Edge of Running Water*]

CAST: Boris Karloff...Dr. Julian Blair, Richard Fiske...Dr. Richard Sayles, Amanda Duff...Anne Blair, Anne Revere...Blanche Walters, Ralph Penney...Karl, Dorothy Adams...Mrs. Marcy, Walter Baldwin...Seth Marcy, Kenneth MacDonald...Sheriff Ed Willis, Shirley Warde...Helen Blair, Erwin Kalser...Professor Kent, Wheaton Chambers...Prof. Saunders

David H. Smith is a lifelong aficionado of horror, science fiction, and fantasy cinema. Although the interest is not necessarily shared, he lives with his complaisant wife Lynn and their son in south Florida amidst shelves of unlabeled videocassettes, closets overflowing with dog-eared comic books, and a singularly lackadaisical black cat named Lobo (Spanish for "wolf" or short for "lobotomy," anyone's guess). David has contributed to *Midnight Marquee Actors Series: Bela Lugosi, Cinematic Hauntings*, and will continue to retrospect on forgotten, impugned, and/or ignored films in the future.

THE BODY SNATCHER (1945)

by John E. Parnum

Some forty-five years ago, at the age of fifteen, I saw Boris Karloff backstage after his performance in *Peter Pan*. It was a unique role that my idol enjoyed—rather two unique roles, since he played both the kindly father Mr. Darling, who romped with his children and enormous St. Bernard, and the nefarious Captain Hook, the terror of the seas surrounding Never-Never Land. This was not the first time that Mr. Karloff essayed good and evil characters in the same show. In 1935, Boris portrayed twin brothers—the evil Gregor and the benevolent Anton—in the Columbia release *The Black Room*. It was a challenge that most actors welcome in their career, and Karloff, was superb.

His interpretation of the Monster in the first three Universal Frankenstein films brought him fame because he made us feel sympathy for the scientist's malformed creation as well as terror. And in how many of those mad doctor movies did Karloff's character begin as a kindly humanitarian researcher who through undeserved humiliation or rejection turns to less ethical means such as murder in order to pursue his goals? Even in films in which his role is totally evil, this kindly actor can elicit sympathy and understanding. As the diabolical mad Doctor Niemann in the 1944 *House of Frankenstein,* we first meet him as a wild-eyed prisoner in Neustadt Prison, reaching through the barred window of his cell to strangle a guard: "Now will you give me my chalk?" he rasps threateningly. Only a moment later, chalk in hand, he casually lectures the hunchback (J. Carrol Naish) in the adjacent cell on the fine art of anatomy. "And now, friend Daniel, shall we go on with our work?" he gently instructs the other prisoner, promising to cure the hunchback of his deformity.

And the duplicity of personalities go on: In *The Haunted Strangler* (1958), Karloff, as the kindly writer James Rankin, faints upon watching a prisoner whipped, but the sight of a scalpel transforms him into the sadistic Haymarket Strangler. However, the most contradictory personalities occur in his portrayal of cabman John Gray in the RKO 1945 Val Lewton-produced *The Body Snatcher.* Directed by a young Robert Wise (*The Curse of the Cat People, The Day the Earth Stood Still,* and *The Haunting*), Gray's charming attention to a paralyzed child is offset by his ghoulish pilfering of Edinburgh cemeteries in 1831 and his tenacious hold over the noted Dr. MacFarlane (Henry Daniell). This is a film of dark contrasts and Karloff's performance is perhaps the most complex of his career. Some critics have called *The Body Snatcher* the finest of all Lewton's films, even ranking it among the top ten horror films of all time, with Karloff at the peak of his career. The critic for *Time* raved "...the last passage in the picture is as all-out, hair-raising a climax to a horror film as you are ever likely to see."

The film opens with the young medical student Fettes (Russell Wade) sitting in a cemetery eating his lunch—a daily life-sustaining function amidst the finality of death. He is disturbed when a grieving mother (Mary Gordon) informs him that her deceased son's little dog Robbie has continuously watched over the young boy's grave to guard it from spoilers who sell corpses to medical schools. Wade appeared earlier in another Lewton film *The Ghost Ship*, while Gordon was Mrs. Hudson, the landlady of 221 Baker Street in the Sherlock Holmes series from 1939 through 1946, as well as being cruelly dispatched by the monsters in both *Bride of Frankenstein* (1935) and *The Mummy's Tomb* (1942).

Fettes, however, is in a quandary. While he desperately wants to continue his studies, he is on his way to inform his mentor Dr. MacFarlane that he must drop out because of insufficient funds. But before Fettes arrives at his destination, MacFarlane receives two other visitors: Mrs. Marsh (Rita Corday) and her crippled daughter Georgina (Sharyn Moffett), brought to the learned doctor's home by cabman Gray, who lifts the child from his black carriage and lets her pet his white horse. When MacFarlane's housekeeper Meg (Edith Atwater) greets them, troubled glances pass between Gray and her. As Edmund G. Bansak points out in his excellent book on the career of Val Lewton *Fearing the Dark* (McFarland & Company, Inc., Jefferson, NC and London, 1995), "...there is a momentary hint of menace in Gray's smiling expression before he goes on his way."

When MacFarlane coldly questions Georgina about her symptoms, he elicits no response from the little girl and suggests that Fettes, who has just arrived, try his bedside manner on the patient. Fettes, of course, is successful—the inexperienced student achieving what the learned doctor could not accomplish. Henry Daniell was a perfect choice to play the stern and humorless MacFarlane and has chilled audiences as Sherlock Holmes' nemesis, Professor Moriarty, in *The Woman in Green* (1945) and as the scientist with a transplanted head in *The Four Skulls of Jonathan Drake* (1959). Rita Corday appeared with Karloff again in *The Black Castle* (1952) while Edith Atwater graced William Castle's *Strait-Jacket* (1964) and Alfred Hitchcock's *Family Plot* (1976).

While MacFarlane unsympathetically refuses to operate on Georgina because he doesn't have the time, he generously agrees to let Fettes continue his studies by becoming his assistant, with paying Gray for deliveries of cadavers as one of the job requirements. Meg is distressed by MacFarlane's self-serving generosity and reminds the doctor that Fettes is "...a good lad—bright and able"

The Body Snatcher **is a film of dark contrasts, and Karloff's performance is perhaps the most complex of his career.**

and that helping MacFarlane will spoil him. Meg herself is living a life of duplicity: an outwardly formal housekeeper by day and passionate mistress by night—"a fey creature with mad ideas," as MacFarlane calls her. The house they occupy is a structure of contrasts also, symbolizing the doctor's dual per-

As Gray the cabman, Karloff, with the cruel line of mouth, gives way to a genuine smile of compassion for the little crippled girl Georgina (Sharyn Moffett).

sonality. J. P. Telotte describes it in *Dreams of Darkness* (University of Illinois Press, Urbana and Chicago, 1985): "The layout of the house corroborates MacFarlane's attitudes by demonstrating his tendency to compartmentalize his life. His lodgings occupy the second floor and part of the first, his office and examining rooms the remainder of the first, and the medical facility—including the dissection tables, lecture room, and storage facilities—is left to the basement. This arrangement suggests how MacFarlane tries to shut out the more unpleasant aspects of his profession with the close of a door or figuratively hold himself above the grisly matters he has relegated to Fettes as his assistant and Gray as his henchman. This effort at demarcation, however, only further amplifies the nature of the paradox between the appearances which MacFarlane has to maintain and the reality to which they correspond."

Telotte then describes the disparity between MacFarlane's and Gray's lodgings, the latter "...located in the rear of a barn on a dead-end street....we see Gray in long-shot, a small figure framed first in the doorway of his lodgings, then, as the camera tracks back, through a portal of his door. Diminished and confined by the multiple frames, bound within darkness, he seems pitiable and menacing, firmly locked in by environmental pressures to a round of gruesome activities he has made his life....we view him through the bars lining his stall; it is a composition that affirms his imprisonment, even as it marks an internal tension as well...." "Bad news, boy," Gray says to his horse; "we have to go out again" after Fettes tells him that MacFarlane has agreed to operate on Georgina but is in need of a cadaver to study.

MacFarlane's change of heart comes about through badgering by Gray and it is obvious that the lowly graverobber has a tenacious hold on the noble surgeon. At the local inn, Gray laughs when he invites MacFarlane to join him for a drink. "The great Doctor MacFarlane wants to sit here with the commonality." He needles the surgeon to operate on Georgina, but it is as self-effacing a gesture as MacFarlane's hiring of Fettes as an assistant. "You only want me to do it because I don't want to," MacFarlane argues, to which Gray answers, "You and I have two bodies; aye, two very different sorts of bodies. But we're closer than if we were in the same skin....for I saved that skin of yours once, and you'll not forget it."

Gray's comment refers to an event in the past when MacFarlane and he procured bodies for the real life Dr. Knox who also used the services of the notorious Burke and Hare. Gray took the blame for the crimes, while MacFarlane—then Knox's assistant—was exonerated. MacFarlane became the respected surgeon, while Gray remained a cabman and body snatcher—transporting the living by day and the dead by night. We first see his ghoulish activities as he enters the darkened graveyard and crushes the little guard dog, Robbie, with his shovel—a shocking scene that follows soon after his pleasant repartee with the crippled Georgina.

Now, with the kirkyards guarded and MacFarlane in need of a cadaver so he can operate on Georgina, Gray must resort to murdering a blind street singer in one of Lewton's famous "walk" scenes. The pretty beggar girl makes her way slowly along the cobblestone streets, the pleasant ballad she sings in harmony with the clip-clop, clip-clop of Gray's horse and carriage following her in the darkness. They disappear into the shadows of an alley as the camera remains on the empty scene, with only the melodic voice and the hollow clip-clop indicating their passage. Suddenly, the blind singer's song is cut off in mid-verse. We do not see the action, but Karloff's ability to previously show his transformation from friendly cabman to heartless brute forms that action in our minds and we can vividly picture what has transpired.

MacFarlane operates on Georgina, but she still cannot walk. Possessing an almost Messiah-like image of himself, MacFarlane demands "Child, I say to you, get up out of that chair and walk!" Fettes, on the other hand, sympathetically comforts Mrs. Marsh by explaining that, "She wants to but doesn't want

Gray's demeanor turns ugly as he "Burkes" Joseph (Bela Lugosi).

to." When MacFarlane later drowns his failure at the community pub, he admits his frustrations to Gray. He stacks glasses on top of each other and tells Gray that Georgina's spine is like a series of building blocks. But Gray reminds MacFarlane that "you can't build life the way you put blocks together, Toddy.... Could you be a doctor, a healing man, with the things those eyes have seen. There's a lot of knowledge in those eyes—but no understanding." Later, Fettes echoes the same sentiments to Georgina's mother when he tells her that MacFarlane "taught me the mathematics of anatomy, but he couldn't teach me the poetry of medicine." As Scott Allen Nollen sums up in his book *Boris Karloff: A Critical Account of His Screen, Stage, Radio, Television, and Recording Work* (McFarland & Company, Inc., Jefferson, NC and London, 1991), "...MacFarlane is primarily the 'healing' agent and Gray is seen as preying on both the living and the dead, but the distinctions are consistently blurred. The poor 'resurrection man' Gray actually possesses a greater understanding of humanity than the 'learned' Dr. MacFarlane does."

Fettes is distressed when he finds that the last body Gray has delivered is that of the blind street singer. When he accuses the cabman of murder, the

278

conversation is overheard by MacFarlane's servant Joseph (Bela Lugosi in one of his last roles). Joseph pays Gray a visit one night and threatens to blackmail the grave robber. Gray generously gives Joseph 16 pounds and several glasses of wine, cajoling the dimwitted servant who asks, "I have made you give me money, but you smile. Aren't you angry?" Gray explains how together they could form a team, like the notorious Burke and Hare who supplied cadavers to Edinburgh's Dr. Robert Knox, an historical incident upon which Robert Louis Stevenson based his short story *The Body-Snatcher* which subsequently inspired this film's screenplay by Philip MacDonald and Val Lewton (under the pseudonym Carlos Keith). An account of the dastardly pair's activities is described in Gregory William Mank's *Karloff and Lugosi: The Story of a Haunting Collaboration* (McFarland & Company, Inc., Jefferson, NC and London, 1990): "With the aid of Burke's mistress and Hare's wife, the duo managed to kill an additional 14 to 28 drunks, hags, and whores, all of whom were plied with liquor and held down by Burke while Hare 'Burked' them (i.e., held his hand over their nose and mouth until they smothered). All victims ultimately were delivered to Knox's cellar. Burke and Hare's downfall finally began when they 'Burked' Mary Patterson, a beautiful 18-year-old voluptuary instantly recognized by Knox's young anatomy students—several of whom had known her to have been very well, and alive, when they had recently enjoyed her favors."

Joseph still does not understand and Gray graciously and jovially explains how they'll "Burke" their victims, all the while singing merrily about "The ruffian dogs, the Hellish pair; the villain Burke, the meagre Hare." When Joseph, befuddled by the brew, asks Gray to show him how they did it, the cabman's pleasant voice turns sinister. "I'll show you how they did it, Joseph. I'll show you how they 'Burked' them. No, put your hand down. How can I show you, man. This is how they did it, Joseph!" Gray's demeanor turns ugly and he "Burkes" the unsuspecting Joseph. But in the aftermath of the struggle, Gray's gentleness returns in a most unique manner as described in Scott Nollen's *Boris Karloff* book: "During an earlier conversation with Fettes, Gray is shown tenderly petting his cat (an interesting contrast to his earlier killing of the dog). This image recurs, in more subtle form, as Joseph lies expired upon the floor. Creating one of the most profound gestures in his cinematic career, Karloff removes his hands from Joseph's mouth and gently reaches over to pet the cat, allowing the animal's tail to slide through his palm."

When Gray deposits Joseph's body in the brine vat in MacFarlane's cellar, the doctor is livid and goes to the cabman's quarters to pay him off and be rid of him forever. When MacFarlane threatens Gray, the body snatcher scolds him: "Surely you're not threatening an old friend." "We've never been friends!" snaps the surgeon. Gray refuses the payoff: "That wouldn't be half so much fun for me to have you come here and beg. You're a real pleasure to me, Toddy." Then Gray sums up all his feelings about MacFarlane and why he enjoys humiliating him in the film's famous "small man" speech. It is to Karloff's credit that he can encompass so many emotions, so much feeling, in this one short paragraph: "I am a small man, a humble man, and being poor I have had to do much I did not want to do. But as long as the great Dr. MacFarlane jumps to my whistle, that long am I a man. And if I have not that, I have nothing. Then I am only a cabman and a grave robber. You'll never get rid of me, Toddy." The two men struggle, and the next time we hear the clip-clop, clip-clop of Gray's horse and carriage it is MacFarlane arriving home with the cabman's corpse.

Ironically, it is another clip-clop, clip-clop which miraculously cures little Georgina. Sitting in her wheelchair atop a castle turret while Fettes tells Mrs. Marsh of his decision to quit school because of MacFarlane's unorthodox method of acquiring cadavers, Georgina hears what she thinks is Gray's horse. Unable to see over the wall, she calls to her mother and Fettes who are so engrossed in conversation (a romance is never even hinted) that they do not hear her. Bravely she rises from the wheelchair and walks slowly to the wall, her disappointment of it not being the white horse immediately overcome by realizing she is no longer an invalid. The only way she could walk again was her wanting to do it badly enough. Overjoyed with Georgina's cure, Fettes seeks out MacFarlane at the inn to tell him the good news. In the story's only weak development, MacFarlane persuades Fettes to aid him in exhuming a body whose family mourns in the adjacent room. This illogical plotting is soon lost to one of the most spine-tingling climaxes in classic horror-film history.

Using a time-honored atmospheric backdrop, the conclusion of *The Body Snatcher* takes place during a blinding thunderstorm as MacFarlane and Fettes shovel away at the grave of the recently buried woman. With their unearthed prize in their possession, they gallop away in a carriage, the shrouded corpse between them. But the bumpy road causes the dead body to fall over onto MacFarlane. Through the howling of the wind, the surgeon keeps hearing Gray's voice: "Toddy... Toddy... Toddy." Once again the corpse tumbles over onto MacFarlane, and Gray's ominous words echo in his ears: "Never get rid of me... never get rid of me...." MacFarlane demands that Fettes stop the carriage, telling him that the shrouded body has changed, that it is no longer the woman. "Hold that lamp up; I must see her face!" As MacFarlane pulls open the grave cloth and the lamp shines on the corpse's face, he shouts in terror: "Gray!!" The startled horse rears up and gallops away, leaving Fettes behind and MacFarlane in the front seat with Gray's illuminous naked body embracing him in a death hold. The carriage topples off an embankment. Fettes runs to assist, but discovers his mentor dead. He checks the shrouded corpse and finds it is the dead woman. Fettes climbs back onto the road and heads toward Edinburgh. The rain has stopped. A quotation by Hippocrates appears over the scene as Fettes walks toward the brightening horizon: "It is through error that

"I am a small man, a humble man, and being poor I have had to do much I did not want to do," says Gray to Dr. MacFarlane (Henry Daniell).

man tries and rises. It is through tragedy he learns. All the roads of learning begin in darkness and go out into the light."

Boris Karloff, of course, was the ideal choice to play John Gray. The contrasting nature of the character required the talents of both a meticulous actor and one with the necessary physical attributes. Gray is an older man, but still burly enough to lug dead bodies over his shoulder. Karloff's tenure as a truck driver during his "lean" years aided him in achieving a powerful appearance, even though he suffered from excruciating back problems. Those bushy eyebrows, the dark features, and the deep husky voice lent themselves to villainous roles. Brooks Atkinson in his *New York Times* review of *The Linden Tree* commented specifically on Karloff's eyes: "He has warmth and magnetism and those beetling brows, which can scare you in his shiver plays, can soothe you with wisdom when he is in a benevolent mood." Portraying Jonathan Brewster in the stage version of *Arsenic and Old Lace*, he even spoofs himself when he tells an accomplice that he killed someone because "...he said I looked like Boris Karloff!" But behind that facade, behind the bushy eyebrows, there is a gentleness, a sparkle, that expresses goodness and even a sense of humor that provided his portrayal of Frankenstein's Monster with an element of sympathy even though it had committed terrible deeds. Likewise, in *The Body Snatcher*, when Gray says to his horse, "Bad news, boy. We have to go out again," those eyes, while implying evil acts to come, impart a kind of sadness in them that causes us to feel sorry for the cabman's lowly station in life.

Karloff's mouth was perhaps an even greater factor in expressing his feelings. Under a heavy mustache which he sometimes wore to hide his prominent upper lip, that mouth created a wide range of expressions. As I noted in my contribution to Greg Mank's *Karloff and Lugosi* book, the actor's mouth could display "the sinister snarl of the Monster as it wrestles with Frankenstein on the mountain top, the trembling lower lip when he is rejected by his mate in *Bride of Frankenstein*, the smile of anticipation when offered a glass of wine by Dr. Pretorius. Or as Gray, the cabman in *The Body Snatcher*, with a cruel line of mouth giving way to a genuine smile of compassion for the little crippled girl petting his horse." Watch how Gray's mouth changes as he describes the Burke and Hare story to Joseph just before he kills him. That mouth could be telling a fairy story to a group of small children—something that Karloff actually did in his later years as a sideline. Even when he places his coarse hand over Joseph's face, there is a kindness in the smile, a gentleness in his voice. And then the mouth line turns down, becomes ugly and vicious, and finally reveals a hint of affection as he strokes his cat by Joseph's corpse. Cynthia Lindsay in her biography *Dear Boris* (Alfred A. Knoff, New York, 1975) describes director Wise's initial meeting with Karloff: "When he first walked in the door I was startled by his coloring, the strange bluish cast—but when he turned those eyes on us and that velvet voice said 'Good afternoon, gentlemen.' we were his, and never thought about anything else."

Karloff's rise to fame as an actor was slow coming. His early theatrical tours in Canada earned him little money. With only bit parts in Hollywood films, he never knew from where his next meal was coming. To bring in extra money he would drive a truck and do other menial labor that caused him the severe back problems mentioned earlier. Perhaps the pain, both physical and emotional, of these early professions are reflected in the pain and loneliness of the characters he played. When Gray says, "I am a small man, a humble man, and being poor I have had to do much I did not want to do," we can perceive Karloff's struggling years in Gray's eyes as if he is relating to his own personal experiences.

Anyone who has ever met Boris Karloff has had only wonderful things to say about this gentle and refined Englishman—with one exception being Elizabeth Russell, who worked with him in another Val Lewton film, *Bedlam*. Forrest J Ackerman has christened him Boris the Benign, and even one of Karloff's ex-wives, Pauline, refused to say anything unkind about the actor when the press

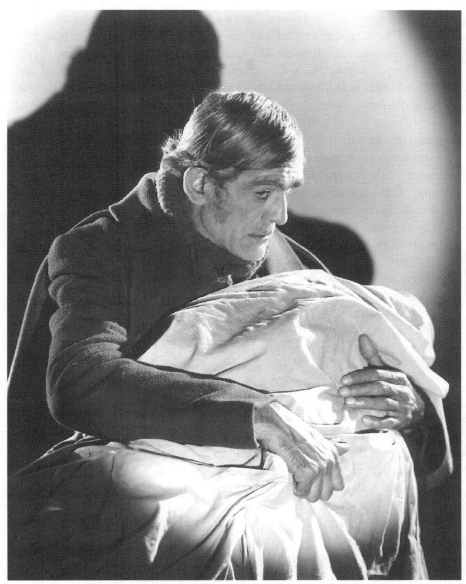

Karloff's mouth was a great factor in expressing his feelings. Under a heavy mustache which he sometimes wore to hide his prominent upper lip, that mouth created a wide range of expressions.

went looking for juicy tidbits after he became famous. This leads me to believe that Ms. Russell's accusations in a *Scarlet Street* interview of Karloff being snobbish and "in love with himself" may be a problem of Ms. Russell herself. In my opening paragraph I mentioned how I saw Boris Karloff backstage when he was touring in *Peter Pan*. Two years before that, at the age of 13, my aunt took me to see him in *The Linden Tree,* a J. B. Priestley drawing room comedy with social overtones, at a matinee at the Walnut Street Theatre in Philadelphia. I would like to add my experience of meeting him to the allocades expressed by others. My aunt gave the usher a note (and a generous tip) to take to Mr. Karloff asking him if he would say a few words to her nephew after the play. He agreed and we were escorted backstage to my idol's dressing room. With pounding heart and trembling voice I bragged "Gee, Mr. Karloff; I've seen all your movies," to which he replied in that wonderful resonant voice of his: "Well, my boy, you just forget about those movies and concentrate more on what you've learned here this afternoon." It was a comment that, though disappointing at the time, now leads me to believe he really did want to shed the monster mold to which he often claimed he owed so much. Taking a pencil from his dressing table, he signed my autograph book which I had purchased just for the occasion and said, "Is this your pencil?" "Oh no, Mr. Karloff," I answered. "That's your pencil." My aunt told me later to my dismay that he had been offering me a souvenir—a personal item that he had touched which he thought I might want. It was something that he certainly didn't have to do—a gesture that affirms his generosity and kindness.

In *The Body Snatcher*, Boris Karloff brilliantly shows us the two faces of John Gray, just as he portrayed good and evil brothers in *The Black Room*. But as Greg Mank points out in *Hollywood Cauldron* (McFarland & Company, Inc., Jefferson, NC and London, 1994), after the evil Gregor murders the kindly Anton, he assumes the good brother's personality—even pretending he has Anton's paralyzed arm. "It is actually Karloff's third performance of the movie: he impersonates his charming brother persuasively, but with a sly, evil glee, as if he's enjoying the fakery and laughing at those fooled by it." I like to think, however, that there is a fourth face, not just in *The Black Room* and *The Body Snatcher*, but in all of Karloff's performances. In addition to Karloff *the actor* portraying a good character, a bad character, or a bad character impersonating a good one, there is Karloff *the gentle and considerate man* living all of these roles, no matter how evil or cruel he is pretending to be. It is Boris Karloff's inherent kindness and gentility that has embellished his many portrayals, causing audiences of all ages to remember him as one of the great actors of our time.

CREDITS: Producer: Val Lewton; Executive Producer: Jack J. Gross; Director: Robert Wise; Screenplay: Philip MacDonald and Carlos Keith (Val Lewton) from a short story by Robert Louis Stevenson; Director of Photography: Robert de Grasse; Camera Operator: Charles Burke; Music: Roy Webb; Musical Director: Constantin Bakaleinikoff; Editor: J. R. Whittredge; Art Directors: Albert S. D'Agostino and Walter E. Keller; Set Decorators: Darrell Silvera and John Sturtevant; Sound Recorder: Bailey Fesler; Re-recorder: Terry Kellum;

Costumes: Renie; First Assistant Director: Harry Scott; Second Assistant Director: Nate Levinson; Script Clerk: Pat Betz; Assistant Cameraman: Tex Wheaton; Men's Wardrobe: Hans Bohnstedt; Ladies' Wardrobe: Mary Tate; Make-up: Frank LaRue; Hairdresser: Fay Smith; Gaffer: Leo Green; Best Boy: Frank Healy; First Grip: Marvin Wilson; Second Grip: Harry Dagleish; First Propman: Milt James; Second Propman: Dean Morgan; Boom: D. Dent; Laborers: Joe Farquhar and Fred Kenny; Painter: Joe Haecker; Dialogue Director: Mrs. Charlot. Songs: "We'd Better Bide a Wee," "When Ye Gang Awa," "Jaime," and "Will Ye No Come Back Again?" (sung by Donna Lee); "Spit Song" (sung by Jack Welsh); RKO; filmed in black and white; 78 minutes; Released on Video: Turner Home Entertainment; Laser: Image

CAST: Boris Karloff...John Gray, Bela Lugosi...Joseph, Henry Daniell...Dr. MacFarlane, Edith Atwater...Meg, Russell Wade...Fettes, Rita Corday...Mrs. Marsh, Sharyn Moffett...Georgina, Donna Lee...Street Singer, Mary Gordon...Mrs. Mary MacBride, Robert Clarke...Richardson, Carl Kent...Gilchrist, Jack Welsh...Boy, Larry Wheat...Salesman on Street, Jim Moran...Horse Trader, Aina Constant...Maid, and Bill Williams

Many thanks to Laura Parnum for editing.

John E. Parnum finished his chapter on *The Body Snatcher* several days before entering the hospital for quadruple cardiac bypass surgery, and his last thought before drifting off under anesthesia was, "Thank God for grave robbers like cabman John Gray who paved the way for anatomical studies of the human body." John has been a frequent contributor to Midnight Marquee Press books and *Midnight Marquee,* the magazine. He has written for *Photon, The Monster Times, Bits and Pieces, Monsters From The Vault, Gateways, The Scream Factory,* and *Movie Club.* And thanks to body snatchers such as Gray, John has recovered and is submitting more chapters for upcoming Midnight Marquee Press publications.

FRANKENSTEIN 1970 (1958)

by Don G. Smith

In 1958, it was exciting to be, as I was, a ten-year old boy in love with horror/science fiction films. Only one year earlier, Shock Theater television packages introduced a new generation to the classic horror films of the thirties and forties, and Great Britain's Hammer Films revived the classic themes, initiating a new Frankenstein series with *The Curse of Frankenstein.* In 1958, the entertainment pages of city newspapers were daily filled with ads promoting such William Castle horrors as *Macabre* and *House on Haunted Hill.* As children, we were unaware that the great fifties' science fiction craze was declining in quality. We certainly could not tell anything was amiss from the number of science fiction films released—tantalizing AIP double features and ads promoting *The Blob*: "It creeps, it crawls, it eats you alive!" I still remember my aunt driving me past a major St. Louis theater that tantalized me with a one-sheet poster from a film incredibly titled *Attack of the 50 Foot Woman.* Obsessed by this imaginative environment, I had begun clipping and regularly poring over a growing collection of newspaper ads from horror/science fiction films.

Then, one day in November or December, I opened the St. Louis newspaper to my favorite pages and saw a large ad for a film called *Frankenstein 1970.* As in so many such ads of the period, a young woman cowered in fear from an approaching "horror." That horror, as portrayed in the ad, was frightening indeed: a gnarled claw, sutured above the wrist, a bolt through the wrist joint! "The Monster of the Future!" the ad proclaimed. "See it born in an atomic reactor! The Thing that will frighten your children's children!" And there, above the title was the name Boris KARLOFF. As the week progressed, other ads appeared for the film showing more of the monster itself (but always from behind). Yes, it wore the clothing worn by Karloff in *Frankenstein* (1931), and the contours of its head left no doubt that Mary Shelley's creature was rising again as a product of the nuclear age. I knew that I would be 22 years old in 1970, and I wanted so badly to glimpse this horrific vision of the future. Unfortunately, despite my pleas, my parents did not take me to see *Frankenstein 1970*, but I would later watch it many times on television and on video.

The pressbook for the film was impressive, including a large fold-out herald with shock graphics announcing that "Boris Karloff brings you the new demon of the atomic age!" The exploitation pages encouraged theater owners to "Go after the horror fans!" Along with the old standbys of having a nurse and ambulance ready at the theater in case customers fainted, theater owners were told to run a five-day Boris Karloff contest in which people were to look at photographs representing "Karloff, in five of his most famous roles" and name the films represented by the pictures. Though one might quarrel with some of the films chosen as Karloff's most famous, they were *Tower of London, The Old Dark House, The Mask of Fu Manchu* (incorrectly identified as *Mr. Wong in Chinatown*), *Son of Frankenstein,* and *Abbott and Costello Meet Dr. Jekyll and Mr. Hyde.*

The focus of this chapter is, of course, Boris Karloff, the man described on the half-sheet poster from *Frankenstein 1970* as "the one...the only KING OF MONSTERS." *Frankenstein 1970* receives whatever serious attention it garners today because of Karloff's presence. That is because the film itself is almost universally pilloried by critics as a sorry failure. While I do not plan to mount a serious argument against that conclusion, I am prepared to argue that the film is better than most critics judge it to be, and that Karloff's performance is a little better than generally assessed.

For context, let us return again to 1958. In his (almost) definitive critical biography *Boris Karloff* (McFarland and Company, 1991), Scott Allen Nollen correctly places the film within the "nuclear terror" category common to science fiction films of the fifties. Anyone living during those years remembers the horrors subsequent to the atomic bombing of Hiroshima and Nagasaki. What would the future hold? To illustrate, I remember the tour my uncle gave me of his "bomb shelter." Expecting nuclear devastation at any moment, many Americans built basement shelters stocked with non-perishable foods of all types. *Frankenstein 1970* is born of this mentality. Also inspirational was the box office success of Hammer's *Curse of Frankenstein* and AIP's *I Was a Teenage Frankenstein* (1957). Frankenstein was hot again, and that meant money!

Intent as they were on making a horror film of the atomic age, the producers did not have a budget up to the task. These pecuniary problems forced the film into the mold of such fifties' anachronisms as *The Strange Door* (1951, with Karloff), *The Black Castle* (1952, with Karloff), and *The Black Sleep* (1956, with Basil Rathbone, John Carradine, Lon Chaney, Jr. and Bela Lugosi), all of which worked on the assumption that mimicking the look and atmosphere of forties' horror films with forties' horror film stars was still a marketable approach. Indeed, *Frankenstein 1970* is a forties' concept, decorated with atomic age paraphernalia, and transported unsuccessfully to the late fifties. It is an atomic age film with a thirties' and forties' horror star working in an isolated German

Director Howard Koch, Boris Karloff, and Mrs. Karloff on the set of *Frankenstein 1970.*

castle, mouthing dialogue about atomic reactors and storing body parts in a 1950s' refrigerator.

So why did Boris Karloff, normally judicious in his choice of films, accept the part? He had played the Frankenstein Monster three times in the thirties but had abandoned the series when the quality of scripts declined and when offers from live theater proved artistically irresistible and financially promising. He agreed to play a mad scientist in *House of Frankenstein* (1944) but otherwise avoided Frankenstein projects. At the time of *Frankenstein 1970* he was under contract with producers Aubrey Schenck and Howard W. Koch to make three pictures. How much control he had over the projects, if any, I do not know. My guess is that financial considerations prompted Karloff to sign the contract. For example, the actor had recently purchased a half dozen lots near California's Malibu Beach—one lot as a potential home site and the other five for investment. Since a good chunk of the production money went to pay Karloff, I assume the actor swallowed his artistic pride and accepted the role. Still, despite Karloff's good sense in the thirties and forties, his choice of film roles in the fifties was aesthetically spotty at best. *The Strange Door* is rightly considered mediocre by critics, as is *The Black Castle* in which he and Lon Chaney, Jr. are reduced to minor roles. *Abbott and Costello Meet Dr. Jekyll and Mr. Hyde* (1953) was not one of the comedians' best, and *Monster of the Islands* (1953) was probably the worst film of Karloff's entire career. *The Hindu* (1953) is unremarkable, and *Voodoo Island* a painful bore. Only *The Grip of the Strangler* (1958, aka *The Haunted Strangle*r) and *Corridors of Blood* (1958, released in 1963), both filmed in England, can be considered enhancements to Karloff's career.

Filmed under the working title *Frankenstein 1960,* the plot is fairly simple: Baron Victor von Frankenstein (Boris Karloff), tortured, disfigured, and probably castrated by the Nazis during World War II, allows an American television troupe to use his German castle as the setting of their latest production. The troupe consists of producer-director Douglas Row (Donald Barry), his ex-wife Judy (Charlotte Austin), performers Carolyn Hayes (Jana Lund), Hans (Mike Lane), press agent Mike Shaw (Tom Duggan), and cameraman Morgan Haley (John Dennis).

Frankenstein hopes to use advances from the project to finance an atomic reactor for the purpose of reviving the Monster. When Frankenstein's servant Shuter (Norbert Schiller), Stevens, and Haley disappear, Frankenstein's friend Wilhelm Gottfried (Rudolph Anders) suspects foul play. As a result, he too soon disappears. Inspector Raab (Irwin Berke) investigates and discovers that Frankenstein, sometimes with the aid of the monster, is using the body parts of the missing persons to complete his work. Atomic steam from the nuclear reactor kills both Frankenstein and his creation. Removal of the bandages from the Monster's face reveals that Frankenstein has given the Monster his own visage.

Let us now examine elements of the film and of Karloff's performance in greater detail. The production gets off to a smashing start as the credits appear over a night-bound, fog-covered pond with gnarled trees. Then the story itself begins with Lund fleeing toward the pond away from a pursuing monster. The camera does not show the monster's face. Instead it lingers on the monster from the neck down as it stoops to a near kneeling position, exercising its claws in anticipation of catching the girl. The screaming Lund wades out into the pond, but the Monster follows, hovers over her, and thrusts her head under the water. "Cut," yells director Row, revealing this tense opening as only part of a film being shot on the grounds of Frankenstein's castle.

Most critics hail this opening scene as the best in the film, but they are appalled at the trick played on the audience, a trick that dissipates the well-created atmosphere and horror. Apparently Allied Artists liked the scene well enough to use it in an effective dream sequence in TV prints of their *Daughter of Dr. Jekyll* (1957). Yes, it is true that the opening scenes are the best in the film, but they do more than just offer a taste of what might have been *most* interesting, the monster is an amalgam of Universal's classic monsters. It has the dragging leg of the mummy, the claws of a werewolf (sans hair), the shoulders of a

Baron Victor von Frankenstein (Karloff) allows an American television troupe to use his German castle as the setting for their latest production.

hunchback, and the platform shoes and general build of the Frankenstein Monster. But it does more than just pay homage to the classics. The dragging leg of the actor as monster is a trait also found in Dr. Frankenstein (Karloff) as a result of his torture at the hands of the Nazis. In effect, the scene lays the foundation for identifying Dr. Frankenstein (and Karloff himself) with a man playing the role of the Frankenstein Monster, a motif that cleverly recurs throughout the film. This is a part written for Karloff (as was his part in *Targets* [1968]), and, like *Targets,* it allows Karloff to be Karloff, to say something about the business that had both made him and betrayed him.

Beyond the "trick," played on the audience, if there is a problem with the opening scenes, it is that they conjure a thirties' and forties' atmosphere in a film advertising itself as futuristic. Unfortunately, there is truly nothing futuristic about *Frankenstein 1970.* Of course, part of the problem is budget. For a product of the atomic age, Frankenstein's lab falls far short of the grandeur of Ken Strickfaden's work in *Frankenstein* (1931). In fact, it is only slightly better than the lab haunted by Lugosi in Ed Wood's financially-challenged *Bride of the Monster* (1955). In addition, Frankenstein stores body parts in a 1950s' refrigerator and flushes human remains down a glorified commode!

291

Frankenstein is a desperate man with important work to perform.

Early in the film, Frankenstein recounts the story of the creation of the Monster for Haley's camera. Interestingly, the account relates little to either Mary Shelley's novel or the Universal Pictures mythology. In Frankenstein's account, the Monster's deeds are motivated by survival, yet Frankenstein calls the Monster evil. Of course, Frankenstein himself has committed "unholy" experiments in order to survive Nazi captivity. Is he evil too? The implication seems to favor that interpretation. Again, the film links scientist (Karloff) and monster, undoubtedly to remind audiences that it was Karloff who, in the 1930s, brought the monster to cinematic life. Row soon comments that Frankenstein ad-libbed his lines but did a great job anyway, leading to the conclusion that Frankenstein's own terrible experiences color his unique understanding of the Monster.

At one point in the film Karloff chuckles, "Good, good!" sounding very much as he did in *Bride of Frankenstein* (1935) when the Monster smokes a cigar given to him by the blind hermit. Again, scientist (Karloff) and Monster (Karloff) are linked.

Frankenstein then feeds his fish and remarks that "the struggle for survival in their world is just as fierce and ruthless as it is in ours." The struggle for survival is a recurring motif in *Frankenstein 1970*. The fish in the tank struggle for survival as Victor Frankenstein and the Monster have struggled. Unable to further the Frankenstein line (a form of survival), Victor sublimates his unfulfilled desire for children by reviving the Monster. Interestingly, the concept of Monster as child was one of the most important aspects of Karloff's performance in the 1931 *Frankenstein*. Ignored for the most part in other Frankenstein films, it appears twenty-seven years later in what would turn out to be one of Karloff's lesser vehicles, though not his worst by far.

Another recurring motif is Victor Frankenstein's distaste for "show people" and cheap entertainment. Frankenstein is a desperate man with important work to perform. On the other hand, director Row glad-hands Frankenstein like a cheap huckster, giving no indication that the Frankenstein history means any more to him than a quick buck. I submit that Karloff probably shared some of Victor Frankenstein's sentiments, though certainly not to the same degree since Karloff always spoke lovingly of his Monster. Whenever Row puts his hand on Frankenstein's shoulder, Frankenstein tries to brush him off as though he were an insect. Later in the film, as Inspector Raab searches the castle cellar at Row's request, Frankenstein dismisses the disappearances by demeaning people in show business: "Inspector, you must make allowances for these show people. They live in the world of fanciful dreams, hidden doors, sliding panels—even sudden disappearances—the nonsense of things that don't exist, a world of make believe." Karloff, in an effective moment, almost spits out the words "make believe."

Frankenstein apparently does consider the servant Shuter and his friend Gottfried to be human beings deserving of life, a consideration he does not extend to "show people." When Shuter accidentally stumbles upon Frankenstein in his laboratory, Frankenstein sadly muses, "Ah, poor Shuter. Why did it have to be you?" If the intruder had been a show person, one surmises that Frankenstein's sentiments would have been different, as they are when he does away with Stevens and Haley. As it stands, Frankenstein's regret at having to kill Shuter elicits Karloff's most (and possibly only) moving lines of the film. Still, Frankenstein can console himself with the knowledge that Shuter's brain will live again in the Monster. With regard to Gottfried, Frankenstein warns him on several occasions not to keep asking questions about matters that don't concern him. Gottfried, a moral man, presses on and soon finds himself in the cellar facing the Monster. In another fine scene, the camera freezes on a close-up of Gottfried's face, then pulls back to reveal Gottfried's eyes in the head of the Monster.

Another well-mounted scene is that in which cameraman Haley pans his hand-held camera across the cellar, only to stop in horror as the Monster comes into view. Frankenstein flushes away Haley's eyes, however, when he discovers that Haley's blood type is not the same as that of the Monster. Perhaps

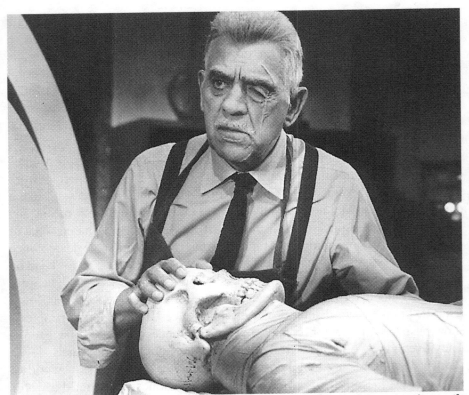

Watching Karloff play Dr. Frankenstein for the only time in his career is worth the "price of admission."

Frankenstein remembered what went wrong for Lionel Atwill and Lon Chaney, Jr. in *The Ghost of Frankenstein* (1942).

There are a few other interesting subtle touches. For example, in a scene of ironic humor, Frankenstein, with hypnotism his goal, tries to interest Shaw in his collectibles, saying, "This castle is filled with rare old treasures." With regard to the Monster, the statement is clearly true! Another nice touch occurs in the scenes in which Frankenstein hovers over the reclining Monster, its head an exposed skull. All the while, the contours of Frankenstein's surgical mask give the impression of a skeletal grin— another device linking scientist (Karloff) with monster. Of course the strongest scenes linking scientist Karloff with the Monster he once played are those at the end of the film in which the Monster's facial bandages are removed to reveal the unblemished face of Karloff. As the film concludes, Inspector Raab plays a tape on which Frankenstein/Karloff says, "I made you in my image so the name of Frankenstein could survive." Since the audience has already seen Frankenstein molding a face from a photo of himself, the ending is not the surprise that it was probably intended to be. Still, there is more than a little message in Karloff's taped words.

294

Now, it is certainly possible to take *Frankenstein 1970* too seriously. Still, so much negative has been written about the film that I have chosen to focus on positive aspects largely ignored by other critics. The film is certainly no classic. On the negative side, which clearly outweighs the positive, Karloff, Barry, and Schiller all overplay. Unlike Lugosi, an overplaying Karloff cannot save a weak film. Tom Duggan is just plain bad, and Don Barry looks uncomfortable throughout the film's first half, probably wishing he were riding the range again as cowboy hero Don "Red" Barry. In fact, the best performances in the film are those of Charlotte Austin and Rudolph Anders. The Monster exhibits no personality at all, a major flaw in a film of this sort. Though blind, it wanders about the house on missions. In one scene designed to elicit suspense, Lund walks backwards into a dark recess of the cellar as Haley films her movements. Unknown to her, the Monster stands behind her, ready to (what?). Also unhelpful is the monster's appearance as a thing bandaged from head to foot with what resembles an overturned waste can for a head. The budget is largely responsible for the film's more disappointing qualities, but much more could and should have been done with the existing money. For example, could the screenplay not have done much more with the Monster and futuristic aspects of radiation, etc.? A futuristic film that looks at least fifteen years older than the year it was made has little chance of earning even a mediocre rating! Here is a smattering of the negative critical opinion leveled at *Frankenstein 1970*.

"The film was an ill-conceived attempt in CinemaScope to mix the Frankenstein monster with hypnotism and atomic steam."—(Peter Underwood, *Karloff*, 1972)

"Dismal."—(Donald C. Willis, *Horror and Science Fiction Films*, 1972)

"A strange mixture of gothic and atomic-age horrors with one of Boris' hammiest performances."—(Michael Weldon, *The Psychotronic Encyclopedia of Film*, 1983)

"Film is slow, monster unexciting, and Karloff hammy. [A] Bomb."—(Leonard Maltin, *Leonard Maltin's 1996 Movie and Video Guide*)

Stephen Jones gives the film 2 stars out of a possible 5 in his *The Frankenstein Scrapbook*, 1995.

Still, I find the film fun at a certain level. Despite its weaknesses, I like it. Call it a guilty pleasure. It is a little better than most critics have judged it, and watching Karloff play a Dr. Frankenstein for the only time in his career is worth the "price of admission." In a nice touch, the script even gives him the name—Victor—the same name as Mary Shelley's original Frankenstein. Universal, of course, gave Colin Clive, the sound era's original Frankenstein, the name "Henry."

Karloff certainly traversed a great deal of cinematic ground between 1931 and 1958. His performance in *Frankenstein 1970* falls far short of those in *The Black Room* (1935) and *The Body Snatcher* (1945), but it can stand alongside or surpass his work in *House of Frankenstein* and most of his other 1950s' pictures.

I want to make one last point. In *Classics of the Horror Film,* William K. Everson divides Karloff's performances into three categories: "those where he genuinely respected the film and role and gave of his best; those like both versions of *The Raven* and *The Mask of Fu Manchu,* where he realized that the roles could never be taken seriously and approached them in a bravura, tongue-in-cheek style; and the *Voodoo Island* and *Frankenstein 1970* roles, where he merely walked through the films without undue effort, apparently on the theory that for such junk the prestige of his name and presence was contribution enough."

In *Boris Karloff,* Scott Nollen quotes Everson and elaborates:

> Saddled with inane situations and dialogue, Karloff, for the most part, does walk through *Frankenstein 1970,* but he probably had few alternatives. He does manage to bring his quiet menace to some scenes, but it is doubtful that any actor could give a serious performance while removing chilled human organs from a 1950s' refrigerator!

Some earlier critics of the film suggested that the director may have encouraged Karloff to overact in *Frankenstein 1970.* In an interview with Tom Weaver, however, director Koch revealed that he just "let him go" because he "was afraid to say to him that it was too much." It appears, then, that Karloff's approach to the picture was his own. So, if Everson's assessment of Karloff is correct, it points out a flaw in Karloff's approach to acting that most critics (including Everson and Nollen) seem to excuse. Karloff accepted the role for money. The producers were giving Karloff $25,000 to act in the picture, a hefty chunk of their $105,000 budget. If the script, sets, and supporting cast were inadequate, Karloff should have risen above them. Not only did Karloff's negative attitude shortchange the producers, but it also shortchanged the people who spent their money at the box office to see Boris Karloff. Performers of all types owe paying customers their best. That doesn't mean that performers will always be at their best; illness and personal circumstances can certainly make a well-intentioned performance lackluster. But all performers owe it to everyone concerned to give the best they've got. To intentionally take producers' money and "walk through" a film is professionally inexcusable.

Consider the contrasting approach of Bela Lugosi. Regardless of the quality of the script, the director, the budget, or the supporting cast, Lugosi always gave one hundred percent. In so doing, he often saved films that would otherwise be unwatchable. Nobody could ever walk out of a theater saying he had been cheated by Bela Lugosi. So, to refute Nollen's thesis, Bela Lugosi could give a serious performance while removing chilled human organs from a 1950s' refrigerator.

In fairness to Karloff, I should quote Peter Underwood's dissenting opinion:

> It was said that he held his own and often gave a good account of himself from his earliest films as he did right through most of the forties, but later there is some justification for comments that he occasionally "walked through" a role which he did not respect and one thinks in particular of *Voodoo Island* and *Frankenstein 1970*; neither film had much cinematic quality or opportunity for expressing acting ability. In fact Karloff's varied interpretation and intelligent delivery enabled him to rise above mere character acting. The charge that he gave slovenly performances on occasions does not bear scrutiny.

So, did Boris Karloff cheat us all in *Frankenstein 1970?* If he didn't, then fine; but if he did, then shame on Boris Karloff!

CREDITS: Producer: Aubrey Schenck; Director: Howard W. Koch; Screenplay: Richard Landau and George Worthing Yates; Story: Aubrey Schenck and Charles A. Moses; Cinematography: Carl E. Guthrie; Editor: John A. Bushelman; Sound: Francis C. Stahl; Music: Paul A. Dunlap; Makeup Supervisor: Gordon Bau

CAST: Boris Karloff...Baron Victor von Frankenstein, Tom Duggan... Mike Shaw, Jana Lund...Carolyn Hayes, Donald Barry...Douglas Row, Charlotte Austin...Judy, Irwin Berke...Inspector Raab, Rudolph Anders...Wilhelm Gottfried, John Dennis...Morgan Haley, Norbert Schiller...Shuter, Mike Lane...Hans

GRIP OF THE STRANGLER (1958)
CORRIDORS OF BLOOD (1958)

by Tom Johnson

The fifties were an odd decade for Boris Karloff. Although the period resulted in nothing on the level of *Bride of Frankenstein* or *The Body Snatcher,* Karloff became more popular than ever. Through his sixty-plus television appearances, children's recordings, and Broadway performances (especially *Peter Pan*), by the decade's end, Karloff had been transformed from ghoul into grandfather. But he did not go quietly into a rocking chair. The horror movies were still there, including two of his most interesting—*Grip of the Strangler (The Haunted Strangler,* USA) and *Corridors of Blood*—but these are rarely spoken of in the same sentence as, say, *The Raven* (1935). One may wonder why. These two British productions almost stand with Karloff's better pictures from any decade.

Grip of the Strangler (first titled *Stranglehold,* then *Judas Hole*) was filmed at Walton, Britain's oldest studio, in August, 1957. The picture was trade shown on October 2, 1958 and premiered at the London Pavilion (with *Challenge the Wild)* on October 24. Karloff, as novelist James Rankin, returned to familiar country *(The Man They Could Not Hang, Black Friday)* as an essentially decent man caught up in events that got away from him. In the London of 1880, Rankin researches a twenty-year-old murder spree committed by the "Haymarket Strangler"—one Edward Styles, who was hanged for his crimes. Rankin comes to believe that a mysterious Dr. Tenant may have been involved... and comes to learn that he actually is Tenant. His long-buried memory of the killings is triggered by finding "Tenant's" scalpel. While clutching it, Rankin is transformed into a grotesque, half-paralyzed monstrosity. As an indication of Karloff's involvement with the part, he achieved Rankin's twisted look largely without makeup... and by removing his false teeth! Like many Karloffian creatures, Rankin dies while trying to do the right thing—shot by a policeman as he attempts to re-bury both the scalpel and his haunted past in Styles' coffin.

While there is little new in this variation on the time-honored Jekyll-Hyde theme, what stands out, in addition to Boris Karloff's superior performance, is the faithful recreation of the seedier aspects of Victorian London. The opening sequence—Styles' hanging—is disturbing to watch even in our jaded times;

the spectators, in their casual search for free "entertainment," are more horrifying than the psychotic killer. Anthony Dawson added able support as Rankin's skeptical Scotland Yard ally, but, other than Karloff, the picture's real star was designer John Elphick, whose sets would not look out of place in a major blockbuster. *Kinematograph Weekly* (September 13, 1962) felt, "artfully spaced scenes of the bawdy night life of its times effectively punctuate the eerie. Boris Karloff runs the gamut..."

Originally titled *Doctor from Seven Dials,* a notorious section of central London, *Corridors of Blood* was shot at Borehamwood during the spring of 1958. Due to problems with the distributor (MGM), the picture vanished and resurfaced four years later. Following a London trade show on September 6, 1962, the picture premiered a week later.

True to form, Boris Karloff was cast, again, as a good man forced into evil behavior by events beyond his control. Dr. Thomas Bolton, an eminent London surgeon, believes that "pain and the knife are not inseparable" and experiments with drugs to create an effective anesthetic. After a failed demonstration—the patient awakens while being cut—Bolton is disgraced and suspended from the hospital. Worse, he falls in with Black Ben (Francis DeWolff) and Resurrection Joe (Christopher Lee), grave robbers and sometime murderers who supply bodies for dissection. When Bolton becomes addicted to his own drug, the pair blackmail him into signing fraudulent death certificates. Bolton rallies to cause the destruction of the ring at the cost of his own life, and his son (Francis Matthews) carries on his work.

Although Boris Karloff could play this type of role while asleep, he still managed to make it look new. He successfully alternates between scientific fervor, arrogance, and pathetic drug addiction, and engages our interest in his fully drawn character. Francis DeWolff and Christopher Lee are as sleazy a pair of villains as one could wish for; Lee's menacing of Yvonne Romain is a highlight. As in *Grip of the Strangler*, the set designer, this time Anthony Masters, is one of the real stars. The picture echoes *The Body Snatcher,* both in its plot elements and in Christopher Lee's top-hatted Resurrection Joe, surely a cousin of Karloff's John Gray in the Lewton picture. *Kinematograph Weekly* (September 13, 1962) was reasonably impressed, calling the picture a "robust clinical melodrama. The plot makes no concessions to the squeamish... Boris Karloff acts in all seriousness..."

Both pictures were the brainchildren of Richard Gordon, the only producer to work with Karloff, Bela Lugosi, Peter Cushing, and Christopher Lee. Born in London in the mid-twenties, Gordon became a movie fan as a child. With his older brother Alex, he followed his dream to America in 1947. Richard eventually set up a film importing/distributing company in New York (which he still operates today), and Alex went west, becoming a founding father of American International Pictures.

In *Corridors of Blood* Karloff was cast as a good man forced into evil behavior by events beyond his control.

Boris Karloff played an important role in Richard Gordon's life, as well as in his pictures. Gordon, despite being in the movie business for over forty years, never got over being a fan, and is almost as well known in this guise as he is as a filmmaker. He has both strong memories and feelings about Boris Karloff and is always willing to share them, fan to fan...

"The first time I ever saw Boris Karloff and realized that it *was* Boris Karloff, was in *House of Rothschild*.[1] I heard the name so often, that I was impressed by finally being able to see him—it was a very imposing performance. It was pretty hard to upstage George Arliss under *any* circumstances, so I was especially impressed with Karloff. It made me very much interested in seeing his horror pictures, which were not easy to see in England at that time—especially for children—they were allowed for 'adults only.'

"I met Boris in 1948, in New York with my brother Alex—we had come over from England to get into the business. We were writing for a British fan magazine and hoped to get an interview. They were specifically interested in *personal* interviews, not publicity stuff, so we went after actors doing summer stock, Broadway... we certainly couldn't afford to go to Hollywood!

301

Although Boris Karloff could play this type of role while asleep, he still managed to make it look new.

"Karloff was in New York doing *The Linden Tree* which, unfortunately, was *not* a success. We got to meet him backstage first, then he invited us to go to his hotel—the Meurice on 58th Street. I was only twenty-three—a real amateur! He was the kind of person who said, 'Here are two enthusiastic kids, the least I can do is to go along with it.' We weren't looking for anything controversial—it was a fan piece. By that time, we had seen his old horror pictures and were very familiar with them. He was very friendly—we went there a couple of times!

"He returned to New York for *The Shop at Sly Corner*. We went backstage to say hello, then lost contact with him for a while. When we met again several years later (I had told him about my ambitions to produce), he showed me a story that had been written for him by Jan Read—an outline, really, called *Stranglehold.* One thing led to another, and he said, 'If you can set this up for production in England, I'm willing to do it.' I'd only done seven co-productions at that point, supplying American artists—this was a *real* challenge! I felt I was ready, and when Karloff gave me the opportunity... I formed a company—Producers Associates Ltd. It says a lot for him that he was willing to give me the free option to set it up—I had no real experience other than as a co-producer. He gave me a real chance!

"I arranged for Jan Read to write the screenplay and with John Croydon, a British producer, to become part of Producers' Associates to take over the physical details—I didn't have the experience to do it alone—and took the package to Eros Films. They wanted a second feature to put out on a double bill: Alex sent me a story called *Thought Monster* out of *Weird Tales* magazine. Eros didn't care too much what the second picture was—they wanted the *Karloff* picture! It became *Fiend Without A Face*—one of my favorites! John Croydon suggested Robert Day as director—he'd done a few interesting things—and I agreed he'd be perfect for *Grip of the Strangler,* as it was to be called.

"There's been so much said about Boris Karloff, that no one has much to say that's new—including me! It seems as though recently, in order to say *anything,* some people are now taking a negative approach. An actress recently, in a magazine, made some obnoxious comments about Karloff during the filming of *Bedlam*... 'He was so *old,* and had a *lisp!*' I can only repeat—he was one of the most courteous, friendly, gentlemanly, and good-natured people I've ever worked with—or met! He was the perfect gentleman—he was as he had always been portrayed—until it has become recently fashionable to knock him—and other celebrities. A *typical* Englishman—the garden, cricket, the 'country squire'—part of the Hollywood 'English Colony.'

"Anyone can have a bad moment—or bad day—and some, in recalling their experiences with Boris, choose to dwell on them. Like so many who were as *professional* as Karloff was, he *could* become intolerant with those on the set who were not—who were not pulling their weight. There *were* moments during my two pictures with him when there was tension on the set. He was not tolerant of people stumbling around, not knowing what they were doing, or telling him to do something that was patently wrong—he didn't have any time to waste. Then, when it was over, it was over—it blew over quickly and that was the end of it... no hard feelings.

"He was a very private person—there's much about his personal life—marriages, relationships, whatever—which has not been explored... his family background, his association with India... People have been, for whatever reason, looking for a 'dark side' of Boris Karloff, which may very well have been there, but was certainly not evident to those who actually knew him, and it certainly didn't interfere with his work, even if it did exist. Even if it did exist—

Director Robert Day (far left), Boris Karloff, and Elizabeth Allan on the set of
Grip of the Strangler. **[Courtesy of Richard Gordon]**

it was a very small part of his life and has *absolutely* no importance! And there's no point in dragging it out.

"Karloff, then, was represented by MCA—a tough agency—and like all agents, wanted to protect their actors—to keep them out of 'small pictures,' if possible. They want a major deal at a major studio where, of course, the agent can get a larger commission! It was a tough negotiation, but I knew Karloff really wanted to do *Strangler.* After all, he brought me the Jan Read story! Part of the deal was an option on a *second* film to be exercised within a certain period of time—subject to Karloff's availability, naturally.

"The idea we came up with, in retrospect, may seem slightly absurd, but the idea was... a new version of *Dracula!* As everybody who has ever tried a new version says, 'Let's go back to the book and do it properly'—but no one ever really does! We were led to believe that *Dracula* was in the public domain, that we'd have nothing to fear from Universal, but we were wrong! This was *before* Hammer did *Horror of Dracula* with Universal. MGM was exhibiting

Boris Karloff "never looked down on any picture or any audience. I think he'd be very surprised—and grateful—for the continued interest in his life and career."

Grip of the Strangler by this time, and we sought their involvement. They were interested—in color and Cinemascope! We did have a script done which, unfortunately, no longer exists. It would be worth a fortune! When we got into the legalities, MGM discovered that *Dracula* was *not,* in fact, in the public domain. It *was* in Europe, to be exact, but *not* in the USA! And that was *that.*

"When *Dracula* fell by the wayside, John Croydon and I were in a quandary—the contract with MCA was 'play or pay.' We needed a subject—quickly—that would please Karloff! The idea we came up with was not a bad one, but, with its combination of horror and historical reality, it fell between two stools. Like *Bedlam, Corridors of Blood* combined two different concepts, but I'm afraid that *mine* wasn't as consistent—it jumped around, back and forth... *Bedlam* was more consistent and more successful.

"A problem beyond our control occurred when MGM changed management in the midst of production—the new guys were not interested in financing 'little' pictures. They were not interested in releasing it... for the time being. We had no way of getting anybody else to put up the money to reimburse

"Boris Karloff was a very dedicated actor, very much appreciative of the success he had."

MGM to take over the film, so it languished for a while until MGM, in one of their other, later management changes, came back to the idea of forming a secondary unit to release pictures of this type. They hired a guy, Fred Schwartz, who'd been an exhibitor to head up the operation. I knew him quite well from my distribution days, so that was fine with me! The question then was, what to release with *Corridors of Blood*? I didn't have another picture, and after my experiences with MGM, I wasn't prepared to make *another* film for them to put out with *Corridors,* so Fred Schwartz acquired *Werewolf in a Girls' Dormitory*—it had a song called 'The Ghoul in School!'

"I prefer *Grip of the Strangler* to *Corridors of Blood,* and so did Karloff. *Strangler* is what it is—what you see is what you get. I think it worked rather well. Karloff wasn't terribly happy with *Corridors,* even though it may be the 'classier' production and more 'mainstream,' despite the title! It isn't an out-and-out horror picture. It was based on a serious subject, made with as much authenticity as we could afford—the period was nicely suggested. It helped shooting it at MGM! But, it's not really for the horror fans, yet too horrible for 'regular' audiences. People were put off by the title.

"We got a real break getting Christopher Lee for the picture. James Carreras, head of Hammer, was a real gentleman and always willing to help other filmmakers. He tipped me that Lee was about to become a hot horror property after *The Curse of Frankenstein* went into general release, and that I could get him fairly cheaply if I acted *quickly*. Sir James really made me a present of him! Unlike my feelings for Karloff, I found Lee to be, from the start, a bit cold and calculating, and I thought, arrogant, both in his attitude toward Karloff and in his evaluation of his own acting ability. I *do* think he played his part *very* well. It was a nice pairing with Karloff, and I'm happy that we got him. He added a great deal to the residual value of the picture, both on TV and in home video. I'm grateful for that.

"I felt that Boris Karloff's greatest strength as an actor was that if he accepted a role, from the moment he signed on, he treated it as a professional and would give the best possible performance—he never walked through a part—it wasn't his nature. He felt a very strong obligation toward his employers—if he was taking their money, they were entitled to their money's worth. And, of course, he was protecting his own future. If he developed a 'walk through' reputation among producers, he might not get the better parts.

"That's not to say that he wasn't better in some parts than in others—every actor is, and sometimes it's beyond an actor's control... the script is weak, the direction is poor... that should not imply that the actor didn't care! Budget, time allowed, many things influence an actor's performance.

"Karloff and Lugosi... the two continue to be tied together, and probably always will be. I never heard Karloff say a bad word about Bela Lugosi. He did feel sorry for Bela—that he was really his own worst enemy due to the mistakes he made in his career—they could have been avoided, and Karloff felt sorry that they weren't! He never derided or wanted to hurt Lugosi—Karloff was *not* that kind of person. On the other hand, he didn't consider himself to be responsible for Bela's downward spiral. He didn't go out and *campaign* for *Frankenstein*—he was chosen after Lugosi turned it down. Then, what happened, happened. He certainly felt no guilt—only that Lugosi used poor judgment.

"Karloff, with his versatility, lived long enough to see himself become a legend, although Lugosi today may be the more popular. Although he was more on 'one note,' he was more colorful than Karloff. His involvement with Ed Wood and Monogram makes him somehow more appealing to many fans.

"Boris Karloff was a very dedicated actor, very much appreciative of the success that he had. He felt an obligation to audiences as well as producers. He believed that if people paid to see him, he owed them the best of his ability.

"He never looked down on *any* picture or *any* audience. I think he'd be very surprised—and grateful—for the continued interest in his life and career so long after his death."

Like Richard Gordon, Robert Day has fond memories of Karloff two decades after directing him. "Boris Karloff was very much like Peter Cushing," Day recalled. "Both were highly professional actors, friendly, and considerate of all those with whom they worked. They were real 'old school' actors—a school with too few students these days."

With tight direction by Robert Day,[2] authentic period "feel," and excellent supporting actors, including Anthony Dawson, Elizabeth Allan, and Jean Kent (*Grip of the Strangler*), and Francis DeWolff, Christopher Lee, Adrienne Corri, and Francis Matthews (*Corridors of Blood*), this pair of aces are good bets for all fans of Boris Karloff. With the exception of *Targets,* he would have no future roles that gave him the opportunities presented here. And, while sentiment and tradition draw us to the "Golden Age" of thirties' and forties' horror, *Grip of the Strangler* and *Corridors of Blood* can hold their own in that company, too.

Grip of the Stangler (*The Haunted Strangler,* USA)

CREDITS: Director: Robert Day; Executive Producer: Richard Gordon; Producer: John Croydon; Screenplay: Jan Read, John C. Cooper [John Croydon], based on Jan Read's story; Director of Photography: Lionel Banes; Special Effects: Les Bowie; Editor: Peter Mayhew; Art Director: John Elphick; Music: Buxton Orr; Musical Director: Frederick Lewis; Dresses: Anna Duse; Camera: Leo Rogers; Assistant Director: Douglas Hickox; Sound: H. C. Pearson; Dubbing: Terry Poulton; Makeup: Jim Hydes; Continuity: Hazel Swift; An MLC/Producers Associates Production filmed at Walton Studios; Released by MGM; 78 minutes; 1958; U.K.

CAST: Boris Karloff...James Rankin, Jean Kent...Cora Seth, Elizabeth Allan...Barbara Rankin, Anthony Dawson...Supt. Burk, Vera Day...Pearl, Tim

Turner...Kenneth McColl, Diane Aubrey...Lily, Dorothy Gordon...Hannah, Peggy Ann Clifford...Kate, Leslie Perrins...Governor, Michael Atkinson...Styles, Desmond Roberts...Dr. Johnson, Jessica Cairns...Maid, Roy Russell...Medical Supt., Derek Birch...Hospital Superintendent, George Hirste...Lost Property Man, John G. Heller...Male Nurse, George Spence...Hangman, Joan Elvin...Can-Can Girl

Corridors of Blood

CREDITS: Director: Robert Day; Executive Producer: Richard Gordon; Producer: John Croydon and Charles Vetter, Jr.; Associate Producer: Peter Mayhew; Screenplay: Jean Scott Rogers; Director of Photography: Geoffrey Faithfull; Art Director: Anthony Masters; Film Editor: Peter Mayhew; Music Composed and Conducted by Buxton Orr; Production Manager: George Mills; Camera Operator: Frank Drake; Assistant Director: Peter Bolton; Sound: Cyril Swern, Maurice Askew; Dubbing Editor: Peter Musgrave; Continuity: Susan Dyson; Makeup: Walter Schneidermann; Hairdresser: Eileen Warwick; Dress Designer: Emma Selby-Walker; Wardrobe: Doris Turner; A Producers Associates Production filmed at MGM Borehamwood; Released by MGM; black and white; 85 minutes; 1958, U.K.

CAST: Boris Karloff...Dr. Thomas Bolton, Betta St. John...Susan, Finlay Currie...Supt. Matheson, Christopher Lee...Resurrection Joe, Adrienne Corri...Rachel, Francis DeWolff...Black Ben, Francis Matthews...Jonathan Bolton, Frank Pettingell...Dr. Blount, Basil Dignam...Chairman, Marian Spencer...Mrs. Matheson, Carl Bernard...Ned the Crow, John Gabriel...Dispenser, Nigel Green...Inspector Donovan, Yvonne Warren (Romain)...Rosa, Howard Lang...Chief Inspector, Julian D'Albie...Bald Man, Roddy Hughes...Man with Watch, Robert Raglan...Wilkes, Charles Lloyd Pack...Hardcastle

Thanks to Robert Day, Richard Gordon, and Tom Weaver.

1. *House of Rothschild* (1934) starred the then-famous George Arliss as the head of the once-famous European banking family. Karloff, as Count Ledrantz, the anti-Semitic villain, was enjoying his second (with *The Lost Patrol)* "straight" part that year after becoming a horror star.
2. Robert Day directed Peter Cushing in Hammer's remake of *She* (1964) with Ursula Andress, John Richardson, and Christopher Lee.

Tom Johnson is a well known Hammer fanatic who has co-authored *Peter Cushing: The Gentle Man of Horror* and *Hammer Film: An Exhaustive Filmography* both from McFarland. He has also contributed to many film magazines including *Midnight Marquee, Filmfax,* and *Monsters from the Vault.*

THE COMEDY OF TERRORS (1964)

by John Stell

What if your landlord was threatening to evict you from your once flourishing, but now bankrupt, funeral parlor, which is presently being run by your son-in-law, who is trying to kill you, while your daughter, who never lets you have your medicine, is flirting with an escaped convict, who is also in your employ? Well, if you're Boris Karloff, and your landlord is Basil Rathbone, your in-law Vincent Price, your daughter Joyce Jameson, and your employee Peter Lorre, you don't do anything because, you see, you're oblivious to what's going on. That's basically Karloff's function in *The Comedy of Terrors:* to sit around and do nothing while the others have the fun. Well, almost nothing. Dear Boris does have several brief but memorable moments in Richard Matheson's uproarious ode to Poe (premature burials), Shakespeare (Rathbone's ravings), and Roger Corman (just look at the cast). *The Comedy of Terrors* is a grand teaming, which gave Karloff, in his ailing years, a chance to work with his peers, Lorre, Rathbone, and Price, the successor to his crown.

The plot is straightforward enough. Waldo Trumbull (Vincent Price) runs father-in-law Amos Hinchley's (Boris Karloff) funeral business. Trapped in a loveless marriage, Trumbull only married wife Amaryllis (Joyce Jameson) to get her old pop's money in the first place. Now, she's falling in love with Felix Gillie (Peter Lorre), Trumbull's assistant whom Trumbull is blackmailing into servitude.

Unfortunately, the funeral business is slow and one year's rent is owed to the landlord, Mr. Black (Basil Rathbone). To "kill two birds with one pillow," Trumbull has Gillie try to kill Black, who promptly has a cataleptic seizure and thus appears to be dead. When Black is laid in a crypt to rest, however, the not-quite-dead landlord escapes, gets an ax, and goes after Trumbull and Gillie.

All ends up okay, however, since Black has another seizure before doing in anyone. Gillie and Amaryllis run off together, leaving behind Trumbull and Hinchley. But Hinchley, finding his son-in-law passed out on the stairs, gives the inebriated no-good "a dose of your own medicine," that is, a taste from the little vial of poison Trumbull keeps in his own pocket. Trumbull becomes a victim of his own treachery, as "dad" goes back to bed.

Do not make the mistake of thinking *The Comedy of Terrors* is about its plot: it isn't. The film gives us the opportunity to see many of our favorite genre stars conspire to spoof their notorious images, each bringing his own eccentricities to the roles. Price is the only true villain, and thus he's the only main character who actually dies, a rather ironic twist given every other person appears dead, or is close to death, in the film. The stars are having fun, and it's easy to get into the spirit of things.

Price's character doesn't have a kind word for anyone, as demonstrated by the following comments about:

Wife Amaryllis' singing: "The vocal emissions of a laryngitic crow."

Wife Amaryllis in general: Her dad did "more than collect curious objects. He also fathered one."

Mr. Black: A "penny pinching old pig."

Felix Gillie: "...probably the most inept house breaker in all of New England."

Amos Hinchley: An "old goat" and "an old fool."

Women in general: "As soon put your trust in them as put a pistol to your head."

As one can gather, Waldo Trumbull is not a particularly positive person. He is in love with the sound of his own voice, a drunkard who likes his booze and his cash. Trumbull has no redeeming qualities: he's a thief and a murderer. That he "gets it" in the end is no surprise.

Lorre's Felix Gillie, on the other hand, is a teddy bear—a sweet, gentle soul who one can't imagine robbing banks. ("I never confessed. They just proved it.") Trying to make the best of his situation, however, he builds a coffin, which Trumbull promptly destroys ("No one in their right mind would be caught dead in that thing!"), attempts to talk Trumbull out of murder ("There must be a little more honest way to conduct a funeral business," to which Trumbull responds, "I might expect that kind of talk from a criminal."), and falls in love with Amaryllis, who, for Gillie, has the voice of "a nightingale." But the mousy Gillie pretty much does nothing confrontation-wise until he believes Waldo has strangled Amaryllis.

Mr. Black, as portrayed by Basil Rathbone, is a businessman with a rather intense, all consuming passion for Shakespeare. How intense? So caught up in reading aloud from the bard is he that, getting up from his bed, he grabs a sword and starts "fencing" with his belongings, traveling from room to room, never pausing in his recitation. Subject to cataleptic fits, he dies several times, awaking from each "death" wondering aloud, "What place is this?"

The Comedy of Terrors **is a grand teaming which gave Karloff, in his ailing years, a chance to work with Lorre, Rathbone, and Price.**

In certain circumstances, Black can be more polite than the situation warrants. For example, while Trumbull and Gillie are trying to keep him locked in a coffin, Black comments, "I regard your actions as inimical to good fellowship." This is much more eloquent than a simple, "Up yours, fella."

And of course, we have lovable Boris Karloff as the blissfully ignorant Amos Hinchley. Not once does Hinchley have a clue as to what's going on. Trumbull tries to poison him on several occasions, which Hinchley welcomes because he thinks he's being given medicine. When his daughter takes it away, he's upset: "Why do you always take my medicine away? Don't you care nothing about my health?" he cries as he bangs his silverware on the table and goes into a boo-hoo-hoo routine. Later he whines, "There you go keepin' my medicine away from me again. I don't believe you care whether your poor old father lives or dies!"

Hinchley has little hearing left, and thus has a hard time comforting his daughter while Trumbull hurls his endless insults. He just sits at the table, eating his soup or drinking his tea, as Trumbull goes on. When she looks at Hinchley pleadingly, he simply passes her the sugar: "I gave the sugar to you once," and, "You're eating much too much sugar. You know that, don't you?" are his typical responses.

Despite his near-deafness, Hinchley does deliver two of the funniest "speeches" in the film. During his eulogy for Mr. Black, Hinchley forgets the guy's name and refers to him as, "what's his name," and "Mrs., uh, Mr. You Know Who." He comments, for all to hear, "Hmm. That's pretty good," about his own sermon. And he fumbles for the word coffin, giving a laundry list of alternate terms.

Even better is the kitchen scene where, out of nowhere, he starts talking, with much delight and amusement, about certain idiosyncrasies of death:

"Old Ben Jonson, buried standing up. Edward III, buried with his horse. Alexander the Great, embalmed in honey so they say. Heh, heh. Egyptians used to hollow 'em out and pour 'em full of resin. Egyptians used to bend them in two and stick 'em in a vase of saltwater. And give 'em false eyes. Yank their brains out with a hook."

It's an hysterical moment, with poor Amaryllis trying several times, unsuccessfully, to keep him quiet.

Thus *The Comedy of Terrors* is really about giving four gentleman who made their living trying to scare us a chance to make us laugh. And they succeed. Who "steals" the movie is open to debate: Price's nonstop insulting one-liners (at the funeral while Amaryllis sings "He Is Not Dead but Sleepeth," Price quips, "I wish her vocal chords would snap."); Lorre's self-deprecating humor (when Price says he's a most inept thief, Lorre responds, "That's true."); Rathbone's blustery and unusual way of phrasing his lines ("What jiggery pokery is this?" he asks when he finds he's in a coffin); and Karloff's innocent delivery of killer comments ("That ought to take care of you nicely," he says after giving Price the "medicine") make the determination of a "winner" almost impossible.

The humor in *The Comedy of Terrors* exists at many levels. We have slapstick in scenes such as the cat watching the spouses go at it, ultimately

Karloff and the successor to his crown, Vincent Price, ham it up in *The Comedy of Terrors.*

"gulping" when Price tries to give Karloff some poison. Joyce Jameson hits high notes that make hats fly off, glasses shatter, flowers wilt, and vases crack. (Karloff says of her singing: "Must have been an earthquake.") Sound effects are employed as characters are conked on the head, and Price's eyes "ping" open when he realizes he's been poisoned. Several scenes include sped up photography, like the duel between Lorre and Price at the end. The best moment of sight-gag comedy though is when Lorre backs into a bust perched on the steps, knocking it backward and creating a domino effect as the other busts crash into each other.

The film also features several running gags. Lorre is always pronouncing Trumbull as "Tremble," and, when corrected, replies, "I said Mr. Tremble." As mentioned Price is always trying to slip poison in Karloff's tea, and Rathbone can be heard to ask "What place is this?" every time he revives from a cataleptic attack.

Yet another source of humor can be found in some truly ironic bits of dialogue. Price asks, "Is there no morality left in this world?" when he finds

There's something very wonderful about the thought of these respected thespians sharing a good time together.

that the widow of the man he's just killed ran off to Boston without paying the funeral bill. As Rathbone tries to get out of the coffin, Lorre suggests, "Be a nice boy and stay in there where you belong." Also, while Price and Jameson go at it, we see a sign which reads "Honor, Patience, Tranquillity" hanging in their kitchen.

And of course, there are plenty of "just plain funny" ideas and moments. Price and Lorre have been using the same coffin for thirteen years, burying people "naked," and yet act genuinely upset when, thanks to Mr. Black being buried in a crypt, they realize they'll have to buy a new one. Disgusted after learning he's to be evicted, Price knocks over a complete stranger, who then looks blankly into the camera. Karloff gets a ladle full of soup in his face when Jameson spins during a musical interlude. Lorre nearly falls off the roof when trying to break into Rathbone's home and matter-of-factly comments, "I don't think this is a good idea." When Rathbone discovers he's "dead," he indignantly exclaims, "The hell I am!" Lorre, while being pursued by Rathbone, takes the time to open a door that has mostly been hacked to pieces. And when Price is bitten by Rathbone during their screwball chase, Price says disbelievingly, "He bit me. The son of a bit me."

Certainly, then the humor is a combination of the physical and the verbal, both of which compliment each other nicely. But the humor, and thus the film, work because we are familiar with the preceding work of the actors who are playing these characters. This film would not have worked if some unknowns had been given these roles. Sure, there would still be laughs. But the contrast of a humorous scenario played out by the classic horror actors would be gone. Thus the reason for the film's being is in the casting.

Richard Matheson drafted a wonderful and witty screenplay for the players in *The Comedy of Terrors*. The author of such novels as *I Am Legend* (1954) and *The Shrinking Man* (1956), both of which were made into films, was very busy during the 1960s. He had scripted several other films featuring Vincent Price including *House of Usher* (1960), *Pit and the Pendulum* (1961), *Tales of Terror* (1962), and *The Raven* (1963). He was also writing teleplays for *The Twilight Zone* during this time. Although Matheson has always had a penchant for blending humor and horror, this was his first real comedy.

Matheson takes the opportunity to poke fun at subject matter he knows to a tee. There's a good in-joke which has Price reciting lines from *The Raven* as he waits for a victim to be discovered. Since many of his Poe adaptations for Roger Corman featured characters who were buried alive, Matheson gives us Mr. Black who refuses to stay buried. Furthermore, by giving Mr. Black a love of Shakespeare, Matheson works in several Shakespearean references. A clever *Romeo and Juliet* reference has both Lorre and Jameson think, at one point, the other is dead. The cat is named Cleopatra. When Price starts strangling Jameson, one is reminded of the jealousy in *Othello*.

Matheson can't refuse to throw in some literary devices, namely foreshadowing. For instance, early in the film Jameson tells Price, "Demon rum will get you yet." Of course Price is poisoned at film's end. Matheson also uses colorful descriptions to give the dialogue more zing. Lorre's crimes aren't crimes, they're "sundry illicit peccadilloes." The screenplay is a nice fusion of frivolity and fright, winding up with Black attempting to ax anyone who gets in his way, Trumbull shooting Black several times, and Gillie and Trumbull dueling to the death. Matheson is at his humorously nasty best here.

Another surprising touch in making *The Comedy of Terrors* was having, as its director, Jacques Tourneur, the man behind the camera on such classics as *Cat People* (1942), *I Walked With A Zombie* (1943), the film noir *Out of the Past* (1947), and *Curse of the Demon* (1957). (In fact, his last film was the Vincent Price effort, *War-Gods of the Deep*, in 1965.) For this comedy, however, Tourneur shows another side to his directing talent.

Much of the time Tourneur plays up the comedy. The opening sequence starts out at a funeral, with Price and Lorre wearing long faces. When the mourners leave, however, they quickly spring into action, while the film speeds up as if we were watching a silent movie, as the two dump the corpse and put the coffin back onto their carriage. The camera follows Rhubarb the cat as she enters the funeral home through the cellar, climbs the stairs, and then sits on a kitchen chair to watch her "parents" argue, moving her head from side to side as if she were watching a tennis match. Many times Tourneur's camera simply focuses on the actors as they hurl one-liners and barbs. An early scene, however, does have Lorre contemplating his options on how to deal with Price's treatment of Jameson: "If he keeps mistreating you like that I won't know what to do." We then cut to Lorre bringing down an ax on would-be fire wood.

But as the finale commences the proceedings take on an ominous tone. We begin with Karloff playing the fiddle as Lorre and Jameson dance together, and Price "bathes" in silver pieces. The scene becomes feverish as the editing cuts back and forth among fiddler, dancers, and bather with increasing speed. When Rathbone leaves his coffin, still quoting Shakespeare, his voice becomes deeper and he speaks slower, indicating his deranged state of mind. Thunder booms and lightening flashes above. The old reliable "knocking door" gimmick causes Price to arise from his drunken stupor and search the house, commenting, "Something's been opening doors around here. But what?" He then steps on the cat, which dutifully squeals. The camera follows Rathbone's footprints up the stairs as we await his first attack. When he does finally begin his revenge, he brings down his weapon, just missing Jameson's head. The film, however, gets back to its comical tone during the ensuing chase where Lorre falls down the stairs, and Rathbone starts talking again just when you think he's finally finished. While the film never becomes an all-out horror show, there are some amusingly suspenseful moments.

The other major player in *The Comedy of Terrors* is Joyce Jameson as the neglected Amaryllis, who gave up her "promising" opera career to marry Waldo Trumbull. Jameson, through no fault of her own, is given a rather one-joke part. In other words, Amaryllis can't sing worth a damn, so time and time again she bursts into song, causing us to cringe. Jameson is good in the role of Amaryllis, but she's just there to be abused by Price and is not given the screen

The Comedy of Terrors is really about giving four gentlemen who made their living trying to scare us a chance to make us laugh.

time her co-stars are. Interestingly, in "The Black Cat" segment of 1962's *Tales of Terror*, Jameson was married to Lorre and had an affair with Price. Now, she's switched men. It's yet another of the film's in-jokes.

The Comedy of Terrors marks the first and only time all four stars—Price, Lorre, Karloff, and Rathbone—worked together. Price, Karloff, and Rathbone appeared in the melodrama *Tower of London* (1939), while Price, Karloff, and Lorre had shared time on *The Raven* (1963). Impressively, the four don't seem to be trying to outdo each other, but rather play their parts so that everyone generates his fair share of laughs. There's something very wonderful in the

thought of these respected thespians sharing a good time together. One could have only wished for a re-teaming.

What is even more important for true horror fans is that Boris Karloff was appearing in a few good movies in the final phase of his career, unlike his comrade Bela Lugosi, who slummed it with Ed Wood. Karloff still had several more accomplishments ahead of him: voicing the Grinch in Dr. Seuss' *How the Grinch Stole Christmas* (1966) and playing basically himself in the acclaimed *Targets* (1968), a reflection on movie horror and real-life violence.

It is, perhaps, a shame that Karloff couldn't do more in *The Comedy of Terrors*. But the fact is, he was not to far away from being mostly confined to a wheelchair, and thus any great physical exertion on his part for this film would have been asking way too much. As his part is, he seems to perhaps be playing a character very much like himself: quiet, gentle, and full of good cheer. One could imagine this poor fellow bursting into tears if he knew what was really going on around him. His ignorance is our bliss.

Price and Rathbone are wonderfully hammy. Karloff, like Lorre, is marvelously low-key. Karloff sits at his table, not intentionally drawing attention to himself, waiting until he's asked to pass the sugar. That one of Karloff's greatest gifts is his voice (in fact, all the stars of this film have great voices) is time and time again proven in this film when he's called to be vocal. The delight in his voice as he talks about burial practices gives the scene its humor, since the dialogue itself is merely a list of facts. Likewise Karloff speaks with passion and empathy during his eulogy, but really doesn't know the first thing about the guy he's eulogizing. His abrupt pause to be delighted by his own words is perfectly expressed.

Aside from his fiddle playing, Karloff sits it out during the climax. He returns to deliver the final punchlines as he innocently poisons Price. Perhaps Hinchley's lament of years gone by, "Everything seems to be in order... Nothing ever happens around here... Now when I was young, we knew how to live," has double meaning in speaking about horror films of past and present. Although if this were the case, perhaps he should have said, "We knew how to die."

For horror fans in general, *The Comedy of Terrors* is the perfect vehicle to laugh away those jitters that Price, Lorre, Karloff, and Rathbone had left us with in films such as *House of Wax* (1953), *Mad Love* (1935), *Frankenstein* (1931), and *Son of Frankenstein* (1939). And for Karloff fans in particular, *The Comedy of Terrors* is yet another example of horror's greatest star playing a part that, although brief, attests to the claim that he gave his roles his all.

CREDITS: Producers: James H. Nicholson and Samuel Z. Arkoff; Director: Jacques Tourneur; Screenplay: Richard Matheson; Co-Producer: Anthony Carras; Associate Producer: Richard Matheson; Production Manager: Joseph Wonder; Cinematographer: Floyd Crosby, A.S.C.; Production Designer and Art Director: Daniel Haller; Editor: Anthony Carras; Music: Les Baxter; Music Coordinator: Al Simms; Released December 25, 1963 by American International Pictures; 83 minutes; Alternative Title: *The Graveside Story*

CAST: Vincent Price...Waldo Trumbull, Peter Lorre...Felix Gillie, Boris Karloff...Amos Hinchley, Joyce Jameson...Amaryllis Trumbull, Joe E. Brown...Graveyard Guard, Beverly Hills...Mrs. Phipps, Basil Rathbone...John F. Black, Rhubarb...Cleopatra, Alan DeWitt, Buddy Mason...Mr. Phipps, Douglas Williams, Linda Rogers...Phipps' Maid, and Luree Holmes

John Stell, a CPA residing in Baltimore, contributes to *Movie Club, Monsters from the Vault*, and *Midnight Marquee*. He has contributed to *Midnight Marquee Actors Series: Bela Lugosi* and is currently working on a book, *Psychos, Sickos, and Sequels*, detailing horror films of the 1980s.

322

DIE, MONSTER, DIE! (1965)

by David H. Smith

"Things do not change; we change" —Henry David Thoreau

Hindsight is indeed 20/20, and missed opportunities for film icons weigh heavily on fans' minds. With the resurgence of interest in Gothic horror films in the 1960s precipitated by the fairly recent release to television of the Universal classics and by the color-drenched product of Hammer Films and AIP lighting up theater marquees, it's a pity AIP was so shortsighted with its new contractee, Boris Karloff.

True, the omnibus *Black Sabbath* (*I Tre Volti della Paura*) was a marvel of filmmaking, and even today, it remains a touchstone for European horror. Aside from his avuncular introductions to each, Karloff's performance in the third of its three stories is as magnificent as its many reviews have stated. Even though today the film and its director, Mario Bava (1914-1980), are fast becoming over-analyzed, *Black Sabbath* (1964) stands as a testament to Karloff's thespian talents as he effortlessly bridged the generations of horror movies of the past to the present.

But for AIP this was the exception rather than the rule. For sheer bewilderment, there was *The Terror* (1963), a meager film crafted from oddments no amount of expository dialogue could rescue. From an outsider's point of view, it looks like they had the best of intentions with Boris. They put him in what appear ostensibly to be topflight product, helmed by master craftsmen like Roger Corman (b. 1926) and Jacques Tourneur (1904-1977). Amid Daniel Haller's efficient yet lush set decorations and reciting dialogue by screenwriters as felicitous as Richard Matheson, Boris was nevertheless remaindered in some of his worst features.

Whether indelicately shoehorned for a cameo into an Annette Funicello/ Frankie Avalon surf romp (*Bikini Beach*), or even sharing top of the bill in horror parodies with genre luminaries like Basil Rathbone and Vincent Price, Karloff always looked to be the odd man out, consigned to thankless roles, and seemed, like his late associate Bela Lugosi (1882-1956), on the verge of living out his years becoming a victim of his own image.

Unlike Lugosi, however, Karloff did not need the work for monetary reasons. He did it out of love for the acting profession, relishing opportunities

Die, Monster, Die! **was a return for Karloff to the true horror film.**

to perform in any venue, and grateful there were audiences that wanted him. Already a triumph on the big screen, his acclaimed Broadway stage work in *Arsenic and Old Lace* (1941-4), *The Linden Tree* (1948), and *Peter Pan* (1950-1), longtime radio work and television success with *Colonel March of Scotland Yard* (1956-8) and *Thriller* (1960-2) had earned him a comfortable retirement in which he wanted no part. Karloff probably saw the moody Poe adaptations that AIP was releasing as a nostalgic return to the period melodramas in which he had first made a name for himself. The stage was set, the lights were dimmed, but AIP almost dropped the tableau curtain before their star had a chance.

    Die, Monster, Die! was a return for Karloff to the true horror film. Albeit set in modern day, the trappings were very Gothic and, save for its radioactive *deus ex machina*, could very well have been set decades earlier. It also adapted for only the second time on screen a writer whose influence has shaped a whole generation of fiction writers (particularly Clive Barker) and filmmakers. Howard P. Lovecraft (1890-1937) was Edgar Allan Poe's successor in horror fiction. As Chauncey Mabe described his "overheated pulp" in the *Fort*

Lauderdale Sun-Sentinel, Lovecraft was "among the first to grasp the terrors possible in a universe governed not by God but by Darwinian biology and quantum physics." Lovecraft's purple prose is indeed sometimes a struggle to wade through, but his tales of tentacled Cthulhu, slithering Shoggoths, and various New England wizards who can come back from the dead can indeed inspire a chill up the reader's spine.

For this movie, veteran science fiction writer Jerry Sohl adapted Lovecraft's "The Colour Out Of Space," which had been first published in the September 1927 issue of *Amazing Stories.* A quiet understated account, it is one of Lovecraft's finest works, wherein a meteorite's surreptitious influence blights a remote area and drives a family to madness and mutation. With "The Colour Out Of Space," Lovecraft created, as Drake Douglas described it in *Horrors!,* "both horror and science fiction at its best."

Sohl wrote his screenplay "on spec," and, as he later told *Starlog* magazine, found a delighted buyer in American International co-founder James Nicholson (1916-1972). But Sohl was not so pleased when the film was flagged as the directorial debut for Daniel Haller, set designer for Roger Corman since 1957, and was further incensed by the tyro director's rewrites.

Born 1926 in Glendale, California, Haller was under contract to AIP and had been offered opportunities to direct before, but had held out for a project that particularly interested him. According to an interview with James Delson in *Fantastic Films*, Haller found Lovecraft "a very difficult writer to interpret for film," and that *Die, Monster, Die!* emerged as "a flawed film, but... fun to do."

With a solid script and a director with a decided eye for visual effect, the cards were definitely stacked in AIP's favor to produce a horror film worthy of competing with the polished products of Hammer, and Amicus. What was released is, subjectively, another matter altogether.

American Stephen Reinhart (Nick Adams) arrives by train at the small English town of Arkham. When he tries to hire the town's lone taxi to take him to the Witley estate, the cabby (Harold Goodwin) demurs and leaves Steve in a lurch. Throughout the town, at every mention of the Witley name, Steve is met alternately with laughter and derision. Even the local bicycle shop proprietor refuses to rent him his wares, leaving Steve to hike out onto the back country roads to the Witley estate on his own.

On his way, Steve sees a vast area bereft of all plant and animal life. When he reaches for a tree branch, it crumbles to dust at his slightest touch. Steve continues on to the high walls of the estate, fog swirling about him. He finds the entry gate chained and locked shut, but determinedly cuts through a broken section and knocks on the door. Receiving no answer, the door swings open on its own. Steve enters and calls out, and is surprised when he is suddenly confronted by an elderly gentleman (Boris Karloff) in a wheelchair.

"The signs clearly say to stay out," the old man barks. "You must have seen them."

"Yes," Steve begins, "I saw them—"

"Then by what right have you entered this house?"

"I've come to visit the Witleys."

The man raises an eyebrow. "Oh? I am Nahum Witley."

"Well, sir!" Steve gulps, "Actually it's Susan I came to visit."

"Susan? My daughter is not receiving visitors. I must ask you to leave."

Steve stands his ground. "Is this the way you treat all your guests?" he asks.

"Guests?" Nahum rejoins sarcastically. "Guests are invited. I don't remember having invited you."

Steve produces a letter from Mrs. Witley inviting him. Nahum recognizes Reinhart's name from conversation with his daughter. When Steve recounts how he met Susan in a science class at the US university they both attended, Nahum's eyes narrow. "*Science*," he harrumphs, then again insists Steve leave immediately.

When Susan (Suzan Farmer) appears at the top of the staircase, plainly overjoyed, Nahum mutters to Steve he must depart posthaste, but the American ignores him to embrace the pretty girl. Similarly ignoring her father's entreaties, Susan leads Steve up the stairs to meet her mother. On the way they pause at a couple of portraits (variations on Karloff's visage) with Susan identifying the subjects as her forefathers. "And what did he do?" Steve asks about Corbin Witley, Susan's grandfather. "He went insane," Susan replies blithely as they trot up to the second floor.

Steve and Susan enter the master bedroom, with Susan's mother Letitia (Freda Jackson) hidden by heavy veils and black draperies in her bed. Letitia dismisses her daughter to speak with the American alone. The elder woman pointlessly tantalizes Steve with a rambling story about a earring lost by a housemaid who "went down with some terrible disease" weeks before, and who had since disappeared. Finally reaching her point, Letitia makes Steve promise to take Susan away from this house of mystery.

Meanwhile, Nahum and his feeble manservant Merwyn (Terence De Marney) gather chains in the cellar to seal up the greenhouse. Nahum fondles the links, smiling, "Chains for demons..." A tarantula ambles by (boo!).

Later, Nahum castigates Letitia for inviting the American. This is clearly Karloff's most memorable scene, and the actor unhesitatingly gives his all. "Let me warn you: *Nothing* is going to deter me from my purpose," he tells his wife.

"Yes, that's what Corbin said," Letitia sighs wearily.

"But he's *dead*, Letitia," Nahum reminds her. "He's been dead for a long time. If there *was* evil, it's buried with him. All that remains of Corbin is a few

Die, Monster, Die! is, in itself, not a bad little horror film.

harmless objects in the cellar." Glimpsed earlier, these objects are sundry demonic paraphernalia, saw-toothed devil masks, and satanic inscriptions on the basement walls.

"I wonder if you realize how like Corbin you've become," the shrouded woman remarks.

Nahum is indignant. "There's no similarity whatsoever," he declares. "I've uttered no incantations, neither have I cried out to any of the other so-called *creatures of evil.*"

"It's only your methods that differ," Letitia huffs.

"And you know why?" her husband asks. "Because I don't believe in it, any of it! I never *have* believed it! It is you who would perpetuate these blasphemies, these absurdities."

Letitia believes Corbin's invocation at his death is at last coming full circle, and tells Nahum she asked Steve to take Susan away. Nahum grudgingly allows Steve to stay for a while.

This was truly Karloff's showcase scene, played to an unseen conversant, his every line laced with a different emphasis. With aplomb, he ranges from indignation to amusement to pleading to resolve. Karloff shrewdly underscores

327

Nahum (Karloff) tries to smash the meteorite with an ax.

significant words, stresses the absurdity of belief in otherworldly forces, and seems at once in control of the situation and simultaneously at a loss to explain it all.

Unfortunately, the following scene so hilariously tries for *misterioso* effect that it undoes much of the mood already achieved. At dinner, while Susan and Steve sip bouillon, Nahum sits glumly at the head of the table, declining to eat. Steve makes a feeble attempt at conversation by commenting about the dining room's dimensions. Getting nowhere, they continue to spoon their soup, until a unworldly wail shatters the silence. No one but Steve seems to notice, and his nonchalant inquiry as to its origin is met by Nahum's dour glare. Shrugging it off, Steve asks about the barren area he walked through on his way to the estate, which is dismissed as being the result of a fire, nothing more.

Serving the main course, Merwyn collapses, dragging the tablecloth and dishes to the floor with him. Nahum urges Steve and Susan to leave so he can take care of the servant himself.

Sometime later, when Susan brings a dinner tray to her mother's room, Letitia shushes the girl so she can listen to the "voices" speaking to her.

As she prepares for bed, Susan is startled by a shadowy figure peering in at her through her bedroom window. Her scream interrupts Steve as he thumbs his way through some esoteric occult books in the library. When he rushes in to comfort her, he finds nothing amiss, and tries to convince her to leave with him that night, but she refuses due to her mother's malaise.

Later that night, Susan and Steve venture out and downstairs when another, similar wail pierces the night air. A disheveled Nahum bars their way to the basement, announcing Merwyn has died. When Steve demands details, Nahum cuts him off, proclaiming, "This is my house, I must ask you to allow me to run my own affairs my own way!"

Still later, Steve sees Nahum burying Merwyn out back (no mean feat for a paraplegic), and also notices the greenhouse pulsing with viridescent light. As Steve examines the chains securing the door, Nahum hears their clinking and rolls to investigate. Steve bolts back to the main house, races upstairs, and dives beneath the covers of his bed even as Nahum, restricted as he is, rolls in at his heels. Convinced the American is asleep and unaware, Nahum hefts a weighty candelabra as if to bludgeon him but thinks better of it and leaves the room.

The next day, Steve heads back to Arkham in search of answers. He is waylaid by a cloaked figure on the way, briefly tussles with it, and continues on. He finds a doctor's address in a telephone directory, and, after admittance by a reluctant housekeeper (Sheila Raynor), questions the doctor (Patrick Magee) about the town's fear of the Witleys. The doctor, no longer in practice and a bit of a tippler, refuses to answer and sends him away. Escorted out by the housekeeper, she tells Steve the doctor has never been the same since attending the deathbed of Corbin Witley.

Steve tells Susan about his journey to town, and about his belief his attacker was the missing housemaid, grotesquely changed by her illness. After describing to her the peculiar glow at the greenhouse, Susan shows him a secret entrance into it. Therein, they find all sorts of enormous plant life, including outsized tomatoes. The strident wail heard at dinner the night before comes again, and when they investigate an adjoining potting shed, they see cages full of writhing, unidentifiable mutations. "Looks like a zoo in hell," Steve mutters. "A menagerie of horrors!" Susan adds.

Steve finds chunks of glowing rock in the soil around each mutated plant, and rationalizes them to be radioactive, chipped from some larger stone. One particularly precocious plant manages to entangle Susan in its vines, but Steve hacks her free and they hurry back to the house.

While Susan goes to pack, Steve (evidently not worried about future virility) goes to the basement to find the mother lode of radioactivity, encountering unaffected bats and even a clattering human skeleton (boo!) hanging on a wall. When he finds the large glowing rock beneath a grating, the irate Nahum argues with him about its effects.

The radiation from the meteorite mutates the crippled Nahum into a walking metallic superman.

Suddenly, Susan screams from upstairs, and the two men race to her aid. Letitia's face has metamorphosed into a lumpy travesty of human features, and the old woman has ventured out of her room. Deranged, she attacks Steve, crashing through oak-paneled doors, before the American feints and makes her stumble out onto a balcony into the rain. The water inexplicably makes her putrefy before their eyes.

At her grave the next day, Nahum reveals the stone to be a meteorite, but he now believes, in a peculiar volte-face, that it has been sent there "from the other side by the hand of Corbin reaching out to us from beyond the grave." Characterization is at its worst here, with Nahum setting aside his earlier intransigently-held scientific rationale in favor of the supernatural. Nahum tells Steve to take Susan away while he destroys the stone.

Nahum moves to smash the meteorite with an ax, but just then the mutated housemaid bursts in and throws herself upon the luminous rock. She dies, it crumbles, and the sudden outpouring of radiation mutates the crippled Nahum

330

into a walking metallic superman with, as Michael Weldon described it *The Psychotronic Encyclopedia of Film*, "a head like a raspberry." After a desultory struggle with Steve and a bit of stalking his daughter, the glowing "Nahum" crashes through a second story railing and plummets to the floor below, unaccountably exploding in a shower of sparks that sets the house on fire.

According to *Castle of Frankenstein*, a visit to the set had Karloff in test footage donning longhaired makeup for the monster's part, but AIP wisely chose to let the arthritic trouper sit it out and had an anonymous stunt player suit up for the part. As Susan and Steve make their escape from the inferno, she inquires of her beau, "Why did all this have to happen?" Such sentiments sometime fill the minds of Lovecraft purists and Karloff fans as well.

Die, Monster, Die! is, in itself, not a bad little horror film. Unfortunately, it has two very vocal factions ready to pounce on its inadequacies The first of these is the burgeoning legion of H. P. Lovecraft aficionados, most of them retroactive converts to the Providence, Rhode Island-born writer's works after Stuart Gordon's rip-roaring *Re-Animator* (1985), a movie just as antithetic to Lovecraft as *Die, Monster, Die!* As an adaptation of "The Colour Out of Space," the movie has a plethora of divers and disparate opinions.

"One of the better efforts" to adapt Lovecraft, Deanne Holding declared in *Shivers* #15. An "atmospheric" adaptation is how the *Blockbuster Guide to Movies and Videos* interpreted it, but Ed Naha's *Science Fiction Aliens* saw it only as a "fair" one.

A "weak" adaptation, said Stephen Jones in *Fear* #22; a "poor" adaptation, said Scott Allen Nollen in *Boris Karloff*; a "miserable" adaptation, said Gary Gerani in *The Monster Times* #17; a "loose-as-a-goose" adaptation, said John Stanley in *Revenge of the Creature Features Movie Guide*. Tom Weaver wrote in *Cult Movies*, "Viewers unfamiliar with H.P.'s works will find it indistinguishable from the average AIP Poe movie."

If not wholly successful as an H. P. Lovecraft movie, then at least David Pirie, in *A Heritage of Horror*, saw it and the earlier Lovecraft film, *The Haunted Palace* (1963), as "honorable failures." And Carlos Clarens, in the pioneering *An Illustrated History of the Horror Film*, knew things boded well for the future of Lovecraft in the cinema when he saw signs in *Die, Monster, Die!* "of an affinity that points the way to fresher, more adventurous collaborations."

And when viewed as a Boris Karloff movie, opinions are just as variegated. Rather than as a last respectable effort in the genre that made him, some critics shook their heads at Boris' involvement. Randy Palmer and Steve Biodrowski saw *Die, Monster, Die!* only as a "monster-on-the-loose fiasco" in their retrospective of Lovecraft movies in an issue of *Imagi-Movies*, with Karloff "in a retread of his *Invisible Ray* role" of 1936. Bruce Lanier Wright, in *Nightwalkers: Gothic Horror Movies The Modern Era*, saw this "tedious adaptation" as "a sad example of the sorts of things Boris Karloff found himself doing in the later 1960s." Still, Wright thought Boris was "magnificently sinister, doing his best to rescue [the] lame dialogue." This criticism of the script, "which thumbs its nose at Lovecraft's more ambitious horror," was embellished by Gene Wright in *Horrorshows.*

Karloff is the one constant above reproach in *Die, Monster, Die!* so much so that *Castle of Frankenstein* #9 thought he "deserves better." While Edward Edelson did not think the film was "particularly earthshaking" in *Great Monsters of the Movies,* he did say Karloff "gave a creditable, honest performance." Peter Haining said "the picture contains one of the last really fine performances by Boris Karloff" in *The Ghouls,* an adulatory sentiment somewhat undone by the inclusion of a miscaptioned still from *The Ghoul* (1933).

While the *Motion Picture Herald* remarked Karloff was "in top form," it also rightly proclaimed "there really isn't anything original about *Die, Monster, Die!,* but all the elements necessary to make a good tale of terror can be found in the film." Hammer inarguably ruled the roost of horror films in the sixties, and producers and studios did their best to copy the studio's profitable output. *Die, Monster, Die!,* from casting to sound effects (listen for the distinctive Hammer *crick-cows* of the thunderpeals) to set decoration to musical score, emulated Hammer.

Even beneath the prefacing AIP logo of the Capitol building, the fortissimo theme of *Die, Monster, Die!* mimics the insistent, redundant Hammer leitmotifs of cascading strings, moaning basses, strepitous brass, and militaristic snare drums. No wonder though, with music composer Don Banks and arranger Philip Martell freelancing from their normative stomping grounds. In fact, the similarities in Banks' scores for *Die, Monster, Die!* and *The Evil of Frankenstein* (1964) are startling. But, in this case, American International knew a good thing when they had it, and the leisurely unfurling of opening credits behind the blaring music and swirling Les Bowie "colours out of space" certainly set the scenes.

Those scenes, despite Richard Bojarski's and Kenneth Beals' assertion in *The Films of Boris Karloff* that *Die, Monster, Die!* was filmed at the Elstree Studios of Associated British Pictures in London, were in fact shot at Shepperton Studios. The imposing Witley manse was really Oakley Court, an English mansion located near Bray Studios, Hammer's home base.

Along with Karloff in the film, despite its budgetary limitations, appeared genre actors of the highest caliber. Freda Jackson, shrouded and unseen until her unveiling as a nodous mutated gnome, has long and rightfully been extolled for her memorable cackling performance as "Greta" in Hammer's otherwise overpraised *The Brides of Dracula* (1960).

Irish-born Patrick Magee, similarly shortchanged in his brief role as the doctor, was a member of the famed Royal Shakespeare Company there in England, and was on the verge of success on Broadway for his role as the

According to *Castle of Frankenstein*, AIP had an anonymous stunt player suit up for the part of the monster.

sadistic marquis who organizes the inmates of an asylum against his one intellectual rival in *Marat/Sade*. For it, he won a Tony Award, reprised the part for the film version (1967), and continued to appear in fantastic cinema, e.g. *A Clockwork Orange* (1971), *And Now The Screaming Starts* (1973), *The Black Cat* (1980), and many others.

The less said about pretty Suzan Farmer may be for the better; optimistically, the problem is not in her performance but in what little the script makes of her character. Cloyingly oblivious to all the weirdness about her, she is left with little but the occasional reprimand of her boyfriend to calm down and not make trouble, even as the household staff is dying off and her own mother is mutating into a curmudgeonly fungus. Miss Farmer fills out her endless wardrobe of peignoirs and pink sweaters well, and shrugs off the most outrageous happenstance with good cheer. Even with cannibalistic vines undulating about her, she finds only room to complain about the sickly sweet odor of compost. The ingenue, briefly a Hammer film fixture, costarred with Christopher Lee in *Dracula, Prince of Darkness* and in *Rasputin, the Mad Monk* later that year.

Die, Monster, Die! is a Boris Karloff movie that stands the test of time. It's good Karloff, and in this case, that's enough.

For appeal on the other side of the Atlantic, AIP cast Nick Adams (1931-1968). Despite legitimate and critical success on television and in the movies (even earning himself an Academy Award nomination in 1963 for *Twilight of Honor*), Adams was being offered fewer parts as the years went along, and even those were hardly good ones. Immediately after completing *Die, Monster, Die!*, Adams, probably too embarrassed to say good-bye to his costar, flew off to Japan to top the bill in *Frankenstein Conquers the World* (1966), a substantiating rote of everything Boris bemoaned about the decline of Frankenstein films since his last essaying of the Monster's role in 1939.

Above all, it was the 77-year-old Karloff's last hurrah in horror films. Hustled from film to torpid film, Karloff was understandably indifferent about

Die, Monster, Die! during production. According to Cynthia Lindsay's deferential *Dear Boris: The Life of William Henry Pratt,* when asked about the plot line, he piffled, "Oh, I can't remember—all I know is I end up in a mass of fungus." Even the *Chicago Tribune* called it "a sporing experience."

The henpecked psychic dilettante Karloff played in *The Sorcerors* (1967), uncomfortably living in "Swinging London," and the antediluvian patriarch of horror films he "enacted" for *Targets* (1968) were still in the offing in 1965; worthy films both, but neither comparable to the man's Universal and RKO antetypes. And despite the feeble protests of perfervid Boris fanatics and their interminable recitations of the scores of movies he made before *Frankenstein* (1931), horror films made Boris Karloff the icon he became and remains. Film fans are hardly clamoring for the licensed videocassette releases of *Tonight or Never* (1932) and *Tap Roots* (1948), but bootleggers can hardly keep with the demand for dreck like *Il Mostro Dell' Isola* (1953) and *Voodoo Island* (1957).

Die, Monster, Die!, even with all its inadequacies, its bastardization of a quality literary source, the disparaging reviews, and the film's hackneyed derivativeness, is a Boris Karloff movie that stands the test of time.

"Astounding! Strange! Weird!" read the cover copy of Dell's comic book adaptation of the film and the saga of the Witley family. The movie is all that, oppressively gloomy, more than a little stilted, and frequently illogical; but it's good Karloff, and in this case, that's enough.

CREDITS: Director of Photography: Paul Beeson, B .S. C., Editor: Alfred Cox; Art Director: Colin Southcott; Assistant Director: Dennis Hall; Camera Operator: R. C. Cooney; Sound Recordists: Ken Rawkins and Robert Jones; Sound Editors: Alban Streeter and Alan Corder; Continuity: Tilly Day; Make-Up Artist: Jimmy Evans; Hairdresser: Bobble Smith: Wardrobe Mistress: Laurel Staffell; Special Effects: Wally Veevers and Ernie Sullivan; Titles: Bowie Films; Westrex Sound Recording; Music Composed by Don Banks; Musical Director: Philip Martell; Screenplay: Jerry Sohl; From "The Colour Out Of Space" by H. P. Lovecraft; Producer: Pat Green; Director: Daniel Haller; Copyright 1965 by Alta Vista Productions; Released by American International Pictures; 78 minutes; Filmed at Shepperton Studios, England; Alternate Titles: *Monster of Terror* (Great Britain); First announced as and produced under the title, *The House at the End of the World*; Released in October 1965

CAST: Boris Karloff...Nahum Witley, Nick Adams...Stephen Reinhart, Freda Jackson...Letitia Witley, Suzan Farmer...Susan Witley, Patrick Magee...Dr. Henderson, Paul Farrell...Jason, Terence De Marney...Merwyn, Sydney Bromley...Pierce, Billy Milton...Henry, Sheila Raynor...Miss Bailey, Harold Goodwin...Cabby, Leslie Dwyer...Potter

BORIS KARLOFF AND THE *MAD MONSTER PARTY* OF THE 1960s (1966)

by Bob Madison

At an age when most men contemplate retirement, Boris Karloff was busy on a multiplicity of projects for the entire decade of the 1960s, his career ending only with his death in 1969.

During those 10 years, Karloff did television guest spots, narrated records, appeared in films, did product endorsements; his face appeared on the covers of monster magazines regularly. To a whole new generation of young devotees, the man who was the Frankenstein Monster had evolved into "Uncle Boris."

But what was the root cause of this heightened activity?

Simply that the 1960s saw the greatest surge of popularity of both Boris Karloff and the classic monsters he portrayed. Never throughout the long years of his career was Boris Karloff more famous, more popular, more beloved than he was during the 1960s.

In fact, with its hit records and revival of interest in classic horror films, its flock of new horror pictures at bijous and drive-ins, funny-scary television shows, the just-created monster magazines and model kits, let alone the endless monster merchandise including everything from latex masks to jacket patches, it is safe to say that the whole decade of the 1960s was one, long Mad Monster Party.

Fondly remembered by legions of adult genre film aficionados, the Mad Monster Party of the 1960s found its roots in the renaissance of sorts the horror film experienced in the late 1950s. The still controversial horror comics of E.C. and the short-lived mania for KABC-TV's Vampira, both of which expired in 1954, led producers to the realization that kids bought monster merchandise, and that the undead was a lively business. It was time for Hollywood, which had relegated the horror genre to Big Bug and Horror-Science Films, to take notice.

The movies' twin obsessions of adolescents and monsters came together in the improbable *I Was a Teenage Werewolf* in 1957, and *I Was a Teenage Fran-*

kenstein in 1958. (As a result of his imitation of a hirsute James Dean in *Werewolf*, Michael Landon won a coveted role in *Bonanza*, starting a long and profitable television career.) Both films, hugely successful, spelled out the simple truth: monsters spoke to young people.

The results were felt in Hollywood. Monster-meisters started to actively court the youth market. The most flamboyant of producers during this period remains William Castle, whose sense of fun and games helped set the tone for the subsequent Mad Monster Party.

Castle first learned how to play his audiences as a young boy while watching the crowds at repeat viewings of Bela Lugosi's stage turn as Dracula. It was a lesson he learned well.

After a desultory career in big-studio publicity departments and directing a few minor B melodramas, Castle hit Halloween Hokum with 1958's *Macabre*. Castle had the prestigious Lloyds of London insure any patron who died of fright while viewing the film. No one died of fright, but Castle did lay them in the aisles.

He found success again in 1958 with *House on Haunted Hill*, the picture that cemented Vincent Price forever into the horror genre, making him the dominant figure, with Karloff, of The Mad Monster Party. The party favor for *House* was particularly memorable: theater patrons were treated to a process called Emergo, where the papier mâché skeleton used by Price in the film left movie screens and flew over the heads of the audience. This effect, a cheap skeleton on a clothesline, was most often met with howls, the skeleton pelted with popcorn until it sought refuge once more behind the screen.

Castle created the ultimate Monster Party romp with 1959's *The Tingler*. In this film, a microscopic organism wrapped around the spine of every human being is finally discovered, a parasite that seems to grow during moments of extreme fright. As terror mounts, this parasite attacks. Screaming, it seems, neutralizes it, causing the entity to shrink.

After a deaf-mute is scared to death, and her Tingler removed, the fun starts. Needless to say, the monster escaped into a crowded movie theater (a revival house, filled with very young people), and Price admonished patrons to scream.

Castle had the seats in selected theaters wired with little motors, causing them to tingle. The perfect date film.

Monsters were suddenly green once more, not with fright, but with the color of money. A 1959 issue of *Playboy* magazine stated that horror films had been big box office for the past five years, with 52 horror films produced in 1957, 75 fright fests in 1958, and a projected 100 horror films in 1959.

Boris Karloff would become a large part of this great wave of interest, often working with his successor to the throne of the Grand Old Man of Horror, Vincent Price. After so many years of watching the elderly, avuncular Price, it is indeed difficult to remember that in the 1960s he was part of the avant garde

John Zacherle dusted off his undertaker character and brought *Shock Theater* to a new generation of horror fans.

of horror films, playing JFK to Karloff's Winston Churchill. And while movie-goers looked forward to each Price-Castle and later Price-Corman film, it was Karloff that was venerated.

But the music of the Mad Monster Party in the late '50s did not play exclusively to teenagers on movie dates Friday and Saturday nights. The music played, perhaps even more importantly, for the younger kids at home as well.

In 1958, John Zacherle exhumed the character of an Old West undertaker he had created for a local afternoon program playing cowboy films to host a new package of horror films. Universal Pictures released 52 of its classic horrors to television under the title *Shock Theater*. As host, Zacherle dusted his undertaker character off, added a few more macabre touches, and "Roland" was born.

Thanks in part to Zacherle's antics, *Shock Theater* became a huge success in Philadelphia. Zacherle later took his Cool Ghoul on the road to New York to even bigger ratings and greater success, changing his character's name to Zacherley. And a legend was born.

And others reborn. Thanks to television, Universal's classic horror films, first released when the parents of this first generation of Monster Boomers were children themselves, found a larger audience and greater popularity than they had known when first released.

Monsters that had been closeted during the Atomic Age of Horror came out with a vengeance. Frankenstein's Monster, the Mummy, Dracula, and the Wolf Man as seen by Universal all became part of a unified myth for a whole generation of young Americans. Monsters were everywhere on television, and in the minds of boys and girls across the country.

Karloff's Monster had a particular resonance for young people. His plight could be seen as a macabre mirror-image of the problems of adolescence. Cast adrift in a world not of his making, the Monster was always an outsider, and constantly struggling with feelings difficult to express. Acutely aware of his own ugliness—as many teens are overly conscious of their own looks—and terribly awkward, the Monster fought for acceptance in a world that did not understand him. Karloff's skillful playing allowed the Monster to be an innocent, sinning more through circumstance than evil, which also touched a chord with American youth. Little wonder that the Monster would become the most potent of all monster icons during this period.

Zacherley himself became part of the mythos. As caretaker of the monsters and official host of the Monster Party, Zack (as he was affectionately known) found himself on magazine and paperback covers, record albums, and a host of other monster-related goodies. His record, *Dinner with Drac*, a collection of ghoulish limericks, became a Halloween perennial with Dick Clark. For a whole generation of genre film buffs, the black and white television glow of Zacherley's undead face is as much a part of the Universal legacy as Boris Karloff and Bela Lugosi.

It is important to remember in this video age what an event *Shock Theater*, and subsequent horror film programs, would become. Such classic Karloff films as *Bride of Frankenstein* or *The Mummy* would run only once a year, and kids (and their parents) made plans to watch them accordingly. Kids would nap in the afternoon to catch a late-night film, or arrange intricate "deals" with parents for the privilege of a couple hours of uninterrupted communion with monsters. And while video tape has made all of these films wonderfully accessible, the thrill of this stolen time with favorite fright figures is gone.

340

This family tree of ghouls and goblins galvanized the imagination. Kids formerly conversant with cartoons and cowboys were now privy to dark secrets and gothic legends. The causes and cures of lycanthropy were better known than many mathematics formulas, the tell-tale signs of vampirism as familiar as the alphabet, and the shambling walk of Frankenstein's Monster an easy exercise done during recess.

Thanks to television's mining the treasures of horrors past, monsters became heroes. And kids from state-to-state wanted even more.

Boris Karloff reads a copy of *Castle of Frankenstein*, **a more adult version of** *Famous Monsters.*

The year 1958 also saw the publication of a new type of magazine. That year, Hymie Taubman was a young entrepreneur with visions of creating his own version of Hugh Hefner's *Playboy* empire. Like many of the monsters he would later celebrate in the pages of his magazine, Taubman died only to live again as another human being, resurrecting himself as a top-drawer publisher now named James Warren.

After a few false starts with various types of publications, Warren hit upon the idea of creating a special, one-shot magazine that would sell to America's monster obsessed youth. His editor, a collector and sometimes literary agent named Forrest J Ackerman, suggested the name *Wonderama*. Warren opted for *Fantastic Monsters of Filmland*. Their distributor suggested changing *Fantastic* to *Famous*, and *Famous Monsters of Filmland* was born.

The first issue of *Famous Monsters* premiered in February of 1958, during a record blizzard on the East Coast. Some 150,000 copies braved the snow, causing publisher Warren to anticipate the worst.

Famous Monsters became an unprecedented hit, proving it could survive all obstacles except lack of interest, fading in 1983, long after the Mad Monster Party had ended.

Famous Monsters opened the floodgates, creating a whole new market for other, better monster magazines. Revelers at the Mad Monster Party could now page through such publications as *Castle of Frankenstein* and *The Monster Times*, or laugh at the intentionally hilarious *For Monsters Only*.

But *Famous Monsters* has a special place in the hearts of Monster Boomers everywhere. Never a distinguished magazine, *Famous Monsters* cannot take credit for creating horror film scholarship, but it did inspire future generation world-class genre film historians like David Skal, Greg Mank, and Tom Weaver. The toe-the-party-line tone of *Famous Monsters*, along with its sometimes bullying stance positioned by editor Ackerman, really kept it from being the magazine it should have become. More damningly, the magazine seemed perversely devoted to a mock-humorous, talk-down approach to young film buffs, refusing to grow up as its audience did. (In fact when recently revived, *Famous Monsters* continued its juvenile approach, completely alienating the now-grown Monster Boomers hungry for nostalgia.)

Unfortunately, this official organ of the Mad Monster Party also did future film scholars a great disservice by not taking its subject matter more seriously. At the height of the Monster Boom, *Famous Monsters* had access to such still-living genre giants as Boris Karloff, Edward Van Sloan, and Lon Chaney, Jr., among others, but nowhere in its pages are there in-depth interviews or serious career retrospectives. Editor Ackerman sadly left this vital resource untapped, leaving the clean-up scholarship to the *Famous Monsters*-inspired, true film scholars who followed him.

After monsters appeared on movie screens, television sets, and magazine racks, the next logical step was to manufacture monsters so kids could have them in their own homes.

And in 1962, Aurora Plastics of Hempstead Long Island did just that. With the creation of a whole line of nine-inch monster models, America's youth could now have their favorite movie monster, fully painted or glow-in-the-dark, on their night tables, bookshelves, or windowsills. The monsters immortalized in plastic ran the whole gamut of creature features: not only Frankenstein's Monster, Dracula and The Wolf Man, but The Phantom of the Opera, The Hunch-

Aurora wisely capitalized on the off-screen lives of its monster toys.

back of Notre Dame, King Kong, The Creature from the Black Lagoon, and Mr. Hyde.

These models became part of the cover-charge for entrance into the Monster Party, and their purchase and construction is something close to a great communal experience for Monster Boomers. Many kids would dote on their creation with all the attention and pride of Dr. Frankenstein himself, painstakingly painting them, or creating elaborate backdrops for the proper display of their favorite creature.

344

Some simply played with them, building them simply to blow them up with firecrackers or burn them in backyard funeral pyres, only to buy the monsters once more and recreate the process, proving that these figures were truly eternal and undying.

Equally important is the kind of daydreams these horrific effigies (and the whole Monster Party) would inspire. The private lives of the monsters became a source of endless speculation: friendships and alliances, enemies and tests of power. These musings could produce endless summer-night speculation, usually ending with questions like: "if Dracula and the Wolf Man were in a fight...?" Also interesting was speculation on the day-to-day grind of a monster's life, imaginings of the little homey touches in our lives, rendered monstrous. (Without a reflection, how does Dracula comb his hair?)

Aurora wisely capitalized on the off-screen lives of its line of monster toys with brilliant bits of advertising. In one memorable ad, the Frankenstein Monster goes to the gothic castle of Dracula, lonely and looking for a mate. Acting as mad scientist, the Vampire King creates a bride for the Monster, with King Kong, The Mummy, and other monsters in attendance at the wedding.

Aurora was not the only guest at the Monster Party that year. Bobby "Boris" Pickett and the Crypt-Kicker Five released the best-selling record *The Monster Mash*, and the Monster Party had found its anthem.

It is no accident that the "voice" of *The Monster Mash* was that of Boris Karloff. Pickett, a monster buff who remembered seeing the classic monsters in movie theaters, may have been the first Monster Boomer. Instead of keeping snapshots of family members or singing stars in his wallet, Pickett carried photos of Karloff and Lugosi. He had won some amateur contests singing pop songs in an eerie imitation of Karloff's voice and later transferred that talent into the creation of the Monster's signature tune, a pop novelty classic.

Pickett created a whole album of Karloff-voiced monster inspired tunes, again reflecting on a monster's lot in life. *Monster's Holiday* told us of Christmas time with the monsters, and *Graveyard Shift* had Karloff admonishing Ygor to get up and go to work. A Lugosi-voiced Dracula warbled *Blood Bank Blues*, and the Lord of the Undead tried to create his own dance craze with *The Transylvania Twist*.

The Monster Mash was a true 10-day wonder, staying on Billboard's number-one spot for two weeks. It created as much publicity for Boris Karloff as it did for Pickett. For many young monster fans, there was no distinction, this was just the same Uncle Boris, packaged in a different way. The myth became reality when Karloff himself, as a guest on the popular rock-and-roll program *Shindig*, performed *The Monster Mash* himself.

The Mad Monster Party continued on, throughout the decade, producing in 1964 such now classic television programs as *The Munsters* and *The Addams Family*. *The Munsters* featured the Universal Monsters in a middle-class Ameri-

During the Mad Monster Party of the '60s, monsters could be found everywhere!

can milieu. Karloff's Frankenstein Monster, now played by comedian Fred Gwynne, was a hen-pecked husband, married to his vampire bride Lilly, played by former screen siren Yvonne DeCarlo. The cultural assimilation of the Karloff figure was now complete: Frankenstein as father figure.

Interestingly, it was *The Addams Family* that was the better show. Based on the celebrated cartoons of Charles Addams that appeared in *The New Yorker*, the upscale Addamses had a smarter edge and greater sophistication than the Munsters. They would also prove equally indestructible, providing the fodder for two Saturday morning cartoons series, and returning to the big screen more than 20 years after the cancellation of the program in two big-budget movie adaptations.

Both programs had hoped to get Karloff as a guest star, but final plans never materialized. But by 1966, when both shows were canceled, Boris Karloff was busy creating the most interesting artifact of the Monster Boom.

Mad Monster Party? (the question mark is in the film's title card, but not all of its promotional material) would become a pure distillation of all the monster mania that came before it. The film is also the first fully animated, puppet monster film with music, decades before Tim Burton's *The Nightmare Before Christmas*.

Produced during a decade that saw some of Karloff's most interesting projects—*Black Sabbath, Targets, How the Grinch Stole Christmas*—*Mad Monster Party?* remains one of the great bogeyman's most enjoyable romps, and is a vivid realization of Karloff's place of honor in the Monster Craze.

Karloff gives voice to Baron Von Frankenstein, venerable leader of the world wide organization of monsters. Working in his isolated castle on a remote jungle island, meddling in forbidden science and trafficking with monsters, he is also a charming, benevolent, sweet old man. The man who creates the formula which destroys all matter—capable of dematerializing any thing, any body, any place—is also "Uncle Boris" to his nephew (and to legions of young monster fans).

Scripted in part by Harvey Kurtzman of *MAD* magazine fame, *Mad Monster Party?* is an affectionate valentine to both Boris Karloff and the monsters who were suddenly famous all over again. The screenplay also charmingly plays on childhood monster fantasies, fully realizing the dream of a complete monster rally, and the hierarchy of the monster world.

Happily, the film never relies solely on the monsters for its affects, and in a kooky way, *Mad Monster Party?* remains a parody of many of the obsessions of the 1960s, including Batman, The Beatles, and James Bond.

Mad Monster Party? is also delightfully funny. Working on two levels, children's picture and adult comedy, *Mad Monster Party?* is like the classic Warner Brothers cartoons, filled with jokes too adult for children to get.

The Karloff and Monster puppets were designed by former E.C. horror comic illustrator (Jolly) Jack Davis. With his shock of white hair and dark eyebrows, high cheek bones, and formal morning coat, the Karloff puppet is remarkably like the real thing. Always an original, Karloff is impossible to mistake even in simulacrum.

The other monster figures are equally well designed. Frankenstein's Monster also looks like Karloff, and the shots of the Karloff and Monster puppet together are eerily reminiscent of *Frankenstein 1970*, where Karloff took great pains to recreate himself in monster form.

The Dracula figure is old-world Continental, complete with bat-wing cape, monocle, and bird-like profile. The voice is not a pure imitation of Lugosi, but rather a passionate reminder of the old actor. Dracula is also, after Karloff, the films' finest example of the animator's craft. This vampire is full of Lugosi-like histrionic motions, with sweeping cape, hand gestures, and melodramatic stance.

Mad Monster Party? also makes much of the Karloff vs. Lugosi myth that was largely created during the Monster Boom. Of all the creatures in the film, the only real threat to Karloff's throne as King of the Monsters is the Lugosi-Dracula figure. The action of the film is generated by Dracula's scheme to gain Frankenstein's secret to destroy matter and become ultimate ruler of the monsters himself—a Lugosi dream of conquest if there ever was one!

The other monsters fare equally well. Frankenstein's houseboy is a Peter Lorre clone in face and voice named Yetch, his round moon-face pockmarked with craters. The Hunchback of Notre Dame looks suspiciously like Disney's later incarnation, and the Invisible Man has the rotund shape and voice of Sydney Greenstreet, keeping his *Casablanca* fez.

Phyllis Diller joined the cast as the Monster's Mate, and her presence is not as jarring as one might think. Diller gives a wonderful line-reading of the part, managing to be both funny and treacherous at the same time. The figure for the Monster's Mate recreates the comedienne well, with its pointy nose and chin, and thin bird legs in big boots.

Amazingly, Diller never met Karloff during the making of the film, despite the fact that they share scenes together. The voice tracks for both stars were recorded separately.

With its secret formula, island stronghold, and beautiful woman, the plot runs like a James Bond film gone *MAD*. The film opens with Dr. Frankenstein in his laboratory, mixing the final compounds of his formula to destroy matter. Infusing it with energy, he places it on a mounting table that lifts to the ceiling, a clever parody of Karloff's own creation scene in the original *Frankenstein*.

It also underlies a subtext evident in another of Karloff's earlier forays into the Frankenstein family tree. In *Frankenstein 1970*, Karloff uses atomic energy to create his new monster while still holed-up in his gothic castle stronghold. In *Mad Monster Party?* the doctor's formula results in a very Hiroshima-like mushroom cloud—the seeds of our atomic destruction are found rooted in our Gothic past.

Thrilled with the results, Frankenstein immediately invites monsters from around the world to a convention at his jungle island home. We first see the monsters as these invitations, carried by bat messengers, reach their respective homes.

Also invited is Frankenstein's nephew, Felix Flanken. Thin, bespectacled, frail, and highly allergic to everything, Flanken is the exact antithesis of the Frankenstein image. Nor is he great shakes as a scientist, working as a pharmacist in a drugstore. (Seeing how a drugstore operated in the 1960s—complete with lunch counter and paperback books, is a nostalgic delight.) Sent an invitation with a Karloff stamp on the envelope most fans would kill for, Flanken heads for the Caribbean, dreaming of white beaches and pretty girls.

Back at the castle, Karloff explains his plans to retire to his secretary Francesca. In a delightful in-joke, Frankenstein mixes a series of chemicals, only to pour them into tea cups as the clock strikes four. It is Frankenstein's plan to give all of his secrets, including his greatest, to Felix.

The monsters board the S. S. Herring (CARIBBEAN CRUISES—PAY NOW, SAIL LATER), the animated captain speaking with the voice of Charles (*Mutiny on the Bounty*) Laughton. He and the first mate are terrified of the monsters, but their fright reaches its peak with Flanken. ("Golly," Flanken says, "What's the matter with those two? Haven't they ever seen a tourist before?")

There is lots of shipboard humor, with Flanken losing his glasses and not seeing the Invisible Man ("I've heard that one before"), and comparing allergy

Mad Monster Party? **is delightfully funny, filled with jokes too adult for children to get.**

medicine with Dr. Jekyll. As the ship nears the Isle of Evil, Dracula demonstrates that he was "the original Batman," and flaps out the window. The other monsters follow him overboard.

On the island, Frankenstein checks his preparations, including the inspection of his army of zombie aviators. This truly lost patrol is to be on the lookout for the one monster not invited, It. ("It was a crushing bore at our last convention," Frankenstein says. "It kept running around, crushing boars, wild boars, in its hands. Very frankly, It disgusts even me.")

The monsters arrive, and we are treated to big introduction scenes for each as they travel down the Baron's grand staircase. Soon the convention is underway, and Frankenstein makes his discovery and plans of retirement known. Dracula and Francesca instantly scheme for control, with the Monster and his Mate planning to protect Frankenstein's interests.

The convention breaks for a musical interlude and a hilarious Beatles parody. A skeleton rock group all in Beatles page-boy haircuts, called Little Tibia and the Phibias, warble *It's the Mummy*.

Dracula and Francesca are caught plotting against the Baron by the Monster's Mate. ("Come, let me kiss you," Dracula says to Francesca. "Women have died for one of my kisses, I'm terrific!") Dracula tries to kill her when he

349

is carried away by the monster and the two women start to fight (with cat screeching on the soundtrack!). Soon, the whole thing descends into a serio-comic brawl, fading into shots of the monsters in their respective rooms, sleeping it off.

The next morning, Frankenstein and Francesca meet Felix on the beach. "Everyone must have had himself quite a time last night," Karloff says. "There was nothing but a huge pile of leftovers in the dining room."

"I wonder who it was?" Francesca asks.

Dracula and Francesca plot to kill Felix (Dracula combs his hair in the mirror, only the comb visible). In the film's comic centerpiece, Francesca takes the bumbling Felix out on a picnic with Dracula and the other monsters try to kill him. (When Felix re-wraps the Mummy around a tree, Francesca says, "Remind me to never sprain my ankle when you're around.")

At the castle, Frankenstein explains that he wants Felix to succeed him as King of the Monsters. Here, Karloff gets to sing the delightful *Stay One Step Ahead*.

Dracula and Francesca plot again, only to be interrupted by the Monster and his Mate. Francesca sees that she is being double-crossed by Dracula, and escapes. She writes to It, summoning him to the island. Followed by Dracula and the others, she jumps into the moat, only to be rescued by Felix. The pharmacist thinks she's hysterical, and slaps her. She falls in love with him, and they kiss, trees falling, waves crashing against the beach, and lightning flashing.

"Does your head feel lighter than air?" he asks. "Is your throat parched, and do you tingle all over? Then you... must have allergies."

Francesca plans to lead him out of the jungle, but Dracula and the monsters are hot on their trail. They carry Francesca away, Yetch yelling in Peter Lorre tones, "Kill! Maim! Decapitate!" Dracula and the others circle Felix, who has a sneezing fit. ("Bless you," Dracula deadpans.) When the hero pulls out a vial of his allergy medicine, the monsters think he is really holding the Baron's formula. He manages to scare the monsters away, only to faint when It (a giant ape cartoon of King Kong) climbs aboard the island.

Soon, the monsters are held in It's gigantic paws, while Frankenstein and his still loyal zombie airmen circle the ape in low-tech bi-planes. The monsters wonder what they are going to do.

"Pray he doesn't start beating his chest," Dracula says.

Karloff's plane is snatched out of the sky by It and, after denouncing the monsters, Karloff drops the vial holding his formula to the Earth far below, destroying the island.

Felix and Francesca, escaping in a rowboat, watch the holocaust. "I know it's wrong," Felix says, "but I have this tremendous urge to sing *Auld Lang Syne*."

350

At the close-out, Francesca confesses that she is a robot, built by Franken-stein and regarded as his masterpiece. Felix sneezes and his voice begins to skip like a broken record, revealing that he too is one of Frankenstein's me-chanical creations.

The musical score of *Mad Monster Party?* is surprisingly good, with lots of moody 1960s' guitars and bongos doing pseudo "scary" stuff. Some of the songs, *Our Time to Shine* and *You're Different*, are quite enjoyable and not the embarrassments that are usually found in pre-*Little Mermaid* children's films.

Mad Monster Party? mirrored the fantasies and dreams of a whole genera-tion of monster-obsessed youths, and is an enjoyable film in its own right. Karloff was such the undisputed King of Horror, that it is impossible to imagine any other genre figure providing the voice of the Baron.

It is not recorded if Karloff ever saw the finished product, but if he didn't, he certainly had no reason to be ashamed. *Mad Monster Party?* is an unbeat-able children's film that monster-obsessed adults will find equally delightful, and is a wonderful artifact of the most popular decade of horrordom.

The Monster Party itself would run for a few more years, the music stilled for a moment by the death of its host, Boris Karloff, in 1969. Its spearhead gone, it would shamble onward another few years, the classic monsters buried forever by the advent of *The Exorcist* and the latter gore films.

In recent years, there has been a minor renaissance in monster culture. Sadly it can only take a small toe-hold in the current atmosphere of interest in this material. The prevailing aesthetic is one of heavy metal biker nihilism—worlds apart from the innocent kids in *Famous Monsters* T-shirts. But as Monster Boomers age, the material generated by the Mad Monster Party of the 1960s is open once again for nostalgic reexamination. It is this revival of interest that is making the genre fun again.

CREDITS: 1966; Embassy Pictures release; a Rankin-Bass Production; Screen-play: Len Korobkin and Harvey Kurtzman; Producer: Arthur Rankin, Jr.; Ex-ecutive Producer: Joseph E. Levine; Director: Jules Bass; Music: Maury Laws and Jules Bass

CAST: featuring the voices of: Boris Karloff, Ethel Ennis, Gale Garnett, Phyllis Diller

Bob Madison has written for *Wonder, Cult Movies, Scary Monsters*, and *Scar-let Street* as well as contributing to *Midnight Marquee Actors Series: Bela Lugosi*. He lives in New York and is putting the finishing touches on a novel as well as several chapters for forthcoming Mid Mar books.

TARGETS
(1968)
by Mark A. Miller

The coda to Boris Karloff's rich and diverse filmic song is most certainly *Targets*, filmed in December 1967. Although Karloff later managed to complete five more films (the mediocre *The Crimson Cult* and four bizarre Mexican horror movies), *Targets* adds the period to his screen career because it is so appropriate, so tailor-made for him, and so lucky a quirk of fate, just as *Frankenstein* (1931) had been.

Karloff basically plays himself in *Targets*, as Byron Orlok, an old horror star who feels out-of-step with the times, a situation that Karloff must have understood only too well. As the film's director Peter Bogdanovich put it in 1968, Karloff "is a symbol of Victorian horror that has been outdated by today's wars and violence."[1]

By designing his film to contrast Karloff's anachronistic image with the horror and violence of a real-life sniper named Charles Whitman, Bogdanovich created one of the most important films of the decade. *Targets* is not, however, a message picture. It simply holds up a mirror and lets the audience see its world with no apologies or explanations. In the process, the film's impact depends on Karloff's unique contribution.

Karloff still owed Roger Corman two days on his contract (equal to $15,000) for *The Terror* (1963), an unforeseen circumstance that would give him his best screen role since his Val Lewton films of the 1940s. At the same time, Corman knew someone dying to make a film, someone who had proved his worthiness by rewriting most of the script and directing the second unit for his biker flick, *The Wild Angels* (1966)—Peter Bogdanovich. After *Angels* was finished, Bogdanovich said that he "had received, in twenty-two weeks, a paid course on just about everything you could do in a picture: scouting locations, writing script, directing... acting, cutting, doing sound work. I learned a hell of a lot."[2]

Corman offered Bogdanovich a package deal. If he would shoot five days of footage of Mamie Van Doren and some other beauties and integrate it into a 1962 Russian sci-fi flick, he would give him the Karloff project. Eventually released by A.I.P. as *Voyage to the Planet of Prehistoric Women* in 1968, the first film offered nothing but headaches to Bogdanovich, who did the movie only so he could make *Targets*. "Well, putting those women in that goddamned picture dragged on for months," complained Bogdanovich in 1968. "It was the worst thing I've ever had to do.... It was so exhausting, much more than anything on *Targets*. Almost killed me."[3]

Once he could turn his attention to *Targets*, Bogdanovich faced more of Corman's edicts:

1. Shoot with a $125,000 maximum budget. (Some sources differ on this, going as high as $150,000.)

2. Shoot the film in 15 days. (It went 10 days over schedule.)

3. Shoot 20 minutes of new Karloff footage in two days.

4. Use 20 minutes of Karloff footage from *The Terror*. (Bogdanovich got it down to around 5 minutes, most of it with Karloff and Jack Nicholson.)

5. Shoot 40 minutes of film without Karloff.

6. Edit the above into an 80-minute feature film!

Bogdanovich wrote the story with Polly Platt, his production designer (and wife at the time). In its original version, Karloff would play an old horror actor who had hated being typecast all his life. Bitter that his career path has not been more like Cary Grant's (!), "he goes into his room... he pushes a secret button, and there's his dressing room," according to Bogdanovich. "He puts on a handsome mask, and he goes out and strangles women in supermarkets. I wanted that, because the floor of a supermarket is great for dollying. You know, you have this shot of a murder, and you pan up, and a sign says, 'PEAS REDUCED THIS WEEK.' This shows you the kinds of ideas you can have when you're desperate."[4]

Realizing that their story would turn into a film as stupid as *Voyage to the Planet of Prehistoric Women*, Bogdanovich and Platt wisely decided to include a modern killer, played by Tim O'Kelly, and let Karloff play himself instead of a heavy. They developed each character's story—"real" horrors (O'Kelly) crosscut with old-fashioned "reel" horrors (Karloff)— so that the two characters and their different worlds could eventually clash at a drive-in, where Orlok makes his last personal appearance and the Whitman character picks off moviegoers with his telescopic rifle through a hole in the screen.

Bogdanovich commented that he was not out to explain the aberrant behavior of the killer, Bobby Thompson, because "the most horrifying thing about these murders is that there doesn't seem to be any reason commensurate with the size of the crime. So I didn't have any socially conscious motivation at all."[5] Nevertheless, Bogdanovich and Tim O'Kelly, in his fascinating portrayal of Thompson, provide shady intimations of Thompson's motivation.

O'Kelly plays his Bobby Thompson as a disturbingly *too* real, quiet, short-haired, all-American boy. His inner rage escapes like rays of sunlight bursting through the holes and cracks of a drafty barn—not enough illumination to see fully, but enough to suspect what trouble lies within. Thompson gobbles Baby Ruths and tosses off bottles of Pepsi as he cruises L.A. in his white Mustang

Orlok (Karloff) tells screenwriter Sammy (Peter Bogdanovich) that "the world belongs to the young. Make way for them. Let them have it."

convertible and listens to top 40 tunes, a picture of youthful normality. During his visit to a gun store, however, his behavior is oddly nervous and quirky. Trying out a telescopic rifle, he focuses it through the shop's window onto Orlok, who happens to be standing across the street. Once he has Orlok's temple in the cross hairs, he squeezes the trigger and "click." Then, in a chillingly affable voice, he says to the clerk, "I'll take it. I've always wanted a gun like this. It's a beauty."

This foreshadowing has followed Orlok's earlier disgusted observation that "the world belongs to the young. Make way for them. Let them have it." Such deliberate contrasts in the story construction enhance O'Kelly's good performance. His toothy grins and polite "sirs" take on sinister undertones in this context, which are confirmed when he opens his car's trunk to reveal an arsenal of ammunition, rifles, and handguns. Thompson's plastic politeness to his wife and parents (with whom they live) contrasts with a private, indefinable discontent that accompanies his sometimes bizarre behavior and cryptic dialogue. On one occasion, he aims his rifle at his father, as he sets up tin cans for them to

Sammy tries to convince Orlok to read the script he wrote for him. Orlok: "My kind of horror isn't horror anymore."

shoot, and almost pulls the trigger. Later, he tries vaguely to communicate with his wife—"I don't know what's happening to me... I get funny ideas"—but she is too consumed with dressing for work to catch the seriousness of his problems.

In comparison to his father, who dominates the household—he even tells his wife when to come to bed—Bobby Thompson appears impotent in his own domestic corner of the house. He cannot even gain his wife's attention, let alone command her to bed. O'Kelly's face subtly reveals Thompson's silent self-disgust at his lack of masculine assertiveness in his marriage and home life.

Perhaps, like many disturbed males who lack sexual power and authority, he overcompensates with firearms. The next morning, Thompson shoots his wife, his mother, and a hapless delivery boy. (Ironically, a 1960s' NRA slogan proclaimed, "Shoot for family fun!") Then he makes a stop at a gun store for more ammo ("Gonna shoot some pigs!"), then heads to a large oil tank at a refinery by the freeway, where he picks off drivers and passengers of passing cars. Finally, he flees to the Reseda Drive-in Theatre, where, by coincidence, Byron Orlok will be making a personal appearance. Thompson, once he starts to kill, does so with unhesitating zeal, fascination, and pleasure, with each victim noticeably providing him with an emotional climax. After Orlok eventually puts a stop to this bloody spree, Thompson brags like a spoiled adolescent: "I hardly ever missed, did I?"

Another trait that adds to Thompson's personality is his mania for neatness and order. He folds his wife's sweater and tucks it into a drawer only hours before shooting her. After he commits the three murders in his home, he meticulously puts the bodies of his wife and mother back to bed and cleans up the blood, in a sequence mirroring Hitchcock's *Psycho* (1960) as Norman Bates cleans up after Marion Crane has been murdered. However, Bogdanovich evidently picked up this detail from the real case of Charles Whitman, which he researched thoroughly.

Bogdanovich's script extends this mania for orderliness throughout the minutia of Thompson's everyday life. Thompson stops a moment to toss an empty Pepsi bottle out of his clean Mustang before he climbs the tall oil tank. Once up there, he carefully unpacks his firearms, ten in all, into two neat rows. Then he relaxes with a packed lunch he has prepared, before causing hideous, bloody disorder. This contradiction between the order and precision of his own life and the chaos and destruction he creates for others underlines Thompson's twisted egoism. If he cannot enjoy life, he can, at least, wipe out that privilege for others. O'Kelly embraces these opportunities in the script, rendering a portrait that is vivid, realistic, and, like the real sniper on which his character is based, unavoidably open to a frustrating number of psychoanalytical interpretations. As Bogdanovich observed, "I felt it was presumptuous to give an answer to something that psychiatrists, sociologists, and humanists don't know. I would rather the audience come out saying 'Why?,' because that's not so complacent an answer."[6]

Bogdanovich's interior settings contribute to characterization, something he worked out carefully with Polly Platt. "We wanted a contrast between Karloff's world and the boy's world," Bogdanovich explained, "so we were careful with the color control. The Karloff sequences were all brown, gold, yellow—warm colors. The boy's sequences were green, blue, white—cold colors. I wanted to make the boy's home, as much as possible, like the homes here in the San Fernando Valley. The houses really are that way—blank walls. We made it even more bare. We wanted a kind of sterility... I just wanted... to convey that the boy is an outgrowth of this kind of society."[7]

Amplifying the "sterility" of the Thompson household is the television newscast reporting grisly, violent crimes that can be heard coming from the living room as Bobby gazes at a tawdry painting of his family and a photo of him with his pretty young wife, two of the few wall decorations. Reports of gruesome crimes continue to be heard while the family says grace at dinner. The family is oblivious, suggesting that they have become desensitized by a

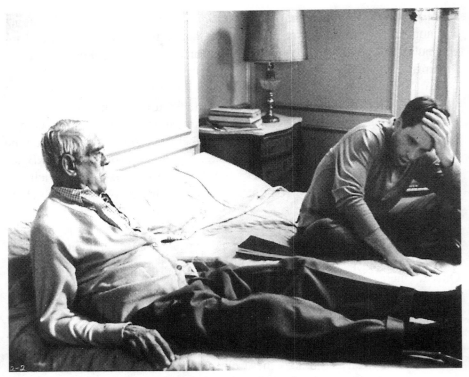

Orlok and Sammy awake after a few too many.

constant bombardment of horror. Small wonder that any hint of Bobby's coming butchery will go unnoticed by them.

Targets is also disturbing because Bogdanovich constantly forces his audience into Thompson's head with subjective shots of his victims, seen through the telescopic lens of his rifle. Thus, Thompson is not alone in lining up the cross hairs on the doomed. Bogdanovich makes us his accomplices, fellow products of his environmental "sterility." Perhaps a little bit of Bobby Thompson's madness exists in all of us.

Bogdanovich's script and direction carefully move Orlok and Thompson into an inevitable confrontation. Along the way, they also reveal Bogdanovich's love for the movies, through cinematic quotes from his favorite filmmakers' works and many in-jokes. For instance, the music, twilight setting, and editing of the kinetic drive-in sequence are reminiscent of *Strangers on a Train* (1951), when Robert Walker goes after his lighter. A shot looking directly down from the top of the oil tank mimics one of Cary Grant running out of the U.N. in *North By Northwest* (1959).[8] After the murders of Thompson's family, Bogdanovich uses a slow, deliberate traveling shot that moves along the floor, past a blood spot and then a slipper that fell off Thompson's wife's foot as he carried her body, finally stopping on a confession Thompson typed and left on a desk. This self-conscious shot calls to mind Hitchcock's similar one in *Psycho*, after Marion Crane's murder, that purposefully leads the viewer from Crane's face past her robe on the toilet, then to a folded newspaper containing the money Crane has stolen, and finally up to a window through which we see the Bates house. Also, the closing shot of *Targets* is a high angled long shot of the drive-in, empty now except for Thompson's car and looking strangely like a graveyard, the car speakers serving as symmetrically placed tombstones. This lingering last shot of the car recalls the last shot of Marion Crane's automobile in *Psycho*. Bogdanovich also attempted to copy parts of the chase sequence from Raoul Walsh's *High Sierra* (1941) in his own short police chase that prompts Thompson to hide in the drive-in.

In-jokes include a drunken writer/director, Sammy Michaels (played by the cost-saving Peter Bogdanovich, in a self-portrait similar to Karloff's), threatening Orlok that he will offer his new script to Vincent Price. Later, a child at the drive-in calls Orlok by the name of "Orloff," humorously and tellingly close to "Karloff." Of course, the vampire in F.W. Murnau's *Nosferatu* (1922) is named Count Orlok.

In one touching sequence, Bogdanovich films Karloff watching himself on television in Howard Hawks's *The Criminal Code* (1931). Sammy remarks, "I saw this at the Museum of Modern Art." Indeed, Bogdanovich, who started as a film critic, had organized retrospectives for his heroes Hawks, Hitchcock, and Orson Welles at the Museum of Modern Art, before he went to work for Corman. More importantly, though, this in-joke contributes to the narrative. The contrast of the young actor in the classic Hawks film with the same man years later, now an old and outdated horror movie star, illuminates Orlok's desire to retire because he does not feel he belongs in the modern world.

This disenfranchisement is occasionally reinforced when Karloff's dialogue sounds as though he were having a candid conversation between shots about his feeling obsolete. "What's it all about?" he asks Sammy. "Everybody's dead. I feel like a dinosaur. Oh, I know how people think of me these days—old-fashioned, outmoded.... You know what they call my films today? Camp. High camp." Showing Sammy a newspaper headline that reads "Youth Kills Six in Supermarket," he concludes, "My kind of horror isn't horror anymore." This embraces Bogdanovich's (still) topical theme—and strangely encapsulates Karloff's career. Later, on his way to the drive-in, Karloff's Orlok dryly observes of Hollywood, "What an ugly town this has become." Karloff, who made his start there nearly a half a century earlier, could very well have felt this way. He seems out of place and uncomfortable in a community of ugly fast food restaurants and gaudy neon. In many respects, his performance is both a conquest over and requiem for Hollywood, old and new.

In the climactic drive-in sequence, Orlok's world is the rational one that emerges victorious when it crosses Thompson's. Orlok's brand of horror is safely confined to the screen in an unrealistic, cathartic form that is harmless and fun, perhaps even purifying. Thompson's type of horror is inexplicable, damaging, and *real*, a reflection of Whitman's pointless killing spree from a tower on the campus of the University of Texas in 1966 (31 wounded, 14 dead, including an 8-month pregnant woman and her unborn child). The senseless killing of so many innocents by Thompson also evokes those real victims then being slaughtered in Vietnam for a questionable cause. The film, too, anticipates the 1968 assassination of Senator Robert Kennedy, probably one of the reasons why it failed at the box office. Bogdanovich may have succeeded too well in depicting modern violence. Many did not wish to witness the carnage of the real world spread across a large screen in the dark, for it was already invading their living rooms in broad daylight on the nightly news.

The confrontation of Orlok and Thompson at the drive-in was suggested by veteran director Samuel Fuller, whom Bogdanovich had asked for advice. "I was more worried about that scene than anything else in the picture," recalled Bogdanovich. "I thought we stood the chance of getting laughed out of the theatre... Sam has a simpler, more basic approach to a story than I do. At first, I found the scene hard to believe in. Then I embraced it as a marvelous kind of melodramatic thing."[9]

Indeed, this sequence offers Karloff a dramatic opportunity that he parlays into a defining moment of his screen career. He spies Thompson in the darkness near the drive-in screen and, in a tone that reveals his own disbelief, says to his secretary Jenny (Nancy Hsueh), "That man has a rifle." Thompson shoots Jenny in her shoulder and, outraged, Orlok storms toward him. Thompson sees Orlok doggedly approach him from opposite directions, both in person and on the big screen, and in desperate confusion, shoots at both images, real and unreal. His inability to distinguish between the two underlines his monstrous incapacity to view murder as anything other than a means for perverted self-fulfillment.

After grazing Orlok's head, Thompson runs out of bullets and picks up another handgun to finish him, but Orlok knocks it out of his hand with his cane, then starts slapping him until Thompson falls, huddled in a corner, weeping.

Karloff handles this sequence with an alarming, triumphant energy that does not seem possible for a 80-year-old, arthritic man suffering from emphysema. When his head is grazed, Karloff stops momentarily, feels the blood, and allows his face to radiate an inexorable mission. Fully rising to the dramatic occasion, Karloff—and everything his *real* screen career as a bogeyman has represented—puts a stop to Thompson, reducing him to a sniveling coward without his weapon. Karloff slaps Thompson as though he is a naughty child, with such authority that we understand and even feel the *real* actor's strict moral code at work, the code inherent in his dark, cinematic fairy tales of a

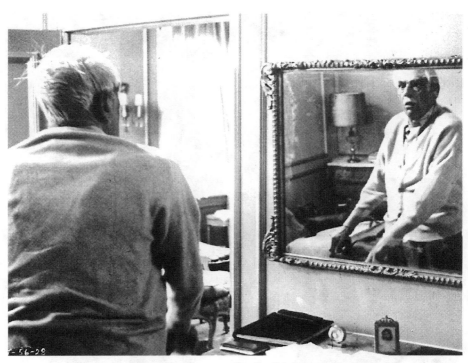

The screen's best bogeyman finally frightens even himself.

bygone era that would not tolerate the immorality of this present-day horror. We can empathize with Karloff's monsters, but never with the likes of Thompson. Such a revelatory climax is only possible because Bogdanovich had Karloff, whose entire career was a prerequisite for this scene's existence and sublime power.

The brave heroics of Karloff were not confined to the screen. Bogdanovich had to get all of his shots involving Orlok's limousine and the drive-in location in one day, the first day of shooting. By 1:00 a.m. Bogdanovich was still shooting at the drive-in, and he begged Karloff to stay longer to complete the needed filming because they couldn't afford to return with him later. The air was extremely cold, which intensified not only Karloff's arthritic pain but also his emphysema. In spite of his severe discomfort, Karloff told Bogdanovich, "All right, we'll do it. It's only for you. It's not for Roger Corman."[10] They finished at 4 a.m.

In fact, Karloff recognized Bogdanovich's potential talent as soon as he read the script for *Targets*. Before filming began, he told the 27-year-old director, "I believe in this picture, but you can't do it in two days." Bogdanovich explained that the money just was not available to pay him for more days. Karloff responded generously: "Take as long as you like." He *gave* him three additional days.[11]

Suffering from arthritis and emphysema, working as late as 4:00 a.m. so that Bogdanovich could get the shots he needed, 80-year-old Boris Karloff still maintained his sublime power before the cameras throughout *Targets*.

Karloff's philanthropy continued throughout his work on this project, with his wife, Evie, always by his side to help. For instance, while Karloff and Bogdanovich rehearsed on a hotel suite set, their wives upholstered banquettes with hammers and tacks on a night club set nearby.[12] When it came time to shoot Orlok's telling of a darkly ironic fable, *Appointment in Samarra*, it was after midnight. An exhausted Karloff suggested that he tell the two minute story with the camera on him, instead of using less effective pans around the room that would have allowed him to recite the long script piecemeal. Karloff, without the script or cue cards, then performed the scene in one shot and one take. Using merely his distinctive, foreboding voice and some subtle facial expressions that translate the tale's terror into visual terms, he manages to chill to the bone. Karloff needed no special effects to frighten. The crew applauded him.[13]

Apparently, the more Karloff worked on the film the more he realized that he was making something special, something lasting and important. His enthusiasm never waned during production. As Bogdanovich recalled, "The only

time I ever had trouble with Boris was when we had worked until three in the morning and he wanted to stay on and read his lines for the other actors—he wanted to help them in reacting in front of the camera. I made him go home and he was mad at me."[14] At one point in the production, Karloff continued to work in the rain and caught a cold, which later developed into bronchitis.[15]

Bogdanovich rewarded Karloff with one memorable scene after another, giving him the richest (and sometimes funniest) dialogue of the film. When an obnoxious, long-haired DJ (Sandy Baron) joyfully tells Orlok that his films "blew my mind," Karloff rolls his eyes and says, "Obviously." As he watches cars race out of the drive-in, and does not yet know of the deadly sniper, only that his new film is playing, he quips, "Well, they seem to be loving it, don't they?" The funniest moment, however, is quite a tribute to Karloff's reputation as the king of monster movies. Half asleep and hung over, he walks past a mirror and jumps when he sees his own image. Of course, we had been doing this for years when *we* saw him on the screen, and so it is a refreshing change of pace to witness Karloff do the same thing to himself!

Although *Targets* received outstanding reviews, with wonderful plaudits for both Bogdanovich and Karloff, the film was not a commercial success. Soon after Paramount bought *Targets* to distribute, Senator Kennedy was shot to death. With the subject matter of the film perhaps too painful and, at this time, too unpalatable, executives added a preachy prologue that pleaded for gun control. As Bogdanovich remembered, "Everybody felt weird about censorship and violence. Paramount thought the gun control notion would be a respected way of selling the picture. I felt that it wouldn't be good for the picture financially, because message pictures are usually box-office poison. But frankly, if they hadn't put that on, I don't think the picture would have been released [that] year. Everybody was scared."[16] The prologue has been removed from prints of the film seen today.

Targets is a matchless intersection of two artists. For Peter Bogdanovich, it was a tremendous *first* step as a director with an entire career before him. His next feature film, after a documentary about John Ford, would be *The Last Picture Show* (1971). For Boris Karloff, it was a courageous, loving *last* step, and one of the best he had ever taken. He played himself—a hugely talented, dedicated, sensitive, intelligent gentleman. Moreover, *Targets* is a lasting film that may offer even more to say today and tomorrow than it did in 1968, as the years—and the *real* horrors of life—continue to multiply, one generation to the next.

CREDITS: Director and Producer: Peter Bogdanovich; Screenplay: Peter Bogdanovich; Story: Polly Platt and Peter Bogdanovich; Photography: Laszlo Kovacs; Editor: Peter Bogdanovich; Art Direction: Polly Platt; Associate Producer: Daniel Selznick; Production Manager: Paul Lewis; Assistant to the Director: Frank Marshall; Sound Recording: Sam Kopetsky; Sound Effects Editor: Verna Fields; Musical Score: Charles Greene and Brian Stone; Makeup: Scott Hamilton; A Saticoy Production; Filmed in Pathecolor, Dec., 1967; Previewed May 2, 1968; Released by Paramount Pictures; 90 minutes

CAST: Boris Karloff...Byron Orlok, Tim O'Kelly...Bobby Thompson, Nancy Hsueh...Jenny, James Brown...Robert Thompson, Sr., Sandy Baron...Kip Larkin, Arthur Peterson...Ed Loughlin, Mary Jackson...Charlotte Thompson, Tanya Morgan...Ilene Thompson, Monty Landis...Marshall Smith, Peter Bogdanovich...Sammy Michaels, Paul Condylis...Drive-in Manager, Mark Dennis and Stafford Morgan...Gun Shop Salesmen, Daniel Ades...Chauffeur, Timothy Burns...Walter, Warren White...Grocery Boy, Geraldine

Baron...Larkin's Girl, Gary Kent...Gas Tank Worker, Ellie Wood Walker...Woman on Freeway, Frank Marshall...Ticket Boy, Byron Betz...Projectionist, Mike Farrell...Man in Phone Booth, Carol Samuels...Cashier, Jay Daniel...Snack Bar Attendant, James Morris...Man with Pistol. Also with Elaine Partnow, Paul Belcher, James Bowie, Anita Poree, Robert Cleaves, Kay Douglas, Raymond Roy, Diana Ashley, Kirk Scott, and Susan Douglas

Special thanks, as always, to Paul M. Jensen. Thanks also to Tom Johnson; Mark Neel; Tom Weaver; the staff of the British Film Institute; Michael and Matthew Dwyer; Jessica, Patrick, Jennifer, and Eric Miller; Drew, Chris, and Ellen Williams; and Nick, Brett, and Jacob Miller

Chapter Notes

1. Stone, Judy. "All Because of Boris Karloff." *New York Times* (15 Sept. 1968).
2. Sherman, Eric and Martin Rubin. *The Director's Event: Interviews with Five American Film-Makers*. New York: Atheneum, 1970: 84.
3. Ibid., 85-86.
4. Ibid., 87.
5. Ibid., 89. (A made-for-television movie based on sniper Charles Whitman was produced in 1975. Starring Kurt Russell as Whitman, *The Deadly Tower* was released on video under the title, *Sniper*.)
6. Stone.
7. Sherman and Rubin, 95
8. Ibid., 91.
9. Ibid., 96.
10. Nollen, Scott Allen. *Boris Karloff: A Critical Account of His Screen, Stage, Radio, Television, and Recording Work*. Jefferson, NC: McFarland,1991: 329-30.
11. Lindsay, Cynthia. *Dear Boris: The Life of William Henry Pratt, a.k.a. Boris Karloff*. New York: Alfred A. Knopf, 1975: 168-69.
12. Thomas, Kevin. *Los Angeles Times*. Quoted in *The Frankenscience Monster* by Forrest J Ackerman. New York: Ace Publishing Corporation, 1969: 53.
13. Lindsay, 172.
14. Ibid.
15. Gerard, Lillian. "The Man Behind the Myth." *Film Comment* (spring 1970): 47.
16. Sherman and Rubin, 89.

Mark A. Miller has contributed articles and interviews to *Midnight Marquee, Shivers, Outré, The Cushing Courier, Santo Street,* and *Filmfax*. He has also penned chapters for a Japanese book, *The Legend of Hammer Horror*, and two Midnight Marquee Press books, *Bela Lugosi* and *Guilty Pleasures of the Horror Film*. His first book, *Christopher Lee and Peter Cushing and Horror Cinema* (McFarland), was published to critical acclaim in 1994. Mark lives in Columbus, Ohio with wife Teresa and teaches English in nearby Gahanna.

Boris Karloff and wife at Toluca Lake in 1934.

Boris Karloff attending *The House of Rothschild* premiere in 1934. Note *The Black Cat* style haircut.

Boris Karloff as Santa Claus

Boris and the Grinch

**Boris Karloff and wife in London
in 1933 visit Hyde Park.**

**Mr. and Mrs. Karloff relax as
Boris reads a script.**

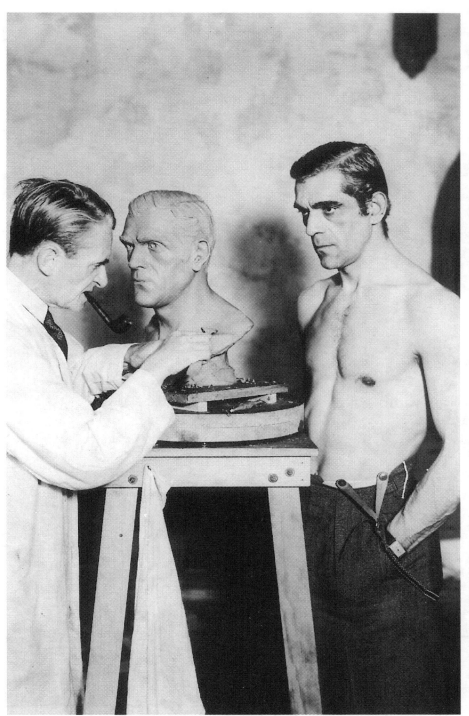

Ivan Simpson sculpts a bust of Boris Karloff.

The Monster as handyman during the filming of *Bride of Frankenstein*.

The Feature Films and Serials of Boris Karloff

Silent Films and Serials

His Majesty, the American (1919)
Masked Raider, The (1919)
Prince and Betty, The (1919)
Courage of Marge O'Doone, The (1920)
Deadlier Sex, The (1920)
Last of the Mohicans, The (1920)
Cave Girl, The (1921)
Cheated Hearts (1921)
Hope Diamond Mystery, The (1921) (serial)
Without Benefit of Clergy (1921)
A Woman Conquers (1922)
Altar Stairs, The (1922)
Infidel, The (1922)
Man from Downing Street, The (1922)
Omar the Tentmaker (1922)
Gentleman from America, The (1923)
Prisoner, The (1923)
Dynamite Dan (1924)
Hellion, The (1924)
Riders of the Plains (1924)
Forbidden Cargo (1925)
Lady Robin Hood (1925)
Never the Twain Shall Meet (1925)
Parisian Nights (1925)
Perils of the Wind (1925)
Prairie Wife, The (1925)
Bells, The (1926)
Eagle of the Sea (1926)
Flames (1926)
Flaming Fury (1926)
Golden Web, The (1926)
Greater Glory, The (1926)
Her Honor, the Governor (1926)
Man in the Saddle (1926)
Nickel Hopper, The (1926)
Old Ironsides (1926)
Valencia (1926)
Let It Rain (1927)
Love Mart, The (1927)
Meddlin' Stranger, The (1927)
Phantom Buster, The (1927)
Princess from Hoboken, The (1927)
Soft Cushions (1927)
Tarzan and the Golden Lion (1927)
Two Arabian Knights (1927)
Burning the Wind (1928)
Little Wild Girl, The (1928)
Vanishing Rider (1928)
Vultures of the Sea (1928) (serial)
Anne Against the World (1929)
Devil's Chaplain, The (1929)
Fatal Warning, The (1929)
Phantoms of the North (1929)
Two Sisters (1929)

Sound Films and Serials

Behind That Curtain (1929)

The first Charlie Chan sound film, starring Warner Baxter, Lois Moran, and Claude King.

King of the Kongo (1929)

A jungle serial starring Jacqueline Logan and Walter Miller. Karloff portrays Scarface Macklin.

Unholy Night, The (1929)

A murder mystery directed by Lionel Barrymore based on a story by Ben Hecht. Starring Roland Young, Polly Moran, and Dorothy Sebastian. Karloff portrays a Hindu servant.

Bad One, The (1930)

A prison melodrama starring Dolores Del Rio and Edmund Lowe. Karloff portrays a prison guard.

Mothers Cry (1930)

Helen Chandler and David Manners appeared in this melodrama where Karloff is a murder victim.

Sea Bat, The (1930)

Deadly sting rays and a convict impersonating a priest are the basis of this film. Karloff portrays a Corsican. Also starring Raquel Torres and Charles Bickford.

Utah Kid, The (1930)

Dorothy Sebastian stars as a schoolmarm who falls in love with a bandit. Karloff portrays a bandit in his last western.

Cracked Nuts (1931)

Mayhem in a fictional kingdom with Wheeler and Woolsey fighting it out for the crown. Edna May Oliver also appears. Karloff portrays a revolutionary.

Criminal Code, The (1931)

Walter Huston and Constance Cummings star in this Howard Hawks prison melodrama. Karloff portrays killer Ned Galloway who murders a squealer and then confesses.

Dirigible (1931)

Jack Holt and Fay Wray star in this Frank Capra-directed film as explorers attempt a trip to the South Pole and must be rescued by a dirigible.

Five Star Final (1931)

Karloff is a reporter who disguises himself as a clergyman to gain to the confidence of an old couple planning their daughter's wedding. The mother, a former murderess, and her husband kill themselves when the photos supplied by Karloff appear in the paper. Starring Edward G. Robinson as the editor who recruits Karloff.

Frankenstein (1931)

Graft (1931)

Regis Toomey stars in this newspaper story of a reporter going after kidnappers and murderers. Karloff portrays a henchman of crooked politicians.

Guilty Generation, The (1931)

A Romeo and Juliet story set in the world of gangsters as Karloff's daughter and his bitter rival's (Leo Carrillo) son fall in love.

I Like Your Nerve (1931)

Douglas Fairbanks, Jr. and Loretta Young star in this action film as Fairbanks saves Young from being sold into marriage. Karloff portrays Luigi.

King of the Wild (1931)

A horse love story (in serial form) starring Rex the Horse. Token appearance by Karloff and other assorted humans.

Last Parade, The (1931)

Jack Holt, Tom Moore, and Constance Cummings star in this gangster film as bootleggers face the electric chair.

Mad Genius, The (1931)

John Barrymore and Marian Marsh star in a Svengali-like tale of ballet. Karloff appears briefly as an abusive father.

Sous Les Verrous (1931)

Laurel and Hardy go to prison and meet gangsters and Karloff in this French-language version of the comics' *Pardon Us.*

Public Defender, The (1931)

Richard Dix and Shirley Grey star in this story of bank failure and an innocent man being sent to prison. Karloff portrays the Professor, who helps the man clear his name.

Smart Money (1931)

Edward G. Robinson and James Cagney star as small-time gangsters who head for the big city to seek revenge and their fortune. Karloff portrays Sport Williams.

Tonight or Never (1931)

Gloria Swanson stars as a singer trying to make it to the Met. Also starring Melvyn Douglas. Karloff appears as a waiter.

Yellow Ticket, The (1931)

Lionel Barrymore and Laurence Olivier star in this melodrama of a young girl who is in trouble with the Russian

Secret Police. Karloff portrays a drunk who tries to molest the girl.

Young Donovan's Kid (1931)

Richard Dix as a gangster takes in young Jackie Cooper. Karloff portrays Cokey Joe, a dope pusher.

Alias the Doctor (1932)

Marian Marsh stars in this surgical melodrama. Karloff appears as an autopsy surgeon but was replaced in some prints when overseas censors regarded some scenes too violent.

Behind the Mask (1932)

Business and Pleasure (1932)

Will Rogers portrays a razor blade manufacturer seeking the perfect steel. He stops a war between desert chieftains by giving them razor blades. Karloff portrays one of the bearded chieftains.

Cohens and Kellys in Hollywood, The (1932)

Two families find and then lose fortunes in Hollywood. Karloff appears as himself.

Mask of Fu Manchu, The (1932)

Miracle Man, The (1932)

Sylvia Sidney, Chester Morris and Irving Pichel appear in the remake of the Lon Chaney silent film. Karloff portrays Nikko, a Chinese restaurant owner.

Mummy, The (1932)

Night World (1932)

Karloff co-stars as a nightclub owner whose wife is cheating on him and sets up his murder. Starring Lew Ayres and Mae Clarke.

Old Dark House, The (1932)

Scarface (1932)

Ghoul, The (1933)

Karloff as Professor Morlant discovers a jewel he is sure will give him eternal life. When the gem is stolen, Morlant rises from the dead to seek revenge.

Black Cat, The (1934)

Gift of Gab (1934)

Bela Lugosi and Karloff appear as part of a radio sketch in this film starring Edmund Lowe, Ruth Etting, and Gloria Stuart.

House of Rothschild, The (1934)

George Arliss, Loretta Young, Reginald Owen, and Karloff star in this banking tale of Napoleon and anti-Semitism.

Lost Patrol, The (1934)

Black Room, The (1935)

Bride of Frankenstein (1935)

Raven, The (1935)

Karloff appears as a criminal seeking the help of Dr. Vollin (Bela Lugosi). He is deformed and enslaved by the insane doctor.

Invisible Ray, The (1936)

Karloff appears as a scientist who discovers an element that contaminates him, leading to a murder spree that includes Bela Lugosi as one of his victims.

Juggernaut (1936)

Needing money to complete his research, Karloff as Dr. Sartorius poisons an ailing husband for a vicious wife. Also stars Joan Wyndham and Arthur Margetson.

Man Who Changed His Mind, The (1936)

Walking Dead, The (1936)

Charlie Chan at the Opera (1937)

Night Key (1937)

Karloff appears as an inventor whose burglar alarm invention is stolen by his partner. Jean Rogers and Warren Hull also appear.

West of Shanghai (1937)

Invisible Menace, The (1938)

Mr. Wong, Detective (1938)

Karloff portrays Chinese detective James Lee Wong. Monogram's version of the Charlie Chan series. Karloff searches for a murderer committing the crimes with deadly gas.

Man They Could Not Hang, The (1939)

Mr. Wong in Chinatown (1939)

Wong (Karloff) along with Grant

Withers seeks the murderer of a foreign princess.

Son of Frankenstein (1939)

Son of Frankenstein marks the last appearance of Karloff as the Frankenstein Monster. Also stars Basil Rathbone, Bela Lugosi, Lionel Atwill, and Josephine Hutchinson.

Mystery of Mr. Wong, The (1939)

Karloff again reprises his role as the Oriental detective, this time seeking the murderer of a gem collector who acquired a star sapphire from China. Also stars Grant Withers and Dorothy Tree.

Tower of London (1939)

The horrors of medieval England are the basis of Tower of London, loosely based on the reign of Richard III. Karloff portrays the murderous executioner, Mord. Also stars Basil Rathbone, Rose Hobart, Vincent Price, Nan Grey, and Ian Hunter.

Ape, The (1940)

Karloff appears as a scientist desperately seeking a cure for polio. In his zeal to find a cure for the disease, he disguises himself as an ape and sets out to acquire spinal fluid from unwilling victims. Also stars Maris Wrixon and Gertrude Hoffman.

Before I Hang (1940)

Black Friday (1940)

British Intelligence (1940)

Devil's Island (1940)

Doomed to Die (1940)

The Mr. Wong series continues as Karloff searches for the killer of a shipping magnate. Also stars Grant Withers and Marjorie Reynolds.

Fatal Hour, The (1940)

Boris Karloff as Mr. Wong seeks the killer of a friend of Captain Street (Grant Withers). Also stars Marjorie Reynolds.

Man with Nine Lives, The (1940)

You'll Find Out (1940)

Peter Lorre, Bela Lugosi, and Karloff as a group of villains out to murder a young heiress. Kay Kyser spoils their plans.

Devil Commands, The (1941)

Boogie Man Will Get You, The (1942)

Karloff portrays an inventor trying to create a race of supermen to help the war effort. Along for the ride are Peter Lorre and Larry Parks.

Climax, The (1944)

House of Frankenstein (1944)

Body Snatcher, The (1945)

Isle of the Dead (1945)

Karloff stars as a Greek general visiting an island filled with a mysterious plague. Also starring Ellen Drew and Alan Napier.

Bedlam (1946)

Karloff in one of his most evil roles stars as the sadistic head of Bedlam. Directed by Mark Robson and co-starring Anna Lee.

Dick Tracy Meets Gruesome (1947)

Karloff portrays master criminal Gruesome who meets the master detective, Dick Tracy (Ralph Byrd). Also stars Anne Gwynne.

Lured (1947)

Lucille Ball helps Scotland Yard track down a murderer. Karloff portrays a dress designer who is a suspect. Also stars George Sanders.

Secret Life of Walter Mitty, The (1947)

Danny Kaye as daydreamer Walter Mitty gets involved in a real-life adventure where he meets Karloff impersonating a psychiatrist.

Unconquered (1947)

Karloff portrays an Indian Chief who leads a raid on a fort and in the process kidnaps the lovely Paulette Goddard, who is rescued from Karloff's clutches by Gary Cooper.

Tap Roots (1948)

Karloff again portrays an Indian in this film starring Van Heflin and Susan Hayward. Karloff and Ward Bond protect a valley and its citizens from the rampage of the Confederate army.

Abbott and Costello Meet the Killer, Boris Karloff (1949)

The comedic duo appear with Karloff in this murder mystery set in the Lost Cavern Hotel. Also stars Lenore Aubert.

Emperor's Nightingale, The (1951)

An animated version of the Hans Christian Andersen fairy tale. Narrated by Karloff.

Strange Door, The (1951)

Karloff portrays a servant in eighteenth-century France who rescues a father and daughter imprisoned by the father's insane brother (Charles Laughton).

Black Castle, The (1952)

A medieval tale in which Karloff appears as a doctor who tries to help victims of an evil Count (Stephen McNally). Also stars Lon Chaney, Jr.

Abbott and Costello Meet Dr. Jekyll and Mr. Hyde (1953)

Bud and Lou star as two American detectives observing Scotland Yard techniques. They meet up with Dr. Jekyll (Karloff) and his evil alter-ego Mr. Hyde.

Colonel March Investigates (1953)

Three episodes of the British TV series, *Colonel March of Scotland Yard* were combined for this film released to theaters. Karloff stars as Colonel March, head of the Department of Queer Complaints for Scotland Yard.

Hindu, The (1953)

In this India-based adventure story, Karloff appears as an aide to a Maharajah. Also stars Reginald Denny and Victory Jory.

Monster of the Island (1953)

In this Italian film, Karloff appears as a drug smuggler who is defeated by an undercover agent.

Voodoo Island (1957)

Karloff stars as a disbelieving investigator of the supernatural whose opinions change radically after a visit to Voodoo Island.

Frankenstein 1970 (1958)

Grip of the Strangler (1958)

Corridors of Blood (1963)

Raven, The (1963)

Karloff, Peter Lorre, and Vincent Price star in this loose adaptation of the Poe work as a group of demented magicians battle each other for more power.

Terror, The (1963)

Karloff stars as a Baron being driven mad by an old witch. Jack Nicholson appears as Andre Duvalier.

Bikini Beach (1964)

Karloff makes a cameo appearance in this Frankie and Annette Beach Party movie.

Black Sabbath (1964)

Karloff appears in this horror trilogy as a vampire who kills his entire family.

Comedy of Terrors, The (1964)

Die, Monster, Die! (1965)

Ghost in the Invisible Bikini, The (1966)

Karloff stars as Hiram Stokeley who is surprised to discover he is dead. He must perform a good deed before being allowed into Heaven in this beach party movie. Also starring Basil Rathbone, Tommy Kirk, and Deborah Walley.

Daydreamer, The (1966)

Karloff provides the voice of The Rat in this live-action/puppet fantasy.

Mad Monster Party? (1966)

Sorcerers, The (1967)

Karloff stars as a hypnotist who invents a device that can control people from a distance. His wife takes control of the device. Also stars Ian Ogilvy.

Venetian Affair, The (1967)

Karloff appears as a political scientist who is being controlled by an enemy agent. Robert Vaughn is the CIA agent who tries to stop him. Also stars Elke Sommer.

Targets (1968)

Crimson Cult, The (1970)

Karloff appears as Professor Marsh,

an authority on witchcraft who saves a young girl from sacrifice. Stars Christopher Lee and Michael Gough.

Cauldron of Blood (1971)

Karloff appears as a blind sculptor whose wife and lover are attempting to do away with him.

Fear Chamber, The (1971)

One of Karloff's four Mexican horror films (all released after his death). In this one, Karloff portrays a scientist who experiments with a living rock.

Incredible Invasion, The (1971)

Karloff appears as a scientist who invents a weapon that attracts the attention of aliens.

Snake People, The (1971)

Karloff appears as the leader of a snake cult terrorizing the local population.

House of Evil (1972)

Karloff appears as the head of a family who invites the relatives to his mansion where they are attacked by tiny robots.

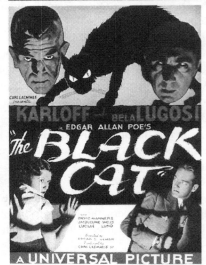

SELECTED BIBLIOGRAPHY

Bansak, Edmund D.: *Fearing the Dark*, McFarland & Company, Jefferson, North Carolina, and London, 1995

Bojarski, Richard: *The Films of Boris Karloff*, Citadel Press, Secaucus, New Jersey, 1974

Brunas, John; Brunas, Michael; and Weaver, Tom: *Universal Horrors*, McFarland & Company, Inc., Jefferson, North Carolina, and London, 1990

Curtis, James: *James Whale*, Scarecrow Press, Metuchen, New Jersey, 1982

Everson, William K.: *Classics of the Horror Film*, Citadel Press, Secaucus, New Jersey, 1974

Everson, William K.: *More Classics of the Horror Film*, Citadel Press, Secaucus, New Jersey, 1986

Gifford, Denis: *A Pictorial History of Horror Movies*, Hamlyn Publishing Group, London, 1973

Gifford, Denis: *Karloff: The Man, the Monster, the Movies*, Curtis Books, New York, 1973

Hardy, Phil: *The Encyclopedia of Horror Movies*, Harper & Row, New York, 1986

Hardy, Phil: *The Encyclopedia of Science Fiction Movies*, William Morris, New York, 1984

Jensen, Paul: *Boris Karloff and His Films*, A. S. Barnes & Company, San Diego, New York, 1974

Katz, Ephraim: *The Film Encyclopedia*, Perigee Books, New York, 1979

Lanchester, Elsa: *Herself: Elsa Lanchester*, St. Martins Press, New York, 1983

Lindsay, Cynthia: *Dear Boris: The Life of William Henry Pratt a.k.a. Boris Karloff*, Alfred A. Knopf, New York, 1975

Mank, Gregory William: *Hollywood Cauldron: Thirteen Horror Films from the Genre's Golden Age*, McFarland & Company, Inc., Jefferson, North Carolina, and London, 1994

Mank, Gregory William: *It's Alive: The Classic Cinema Saga of Frankenstein*, A. S. Barnes & Company, Inc., San Diego, New York, 1981

Mank, Gregory William: *Karloff and Lugosi: The Story of a Haunting Collaboration*, McFarland & Company, Jefferson, North Carolina, and London, 1990

Martin, Floyd, W.: *The International Dictionary of Films and Filmmakers*, St. James Press, New York, 1993

Nollen, Scott Allen: *Boris Karloff: A Critical Account of His Screen, Stage, Radio, Television, and Recording Work*, McFarland & Company, Inc., Jefferson, North Carolina, and London, 1991

Penzler, Otto; and Steinbrunner, Chris: *The Encyclopedia of Mystery and Detection*, McGraw-Hill, New York, 1976

Riley, Philip J.: *The Mummy*, MagicImage Filmbooks, Absecon, New Jersey, 1989

Rovin, Jeff: *A Pictorial History of Science Fiction Films*, Citadel Press, Secaucus, New Jersey, 1975

Skinner, Cornelia Otis: *Life with Lindsay and Crouse*, Houghton, Mifflin and Company, New York, 1976

Stanley, John: *Creature Feature Movie Guide Strikes Back*, Creatures at Large, Pacifica, California, 1994

Telotte, J. P.: *Dreams of Darkness*, University of Illinois Press, Urbana and Chicago, Illinois, 1985

Underwood, Peter: *Karloff*, Drake Publishers, New York, 1972

Weaver, Tom: *It Came from Weaver Five*, McFarland & Company, Jefferson, North Carolina, and London, 1996

Weldon, Michael: *The Psychotronic Encyclopedia of Film*, Ballantine, New York, 1983

Willis, Donald C.: *Horror and Science Fiction Films*, Scarecrow Press, Metuchen, New Jersey, 1972

INDEX

[Courtesy Ronald V. Borst/
Hollywood Movie Posters]

Also Available from Midnight Marquee Press